# NANO NAGLE

ADVANCE PRAISE FOR *NANO NAGLE*

'Meticulously researched, this book offers an insightful analysis of the life and legacy of Nano Nagle.'

*Professor Tanya Fitzgerald, La Trobe University,*
*Melbourne, Australia*

'Nano Nagle's contribution to the education and welfare of Ireland's youth is peerless, but her memory is largely forgotten. This timely volume restores that reputation and demonstrates the significance of her legacy which is global in its scale.'

*Professor Daire Keogh, Dublin City University, Ireland*

'A well-written study of a fascinating woman and her legacy. The authors clearly show that it is time for Nano Nagle and her sisters to take their place in education, religious, and women's history.'

*Professor Margaret McGuinness, La Salle University,*
*Philadelphia, USA*

'Through a meticulously researched thematic study of Presentation education, this groundbreaking book examines the life and the worldwide education legacy of Nano Nagle. The critical analysis of an array of documents drawn from private and public repositories reveals a heretofore untold account of historically significant, resilient women and their women-financed, women-led schools, as they constantly negotiated among their religious communities, the Church, the State and the larger secular society.'

*Professor Elizabeth M. Smyth, University of Toronto, Canada*

# NANO NAGLE

## THE LIFE AND THE LEGACY

DEIRDRE RAFTERY
CATRIONA DELANEY
CATHERINE NOWLAN-ROEBUCK

IRISH ACADEMIC PRESS

First published in 2019 by
Irish Academic Press
10 George's Street
Newbridge
Co. Kildare
Ireland
www.iap.ie

9781788550574 (Cloth)
9781788550581 (Kindle)
9781788550598 (Epub)
9781788550604 (PDF)

British Library Cataloguing in Publication Data
An entry can be found on request

Library of Congress Cataloging in Publication Data
An entry can be found on request

Interior design by www.jminfotechindia.com
Typeset in Minion Pro 11/14 pt

Jacket design by edit+ www.stuartcoughlan.com
Jacket front: Nano Nagle. Oil on canvas. (James Barry RA, attrib.) By kind
permission of the Presentation Sisters Congregational Archives, Cork.
Jacket back: Sister M. Canice O'Shea and pupils, after the 1906 earthquake and
fire, Presentation Sisters 'Refugee School', San Francisco. By kind permission of
the Presentation Archives San Francisco. Photographer, Hugo Weitz.

# Contents

# Presentation Foundations
# in America by 1965

## South Dakota
### ✠ Convents
- Aberdeen
- Holy Family, Mitchell
- Milbank
- St Luke's Hospital, Aberdeen
- Mount Joseph Manor, Aberdeen
- Jefferson
- Bridgewater
- St Joseph's Hospital, Mitchell
- ND Academy, Mitchell
- Brady Memorial, Mitchell
- Woonsocket
- Dell Rapids
- McKenna Hos, Sioux Falls
- Sacred Heart, Aberdeen
- Humboldt
- Madison
- Huron
- St Mary's Sch, Sioux Falls
- O'Gorman HS, Sioux Falls
- Roncalli HS, Aberdeen
- Timberlake
- Winner

## North Dakota
### ✠ Convents
- Fargo
- New Rockford
- Sykeston
- Lidgerwood
- Sheldon
- St Mary's School, Fargo
- St Anthony's of Padua, Fargo
- Holy Spirit School, Fargo
- Nativity School, Fargo
- St Alphonsus School, Langdon
- City hospital, New Rockford
- Carrington hospital, Carrington
- Holy Family Guest Home, Carrington
- St John's, Grafton
- St Joseph's Hospital, Grafton
- Park River
- St Mary's, Langdon

North Dakota

South Dakota

## Washington
### ✠ Convents
- Seattle

## Montana
### ✠ Convents
- Holy Rosary, Miles City
- SH Grade Sch, Miles City
- SH High Sch, Miles City

Oregon

Idaho

U N I T E D   S T A

Wyoming

Nebraska

Nevada

## Utah
### ✠ Convents
- Salt Lake City

Colorado

Kansas

## Iowa
### ✠ Convents
- Key West, Dubuque
- West Dubuque
- Ackley
- West Hill, Dubuque
- Lawler
- Waukon
- Elkader
- Farley
- Clare
- Whittemore
- Dougherty
- Fairbank
- Mt Loretto, Dubuque
- Mason City
- Ryan
- Monona
- Humboldt
- Algona
- Osage
- Storm Lake
- Charles City
- Epworth
- Sheldon
- Ashbury, Dubuque

## California
### ✠ Convents
- Masonic Avenue, San Francisco
- Sacramento
- Upland
- Gilroy
- Powell Street, San Francisco
- Taylor Street, San Francisco
- Berkeley
- St Agnes Academy, San Francisco
- St Teresa's, San Francisco
- OL of Lourdes, Los Angeles
- OL of Loretto, Los Angeles
- St Anne's, San Francisco
- St Patrick's, San Jose
- The Epiphany, San Francisco
- Montebello
- St M Magdalen's, West Los Angeles
- St Elizabeth's, San Francisco
- San Pedro
- San Lorenzo
- St John Vianney, San Jose
- Los Gatos
- Upland, San Diego
- Montclair

## Arizona
### ✠ Convents
- Globe
- Mesa

## New Mexico
### ✠ Convents
- Pecos
- Albuquerque
- San Lorenzo

Oklahoma

## Texas
### ✠ Convents
- San Antonio

M E X I C O

0   200   400   600   800   1000
Scale                    Kilometres

CANADA

**nnesota**
✠ *Convents*
Lake Mound
Willmar
Anoka
Monticello
St Paul

S

Iowa

Wisconsin

Michigan

**Illinois**
✠ *Convents*
• Oregon
• Old Park

Missouri

Indiana

Ohio

Kentucky

West
Virginia

Virginia

Tennessee

North Carolina

Arkansas

Mississippi

Alabama

South
Carolina

**Louisiana**
✠ *Convents*
• Houma

**Georgia**
✠ *Convents*
• Macon

Florida

Pennsylvania

New York

CT

MD

Maine

VT

NH

**Connecticut**
✠ *Convents*
• Riverside
• St Mary's, Stamford

**New Jersey**
✠ *Convents*
• Clifton

**Massachusetts**
✠ *Convents*
• Fitchburg
• St John's, Clinton
• W. Fitchburg
• Our Lady of Rosary, Clinton
• Leominster
• Mount St Mary's, Fitchburg
• Whitingville
• Holy Family, Fitchburg
• Ayer
• St Bernard, Fitchburg

**Rhode Island**
✠ *Convents*
• Central Falls
• Woonsocket
• Conimicut

**New York**
✠ *Convents*
• Watervliet
• Holland Ave, Bronx
• Newburg
• Bronx 66
• Bronx 67
• Goshen
• Kingston
• Yonkers
• Fishkill
• Yonkers
• Chappaqua
• Long Island
• OL of Presentation, Goshen
• Rockaway Bch
• Masterson, Albany
• Sacred Heart, Albany
• Little Falls
• Schenectady
• Latham
• Frankfort
• Altamont

**Staten Island, NY**
✠ *Convents*
• Manhattan
• St Jude's, Manhattan
• Green Ridge
• Grant City
• New Dorp
• New Brighton
• Concord
• Tottenville
• Stapleton

CUBA

# Presentation Foundations Made From Ireland by 1964

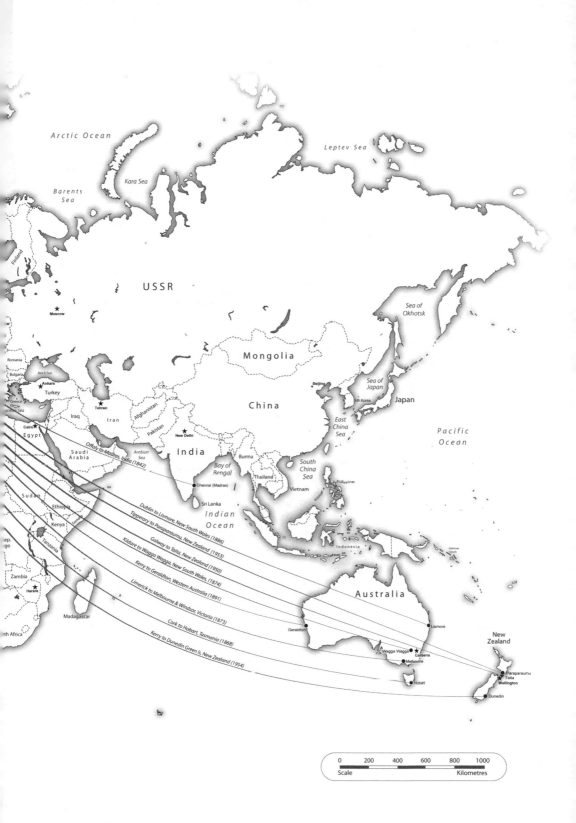

Arctic Ocean

Barents
Sea

Kara Sea

Leptev Sea

Finland

USSR

★ Moscow

Romania

Bulgaria

Black Sea

Ankara

★ Turkey

Greece

Aegean Sea

Cairo ★

Egypt

Iraq

Iran

Tehran ★

Afghanistan

Pakistan

New Delhi ●

Saudi
Arabia

Sudan

Ethiopia

Kenya

Tanzania

Zambia

Harare ●

South Africa

Madagascar

Offaly to Madras, India (1842)

Arabian
Sea

India

Bay of
Bengal

Chennai (Madras) ●

Sri Lanka

Indian
Ocean

Mongolia

China

Beijing ●

Sth Korea

Sea of
Japan

Japan

Sea of
Okhotsk

East
China
Sea

Burma

Thailand

South
China
Sea

Vietnam

Philippines

Pacific
Ocean

Indonesia

Solomon
Islands

Dublin to Lismore, New South Wales (1886)

Tipperary to Paraparaumu, New Zealand (1953)

Galway to Taita, New Zealand (1950)

Kildare to Wagga Wagga, New South Wales (1874)

Kerry to Geraldton, Western Australia (1891)

Limerick to Melbourne & Windsor, Victoria (1873)

Cork to Hobart, Tasmania (1868)

Kerry to Dunedin Green Is. New Zealand (1954)

Australia

Geraldton ●

Lismore ●

New
Zealand

Wagga Wagga ●   ★ Canberra

Melbourne ●

Hobart ●

Paraparaumu ●
Taita ★
Wellington ●

Dunedin ●

| 0 | 200 | 400 | 600 | 800 | 1000 |
|---|---|---|---|---|---|

Scale                                    Kilometres

# Presentation Convents in Ireland, 1775–1965

Donegal

Derry

Antrim

Tyrone

**Belfast**

Down

Fermanagh

Leitrim

Portadown

**Armagh**
✠ *1 Convent*

Sligo

Monaghan

Meath

**Cavan**
✠ *1 Convent*

Bailieborough

**Louth**
✠ *2 Convents*

Roscommon

Granard

Drogheda *(Greenhills)*
Drogheda Town

**Mayo**
✠ *1 Convent*

Keel

**Longford**
✠ *1 Convent*

**Dublin**
✠ *7 Convents*

Mullingar

**Dublin**

Tuam

Headford

**Galway**
✠ *8 Convents*

**Westmeath**
✠ *1 Convent*

Kilcock
Maynooth

Lucan
Clane

Blackrock
Stradbrook
Hall

George's Hill
Terenure
Clondalkin
Warrenmount

Carraroe
Tiernee

Shantalla

**Galway**

Galway City

Athenry

Oranmore

Rahan

**Offaly**
✠ *1 Convent*

Mountmellick
*(Our Lady of Victories)*
Mountmellick Town
Portarlington

**Kildare**
✠ *4 Convents*

Kildare Town

**Wicklow**
✠ *1 Convent*

Clare

Portlaoise

**Laois**
✠ *6 Convents*

Stradbally

Baltinglass

Durrow

Castlecomer

Carlow Town

**Carlow**
✠ *2 Convents*

**Tipperary**
✠ *7 Convents*

Castleconnell

Thurles

Kilkenny

Bagenalstown

Limerick City
Janesboro

**Limerick**

Ballingarry

**Kilkenny**
✠ *4 Convents*

Enniscorthy

**Limerick**
✠ *4 Convents*

Hospital

Dundrum
Cashel

Fethard

**Wexford**
✠ *2 Convents*

Listowel
Lixnaw

Rathmore
Tralee Town
Tralee *(Oak Park)*
Castleisland

Doneraile

Mitchelstown

Carrick-on-Suir

Clonmel

Kilmacow

Mooncoin

Wexford Town

**Kerry**
✠ *11 Convents*

Dingle

Milltown

Killarney

Mill Street

Fermoy

**Cork**
✠ *13 Convents*

Lismore

Waterford City

**Waterford**
✠ *3 Convents*

**Waterford**

Cahirciveen

Killarney

Dungarvan

Sneem

Douglas Street
Blackpool
Turner's Cross
Ballyphehane
Tivoli
Crosshaven

**Cork**

Youghal
Midleton

Bandon

0   20   40   60   80   100
Scale                    Kilometres

# Preface and Acknowledgements

In the year of the tercentenary of her birth, it has been an honour to write a study of Nano Nagle and her legacy. It has also been a great challenge, not least because Nagle's legacy is extensive: there are Presentation foundations all over the world. An early decision was made to focus on her legacy to education immediately after her death and the expansion of Presentation schooling in Ireland, while also paying attention to some of the ways in which the Order quickly expanded outside the country. Each Presentation foundation was an independent house, which meant that it could respond in a practical way to the environment in which it was situated. This prompted many questions: was it difficult to operate without a highly centralised leadership? Or, did Presentation houses have loose ties with each other that sustained them? Were all of the schools different because they were independent of each other? Or was there a particular inflection to Presentation education? As the research developed, drawing on different archival collections, it became clear that, although there were kinship and professional networks that spanned continents, the uniting factor was – without doubt – a profound connection to Nano Nagle and her first foundation in Cork.

I am most grateful to the three Provincials, Sr Eileen Keating (England), Sr Sheila Kelleher (Ireland South West), and Sr Margarita Ryan (Ireland North East), and their leadership teams, who supported this research through the Nano Nagle Postdoctoral Fellowship at UCD. The three leadership teams remained enthusiastic about this project at all times, without ever interfering in the research process.

The Presentation Sisters Congregational Archive, Cork, was an important source of material for this book. Sincere gratitude is expressed to Sr Rosarie Lordan, Congregational Archivist, for her tireless assistance and her enthusiasm for our work. Research in the South-West Province was also generously supported by Sr Ann Coffey, Archivist.

Of equal importance were George's Hill Archives, Dublin. Sincere thanks to Sr Marie Therese King, Archivist (North East Province), who shared her deep knowledge of the George's Hill Collection, and co-ordinated research visits to convents in the North East Province.

Research for this book included visiting many of the Irish Presentation convents, and being given unfettered access to materials. Our thanks to the local leaders and communities who welcomed us at Presentation convents in Bandon, Fermoy, Galway, Kilcock, Killarney, Midleton, Rahan, Tralee, Milltown and Youghal. Gratitude is also expressed to Sr Kathleen Fahy (Galway), Sr Maura Finn (Bandon) and Sr Eucharia Fintan (Fermoy) who supplied photographs.

Sincere thanks to Dr Bernadette Flanagan, Ireland North East leadership team, who facilitated several stages of the planning, and kindly liaised with international houses.

In England, Sr Susan Richert, Archivist, and Sr Carmel Clancy, were most helpful in providing access to all of the relevant collections, and co-ordinating a research visit, for which we are grateful.

Sr Lois Greene, and the community at the Presentation Convent, St John's, Newfoundland, kindly facilitated a research visit. Special thanks to Sr Patricia Whittle who, over several days and evenings, generously shared her knowledge of the congregational archives in Newfoundland. Thanks also to Wanita Bates for her assistance in locating images of the first Presentation convents in Newfoundland.

In San Francisco, Sr Patricia Anne Cloherty and the Presentation community at Turk Boulevard were most welcoming, and Archivist Rachel Foote was very helpful in locating materials, securing permissions, and providing images.

Thanks also to Sr Hermann Platt (Archivist, Dubuque, Iowa), and Sr Enid Storey (Archivist, New Windsor, New York) who provided information on convents that could not be visited within the limits of time. Other Sisters also tried to support this project where possible from a distance; gratitude is expressed to Sr Kathleen Daly (Aberdeen, South Dakota), Sr Lancia Rodrigues (Archivist, Chennai, India), and to Lisa Olson (Conference of Presentation Sisters).

Thanks to the Ursuline Sisters, Blackrock, Cork, for giving access to their archival collection, and to Margaret Lantry, Archivist, for her assistance.

Permission to publish materials has been granted by the Diocesan Archives of Newfoundland, the Dublin Diocesan Archives, and the Galway Diocesan Archives. We acknowledge this with gratitude.

There are many deceased Sisters who have left a legacy to the history of women religious by their preservation of congregational records, and their careful recording of information; these include Sr Rosarie Allen (Archivist) and Sr Pius O'Farrell.

This research on Presentation history has benefited, in different ways and at different times, from insights provided by Professor Bernadette Whelan (University of Limerick), Professor Elizabeth M. Smyth (University of Toronto) and Emilie Papaix (Archives Enfant Jésus Nicolas Barré), for which we are most grateful. The supportive environment of UCD School of Education is also acknowledged, as is the enthusiastic interest of Deirdre Bennett, Ruth Ferris and Ellen Regan, who are completing doctoral research on the history of women religious, under my supervision at UCD.

Special thanks to Catherine KilBride, editorial adviser and manuscript editor; Catherine's expertise at various stages of the research and writing has added immeasurably to the successful and timely completion of the book, and is greatly appreciated.

Finally, many thanks to Irish Academic Press, which was enthusiastic about this project from the outset.

As we went on research trips, lost track of time in archives, and buried ourselves in writing, we were always supported by our families and friends. This book is dedicated to them, with love and thanks.

Professor Deirdre Raftery
University College Dublin
October 2018

# Sources and Referencing System

The research for this book included a substantial period of work at the new Presentation Sisters Congregational Archives, Cork (PSCA). Additional research was undertaken at the Presentation Archives and Heritage Centre, Matlock, England; the Presentation Archives, San Francisco; and the Presentation Archives, Newfoundland. Digital copies of Annals and images were supplied by archivists at the Presentation Convent, New Windsor, New York, and the Presentation Convent, Dubuque, Iowa. Relevant materials were also consulted at the Dublin Diocesan Archives; the Diocesan Archives of Newfoundland; the Provincial Archives of Newfoundland; the Galway Diocesan Archives and the Cork Diocesan Archives.

A substantial amount of the research was conducted in many Presentation convents around Ireland, each of which has its own collection; these are mainly uncatalogued. As part of the ongoing archival planning around the many convent collections extant, the Presentations have recently assigned a unique identifying number to each convent collection. Uncatalogued convent collections are not yet using this identifier, and they are referenced using the abbreviated forms assigned by the Presentation Sisters Congregational Archives.

Where collections have recently been deposited at the Presentation Sisters Congregational Archives, PSCA is indicated as the location. To facilitate readers, and especially those who use this book in the years ahead during which many Irish Presentation collections will be accessioned and catalogued, Sr Rosarie Lordan, General Archivist, Presentation Sisters Congregational Archives, has supplied a list included here. It indicates the new number assigned to each convent collection, the convent name, and the abbreviation used for that collection.

# PBVM References for Irish Collections

| Number | Convent | Abbreviation |
|---|---|---|
| 1 | South Presentation Convent | SPC |
| 2 | Killarney | KLY |
| 3 | George's Hill, Dublin | GHD |
| 4 | Waterford | WAT |
| 5 | North Presentation Convent | NPC |
| 6 | Kilkenny | KKY |
| 8 | Tralee | TRA |
| 14 | Galway | GAL |
| 15 | Rahan | RAH |
| 16 | Thurles | THU |
| 17 | Doneraile | DON |
| 18 | Wexford | WEX |
| 20 | Portlaoise | PLE |
| 23 | Bandon | BAN |
| 25 | Dingle | DIN |
| 29 | Midleton | MID |
| 30 | Youghal | YOU |
| 34 | Sexton Street, Limerick | SSL |
| 35 | Milltown | MLT |
| 37 | Fermoy | FER |
| 40 | Millstreet | MIL |
| 41 | Caherciveen | CAH |
| 42 | Listowel | LTL |
| 46 | Mitchelstown | MTN |
| 48 | Clondalkin | CDN |
| 53 | Ballingarry | BAL |
| 56 | Crosshaven | CRO |

# Glossary

Throughout the book, we refer to place names as they were known during the period being discussed (e.g. Madras, and not Chennai). We use the terms 'nun' and 'Sister' interchangeably, as is common in scholarship.

| | |
|---|---|
| Apostolate | Active works undertaken by a community of religious. |
| Cloister | An enclosed part of a convent or monastery, which is free from entry from outsiders. |
| Convent | A community of nuns; also, the building in which they live. |
| Discreets | Women religious holding offices (Assistant Superior, Bursar, Mistress of Novices). |
| Divine Office | Book of prayer, comprising psalms, hymns and lessons, recited or sung daily in choir by professed religious; it is composed of eight hours (Matins, Lauds, Prime, Terce, Sext, None, Vespers, Compline). |
| Enclosure | Rule of cloistered orders of nuns, by which they live always within the convent and do not go into the outside world, except in special cases provided for by Canon Law. |
| Filiation | Foundation made from another convent; the filiation becomes independent of the 'parent' house. |
| Habit | Distinctive clothing worn by members of a religious order. |
| House of the Order | Convent of an order of nuns. |
| Nun | Female member of a religious order, who has taken solemn vows. |
| | The term refers to women religious who entered contemplative life. Though distinct from 'Sister', the terms are now often used interchangeably. |
| Novice | Person formally received into a religious community to serve a period of formation that determines fitness for profession. |

| | |
|---|---|
| Novitiate | Term used to refer to both the building in which novices live separately from the professed religious, and the time of probation spent under the direction of a Mistress of Novices before a novice is admitted to religious profession. |
| Postulant | Candidate for admission to a religious community who serves a probationary period before being admitted to the novitiate. |
| Prefect Apostolic | Clergyman with jurisdiction over a district of a mission territory. |
| Profession | Act of embracing religious life by taking vows of poverty, chastity and obedience, according to the Rule of the religious order. Some orders have additional vows, such as a vow to educate. |
| Questing | Seeking vocations, usually by visiting schools and Church gatherings to request that aspirants to religious life might come forward |
| Reception | Ceremony at which a postulant is officially received into a religious order as a novice. |
| Right Reverend | Title for high ecclesiastical officials. |
| Sacred Congregation of the Propaganda Fide | Department of the pontifical administration in Rome whose role is to spread Catholicism. |
| Sister | A female religious who has taken simple vows and lives in a religious institute called a congregation. |
| Superior | The Bishop or Ordinary, in charge of a local convent. |
| Superioress | The nun in charge of a convent. |
| Teaching Sisters | Women religious who conduct schools. |
| Temporary Vows | Vows which are temporary and have to be renewed after a period of time. |

# Abbreviations

| | |
|---|---|
| AL | Autograph Letter |
| CICE | Church of Ireland College of Education |
| CSJ | Sisters of St Joseph |
| DDA | Dublin Diocesan Archives |
| DE | Department of Education |
| GDA | Galway Diocesan Archives |
| GHAD | George's Hill Archive Dublin |
| HC | House of Commons |
| IE | Ireland |
| KPS | Kildare Place Society |
| MFA | Microfilm Accessions |
| MS | Manuscript |
| NAI | National Archives of Ireland |
| NAI ED | National Archives of Ireland Education Files |
| NLI | National Library of Ireland |
| NN | Nano Nagle |
| NSW | New South Wales |
| OFM | Order of Friars Minor (Franciscans) |
| OP | Order of Preachers (Dominicans) |
| OSB | Order of St Benedict (Benedictines) |
| OSU | Order of St Ursula (Ursulines) |
| PAHCM | Presentation Archives and Heritage Centre Matlock |
| PASF | Presentation Archives San Francisco |
| PBVM | Presentation of the Blessed Virgin Mary |
| PP | Parish Priest |
| PSCA | Presentation Sisters Congregational Archives |
| QUB | Queen's University Belfast |
| RC | Roman Catholic |
| Rev | Reverend |
| RSCJ | Society of the Sacred Heart |
| Rt Rev | Right Reverend |

| | |
|---|---|
| SJ | Society of Jesus (Jesuits) |
| SPG | Society for the Propagation of the Gospel in Foreign Parts |
| Sr | Sister |
| TB | Tuberculosis |
| TCD | Trinity College Dublin |
| UCB | Ursuline Convent Blackrock (Cork) |
| UCC | University College Cork |
| UCD | University College Dublin |
| n.p. | no page |
| n.d. | no date |
| n.n. | no name |

CHAPTER 1

# Finding Nano: Researching an Enigmatic Irishwoman and Her Legacy

The aim of this book is to examine the life and the education legacy of Nano Nagle (1718–84). Few women have left such a significant legacy to female education, yet Nagle remains almost invisible in scholarship on the history of education, women's history, and in the burgeoning field of the history of women religious.[1] Nagle brought the Ursuline order to Ireland; she also founded the Presentation order which expanded very rapidly, in Ireland and around the globe, in the nineteenth century. Her education legacy can be discussed with reference to hundreds of Presentation schools, thousands of Presentation Sisters who taught in these schools, and tens of thousands of pupils who attended the schools since the first one was founded in 1775.[2] She is at least as important a figure in Irish education as Edmund Rice, founder of the Christian Brothers, yet it is he who has been well served by scholarship.[3] Indeed, while the legacy of Presentation women to global education is on a par with that of other large female teaching orders, such as the Sisters of St Joseph and the Society of the Sacred Heart, it is far less well documented.[4] Equally, Nagle has attracted considerably less attention than Irish-born Protestant women involved in poor relief and education.[5] What kind of attention has she received, and why is she a shadowy figure in the history of education and women's history? These questions prompted the research for this book, undertaken at Presentation archives in Ireland, England, Newfoundland and North America.

Many individual Presentation convents and schools around the world have published their own histories, sometimes for a celebratory event such as a school centenary or bicentenary.[6] There is also a small number of books on Nano Nagle and on the Presentations, written by women religious and by clergymen, between the 1950s and 1990s.[7] The broad narrative of how the Order was founded is therefore already known, and it was decided not to rehearse the chronological accounts that appear in the studies by the Rev T.J. Walsh and Sr Mary Pius O'Farrell, for instance. What has not existed is a thematic study of the schools founded by Nagle and the first generations of Presentations. Though Presentation schools became widespread in Ireland by the end of the nineteenth century, particularly in Leinster and Munster, there is no systematic study of the education they provided. Similarly, there is no study that shows how a system of Irish schools could generate the vocations to religious life, and the skills in teaching and teacher training, that would sustain the first international Presentation missions.

Our aim then, is to focus closely on Presentation education in an attempt at understanding how Irish schools became the bedrock of Nagle's global education legacy. In choosing to write a thematic study, and not a chronological account, we move purposefully away from seeing Nano's legacy as something that can be mapped as a linear sequence of events. However, we recognise that a thematic study presents readers with occasional repetitions, as we move back and forth between the nineteenth and twentieth centuries, and between Ireland and other countries. This is unavoidable, but it has the advantage that it generally allows each chapter to be read independently of any other. For more traditional chronological accounts of Nano and Presentation education, readers can turn to narrative publications that commenced with the eulogy given by the Bishop of Cloyne.

## Publications on Nano Nagle: From panegyric to *Positio*

The earliest attempt to create a chronology of Nano Nagle's life was undertaken by Dr William Coppinger, Bishop of Cloyne, when he delivered a eulogy on Nagle in 1794, to raise funds for a charity, the Cork Amicable Society.[8] This account of Nagle's life had some errors (later corrected), and was written in the style of an eighteenth-century panegyric. Coppinger provided an outline of the trajectory of her early life, but with little concrete detail. This may have been in part because, a decade after her death, he recalled few events from her youth. His comments were general, and favourable: he described the young Nano as a person of 'affable disposition' and suggested – not improbably – that her parents shaped her personality by their own 'good example'. He noted that she was educated for a time in Paris, and that she later tried her vocation at a convent in France. Coppinger praised Nagle for turning her attention to 'the poor Irish', by returning from France 'to contribute to their relief', and his address continued with an overview of her adult life.[9] The text of the eulogy, while providing a broad sketch of Nagle's life, frustrates the researcher. It fails to provide any insight into how Nano Nagle overcame the challenges of being an ambitious woman of faith, operating within a deeply patriarchal Church, in an impoverished corner of a country suffering the severe strictures of penal legislation against Catholics. The eulogy could be dismissed as mere hagiography; however, it is a useful reminder of the complex relations between powerful churchmen and independent secular women. Although the Bishop was fulsome in his praise of what Nagle achieved, he also wrote of Nagle's 'misguided zeal, her shameful indiscretion, [and] her inconsiderate piety', hinting that she needed to learn to sublimate her wilfulness in order to better serve her Church.[10]

The address, despite its limitations, provided subsequent biographers with a handful of details about Nagle's life that they have all reproduced unquestioningly, reminding readers of its *ex Cathedra* position. For example, one such detail is a description of Nano Nagle's experience of epiphany. Coppinger recounted how Nagle, while living in considerable comfort in Paris, saw poor people waiting to attend Mass at dawn one day, and was struck by their faith. The Bishop's interpretation of this moment was that it was 'pointed with a sting of Divine Grace' and he wrote that 'she was edified and confounded at the sight'.[11] Coppinger concluded that the 'charms of dissipation ... lost much of their ascendency on this occasion' and Nagle came 'gradually to despise what a short time before she had deemed so desirable'.[12] There is no way to corroborate this story and the significance of the incident was disputed by one of Nagle's contemporaries, Mother Clare Callaghan, who wrote that 'the love of the poor which animated her young sister, and that sister's premature death, had a more profound influence on Nano's decisions'.[13] However, although Nagle was dead ten years when Coppinger penned the eulogy, she was 'within living memory', and the events of her life contained in his panegyric attained the status of fact in subsequent biographical studies. Arguably the most compelling of the Bishop's recollections was that in her lifetime Nagle 'received the most opprobrious insults' on the streets of Cork. He wrote that she was charged with 'deceiving the world with her throng of beggar's brats ... [and] that her schools were a seminary of prostitution'.[14] These few comments, written against the grain of the otherwise pietistic account of Nagle, challenge the researcher to consider how she may have been viewed by some people in her own lifetime.

The first full biography of Nano Nagle, by the Rev William Hutch, was published in 1874 to mark the centenary of the founding of the Presentations.[15] Hutch penned biographical studies of several women religious and, in the style of the time, his writing was congratulatory in tone. The biography surveyed the growth of the Presentations over a century, and contained a conspectus of schools that remains a useful research tool.[16] In the 1930s, the Presentations in Cork asked Alfred O'Rahilly to write a new study of Nano Nagle and the Presentation Sisters. O'Rahilly was a good choice for many reasons: he had been educated at University College Cork (UCC), and had entered the Society of Jesus (Jesuits), although he left before ordination. O'Rahilly completed a DPhil, returning to UCC where he eventually became president of the university. He had the kind of scholarly background that suggested he would be suited to writing about a religious congregation, and his papers suggest that he commenced the task with enthusiasm.[17] However, his professional commitments prevented him from making significant progress with the book, and he involved a local curate, T.J. Walsh, in the project. Following the death of his wife, O'Rahilly decided to become a Holy Ghost priest, and moved to Dublin to begin his training at Blackrock College. At about this time, he handed all of his research on Nano Nagle to Walsh, and advised the Superioress of South Presentation Convent that while he could not complete the book, he had placed the task in good hands.

Walsh was inspired to write the biographical study of Nagle not only because O'Rahilly needed his support, but because he had family links with the Motherhouse, South Presentation Convent, Cork. His mother had been a pupil there, and had learned about Nano Nagle from 'a dear old Sister Agatha, quite blind, who ceaselessly told the story of Nano's halcyon days in Paris'.[18] Walsh was a worthy successor to O'Rahilly in many respects. His study of Nagle drew on extant manuscript material, and he was painstaking in researching how the Presentation Rule and Constitutions were developed. The book was published in anticipation of the Cause for the canonisation of Nagle, and it provides an overview of how the Presentations began to spread throughout the world.[19] Walsh, however, was not the only researcher on the book: it is clear from extant papers that research was done by Sr Catherine Condon.[20] It was she who contacted all of the international foundations, gathered data, and prepared the genealogical research and some valuable tables and charts. One of the most impressive of Condon's creations was a five-page folding insert, containing a visualisation showing every Presentation foundation in the world, and the relation of each to the other. But because individual nuns were not singled out for attention and praise, Sr Catherine Condon was not acknowledged as a co-researcher on the book; rather, Walsh extended a general word of thanks to all the

Sisters who had supported him. Condon suffered the fate of many women who were the 'helpmeet' of clergymen and male scholars at that time: she remained invisible.[21] Research on Nagle continued in the twentieth century under Sr Pius O'Farrell, a Presentation Sister with extensive knowledge of Presentation records.[22] The impetus to gather materials and provide accounts of Nagle's life arose from the continued efforts towards the Cause for her canonisation, which was presented to the Congregation for the Causes of the Saints, in 1994.[23] Sr Pius O'Farrell published some of the papers used in the *Positio*, providing researchers with a useful collection.[24] Nonetheless, the fact remains that there is only a handful of letters in Nagle's own hand, and very slender evidence about her life.

## Nano's Legacy

For the purpose of this book, it was decided to focus on the most obvious – yet surprisingly uncharted – element of her legacy: the schools which she founded in her lifetime in Cork, and the network of foundations around Ireland which grew from that very first foundation in Cove Lane. These in turn gave rise to international foundations. To explore hundreds of international convents would have been impossible in a single volume, and indeed at this point in Presentation history it is no longer possible to ascertain the founding/closing date of every single house that has ever existed. It was decided to examine the histories of the Irish foundations and the way they contributed to education, and then signal how the nineteenth-century international foundations commenced in response to a growing mission imperative within the Order. In this way, the book could show the different ways in which Nano Nagle's legacy became evident, in the century after her death.

The book commences with a biographical study of Nagle, drawing on extant sources and on the historiography of Ireland in the seventeenth and eighteenth centuries. The impact of penal legislation on families such as the Nagles, the relevance of the 'Irish enlightenment', and the changing face of Cork in Nano's youth, are explored. The study of Ireland in the seventeenth and eighteenth centuries is a rich area in scholarship, to which our study makes a small contribution by placing a lens over one family, and the times in which they lived. The scholarship of Michael Brown, David Dickson, Jane Ohlmeyer, Ian McBride, Thomas O'Connor and Mary Ann Lyons was immensely useful, as we considered Cork, Ireland and Europe in the time of Nano Nagle and her family.[25] There has been considerable growth in medical history, and this has helped us understand Nagle's prolonged illness and death, and the kind of contagious diseases common in boarding schools, novitiates and convents in the nineteenth century. Though health is not a major theme in our study, the book signals the kind of medical information that can be found within convent archives.[26]

The book attempts to make original contributions to the history of education, and the history of women religious. The history of education is a major research field, and areas of research include how schools were founded and funded, how children and adults experienced education, and how education policy was created and worked in the past. Historians also study the materiality of education, and the gendered nature of education.[27] One of the least-explored topics in the history of education is the culture of convent schools, while the education and training provided by nuns demands much more attention.[28] The Presentations, who founded schools in Ireland, England, India, Tasmania, North America and Australia in the nineteenth century, have a place in the history of education, not only because of the education they provided, but because of their contribution to teacher training for women. They coordinated their own internal training systems, and also adopted the monitorial system in many of their large schools. In records concerning every country we examined, we found that women and girls in nineteenth-century Presentation schools were given the opportunity to learn to teach. Indeed, records indicated that the nuns generally were positively disposed to teaching girls to earn their own living. By teaching them to sew, knit and weave, they gave them the means to do paid work, even when married and raising children. In some of their convents, such as the foundation in Youghal, the nuns taught young women how to establish and run co-operatives to sell fine lace work and manage their incomes.[29] In Ireland, when civil service opportunities opened up for Catholic females, the Presentations were quick to prepare girls to take entrance examinations, and they were also enthusiastic supporters of university/further education for young women, though this has not heretofore been written into the historical narrative around female education in Ireland.

The book also shows how, in the early twentieth century, the Presentations globally had to adapt to education change. Nuns began to attend teacher training colleges, university, and seemingly endless summer schools and short courses, as they gained the qualifications increasingly required to run their schools. Though this meant going outside their enclosure, nuns seem to have been willing college students. A major part of the book involves an exploration of how the Presentations engaged with the National System of education, which commenced in Ireland in 1831. Though the system was non-denominational, the nuns found ways to work successfully within its constraints, so that they could take in larger numbers of pupils. Presentation education initiatives in many of the countries outside Ireland in which they missioned are also examined. In particular, we focus on the strategies that they used in order to get their schools built and funded.

This book also adds to the growing field of the history of women religious. The historian and Dominican Sister, Margaret MacCurtain, pointed out in 1995 that while women's history was the most significant new field to develop in the 1980s, there remained a need 'to hear the voices of religious women'.[30] Far from being 'sterile and narcissistic', convent life provides historians with a range of source materials, and MacCurtain has argued that the history of Irish nuns should become 'an integral part of Irish history'.[31] Internationally, scholarship in this area has grown significantly in the last thirty years, and the work of Margaret McGuinness, Rebecca Rogers, Anne M. Butler, Elizabeth M. Smyth, Carmen Mangion, Phil Kilroy and Susan O'Brien has added considerably to the understanding of the lives and work of women religious. In Ireland, work by Caitríona Clear, Mary Peckham Magray, Rosemary Raughter, Bronagh Ann McShane and Máire Kealy has helped to open up the field, with the result that research on women religious in Ireland is attracting attention, and the international reach of Irish women missionaries has also been the subject of recent scholarship.[32]

## Religious Life: Structures, Systems and Missions

The governance of Presentation convents is a compelling area of study, and sources indicated more flexibility on the part of nuns than might have been expected. On the one hand there were clearly defined roles for different community members; on the other hand, over time, adaptations were made to regulations governing religious life. Individual Sisters had to make compromises in order to survive in the different missions in which they found themselves. However, as Presentation houses proliferated around the globe in the nineteenth century, Sisters were unified by their Rules and Constitutions; their *modus operandi* was described in the *Presentation Directory*, written as a single reference source for all Presentation convents.[33] The *Directory* laid down practices to be observed, from the most prosaic house rules to the duties of nuns such as the Superioress, and the Discreets (the nuns who held the offices of Assistant Superior, Bursar, and Mistress of Novices). While the Superioress governed the convent, the 'spiritual and temporal affairs of the Monastery ... [and] the exact observance of the rules and constitutions' were in the authority of the bishop. 'The first and principal Superior of the Religious of the Presentation Order is the Diocesan Bishop, to whose authority they are to yield,' the *Directory* reminded readers.[34] As a symbol of the subservience of the Superioress to the Superior, she had to 'go on her knees, and kiss the [end of his] stole as a mark of her submission, and in acknowledgement of his authority' every time he visited the convent.[35] Because bishops were often 'occupied in the weighty concerns' of the diocese, a convent could be placed in the charge of a priest.[36] Again, the nuns had to show absolute obedience to the appointed priest.

Sisters were taught that the 'possessions of the Monastery shall be in common ... Religious will receive what is necessary, not looking upon it as their own, but as given only for their use.'[37] They were to 'ardently cherish purity of mind and body', and 'excel in the practice of Obedience.'[38] Obedience to the Superioress was crucial to the harmony of the convent, as it was she who governed every aspect of the lives of the Sisters, including the work they did in the schools. She was responsible for ensuring that the Sisters carried out their school duties with 'zeal, charity, and humility, purity of intention and confidence in God' and she was required to visit the schools at least once a week.[39] Furthermore, she was responsible for the appointment of the teaching Sisters in the schools.[40] While she might consult the Discreets, it was the Reverend Mother who decided the classes and subjects that each Sister would teach. However, before Sisters could embark on their role as educators they had first to complete their religious formation.

Religious formation took two and a half years to complete. The first five to six months were known as postulancy. During this time postulants were required to:

> ... attend the schools every day for three hours; the remainder of the time they shall employ in spiritual exercises, and in learning such things as may qualify them for the functions of the Institute, according as the Mother Superior and the Mistress of the Novices shall direct.[41]

After postulancy, there followed two years in the novitiate. Novices had to 'apply themselves to the study and exercises of the interior life', and also learn to teach in the schools. The Mistress of Novices had to 'form' the novices into teaching Sisters by constantly supervising them in the schools.[42] At intervals, the progress of a novice was assessed by the Vocals (professed Choir Sisters with the right to vote), but the group of Vocals determining the progression of a postulant or novice could not include her own 'Sisters, Aunts or Nieces'.[43] There were regulations to prevent nepotism; there were also regulations to minimise the possibility that women without a vocation, and women in poor health, could enter the convent. 'Care should be taken to receive no member who is afflicted with any dangerous malady, or who may be subject to infirmities incompatible with the functions of the Institute,' the *Directory* stated.[44] However, because there were no medical tests for postulants in the nineteenth century, it proved impossible to know much about their health; many entrants were in the early stages of pulmonary tuberculosis, and the disease was not uncommon in convents, schools and institutions at that time.[45]

From 1923, the whole of the first year of the novitiate was known as the 'spiritual year'. The Annals of the Presentation Convent Killarney recorded: 'For the first time in the history of the house novices were withdrawn for one whole year from school work to fulfill obligations of Canon Law by making a Spiritual Year before their first vows.'[46] During the spiritual year, the novice was not permitted to 'be employed in the external charges of the congregation, or even in the special study of letters, the sciences or arts'.[47] The spiritual year was to be dedicated entirely to religious formation and spiritual exercises. Secular studies and work in the schools were prohibited and visitation by family members was restricted. While the second year of the novitiate required further spiritual training and study of the constitutions, the novices were permitted to 'be employed in the work of the community' provided they were not employed 'to supply the want of teachers'.[48] Having successfully completed the two-year novitiate and accepted the Rule of the Presentation Order, the novice was accepted by the Chapter and professed with temporary vows. The period of temporary vows lasted for three years, after which the Sister could attain perpetual profession. A harmonious community depended on nuns continuing to conform to the vow of obedience throughout their religious life. Until the changes in religious life that followed the Second Vatican Council, the understanding within the Presentation Order was that 'blind obedience to the rules and regulations of the house and the Superior was what led to sanctity'.[49]

Like most Orders, the Presentations had both Choir Sisters and Lay Sisters. The distinction between Lay and Choir nuns arose in Western monasticism, in the Middle Ages. Educated women who entered convents brought their maidservants with them; these women did not take solemn vows, rather they did the domestic work that left Choir Sisters free to recite the Divine Office and pursue intellectual interests.[50] The survival of the two-tiered convent system into the late eighteenth and nineteenth centuries meant that in the newer apostolic orders, such as the Presentations, the domestic work of the Lay Sisters freed the Choir Sisters to run the schools. Women who entered religious life to become Choir Sisters were usually educated women who could be trained for professional work, such as teaching, and they could assume leadership roles such as Superioress or Bursar. Some Sisters were noted for their ability to make foundations and manage extensive building projects, and many travelled to found overseas missions. These are the women whose lives are discernible in congregational archives, in convent Annals, financial records, school records and in surviving correspondence.

The women who entered convents to become Lay Sisters (in some congregations known as Converse Sisters, or House Sisters) are much harder to research as they rarely wrote anything, and were rarely written about.[51] 'The number of Lay Sisters shall be small, and particular care taken that they be well chosen,' the *Directory* noted.[52] They needed to be strong, healthy and hardworking; while Lay Sisters only very occasionally appear in convent records, it is always their labour and devoted service that is noted.[53] Because this book focuses on education, it casts little light on the lives of Irish Lay Sisters. Occasionally they were included in lists of founding groups of nuns going to overseas missions, but their work was rarely described in Annals, and generally they could only be identified in Profession Registers by a process of deduction.[54] However, where a Superioress in a nineteenth-century convent wrote about Lay Sisters, it was invariably because these women were vital to the success of the mission. Visiting the Presentation Novitiate in Kilcock, in 1880, one Superioress was delighted to note the arrival of 'two Lay Srs, Invaluable'.[55]

It is a common misconception that the two-tiered structure of convent life was a function of whether or not women entered convents with a dowry, and that women without dowries could not become Choir Sisters. Our research in many Presentation archives confirms what we have noted elsewhere: the possession of a dowry was not a condition of acceptance into most convents in nineteenth-century Ireland, and indeed many women had no hope of raising a dowry.[56] Had convents insisted on dowries, the rapid expansion of congregations in the nineteenth century would simply not have taken place. The *Directory* indicated that 'the fortune and other expenses required' of a novice were to be determined 'according to the times and the wants of the Monastery'.[57] This recognised the possibility that when communities accepted women with very large dowries, that money could support several other Sisters who had nothing. There are many instances in Presentation records that indicate clearly that convents did not expect dowries from every woman, and that Superiors were satisfied to accept women who were educated, who 'showed promise' or who had 'grand voices'.[58] The Superioress in San Francisco in 1878, Mother M. Teresa Comerford, noted pragmatically that 'young ladies in this country seldom bring dowries to the Convents'.[59]

Though the Presentation Order spread around the world in the nineteenth century, it is noteworthy that many Irish-born Sisters lived out their religious life in the convent where they entered. This gave stability not only to the convents, but to novices and Sisters, who knew with reasonable certainty where they would spend the rest of their lives, and where they would be buried. Each house was independent, and mobility between houses was not expected, though it certainly happened. Communities were often small in the nineteenth century, and getting one or two new postulants each year was a good outcome. Often convents attracted girls who had attended their schools, or girls who had cousins and aunts in the convent, making communities even tighter. The process of making a new foundation was regulated very clearly, and it provided for the possibility that a nun sent out to make a new foundation might want to return to her own community.[60]

While much of this book examines Presentation education in Ireland, it also looks at how the Order expanded globally in the nineteenth and early twentieth centuries. There are common patterns to be found in the ways in which missions were made; usually there was an invitation from a bishop or a priest who was related to a Presentation Sister; then there was a flurry of activity to assemble a founding group; then the journey was undertaken, and invariably the pioneers arrived at their destination to find that there was no convent ready for them. It is tempting to think that the early pioneers in Newfoundland, India, Tasmania, Australia and America were excited by the prospects ahead, but it is far more likely that they approached their missions with trepidation. They were not supposed to take any pleasure from their travels, and were not to show the slightest interest in seeing 'the curiosities of those places through which they pass'. However, the surviving records of the travels of missionary nuns show that they were curious about, and appreciative of, what they saw *en route* to their new missions. They were dispensed from the 'fasts, abstinences and other austerities of their rules' while journeying, and some even managed to embrace the hardships of travel with gusto.[61] Nowhere is this more evident than in the illustrated travel diary of Mother Teresa Comerford, which charts the pioneering journey to San Francisco in 1854.

Sr Mary Margaret Mooney described the process by which many new nineteenth-century foundations were made:

> It was not unusual for the Irish convent receiving [a] … request to inquire if other Presentation houses could spare a Sister or two for the new work. The volunteers from two or more houses would together make the new foundation. While the missionary Sister could at any time return to the house of her profession, the new foundation was a self-supporting entity of status equal to the older establishments.[62]

Once a foundation was made, it became 'a distinct establishment'.[63] Yet despite this, it is clear that convents often reached out to each other for support, and Sisters sometimes moved between Presentation foundations. In particular, early overseas foundations relied on the mobility of Irish nuns, and Sisters came home to seek additional support, in a process that was known as 'questing'. The Annals of Bandon convent announced: 'Sisters M. Teresa and Raphael from the Presentation Convent of Aberdeen, South Dakota, arrived today. They have come to Ireland in quest of subjects.'[64] As this book shows, nuns who returned to Ireland questing for vocations were always successful, and in this way they swelled the ranks of their convents, until sufficient vocations were found locally.

Nineteenth-century Presentation foundations developed their own distinct characteristics, and operated independently of each other. However, it is clear that despite limited communication and travel, Presentation Sisters worldwide were unified by their charism and by their roots in one single foundation: Nano Nagle's first convent in Cork.

## CHAPTER 2

# Nano Nagle: Her Life and Times

*I shall tell you how I began … it was an undertaking I
thought I should never have the happiness of accomplishing.*

– Nano Nagle to Miss Fitzsimons, 17 July 1769.

## An Unusual Irish Childhood

Honora (Nano) Nagle had the misfortune to be born a woman in eighteenth-century Ireland, and her baptism as a Catholic conferred on her the added disadvantage of belonging to a Church persecuted by penal legislation. However, she was born wealthy, and that would make all the difference. In her youth, she was protected from the childhood hazards of her contemporaries, such as starvation, disease and premature death. But around her, there was clear evidence of poverty and its consquences. Just a year after her birth in 1718, the foundation stone of the North Charitable Infirmary was laid in Cork.[1] The Cork South Charitable Infirmary was established in 1722. While Nano was learning to walk and talk, at the family estate in Ballygriffin, the streets of Cork and Dublin teemed with juvenile beggars, and smallpox claimed the lives of thousands of children.[2] The country had been reduced to the status of a 'depending kingdom' by the Declaratory Act of 1720, triggering a sense of political disorientation.[3] In the years in which Nano was being educated in France, Ireland witnessed several famines, and so great were the numbers of homeless and orphaned children that many foundling hospitals and orphanages had to be established.[4] Catholics were subjected to penal legislation that prevented them from buying land, pursuing Catholic education at home or abroad, practising their faith, or participating in the electoral franchise.[5] Despite having been sheltered from the many miseries of Irish life, Nano Nagle eventually devoted herself and much of her fortune to the care and education of Irish poor children. What did she experience in her youth, that might have later influenced her to take radical steps to promote social justice?

The family into which Nano was born was the source of her strong Catholic Irish identity, and her financial acumen. Research on Nano's Norman ancestors shows how the name 'Nagle' had numerous iterations including de Nongle, de Nangle, and de Angulo. It was a de Angulo who landed in Ireland in 1170, as part of the retinue of Richard FitzGilbert, Earl of Pembroke (known as Strongbow).[6] De Angulo was given lands in Navan, and one of his sons came into possession of land in Limerick and South Tipperary. The de Nangles also owned considerable tracts of land along the Blackwater and an Anglo-Norman stronghold of the de Nangles was built in Monanimy, Cork, where generations of de Nangles and Nagles lived until the mid-seventeenth century. Recognised as 'one of the most important Catholic landed families to survive the seventeenth-century confiscations',[7] the Nagles were astute in the management of their estates. In addition to holding long leases of land from major Protestant absentee eighteenth-century landowners, including James Barry, 7th Earl Barrymore, they also leased land on the Doneraile and Kingston estates in north Cork, and on the Cahir Butler estate.[8] The Nagle land along the Blackwater was planted with large orchards, and indeed the Ballygriffin estate on which Nano Nagle was born was known to be one of the most productive Irish orchards; orcharding in the eighteenth century supplied a robust market for Munster cider in Dublin, and added to Nagle wealth.[9]

The Nagles embodied a distinctly Irish-Catholic heritage, and over generations they intermarried with many similar prominent families, consolidating their status and wealth. Nano's grandfather, David, was an MP in the parliament of James II, and he married into a wealthy Cork family, the Lombards of Lombardstown Park. David bought a considerable amount of land in the environs of the parish of Blackrock, Cork, and his fortune would eventually benefit Nano. When David died, his lands were gavelled between his sons, Garrett and Joseph.[10] From these men she learned the kind of shrewd strategising that would influence how she built schools and convents, invested in land and shares, and carefully constructed her will to dispose of her remaining wealth as she approached death.

Joseph Nagle, a lawyer, was described by Nano as 'the most disliked by the Protestants of any Catholic in the kingdom'.[11] He was named, along with Nano's father Garrett, as a conspirator in a Jacobite plot in 1731. In 1733, a parliamentary committee was established to investigate the claim that Joseph was remitting funds to James II from Ireland. Further, it was suggested (not improbably) that Garrett Nagle was the Pretender's agent in Flanders.[12] The case collapsed, but both brothers nonetheless suffered the consquences of the Penal Laws, and were identified as practising papists who could, therefore, not hold property. It was not uncommon for Catholic landowners to resort to religious conformity, a legal procedure by which they could 'register a switch of confessional allegiance to the Church of Ireland'.[13] South Munster conformity surged in the 1750s and 1760s, though there is no evidence that Joseph conformed.[14] Through a series of smokescreen transfers of property to Protestant friends, he managed to hold onto much of his land until his death in 1757, and he deliberately died intestate. Intestacy was a procedure used by Catholics at the time, to safeguard the succession of property. A trust replaced a will, and the trust pledged immediate relatives to administer his estate according to his directions. This would ensure that Nano would have sufficient funds to found schools for the poor in Cork, and build convents for the Ursulines and Presentations.

Nano was a mature woman by the time she devoted her life to the poor. Everything that happened before that was, in some way, a preparation for years of self-mortification and the disinterested care of others. Her childhood was spent at the family home in Ballygriffin, where Nano was the eldest of seven children born to Garrett Nagle and Ann Mathew between 1718 and 1730. When Garrett Nagle married Ann Mathew, he connected the Nagles with several distinguished familes: Ann's great-grandfather had married Elizabeth Poyntz, the widow of Thomas, Viscount Thurles, whose father had been Walter, Earl of Ormond and Ossory. Elizabeth Poyntz was herself the daughter of Sir John Poyntz, a Catholic recusant in England. The Ormond line would, in time, furnish Nano Nagle with postulants for her Ursuline foundation in Cork.

Ann Mathew and Garrett Nagle were married in Flanders, where many Jacobite exiles lived, and where Garrett allegedly served as agent to James II. Nano's birth in 1718 did not provide Garrett and Ann with an heir to Ballygriffin, but the following year a son was born. He was named for his Nagle grandfather, David. His birth was followed a year later by the arrival of a second daughter, Mary. By 1830, Garrett and Ann Nagle's family was complete and four more children had been born: Ann (1722), Joseph (1724), Catherine (1726) and Elizabeth (1730). The seven Nagle children were raised on the Nagle estate at Ballygriffin. Ann Nagle's confinements, which came close together, would have kept her busy and she would have had wetnurses to care for each new infant. It was common practice for gentlewomen to have nurses to relieve them of the trouble of breastfeeding, especially if they were expecting another baby. Additionally, it was believed that a healthy nurse, with good milk, could prevent childhood diseases such as *noma*, a gangrenous process in children that usually began with a black gum ulcer that became necrotic and led to deformation and death.[15] Choosing a good nurse included finding a woman who had good moral values; she should 'eat and drink little, enjoy no sexual relations, take little exercise, be between 25 and 35 years old, [and] have good teeth', and she should have given birth at least twice herself.[16]

In addition to overseeing the care of her small children, Ann Nagle would have had responsibilities including managing servants, and hosting occasional 'at homes', dinners and suppers. Garrett Nagle was often away, in France and in Flanders, and following the 'Jacobite plot' accusation of 1733, he spent most of his time out of Ireland.[17] During Nano's childhood, an extensive network of Nagles provided support to each other, and no doubt they socialised together and discussed politics and religion. Strong blood ties kept the siblings close in the decades that followed; Nano's sister Mary, having married her first cousin Pierce Nagle, had many children and thereby linked the Ballygriffin family even more closely to the Nagles of Annakissey.[18] Pierce's father (also Pierce) and uncle (Sir Richard) had married sisters, Mary and Jane O Kearney, and they settled in France, with the result that there were strong family bonds extending to the continent in ways that facilitated business and social networking.[19] For instance, Sir Richard's son, Jacques, looked after the French business interests of Nano's father when Garrett was in Ireland.[20]

Nano, her siblings and her extended family, all continued to socialise with each other in adulthood. Garrett Nagle was sponsor for two of Jacques Nagle's children, when they were baptised in Lille Cathedral in 1723 and 1731. When both David and Joseph moved to Bath in the 1760s, Nano visited there at least once. In 1766, Nano went to stay at the Galway home of her sister, Elizabeth Ffrench, and enjoyed a dinner attended by their distant cousin, Edmund Burke.[21] At around that time, one of Burke's cousins on his maternal side (also named Garrett Nagle), had been arrested in the Whiteboy inquiry of 1765–6, and had 'conformed' to the Established Church. Conforming was rarely an act of faith, and was more usually a pragmatic step to protect land, and there were many 're-conversions'.[22] Nano, doubtless, would have known about this, and would also have known that 'paper converts' usually remained sympathetic to their Catholic friends, and often protected them. They favoured relief measures for Catholics, protected priests, and used their social and political connections to help their former co-religionists.[23]

Within Nano's family, sibling loyalty was evident: Nano was particularly attached to her sister Ann, and her brother Joseph, to whom she would lend £2,150 to buy Calverleigh Manor, in Devon, in 1768.[24] Indeed, the surviving records of Nagle inheritances also point to a close-knit family: Garrett was executor for the will of his cousin, Edward Lombard; Nano's uncle Joseph, having no wife or children of his own, left his fortune to his nieces and nephews. Nano's own will would provide legacies for the three siblings who survived her: David, Joseph, and Elizabeth.[25] It is noteworthy that while Nano left nothing to Elizabeth's son, she made provision for Elizabeth's five daughters, including a generous bequest to the eldest daughter, Mary Ann.[26] This last gesture recognised the importance to women of financial independence, and was the action of a woman who had herself enjoyed financial security and autonomy.

Bonds of kinship and loyalty characterised the kind of resilience shown by the Irish Catholic élite in penal Ireland, and this resilience contributed to the survival of their faith. Nano Nagle was a female exemplar of such resilience, and she knew how to harness her wealth and independence in support of her ideals. To find the source of some of these ideals, it is necessary to look at her education and young adulthood.

## Nano's Education in the Age of Enlightenment

The Nagle home at Ballygriffin has not survived, and there are no images of the house. The surviving outbuildings, which are of cut stone, show evidence of architectural literacy, and it is likely the main house was also a stone building. The typical gentry houses of the era were 'two or three storeys over basement, five to nine bays wide' and testified to 'a family's substance, standing and taste'.[27] An estate like Ballygriffin was designed to provide 'a venue for conspicuous hospitality, social intercourse and polite recreation'.[28] The house would have had a collection of books, as it was the home of men whose lives were bound up with print through their roles in the law and public life.[29] While few eighteenth-century homes had 'libraries', collections of books were displayed on shelves and in cabinets, where vistors could view them, and then discuss them.[30] From the late seventeenth century, Irish readers had access to Latin and Greek classics, and Irish booksellers imported books in English, French and Italian. The country witnessed a robust trade in translations of French literature, and popular periodicals carried extracts from historical works and the writings of Enlightenment thinkers.[31] Writing paper was imported regularly from the continent, and would have been plentiful for wealthy people like the Nagles.

It is reasonable to suggest that the Nagle children had an education not unlike that of other Catholics of their rank. Schooling in early eighteenth-century Ireland was neither institutionalised nor specialised, as it was in neighbouring England and Scotland. While there were a few academies for boys, the young children of gentlemen were usually educated at home by scholar-teachers. These men were often poets, scribes, or translators working on Irish manuscripts, who were offered hospitality in exchange for tuition for the children of the house. This was a patronage system, which remained intact right through the eighteenth century. Many of these scholars and scribes were well-known hedge-school masters who were hired by Irish gentry, and by the rising Catholic families who were ambitious for their children.[32] They sometimes travelled between several homes, and in some cases children went to board with relatives or friends who had a tutor. There was also a custom whereby a few families would join together to hire a tutor who would board for a week in each household.[33] For instance, Eoghan Ó Caoimh was in four households in Cork and Kerry in 1684, and Conchubhar Óg Ó Cruadhlaoich was in at least two, in the years 1721–2.[34] Some scribes and scholars eventually established schools, such as Eoghan Rua Ó Súilleabhán, who was a tutor in the Nagle household in the mid-eighteenth century before becoming a schoolmaster.[35]

Because there is evidence that the Nagles hosted scholars, it is likely that this is how Nano and her siblings started their education. In addition to learning to read and write, David and Joseph would have had tuition in arithmetic, geometry, Greek and Latin. It is very possible that they also had a French tutor; many exiled Huguenot teachers living in Ireland became tutors to Catholic families, and taught children to read in French.[36] The Nagles developed business and investment interests in France, and it would have been prudent for the sons to learn to speak French. The children may have read some of the popular Anglo-Norman tales of chivalry that were used in hedge schools, such as *Guy, Earl of Warwick*, and the Irish abridgement of *The History of Fortunatus*.[37] The latter was a moral tale that taught readers that great riches are a burden, a lesson that certainly would not have been wasted on Nano, who would eventually dispose of her wealth in the interest of others. Children also read editions of *Aesop's Fables*, and Pepys's seventeenth-century abbreviated version of *The Seven Wise Masters* was highly regarded in Ireland, and was widely used to teach reading. Novels such as *Robinson*

*Crusoe*, published in the year of Nano's birth, would remain popular with young Irish readers for over two centuries.

Even when there was a tutor in a house, girls were often taught to read by their mothers, and Nano may have benefited from the undivided attention of Ann Nagle when she was five or six, and her sisters were still in the nursery. Nano's childhood preceded the growth of didactic juvenile fiction, and it was not until the mid-eighteenth century that the genre of conduct literature for girls became popular. But even if the moral tales of evangelical writers such as Hannah More, Mrs Trimmer and Mrs Sherwood had been available, it is most unlikely that they would have been allowed into the Catholic Nagle house.[38] The Nagle parents were far more likely to have been influenced by the thoughts of the French Cardinal, François Fénelon, published in his treatise *De L'Éducation des Filles* (1687). It promoted an education for girls of rank that included practical knowledge: they should understand book-keeping; they should know how to improve the lot of the poor, and they should even be able to set up schools for their tenants. They should also understand the law relating to land, and business matters concerning their estates. Wherever Nano learned her financial acumen and astuteness about managing property, her education certainly reflected the principles of Fénelon's treatise.

When Nano was around ten years old, Ann and Garrett Nagle decided to send her out of the country to be educated at a convent, indicating their respect for female learning and the value they placed on her spiritual formation. To prepare Nano for her convent schooling, her mother would no doubt have introduced her to the lives of the saints, and books of spiritual instruction. The fact that the Nagles travelled meant that it would have been easy for them to acquire books that were not available in Cork.[39] Devotional books popular with women readers included the *Imitation of Christ*, by Thomas à Kempis. They also read the lives of staunch Catholics such as Lady Magdalen Countess Montague, and studied books of Marian devotion that had been translated by confessors to houses of English nuns.[40] All of these books reminded their readers of the kind of burden that virtuous Catholic women had to bear, and encouraged them to model themselves on the female saints.

The lesson that self-sacrifice and worldly suffering could lead to spiritual development was not lost on Nano; she may have been sad to leave her family in order to be educated in France, but this was the price that Irish Catholic gentry paid to secure a Catholic education suited to their station. Indeed, convent education was not just 'a mandatory stage in the life of a young girl from the élite', it was also 'the first step in her transformation into a virtuous

Christian woman.'[41] But it was not a step taken without risks, and the Nagles would have been discreet in preparing Nano for her voyage, doubtless undertaken with other Catholics and possibly with one of her sisters. The illegal conveyancing of Catholic clergy and young scholars between Munster and France was 'conducted in small vessels operating from under-supervised harbours', such as Dungarvan and Clonakilty.[42] From an early age, Nano Nagle was aware of the importance of secrecy, and the necessity for fortitude; this would stand to her in later years.

Nano was sent to the continent for several years. There are no records of her schooling, though she may have attended the Benedictine Abbey at Ypres, in Belgium.[43] The monastery at Ypres had been established in 1665 to provide education and protection to Irish women during the religious persecutions.[44] The house at Ypres had so many Irish vocations that the nuns there were known variously as the Irish Ladies, and the Irish Dames of Ypres. If the young Nano had shown her parents that she had any inclination towards becoming a religious, the monastery and novitiate at Ypres would have been a suitable choice for Garrett and Ann Nagle. Equally, the couple may have chosen Ypres because they wanted a Catholic education for their daughter. English was the language used in the Benedictine Abbey at Ypres, and this would account for Nano Nagle's poor knowledge of French, a disadvantage on which she later wrote.[45] Congregations such as the Ursulines and the Dames de St Maur in Paris were French-speaking, and would have conducted lessons and daily routines through French. In the absence of any surviving evidence of where Nano went to school, her comment about being unable to write in French is perhaps the most compelling evidence for Ypres.

Catholic gentry, such as the Nagles, provided their children with the kind of education that prepared them for a good marriage. Nano's schooling would have included studying catechism, and perfecting some of the 'female accomplishments' such as music and drawing. This kind of education ensured that a young woman would not only make a good mother and wife, but that she would be attractive to potential husbands. For the propertied élite in the eighteenth century, marriage had serious implications; it could provide heirs and 'establish or consolidate valuable relationships'.[46] It could also create new claims and obligations such as the transfer of assets, so marriage had to be managed in a practical fashion.[47] Indeed, Cork witnessed a particularly business-like approach to the marriage market in 1771, as word circulated that Alderman Freeman of Youghal had three daughters 'ready to dispose of in marriage ... [with] £500 to give each'.[48] But most marriages were arranged with discretion, not least because of the risks of the abduction of heiresses that was not uncommon in eighteenth-century Ireland.[49] Though this was a risk more common amongst wealthy Protestants, it was not unheard of amongst Catholics. For wealthy Catholic families, the need to transfer assets discreetly was important. Because men and women married within their own rank, there were rarely fortunes to be made through marriage; rather, a satisfactory and mutually beneficial arrangement was the main precondition to the match.[50]

Catholic gentry families, such as the Nagles, Kenmares and Coppingers, sought out other Catholic families for marriage, but it was a limited market; some men had to look for brides from old English families, and travelled to England to make a match. Other Catholic landowners had to marry down the social scale, or across the denominational divide. Marrying 'out' was unlikely to meet with the approval of the tight network of Nagles, and Nano's siblings chose their spouses well. Elizabeth married into a branch of the Ffrench family of East Galway, Mary married a first cousin, and Joseph married into another prominent Catholic clan, the Mapas family of Co. Dublin.[51]

Nano, however, did not marry. Garrett Nagle's eldest daughter did not connect the Nagles with another prominent Irish Catholic family, nor did she make a marriage with a good French family, like some of her cousins. Indeed, many similar women of independent means did not feel compelled to marry; custom and contemporary law made women inferior to their husbands, and such subordination may not have appealed to Nano. Marriage brought with it other disadvantages: married women had to survive the burden of childbirth, at a time when the maternal death rate was high, and mean family sizes were large; additionally, up to the middle of the eighteenth century child mortality was so high that between a quarter and a third of all children would die before the age of fifteen.[52] Garrett Nagle's eldest daughter – for whatever reason – remained single. Rather than preparing her to be a wife and mother, Nano's convent education deepened her faith and helped to shape her future.

## Becoming a Woman: Formation, Faith and Fatherland

On completing her education, Nano spent some time in Paris with her younger sister, Ann. She returned to Ireland around 1746, after the death of her father, and lived on Bachelor's Quay, with her mother and Ann. If this arrangement was agreeable, it was short-lived: her mother died in January 1748, and Ann died a year later at the age of twenty-six. Nano went to live with her recently married brother, David, at the family estate in Ballygriffin. There would have been no other option for a single woman of Nano's rank, and – like many spinsters in similar situations – she passed her time by taking an interest in the tenants on the estate, and the education of their children. She was struck by their lack of schooling and the absence of religious instruction. She was also, doubtless, struck by how much Cork had changed while she had been in France. Terrible conditions of intense cold and exceptional drought had afflicted the county between December 1739 and late summer of 1741. The exceptional weather conditions resulted in widespread starvation and illness, and a loss of between 300,000 and 400,000 lives.[53] In Cork, a poorhouse-cum-foundling hospital was developed in 1747, in response to dire need; Nano could not have avoided being affected by the misery of the poor.

This may have prompted her to become a nun, for she returned to Paris in 1749, with the aim of entering a novitiate.[54] Records of her postulancy are as flimsy as those of her schooling, but by the time she returned to Cork in 1750 she had developed an understanding of the economics of convent management, and what would now be called property development; these hint at the things that Nano Nagle learned from the women who surrounded her, during her time in a French convent.[55]

Because Nano returned to Ireland to devote herself to teaching catechism to poor children, it seems likely that she spent time with a community that had a vocation to the care of paupers. Such communities had grown in number, in the mid-seventeenth century, as a new kind of woman appeared: the *filles dévotes*, or *filles séculières*.[56] These were pious women who did not want to withdraw from the world by entering an enclosed convent, rather they wanted to be of service to the public. While daughters of the upper ranks had traditionally entered religious congregations suitable to their station, such as the Ursulines, Bendectines and Visitations, there were now women who 'broke ranks' and chose to live alone or in female groups, and walk alone, even though this was considered improper. Their lifestyle was not the only way in which the *filles séculières* challenged norms: they took it upon themselves to catechise, at a time when the 'catechising function was most emphatically forbidden to women'.[57] While the aims of the Counter-Reformation had included preventing such novelties in the Church, the reforming councils also stressed the need to instruct the faithful. Bishops and priests needed women to help in the instruction in religion of children and girls. The grounds on which a woman like Nano Nagle could eventually catechise and teach were slowly being established.

In France for example, a Minim priest, Nicolas Barré, chose to carry out his ministry with the aid of a tiny group of women auxiliaries who had left the luxury of their homes to serve God by catechising children and preparing them to receive the sacraments. In 1662, these women agreed to live in community and by 1669 the group numbered two hundred women, and they were known as the Charitable Mistresses of the Holy Infant Jesus.[58] They ran small schools, teaching girls to read and training them in piety. A house was rented on the rue St Maur, in Paris, which became the novitiate and motherhouse, and the Sisters became known as the Dames de St Maur. In 1686 they became an offical congregation with a religious rule of life. The rapid success of their schools attracted the attention of Louis XVI, and of Madame de Maintenon, when they were planning the academy of Saint-Cyr for the education of noblewomen. Twelve 'of the best sisters' were demanded for Saint-Cyr, and they remained there until 1694.[59] The Charitable Mistresses continued to expand throughout France, using a model that Nano Nagle would consider when she founded the Presentations. A copy of the *Lettres Spirituelles du R Père Nicolas Barré* (1697) bearing Nano's autograph, indicates that she studied them at some point, and it is possible that she became familiar with the *Rule* in Paris in the late 1740s. At that time, the Superior was Catherine de Bosredon. Catherine had been educated at Saint-Cyr and her family mixed with members of the royal household.

There are many similarities between Catherine de Bosredon and Nano Nagle. Catherine turned her back on a life of luxury to teach catechism to the poor, walking about the poorest quarters of the city to find pupils; like Nano, she used her fortune to buy her congregation its Motherhouse and support its dependencies.[60] She was a practical woman who became deeply involved in all of the stuctural improvements to her convent, much as Nano would do in 1771. Throughout her term as Superior, which lasted over forty years, Catherine de Bosredon remained dedicated to the schooling and cactechising of the female poor. If Nano spent time with the Charitable Mistresses of the Holy Infant Jesus as a novice under Mère Ste Catherine, it would account for the education model she had in mind when she founded the Sisters of the Charitable Instruction of the Sacred Heart of Jesus (later Presentations).[61] There were other women who could have acted as guide and mentor to Nano Nagle when she was considering religious life in Paris, but Catherine de Bosredon stands out as a woman with whom she had much in common.

While Nano was in France, both as a pupil and as a postulant, she would have become aware of a range of types of educational provision.

Her own childhood in penal Ireland could not have prepared her for the variety of schools openly operating in seventeenth-century France. There were fee-charging schools, such as the élite boarding schools, or *pensions*, run by religious orders such as the Ursulines, and the Charitable Mistresses of the Holy Infant Jesus. The *pensions* were boarding-schools, which taught languages, literature, and female accomplishments. While the *pensions* were restricted to those who could afford fees, they often had a free school attached. The fees from the boarders helped to finance the free schools. There were also the *petites écoles*; these were primary schools that provided lessons in reading, writing and religion, for a small monthly fee, known as *écolage*.[62] There were also classes provided by master scriveners, and some clerics worked as private tutors. All of these forms of education involved the payment of fees, though in some cases the fees were modest. For those who could not afford to pay for schooling, there were charity schools, such as those within the poorhouses or *hôpitaux généraux*.[63] Finally, there were charity schools run by religious orders, and this was the model that attracted Nano Nagle. There was little difference between the curriculum of the *petites écoles* and the charity schools; they usually taught reading, writing, some arithmetic, and religion. A great diversity of 'deserving poor' availed themselves of the different forms of free schooling, and Nano became aware of distinctions of poverty that she had not heard of in Ireland. The vocabulary of poverty included '*pauvres, pauvres valides et invalides, mauvais pauvres, pauvres honteux, indigents, nécessiteux, misérables, gueux, gens sans aveu, mendicants, vagabonds, gagne-deniers, petit peuple*, [and] *canaille*.'[64] France not only increased Nano Nagle's awareness of poverty, but it also showed her ways in which free education could change the lives of the poor, and she returned to Ireland with a heightened sense of what she could do to alleviate poverty in Cork.

## Nano's Return to Cork and the Establishment of the Ursulines

Nano's time in France was happy; she later wrote that 'nothing would have made [her] come home', if she had not been prompted to return to Ireland by her confessor, a Jesuit priest.[65] He told her that her duty lay in instructing Irish children, and that she should 'run a great risk of salvation' if she neglected that duty.[66] It was with that in mind that she returned to Ireland in 1750, and went to live with her brother Joseph and his wife, Frances, in Cove Lane, Cork. Her brother David was still at Ballygriffin, and her bachelor uncle Joseph was living nearby in Blackrock, so Nano had a family network around her. Several years elapsed before she began her first school, during which time she kept her plans 'a profound secret', as she knew she would 'meet with opposition on every side'.[67] As a member of a distinguished and prosperous family, it could be expected that Nano would have occupied herself with 'gentry pastimes'.[68] Other women of rank in Ireland, such as Letitia Bushe and Mary Delaney, passed their time visiting the houses of friends or 'riding out' with hounds, and they also enjoyed 'reading, prating, walking, backgammon … chess … [and] card-playing'.[69] Socialising reflected a 'more permissive code of behaviour' than would become evident in the nineteenth century; women met to drink tea and have 'a few hours chat'; they drank wine in the evening, and spontaneous singing was enjoyed.[70] They also had access to a wide range of works published at home and abroad.[71] But Nano's dedication to charitable work suggests that she would not have been attracted by the pastimes of leisured women. Rather, this work became an outlet for her benevolent impulses, while also according with social 'expectations of her sex as tender and nurturing'.[72] Because she took a vow to enter religion while in France, it is likely that she led a relatively secluded life of prayer and contemplation, while providing companionship to her sister-in-law Frances, who did not have children. Nano's sister, Mary, who had married their cousin Pierce Nagle, was raising a large family at Annakissey.[73] Her sister Elizabeth, married to Robert Ffrench of Rahasan, Galway, was also busy raising a large family.[74] Nano passed a few quiet years in Cork, which were doubtless made painful by the the death of her infant nephew, Garrett Joseph, in 1753, and her sister, Catherine, in 1754. Grief at the loss of two members of her family may have moved her to begin to carry out the mission that had brought her back from France. She had also been very struck by 'the ignorance of the poor', which she had noticed from talking with 'servants of the house'.[75] It was time to take action.

Living in her brother's house in Cove Lane, Nano became aware of the kind of education provision for poor children in Cork. Very nearby, there was a Blue Coat Charity School for boys that provided education to Protestant boys and to 'popish natives'; there were also several Charter Schools dotted around the county. Charleville Charter School had opened in 1748, and was followed a year later by a Charter School in Castlemartyr; there were also Charter Schools in Kinsale (1749), Dunmanway (1751) and Innishannon (1752). These were part of the system of schooling established by the Incorporated Society in Dublin for Promoting English Protestant Schools in Ireland, which had been founded in 1733.[76] The schools fell into disrepute, because of the way in which children were abused, and because of the poor condition of the schools. The Cork schools that surrounded Nano Nagle were harshly criticised by Sir Jeremiah Fitzpatrick (Inspector General of Prisons). He described the 'ragged' children and damp schoolroom at Charleville Charter School: 'the windows of every room were broken, the beds filthy, and there was not a single sheet in the house for the children's use, whose education was shamefully neglected'.[77] At Innishannon, the 'children were very dirty, their clothes in rags', while a schoolmaster at Dunmanway Charter School at one point refused to enter the boys' dormitory in case he would catch 'a disorder' from the filthy children; the absence of soap in some Charter Schools resulted in the children's clothes being washed in urine.[78] At Innishannon Charter School, like most other similar schools, 'the itch' and 'scald head' were common.[79]

If the conditions of the Charter Schools did little to recommend them to even the poorest Catholics, the aims of the Charter School system would have made them reprehensible to the Nagles. The system aimed to 'promote the pure Protestant faith', to secure loyal subjects for the Crown, and to teach poor Catholic children to 'earn their bread'.[80] The Incorporated Society openly articulated its view of Catholic 'natives': they were superstitious, lazy and ignorant.[81] Having been placed in a Charter School, a Catholic child would be raised Protestant, and given incentives to remain Protestant.[82] The purpose of the schools, as much as their grim conditions, were anathema to Nano Nagle: she would found schools where Catholic religious instruction was at the very centre of daily activity.

Sometime between 1754 and 1755, Nano took her first steps towards quietly starting her first school, by renting a house in Cove Lane and sending her maid to 'get a good mistress, and to take in thirty poor girls' from the streets of the city.[83] The project was not without risks, however, and she knew that her 'immediate family ... would suffer most' if word got out that she was secretly teaching catechism to Catholic children.[84] She was particularly concerned that her uncle Joseph might be made to pay the price for her actions, as he was 'the most disliked by the Protestants of any Catholic in the Kingdom'.[85] Her brother was furious when he accidentally found out about Nano's secret school. But he became reconciled to it, and even supported the venture. Mother Clare Callaghan later recalled how Nano had 'assembled thirty wicked children',[86] who needed religious instruction. Within nine months, she had two hundred pupils and was ready to expand; she then established a school at the opposite side of the city, and attracted an equally large number of children there. Nano took on the responsibility of preparing children for the Sacraments. Each day, 'the schools [were] opened at eight, at twelve the children [went] to dinner', and school ended at five in the evening.[87] The children were taught to read, and to 'say the Catechism in each school by question and answer all together'.[88] Then the boys were taught to write, and the girls were instructed in needlework. Nano ensured that the children heard 'Mass every day … [said] their morning and night prayers … [and went] to Confession every month and to Communion when their confessors think proper'.[89] Older girls stayed in school until after six, to 'say the beads' and their night prayers. The success of the schools surprised Nano, who thought that she 'would not have more than 50 or 60 girls'.[90]

Then, in 1757, Nano's life changed forever when her uncle Joseph died and left her a fortune.[91] Joseph, like many wealthy Catholics in penal Ireland who wished to safeguard the succession of their property, died intestate; a Deed of Trust was created by his immediate family, to divide his estate as he had wished.[92] This 'considerable personal estate' was divided between his nieces, Nano and Elizabeth, and his nephews, David and Joseph.[93] Nano's uncle may have wanted to help Nano's poor schools; equally, he may have wanted to ensure that his niece – a single woman of almost forty years – was financially independent. Either way, she found herself a rich woman. This made it possible for her to support her 'two schools for boys and five for girls', in which the children were taught catechism, and how to read.[94]

A decade after receiving her inheritance, Nano started to develop new plans; she wanted to bring a religious order of nuns to Cork, to establish a convent and a school for girls. She had the support of Fr Francis Moylan, who had been ordained for the diocese of Cork, at the Irish College in Toulouse in 1761. Returning to Cork in 1763, Moylan had quickly become aware of Nano Nagle's work for the poor. Influenced by his Jesuit uncle, Fr Patrick Doran, he agreed with Nano that a female congregation should be established in Cork, and he determined that the Ursulines should be brought from France. Moylan persuaded a young Irishwoman, Eleanor Fitzsimons, to abandon her plans to enter the Visitations in France and instead become a postulant with the Ursulines at the rue St Jacques, in Paris. That convent thereby became the parent-house to the proposed Cork foundation.

Nano herself became involved in the process of finding support for a Cork convent. In 1768, she went to stay for about seven months at the Ursuline Convent, Saint Denis, Paris. Her cousin, Margaret Butler, had entered there in 1763 and had been professed in 1765.[95] Nano wanted Margaret to return to Cork as Superior of the Ursuline convent, which Nano would establish and support. In addition to the vows of poverty, chastity and obedience, the Ursulines had a fourth vow: the instruction of females.

This would have recommended the congregation to Nano, as being suitable for her Cork plans. While in Paris, Nano did not enter the congregation, rather she was there 'to receive training in the different exercises and to learn French'.[96] In this way, she believed she would become familiar with Ursuline life, and would be better able to support her foundation in Ireland. Her hesitation about becoming a professed religious remained, and indeed she would eventually be dispensed of the vow to enter religion that she had taken before returning to Ireland in 1750.

In 1767, the two cousins were ready to leave Paris; at the end of August, the annalist of the Ursuline Convent, Saint Denis, recorded that Margaret was 'to go to Cork, Ireland, [to] start the foundation of an Ursuline Convent. Miss Nagle is the foundress of it.'[97] Margaret was only one year professed when she set sail for Ireland. The Ursulines were willing missionaries: Margaret and Nano knew of the revered Sr Marie de l'Incarnation, who had led a group of nuns to Canada in 1639; more recently in 1727, French Ursulines had made a foundation in New Orleans. Missionary nuns had to be both resilient and resolute, as they often faced danger and outright hostility. Nano Nagle knew that Margaret, as first Superior, might face obstacles, but she believed these could be overcome. Her optimism was, however, premature. Within a year, Margaret Butler returned to Paris, having found that she 'could not adapt to the rigours of a foundation'.[98] How were the 'rigours' of convent life in Cork any different from those in Paris? Firstly, there was still a cloak of secrecy around the establishment of the Cork convent and its Catholic school. Secondly, the enormous task of building up a congregation in Ireland lay ahead and, while this did not daunt Nano Nagle, it daunted her cousin who could not have avoided knowing about the increased sectarian tensions that had driven people, including David and Joseph Nagle, out of the country in the 1760s. Thirdly, Margaret may not have anticipated the hardship she would experience in Cork; she witnessed the 'big freeze' of January 1768, when the city was covered in six feet of snow. There were few comforts, as the south suburb where she and Nano lived was where 'the poorer sort of the inhabitants dwell ... [t]heir doors thronged with children'.[99] Finally, the construction of the proposed convent had not begun, and the whole project was daunting to Margaret, who had become used to life in a quiet French cloister.

All was not lost, however. At the Ursuline Convent in the rue St Jacques, the novitiate of Eleanor Fitzsimons had progressed well. By 1770, three other Irish novices had joined her: Elizabeth Coppinger, Margaret Nagle, and Mary Kavanagh. This little group was enough to get the Cork foundation started, if they could find a French Ursuline willing to travel with them to Cork, as the founding Superior. Mother Margaret Kelly was the Irish-born nun at the Ursuline Convent in Dieppe selected by Francis Moylan for the Cork foundation. She had objections to the plan, but the power of a patriarchal church was in operation: Moylan prevailed upon the Archbishop of Rouen, who ordered Mother Margaret Kelly to go to Ireland as Superior to the newly built Ursuline convent.

The Cork in which Nano Nagle built her convent was a very different place from the Cork in which she had been born in 1718. Catholic merchants were becoming prosperous through the sale and export of butter, salt beef and pork. The city had expanded on reclaimed marshland, and there were new streets and rows of terraced houses. The commercial centre of the city was buoyant, and roads reached out towards an expanding residential area on the southern periphery of the city, where a rising middle class was building large homes with extensive gardens. Nano eschewed the areas that were attractive to rising Catholics, and instead chose to build her convent in Cove Lane, leasing a plot of land which had been owned by the Nagle family.[100] Though Catholics were becoming more prosperous, they still laboured under the penal code, and sectarian tensions that stirred up in the 1760s would have made Nano wary. Her brothers had moved permanently to Bath, and many other Munster Catholics became absentee landlords. Nano Nagle had to protect the convent in which she was investing her fortune. At the outset she sought 'counsel learnd in the law' in order to 'guard against penal laws',[101] and she conducted her business quietly, ensuring that the convent was a modest building, hidden behind a high wall with no formal gateway or ostentatious entrance. In a telling note she reminded Eleanor Fitzsimons: 'we are in a country [in which] we cant doe [*sic*] as we please'.[102]

The convent that Nagle built was not unlike the style of the house in Ballygriffin: it had three storeys and five bays, with chimneys at the gable ends. The cells in which the nuns would sleep were small and without fireplaces, but the reception rooms on the ground floor were more comfortable and were finished with plaster cornices.[103] She kept a close eye on the construction of the convent and, in an effort to have it ready for the arrival of the Ursulines in late 1770, she even paid workmen a full day rate to work through the short days of winter. When the Ursulines delayed their journey to Ireland, she was frustrated by having wasted money on rushing the building project, and decided to suspend the building works until they arrived.[104]

In May 1771, the four nuns arrived, and were temporarily lodged in a little house within the convent enclosure; by September they were able to move into their convent and no doubt expected that Nano would live with them. However, she chose to stay in the little house, living there for nine years and visiting the Ursulines regularly. The community worked quietly at starting a boarding school for young ladies, though their efforts were unpopular with some Cork Protestants. An article in the *Freeman's Journal* criticised the 'nuns brought in from the Continent', saying that the women 'mean to receive Protestants for tuition ... [and] will lose no pains to seduce and make converts of the young and weak minds committed to their care'.[105] The Catholic bishop of Cork, Dr Butler, believed that things would progress more smoothly for Nano if she first consulted with members of Cork's Protestant Ascendancy and sought their approval of her project; unsurprisingly, she did no such thing.[106] Despite a handful of critics, the school flourished, and a large addition was made to the convent in 1772. The extension included a chapel, infirmary, and additional cells which were much needed, as the Cork Ursulines were attracting vocations and growing steadily. The pension paid for novices was usually £15 per annum, for the period of their noviceship.[107] This money, together with school pensions and interest on dowries, would have defrayed much of the costs attached to expanding the convent. Nano Nagle contributed £60 to the building project; she later calculated that her overall investment in establishing the Ursulines in Cork was between £4,000 and £5,000.[108]

## Founding the Sisters of the Charitable Instruction

By 1771, Nano Nagle had realised her ambition to found a convent in Cork, and provide for the education of Catholic girls. It might be expected that she would begin to rest, watch the congregation flourish, and see the new convent school succeed. She was fifty-three years old, and she was already infected with the tuberculosis that would bring about her death in 1784. She had given years to the punishing routine of going around the lanes of Cork, often in rain and freezing conditions, to teach at her cabin schools, and she had worked tirelessly on the project of building the convent for the Ursulines. Rest was to be recommended, but it was not what she chose. Instead, she spent the next decade founding a new congregation, which was given the temporary name of Sisters of the Charitable Instruction of the Sacred Heart of Jesus (later Sisters of the Presentation of the Blessed Virgin Mary).

The Ursuline Annals record that the congregation quickly found their 'members multiplying [and] their exertions crowned with success'. The Annals also note, however, that Nano Nagle was 'greatly disappointed ... when she found that the Ursulines were bound by their Constitutions to inclosure [*sic*] and to the education of the higher orders of society.[109] Nano had wanted to give Cork a congregation of women who would teach the poor, and be free to leave the enclosure in order to seek out those in greatest need. To some degree, the little Ursuline community met her first requirement: they ran a poor school within the Cork enclosure, just as many French Ursuline convents ran *écoles externes*. But the reality was that the convent was proving very attractive to wealthy Irish Catholics, who previously had to send their daughters to school on the Continent. Pupils arrived from Dublin to board, and the novitiate attracted the daughters of prominent Catholic gentry, such as the Coppingers and the Moylans. Indeed it was Dr Moylan, and his uncle, Fr Doran SJ, who had 'strongly recommended the erection of an Ursuline monastery' in the first place, and they knew it met the needs of their family and friends.[110] An indication of the success of this pioneering Catholic boarding school is that it heralded the end of the need to send Irish girls to Ypres.

Not long before Nano's death, the Abbess at Ypres wrote in February 1784 to Nano's friend, Teresa Mulally, asking her to help find Irish boarders: 'I would be grateful to you if you could procure us an encrease [*sic*] of pensioners.'[111] She wrote again in November, urging Mulally to recommend the Abbey at Ypres to any potential pupils.[112] Not alone was Nano's Ursuline foundation attracting exactly the kinds of families who traditionally sent their daughters to Ypres, but it made it possible for other Catholic boarding schools to open their doors.[113] However, if the provision of schooling for the wealthy was improving, the schooling of the Catholic poor was not.

Nano Nagle knew that the Ursuline foundation would never devote itself fully to teaching the poor; with remarkable speed and decisiveness she set about founding an Irish congregation that would not be bound by solemn vows, and that would have a specific mission to the education of the poor. Dr Moylan was displeased, and made every effort to get her to change her mind, but she simply replied that she would take her proposed foundation – along with her money – 'to some other part of Ireland where she should meet with no opposition and more encouragement'.[114] Moylan backed down, and Nano forged ahead with her plan. On 29 September 1776, she described her new foundation as the Sisters of the Charitable Instruction of the Sacred Heart of Jesus. It was a remarkable step, made possible because she was a woman who had independent wealth and the courage to go against male clergy. Her determination resulted in the establishment in Ireland of the first of the 'modern' congregations, and Nano became the first Irish woman to found a congregation on the island since St Brigid.

The new congregation began very simply, as many Continental congregations had done, with a group of women gathering to live together. The group comprised Nano, and three other Cork women: Mary Fouhy, Elizabeth Burke and Mary Ann Collins. On 24 December 1775, they 'commenced their novitiate, delivering themselves up unreservedly to the practice of the most severe monastic discipline'.[115] In 1776, they were professed by Dr Butler, Bishop of Cork, and were known as the Sisters of the Charitable Instruction of the Sacred Heart of Jesus. They lived under a temporary religious rule drawn up by the curé of St Sulpice, and Nano set about examining French religious societies to find a rule and constitutions that would best meet the needs in which her convent operated.[116] Though Dr Moylan had been unsupportive of Nano's initiative, he came around to accepting it, and he usefully brought it to the attention of Teresa Mulally in Dublin. A sincere friendship developed between the two women, which made it possible for the little congregation to spread outside Cork, and begin what would become a lengthy and rapid period of expansion in Ireland. Between 1789 and 1850, Presentation convents would be established in Ireland every two to three years, with the result that by the mid-nineteenth century they would account for just over half of all convents in the country.[117]

Nano Nagle's last 'foundation' was not a convent, or a school. It was an almshouse, or asylum, for the relief of destitute older women. This was a controversial step, taken in 1783 even as illness was consuming her body. The almshouse drew criticism from some Cork people, who suggested that it was supporting prostitutes. Given Nano's sympathy for the most wretched of society, it seems unlikely that she would have shied away from providing shelter to prostitutes. Certainly, she embarked on the project with enthusiasm and pride, writing to Teresa Mulally to say: 'I am building the house I spoke to you about for the old women.'[118] The women were provided with 'meals of plain wholesome food in the dining hall of the establishment' and they prayed together. On their death, they were given a 'decent though simple burial'.[119] Nano's provision for the death of these women may have been prompted by a sharpened awareness of mortality: she would die not long after establishing the almshouse for women.

## Illness and Death

Nano Nagle's life was unusual, for a woman of her rank living in penal Ireland. Certainly, other Catholic women were known for being generous benefactors to the poor, and for attending to the education needs of their tenants. Women who spent substantially on helping the poor, and acted independently of men, included Lady Fitzgerald of Transtown, Lady Kingsborough of Mitchelstown, and Arabella Denny whose 'philanthropy and reformist zeal was principally concentrated on urban poverty in Dublin'.[120] But Nano Nagle occupied a curious space; she chose to remain unmarried and spent much time discerning whether or not to become a vowed religious. She was generous to her family, lending one brother a small fortune to buy an estate with lands in Devon, yet she allowed herself no material indulgences whatsoever. Having decided to bring a congregation of vowed women to Ireland to establish a convent, she then stayed firmly outside it, so that she could go about Cork to teach the poor. She ignored the requests of the Ursuline sisters that she should move into their convent, and openly defied Dr Moylan by deciding to spend more of her fortune on founding a new congregation and building another convent right beside the Ursulines. And Nano only finally chose to become a fully professed religious a few years before her death, indicating that at no time had she felt a need for the kind of protection that cloistered life gave women. Everything about her life suggests an independent spirit, and a fearlessness. Nothing about her life was conventional: she neither pursued the life of a gentlewoman, nor did she vanish inside a cloister. She took inconvenient and even contrary routes to achieve her goals, and seems to have had no concern with what others thought of her.

Sr Francis Tobin, one of the early sisters at Cove Lane, believed that Nano should have 'done less herself, and exacted less of others'.[121] There are many instances when Nano's contemporaries referred to her 'zeal', and to 'the privations and austerities' and the 'laborious and annihilated life' in her convent.[122] Her zeal expressed itself in relentless work: teaching, begging, walking the streets, praying, writing, organising. There are several records of her going around the sodden lanes of Cork wearing clothes that were 'penetrated with rain'; in her final year she had 'repeated neglected colds', and had to use a cane when walking.[123] She prayed for long periods, and 'took the discipline', demonstrating a kind of self-mortification that was both admired and abhorred by those who cared for her.[124]

A consequence of Nano's relentless activity, and a diet that was 'plain and frugal', is that she became weak and ill.[125] At some point she had become infected with pulmonary tuberculosis (TB), probably contracting it from the children she visited in cabins around Cork city. The disease, which is caused by an airborne bacteria that spreads from person to person through coughing or speaking, had reached epidemic proportions in eighteenth-century Europe, but was not fully understood until the late nineteenth century.[126] Neither Nagle nor her contemporaries would have understood how the disease was spread, nor was there any treatment for it at that time.[127] It presented with flu-like symptoms, a cough, the spitting of blood caused by a lung lesion, and general weight-loss; however, an infected person could have periods of remission. Nano commented in a letter in 1769 that her chest was 'not strong', adding: 'I spit blood which I took care to conceal.'[128] Some fifteen years later, after a year in which 'she had been visibly declining', Nano succumbed to the disease. On 7 April 1784, she 'was taken with a spiting [*sic*] of blood at a ladies house', and 'walked home for the last time.'[129] Across the two weeks that followed, her health declined further, and a doctor treated her with some of the standard procedures of the time, including blistering, and the 'letting of blood'; these could have only added to her suffering.[130] Following a pulmonary haemorrhage, Nano Nagle died on 26th April.

Her life had ended; her education legacy was just beginning.

CHAPTER 3

# Founding and Funding: The Establishment of a Network of Irish Convents

*The schools are opened at eight, at twelve the children go to dinner, at five o'clock they leave school ...*

– Nano Nagle to Miss Fitzsimons, 17 July 1769.

In the days after Nano Nagle died the existence of the Society was in serious doubt – a situation that lasted for nearly a decade. Illness and death, the embezzlement of funds, and the scarcity and insecurity of postulants, reduced the small community almost to vanishing point. Nano made provision in her will for the support of both the Ursulines and the Sisters of Charitable Instruction, structuring her estate to provide security for both of the convents that she left behind.[1] Through the misdeeds of the administrator, Thomas Roche, the intended support did not materialise for either convent. It was not until her brother, Joseph Nagle, assumed responsibility for some of these payments in 1799 that their financial position became regularised. Joseph Nagle made further provision for the South Presentation community in his own will of May 1813, and the matter was finally settled in 1814 by Nagle's nephew by marriage, Charles Chichester.[2] However, for many years the fledgling community in Cove Lane often went hungry, and the Annals hint at their despair. Mother Angela Collins guided the nuns and the poor schools through these difficulties, until her own sudden death in 1804.

The courage with which the small group of women met these challenges was matched by the determination they displayed on the journey towards canonical recognition, a journey they shared with Bishop Francis Moylan and Fr Laurence Callanan. Callanan's draft of the new rules and constitutions for the Order was completed in 1793, and in 1802 the bishop was able to present them to the Holy See for approval. The Sisters had determined to have monastic status, taking solemn vows. Though the decision seemed at first to be at odds with Nano Nagle's desire for her nuns to be out amongst the people, they had practical reasons for choosing a cloistered life. They argued that there was 'little security' for anyone wishing to join a congregation with simple vows, as it did not exist on a 'steady foundation'. In contrast, by forming a 'regular Confirmed Order and consequently by [a] strict observance of enclosure',[3] the sisterhood would have firm grounds, and would arguably be more likely to attract vocations. The *decretum approbationis* of the Sisters of the Blessed Virgin Mary was promulgated in Rome on 9 April 1805.[4]

Though the status of the congregation had been uncertain, and the finances were often slender, this did not prevent the nuns from commencing to expand outside Cork, as early as 1793, when they made a foundation in Killarney. A year later, with the founding of the Presentation Convent at George's Hill, the wishes of Nano Nagle for her nuns to serve in Teresa Mulally's school for Dublin's poor were fulfilled. Foundations were also made in Waterford (1798), North Presentation, Cork (1799) and Kilkenny (1800), with the result that there were six convent communities on whom the Final Approbation of 1805 conferred the status of religious order. At the start of the new century these six communities formed the nucleus of the Presentation Order, and are known as the Primary Foundations. As the Order expanded globally in the century that followed, all international foundations traced their history back to the Primary Foundation from which they originated.

Between 1807 and 1830 the Presentation Order experienced its most active period of expansion in Ireland. Twenty-two new houses of the Order were opened in fourteen counties.[5] To understand how this network of convents and schools grew, two important factors will be considered: the mechanisms whereby foundations were brought about, and the ways in which they were funded. Founding was a process that invariably involved one nun from a well-established convent being sent as founding Superioress to lead a fledgling group as they opened a new 'house', or convent. The little group usually comprised one or two novices, and a couple of professed Sisters. In the nineteenth century, the founding Superioress did not always remain at the new foundation; often she returned to her own Motherhouse, and sometimes she went on to make yet another foundation, or went overseas once the Presentations began to grow in India, Newfoundland, North America and Australia. Each house was independent, though records indicate clearly that new foundations saw themselves as filiations of the house from which they were founded. The records frequently refer to novices making their novitiate at one convent, 'for' another; that is, they were trained with a clear view of going to the new house for which they were destined. For example, Sr Catherine Lynch had entered George's Hill to complete her novitiate 'for the Drogheda foundation', and that was where she was then sent when it was being established in 1813.

George's Hill made its first filiation when it established a new convent on James's Street in Dublin on 17 August 1807. The property in James's Street had been left to Mother Xavier Doyle and Mother Ignatius Doran by a friend of Doyle's, Mrs Eliza Cruise. Her wish was that they convert the house into a Presentation convent if it was suitable. If not, they were free to sell it and use the proceeds as they saw fit.[6] No sooner was this convent established, than the onward movement of the nuns began as they commenced more foundations. Along with Sr Angela Biggar, Sr Xavier Doyle opened the second Presentation convent in 1807, which eventually relocated from Fairview to Terenure, in South Dublin.[7] George's Hill established two more convents before 1830: Presentation Convent, Drogheda (1813) and Presentation Convent, Rahan (1817). It was Sr Ignatius Doran from the James's Street convent who went to start the Drogheda house. Mother Angela Biggar and Mother Clare Biggar also left Dublin to establish the Rahan convent.[8] The Fairview/Terenure convent went on to open its own filiations in Maynooth, Kildare (1823) and Mullingar in Westmeath (1825). Mother Xavier Doyle, pioneer in James's Street, was involved in establishing the convent in Mullingar where she stayed for seven years.[9]

Three of the other Primary Foundations opened convents within this period also. Mother Joseph Curtayne and Sr John Sheehy left the Killarney convent to open a new foundation in Tralee (1809). Mother Joseph was an experienced foundress, who had made her novitiate in South Presentation, expressly for the Killarney foundation. Sr John Sheehy had served her novitiate in Killarney with the intention of opening the house in Tralee. Twenty years later the Tralee convent opened a house in Dingle (1829).[10] The Presentation Convent in Waterford opened three filiations before 1820: Dungarvan (1809), Carrick-on-Suir (1813) and Clonmel (1813).[11] North Presentation made its first filiation in 1834, when it sent Sisters to establish a convent in Midleton.[12]

The Primary Foundation in Kilkenny was particularly successful at attracting vocations, and was therefore well positioned to make many foundations. Indeed, by the last quarter of the twentieth century more than a third of the Presentation convents throughout the world could trace their origins back to Kilkenny.[13] Things augured well from the outset, and between 1803 and 1838, sixty-six postulants entered the Presentation Convent, Kilkenny. The convent established its first filiation in Carlow (1811). The Sisters who opened the new house were Mother de Sales Meighan, one of the original group who founded Kilkenny, Mother Magdalen Breen and Mother Agnes Madden. This was the first of seven houses to be established from Kilkenny during the nineteenth century, six of which were open by 1830.

In addition to establishing five Primary Foundations, South Presentation made two more filiations before 1830: Doneraile (1818), and Bandon in May 1829.[14] Most of the Presentation foundations in the nineteenth century were situated in the cities, provincial and smaller towns and villages of the south, midlands and east, and there was a high concentration of convents located in the Dublin and Cashel ecclesiastical provinces.[15]

## Founders, Supporters and the Church Hierarchy

The involvement of bishops and priests in the founding of many nineteenth-century Presentation foundations was similar to that which had characterised the establishment of the South Presentation Convent and the five Primary Foundations. Invariably, the records show a combination of individual effort on the part of nuns, lay philanthropic women (some of whom became nuns), and local clergy, often underpinned by the financial support of the professional and business classes. The successful foundations at Galway, Thurles and Wexford illustrate how this pattern operated in the early stages of the Order's development. On 28 October 1815, the Presentation Convent, Galway, opened in a house in Kirwan's Lane, just one day after the arrival of three founding Sisters from Kilkenny.[16] The community in Kilkenny had responded to a request by the Warden of Galway, Edmund Ffrench, sent a mere eleven days earlier.

Ffrench's letter to Mother Joseph McLoughlin, Superioress in Kilkenny, expressed the desire 'to establish a house of the Order of the Presentation for the religious instruction of our poor female children' and recorded the unsuitability of 'the laity in general to preside over such schools'.[17] He asked for three Sisters to come for an initial period of six years, and proposed the financial arrangements that would be put in place. A bond of £4,400 would be signed over to the community, the annual interest of which would be applied to its maintenance and support. He also pledged to hand over all leases, furniture and funds belonging to the existing Charity School of

St Nicholas.[18] This package of support included £1,000 Government 5 per cent debentures, and the proceeds of a yearly Charity Sermon.[19] Sr Joseph McLoughlin agreed to the proposal, subject to the approval and permission of Kyran Marum, Bishop of Ossory. Sr Joseph had some conditions of her own, which she indicated to Ffrench: firstly, the Kilkenny community 'in case of actual exigency, shall have the power to recall either of the Sisters who shall now be destined to fill the place of subjects in Galway'.[20] Secondly, she proposed that the Warden could send back any of the group of three who proved insufficient within the six-year period and claim a replacement should he wish it. The whole arrangement was agreeable to both parties, and the foundation was made with astonishing speed. In less than a fortnight, Kilkenny had made the first Presentation foundation in Connaught, and the house in Kirwan's Lane became both convent and school, where the nuns provided board and lodging for thirty poor children.[21]

The Presentation Convent, Thurles, opened on 16 July 1817. Several sources of funds were harnessed in support of this foundation, and indeed some had been in place for a long time. On his death in 1791, the Archbishop of Cashel had bequeathed £2,000 to be applied for the benefit of the poor of the town. His successor, Dr Bray, considered that the issue of educating the poor had not been addressed, and he too settled on establishing a convent of the Presentation Order. This proposal met with opposition from the coadjutor bishop Patrick Everard, and some of the principal clergy of the diocese, who argued that a seminary for young men should be built instead, or that the intended convent should be moved to another part of the diocese. Bray persisted, however, and with an additional contribution of £500 from a widow, Mrs Cahill, it was finally arranged to have a Presentation Convent in Thurles.[22] Margaret Cormack, a respectable lady from the town, had entered the convent in Kilkenny on 10 June 1814 to serve her novitiate for the intended foundation. On 19 June 1817, she was professed as Sr Francis Cormack and returned to Thurles where she stayed in the Ursuline Convent until a suitable house was acquired for the new convent.[23] She accepted the offer of a small house in Stradavoher from her brother John and moved into it on 12 July. On 22 July, six days after the official foundation, Sr Francis Cormack was joined by Sr Augustine Power from the convent in Clonmel who was appointed Superioress of the new house. After the enclosure was marked out, the Sisters opened their school and lived in observance of their rule as much as their circumstances allowed.[24]

Just over a year later, the eighteenth convent of the Order was established in Wexford. It was the first convent established in the diocese of Ferns since the Reformation.[25] Two women, Catherine Devereux (Sr Francis de Sales) and Jane Teresa Frayne (Sr Baptist) had gone to the Presentation Convent in Kilkenny for training in the practices of the religious life, with the intention of establishing the Order in the town of Wexford. With the special sanction of Dr John Troy, Archbishop of Dublin, and the permission of Dr John Ryan, Bishop of Ferns, the two women returned to a purpose-built convent in the town.[26] A Mr Carroll, who had at one time lived in the town, bequeathed £1,600 to build a convent there. When the women arrived, the building was unfinished, but they fitted up one of the ground-floor rooms as a chapel. After the celebration of the first Mass and the installation of the Eucharist there, the convent was declared officially open. With Devereux confirmed as the first Superioress, the Sisters opened their school immediately.[27]

By 1837, the Presentation Order had grown to include thirty-four convents, thirty-two of which were in Ireland.[28] On 8 May of that year the thirty-fifth foundation was successfully established in the city of Limerick. The Limerick convent was an example of the more complex arrangements that could result in a new foundation. It came about because of the efforts of Catherine Maria King, and the support and advice of Dr Patrick Hogan, the last parish priest of St Michael's parish.[29] Catherine King was born in Waterford, to wealthy Protestant parents. On the death of her father, she came to Limerick to live with Captain and Mrs Moore of Patrick Street.[30] Mrs Moore, her grandaunt, was Roman Catholic and played an important part in King's conversion to Catholicism. In 1826, she entered the Monastery of the Visitation at Shepton Mallet in England. Her health failed, however, and she returned to live with her aunt and uncle in Limerick.[31] After her return, Catherine began her work as superintendent of the female parochial school in St Michael's, devoting both herself and her money to improving the spiritual and temporal lives of the poor children attending the school. Within a few years she became anxious to establish her work on a permanent basis and decided to open a Presentation convent in Limerick.[32]

King approached the parish priest, Patrick Hogan, for assistance in the venture and he readily agreed to her proposal.[33] A short time previously he had built a house that adjoined his residence costing £3,000, and a schoolhouse in Sexton Street that had cost £1,300. Hogan transferred ownership of the house, school and grounds to Catherine King, who additionally became the sole heir to an uncle and aunt's estate on their death. She was perfectly placed to secure the financial viability of a new convent.[34] She appealed to Sr Joseph Harnett, a Kerry woman who had entered South Presentation in 1823, with the hope of opening a house in

Limerick. Harnett agreed to go, together with Sr Stanislaus Drinan and Sr Francis Cantillon, to Limerick where she opened the new convent on 8 May 1837. With characteristic speed, the Presentation nuns were ready to open a school three weeks later, and accepted 300 pupils.[35] Catherine King entered the convent as a novice in 1840, and was professed on 8 September 1841, taking the name Jane Frances de Chantal. The following November she replaced Sr Stanislaus and Sr Francis in their roles as Assistant and Bursar, when the two Sisters returned to their convent in Cork. Sr Jane Frances de Chantal was elected Superior in June 1843.[36]

After that period of rapid expansion in the first half of the nineteenth century, things slowed down and only one Presentation foundation was opened in Ireland between 1854 and 1861.[37] This was in the small village of Clondalkin on the outskirts of Dublin. It was a filiation of the house in Carlow. The money to establish it came from a local professional family, the Caldbecks. Mrs Eliza Caldbeck was a philanthropist, whose particular interest lay in the education of the poor girls of the area. In 1809 she had opened a small school in the gate lodge of her house where she taught pupils. She subsequently built a large schoolroom in Clondalkin village, where she employed some teachers.[38] After her death in 1840, Eliza Caldbeck's daughter, Anne Frances, carried on the work in the school until her own death in 1844. In her will, Anne Caldbeck left £2,000 to establish a convent of nuns devoted to the education of the poor. The parish priest, Fr John Moore, purchased approximately twelve acres of land for £300, of which he enclosed three to five acres and began to build a Gothic convent and school.[39] On 1 July 1857, Fr Moore successfully approached the Superior of the convent in Carlow for a group of Sisters to establish a convent in Clondalkin. Accompanied by the chaplain of the Carlow convent, three nuns – Sr Joseph Cosslett, Sr Regis Cosslett and Sr Stanislaus Mulcahy – travelled to Clondalkin on 7 December 1857.[40] Once again, no time was wasted in opening a school, and the following day the official foundation of the convent and school was marked by High Mass, after which between 200 and 300 children registered for the school.

What is clear from Presentation records is that Sisters in the early foundations often had to improvise, and rely on charity, in order to furnish their convents and schools. The first pieces of furniture for the Clondalkin convent were sent by the parish priest from his own house, and comprised some carpet, a few chairs and a table. Tables for the refectory were improvised from the scaffolding planks left over from the building work.[41] In many cases, the convents were not ready when the Sisters arrived. The first community in Wexford was met with an unfinished building; similarly the six Sisters who opened the convent in Milltown (1838) had to make do with an unfinished house. The windows in the eight cells had to be taken out because the rain was pouring in between the frames and the sashes. This left the Sisters with only one room that was fit for occupation, the infirmary. For more than twelve months the new community used this room as their dormitory, kitchen and refectory whilst tradesmen worked alternately in the other apartments of the house.[42]

For some communities there was no purpose-built convent, rather the first building was simply whatever dwelling was available. For example, the first home for the Tralee convent was an old and dilapidated house in the centre of the milk market in Blackpool. There the Sisters lived and taught school for three years before they moved to a small house they had built beside the parish church of St John's.[43] In Galway, the convent in Kirwan's Lane was originally a private dwelling, not suited to a growing community and a large number of boarders. In 1816 they moved to a 'commodious house in the Green with the intern children',[44] and in 1819 they moved to their final home in the western suburbs of the city. This building had been a Charter School until its closure in 1798.[45] In spite of its 'ruinous condition' and a high rent, the Sisters considered it suitable for the community and the children. With the financial support of the people of the city, the nuns repaired and renovated the house, garden and enclosure walls.

It took the community in Thurles longer to acquire the building that became their final home. The small house in Stradavoher proved entirely unsuited to their work, interfering with both the observance of their rule and the effective operation of the school. On the advice of friends, the Sisters offered to buy the house and schools of the Christian Brothers. The Brothers agreed, selling the property for £1,000 and moving to a small house until their new monastery and schools were built.[46] In November 1817, the small community moved to their new home, which required many alterations to make it comfortable. However, the schools attached to it were fine and spacious, and the facility of hearing Mass in the parish chapel compensated for the difficulties presented by the house.[47] The numbers in the community grew, and in 1821 the Sisters finally bought an old brewery and some land that adjoined their convent, having made several unsuccessful offers to its owner.[48] The foundation stone for the new convent was laid in May 1824, and the Superioress, Mother Augustine Power, was closely involved in the design and planning for the new convent, which was completed in March 1826.[49]

## Funding the New Foundations

The effort involved in opening a new house of the Order was merely the first step in establishing the foundation on a secure footing. The first attempts at founding a new convent did not always succeed; neither did all foundations endure.[50] Having opened a new convent, one of the challenges that faced the nascent community was how to ensure the survival of the house and attached school. Whatever the source of funding for the opening of a new convent, the members of each new community had to become the main agents in ensuring its continued existence and consolidation. The *Rules and Constitutions* stipulated that the Sisters of the Congregation could not 'receive money, or any other temporal emolument for their instruction.'[51] Given that the communities could not derive any direct income from their primary occupation they had to secure financial support elsewhere. Over the years they fashioned a multi-layered system of funding that drew on a variety of sources.

The source of the initial funding for the establishment of a new convent sometimes provided for continued financial support. For example, Teresa Mulally, the founder of the George's Hill Convent, kept the money and regulated the expenditure of the Convent during her life.[52] Mulally did not become a religious, but she retained a close relationship with the community, for whom she clearly felt great responsibility. In November 1791, she began to build the first of three houses on the property at George's Hill, to generate regular income for the convent.[53] Later, she built two more houses on the property at a cost of £1,500. Each house provided an income of forty guineas per annum.[54] These were reliable sources of income, unlike some other sources that – initially – had been crucial to the founding stages of George's Hill.

The Coppinger, Bellew and Bray bequests that had helped to seal the start of the building programme in the 1780s had not been phrased in explicit terms.[55] This meant that Teresa Mulally had to depend on the good will of the executors for payment of the annual interest. Prior to her death in 1803, she tried to ensure that the claims of the convent on these bequests were fully acknowledged. In an attempt to pay arrears on his brother's bequest, Edward Bellew sent £275.7s.7½d over the following months. After Mulally's death, both Edward and his successors continued to honour the trust, paying just over £1,893 between 1804 and 1832.[56] Although she had tried to come to a definite settlement with John Bray's family, the Butlers of Ballyragget, Co. Kilkenny, Mulally died before the details were finalised. Some months after her death, Mother Francis Xavier Doyle, the first Superioress of the George's Hill Convent, wrote to Mrs George Butler reminding her of Mulally's earlier correspondence and detailing the circumstances of the Bray legacy.[57] Between 1803 and 1827, the Butler family gave just over £3,542 in support of George's Hill.[58] Finally, under the terms of her will, Teresa Mulally left what remained of her fortune and real estate – after the discharge of her debts and bequests to Catherine Toole and four of her relatives – to Frances Doyle and Bridget Doran jointly and to their survivors.[59]

The Presentation Convent in Doneraile is an example of a foundation built largely through the munificence of one woman. The foundress, Mary Anne Flynn (Sr Mary Joseph), was a widow who met most of the expenses incurred in building the convent from the estate of her late husband. She also provided considerable financial support in the early years of the community's existence. The Doneraile Convent Accounts for the years 1818–21 record regular amounts of £30 paid in interest on £500 in her name. In November 1822 the £500 came to the Convent in full, with the entry recording it as 'Mrs Flynn money left by her husband's will'. The Accounts also record varying amounts of money as 'Sister Flynn's profit from the Salt Works' for the years 1818–22; the amounts together came to a total of just over £544. These were in addition to the £100 Annuity paid by Sr Joseph.[60]

In Limerick, Catherine King (Sr de Chantal) had shown 'the most lively interest, sparing neither pains nor money, in her anxiety to promote the spiritual and temporal improvement of the poor children', before entering the convent.[61] When she inherited her uncle and aunt's estate, she provided 'furniture &c [and] one hundred and twenty pounds annually towards the support of the Convent'. [62] On the profession of her final vows on 8 July 1841, her wealth continued to benefit the congregation. The Annals record that in 1842 Sr de Chantal King paid for an organ, silver lamp and Benediction Veil for the chapel.[63]

In convents that did not have the benefit of the wealth of founding members, the moneys for the project – whether from bequests, donations or collections – often had to be stretched to provide a degree of ongoing support once the house was opened. When Edmund Ffrench outlined the arrangements for the intended foundation in Galway, he gave details of the income that would be available to the community.[64] Annual interest on a bond of £4,400 would go towards the Sisters' maintenance and support, and would pay a salary to their chaplain for six years. Ffrench also committed the amount of future annual subscriptions of the people in addition to the proceeds of the yearly charity sermon. Finally, on behalf of the governesses of the Female Charity School of St Nicholas, he pledged all furniture, leases and funds associated with that establishment.[65]

The Presentation Convent, Millstreet, (1840) was built at the expense of the Bishop of Kerry, Dr Egan. He had the convent fitted up comfortably in time for the reception of the new community; the Sisters had no rent to pay on the school building, and had a lease on it in perpetuity.[66] In Clondalkin, Fr Moore had no means of supporting the nuns, but he explained to the founding group that he would attach the parochial church to the new convent, and thereby save the Sisters the expense of paying a chaplain. Fr Moore also used £500 left by Anne Caldbeck to invest in some land on the Alley estate in Crumlin. The rent on this piece of land brought in approximately £22 per annum to the convent.[67]

## Internal Sources of Convent Funding

Members of convent communities provided an important source of income for their houses. The two main forms of income that they brought were the pensions paid during their training in the novitiate, and their dowries. As the Annalist in Clondalkin wrote in 1863: 'The pensions paid by the Novices, the interest on the dowries of a few professed … kept up the house expenses, paid rent, taxes and repairs.'[68]

Traditionally, when a woman entered a convent she brought money with her for her maintenance. Her 'final profession invested the convent with this property and with any other which belonged to the nun'.[69] Under Canon Law income derived in this way could not be spent during the Sister's lifetime; however, dowry funds, if not already in an income-generating format, were invested, and earnings on the investments could be applied to the running costs of the community.[70] On the death of the community member, her money became the property of the community. In the event of a Sister leaving an order, any money that she brought with her was returned to her.[71] For example, Marcella Curtis, who entered in Wexford, had the £50 she brought as dowry returned to her in 1871 when she left the convent. The Annalist remarked that, 'By this act, which was legally sanctioned and confirmed, the Community was freed from any further claim being made by her.'[72]

Women entering convents brought various amounts with them. In the period 1770–1870, a typical dowry in Ireland was set between £500 and £600.[73] However, it was common for as little as £200 to be paid as dowry, while in some instances very large dowries were paid by the families of wealthy heiresses.[74] Whilst a dowry was technically required of all entrants, women were admitted to convents without one. Generally, this was made possible by the entrance of wealthy women who were encouraged to bring with them as much money as they possessed. This meant that one dowry could support several women.[75] Over the course of the second half of the nineteenth century the amounts paid as dowries declined. Additionally, the social background of the women who entered convents began to change, and many religious houses accepted women who had no dowry. In such cases, the education of the entrant was an important factor, and could replace a dowry. An educated girl could be trained to become a teacher, so – even without a dowry – she would be a valuable asset to a convent.

But leniency around dowries and funds was not always possible, especially in the early decades of the Order. The *Rules and Constitutions* of the Sisters of the Congregation of the Charitable Instruction (1793) were brief on the matter of aspirants' funds. They stated that: 'As many shall be received on the Establishment as the funds shall admit of, and no more, unless the Subject brings with her a Sufficient Dowry for her support in every necessary.'[76] In the years immediately following Nano Nagle's death the South Presentation community's problems were significant. The uncertain canonical position of the Institute and physically demanding nature of its work were compounded by its desperate financial position and the lack of new entrants to the community. These factors acted in a cyclical manner. Aspirants did not find the Institute attractive because of the arduous nature of the work and its uncertain status. Without new members bringing much-needed funds, the community remained small, their finances precarious and the burden of work continued. This self-generating situation meant that the community lacked the resources, both in terms of finances and personnel, to establish any new foundations of the Institute from within itself.

What helped to break this cycle was the fact that each of the five Primary Foundations was supported by people who provided the initial funding and resources. The women who came to South Presentation to train for George's Hill, Waterford, North Presentation and Kilkenny, all had their own financial resources and all came from families who lived in comfortable circumstances.[77] These women could afford to pay their annual novitiate 'pension', which covered their upkeep. Then, once the South Presentation Convent established itself on a secure footing, it attracted more new members who brought funding with them to the community. Pension fees varied from novice to novice, and seem to have depended on what families could afford to pay. Between April 1824 and April 1825, the income of South Presentation

Convent included £36 for twelve months pension for Sr Bennett; £30 each as twelve months pension for Sisters Xavier and Joseph Harnett, and £10 as twelve months pension for Sr Madden.[78] In the Doneraile Convent, new members paid annual pensions ranging from £107 to £20,[79] while in Fermoy payments were lower at around £20 per annum.[80] The Yearly Accounts Books for Killarney, Bandon, Mitchelstown and Crosshaven all indicate that the practice of receiving pensions for the board and keep of novices continued across the nineteenth century.[81] The dowries of the novices did not become due until final profession, so pensions provided convents with a crucial source of income in order to survive.

On final profession, new members of a community paid a dowry to the convent. Like annual pensions, dowries could vary in size. In North Presentation in the nineteenth century, they tended to be between £300 and £500. A sum of £450 was paid on behalf of Sr Stanislaus Daly in 1838; £300 was paid on behalf of Sr Josephine Mullaney in May 1847; £500 was recorded for Sr Gertrude Murphy in February 1850. Occasionally, a Sister would bring a substantial dowry, such as the £1,300 recorded for Sr Clare Mahony in September 1862. Other entrants brought additional sources of income. When Sr Francis Xavier Mahoney was professed in January 1833, her father made a Deed of Trust in which he secured the sum of forty guineas per annum on houses he had in George's Quay. This money was to be paid twice a year, in January and July. In 1836, Sr John Baptist Daly took her final vows some days after her brother Maurice paid over to the convent the £500 she had inherited from her mother's estate. On Sr Bernard Maguire's profession, in 1841, her father sent his bond for £400, bearing interest at 5 per cent, along with a bank bill for £100. He subsequently made payments of £100 in February 1843, as well as July and December 1848.

As noted above, while congregations could not spend dowries, they could invest them. Sr Gertrude Murphy's dowry from 1850 was lodged with the Provincial Bank, while Sr Alphonsus Clery's dowry of £200 from August 1860, along with £300 that the community received in a bequest, was given on loan at 5 per cent to a Mrs Kiely in July 1861. Sr Teresa Coveny's dowry of £300, paid in May 1864, was lent to a Eugene Byrne from Bridgefield, Cork at 5 per cent interest. Both Sr de Pazzi Hanigan and Sr Paul Ryan were professed in May 1872 and paid dowries of £200 and £350 respectively. These sums were in turn 'put out at interest to Mr Shanahan South Monastery'.[82] Loans could be secured against dowry funds, and used for practical projects. In August 1874, £200 of Sr Ignatius's dowry was lent for the new Infant School at 5 per cent interest; a year later all of Sr Angela's dowry of £200 was applied as security against a new building and a portion of Sr Catherine's £300 was given over to the same purpose. Later that year a total of £800, the combined dowries of Sr Berchmans and Sr Gonzaga, was invested in Corporation Debentures at 4½ per cent.[83]

Some nuns had specific wishes for how their dowries would be put to use, and these wishes seem to have been honoured. For example, in Thurles, Sr Peter Magan requested that the yearly interest on her dowry of £300 should be used to buy clothing for poor children in the school. And in South Presentation Convent, Sr Josephine Drinan contributed £200 of her dowry towards a new organ for the South Presentation Convent chapel, which was installed in 1848.[84] Sometimes members of a community also made donations of money or items to various aspects of the convent's life on their entrance or subsequently. In December 1859, the inmates of the Alms House, a work that had been started by Nano Nagle, were moved to their new building on the South Presentation campus. Sr Magdalen O'Reilly, who died nearly four years later, instigated that project with a donation of £1,000.[85] When Mary Catherine Burke, from Newport, Co. Tipperary, entered the Clondalkin Convent in March 1878 she brought a 'cottage piano' with her. This was put to use in the school where the pupils who had no piano at home could practise on it.[86] Very occasionally, the relatives of deceased nuns thought that they should somehow be able to benefit from dowries earlier paid over to convents. In 1869, the Annalist in Clondalkin recorded a visit to the convent one Sunday, by a relative of a recently deceased Sister:

> Although he was in good circumstances, he expected that she would leave him part of her property – but she had already given it to God. The fortune £1,400 went to the building fund and was a substantial help towards paying the debt.[87]

## External Sources of Funds

In addition to these sources of finance, convents derived significant levels of support from outside their communities. Wealthy benefactors and local clergy contributed to the early efforts of individual convents to become established. There were bequests, donations of money, and gifts of items used by the nuns in their spiritual, temporal and working lives. Some benefactors helped the Order at crucial moments. In recording the death of Dr Jeremiah Collins in November 1829, the South Presentation Annals note that, 'In a pecuniary way we are also deeply indebted to our dear departed best of fathers.'[88] Collins donated £500 with which the community bought the Ursuline Convent and gardens on the Cove Lane grounds, when the Ursulines moved to Blackrock in 1829. Immediately before his death, Collins gave Mother Clare Callaghan £1,500 in gold coins for the use and benefit of the community.[89]

The George's Hill Annals also record various donations and bequests from the clergy. Cardinal Paul Cullen gave £600 towards new schools that opened in 1862. Dr Yore, confessor to the community and Vicar General to the diocese of Dublin (1839–64), was the first to subscribe to the new schools with a donation of £100.[90] In December 1890, the executors of the parish priest Archdeacon McMahon forwarded £630 to the Superior of George's Hill with the promise of another £70 when the priest's affairs were settled.[91] The George's Hill Annals also record that a stained-glass window was erected in the sanctuary in 1867 through subscriptions from a number of people, two main subscribers being a Mr Robert Healy and a C. Kennedy.[92] In recording the opening of the new Convent Chapel in 1878, the Annalist listed thirty-one benefactors who contributed £2,357 in varying amounts between £6 and £500. This was in addition to those who had been listed as the 'Principal Benefactors'.[93]

The new house beside St John's Parish church that the Tralee community moved to in 1812 was built for them with the help of subscriptions. They taught their pupils in the church until their first school was completed, the construction of which was paid for with a bequest of £200 from a Miss Toomy, and subscriptions from 'other friends' were put towards building the choir. They added a new wing to the convent in 1823, which comprised a community room, chapel, kitchen, refectory and closet, at a cost of £200, £164 of which was contributed by Dr Loughnane, Mr Nickson, Rev Egan and collections made by Michael Mulchenock in Cork and Dublin. In addition to necessary repairs, a new school and cells were built in 1830 which were also financed with the help of subscriptions. Whilst the community paid £100 towards this, Dr Egan and Dr McEnery also contributed £100 to the project.[94]

Although many donations and bequests were made directly to the convents, on occasions the contributions were made through the clergy. Cardinal Cullen gave the Sisters in George's Hill part of a bequest placed at his disposal, to be applied to the orphanage.[95] The convent in Wexford benefited similarly in May 1868, when the parish priest James Roche gave the nuns £100, which was part of a bequest given to him by a former resident of the town.[96] Roche was the conduit of charitable donations in 1869, when Mr d'Arcy MP left a handsome donation to be distributed among the charitable institutions, and again in 1870 when an anonymous friend gave £50 for the education of the poor.[97] The convent in Clondalkin also received a bequest through Rev John Moore in 1871, when he donated the £400 left to him by his cousin, Miss Marianne White; it was used to liquidate the debt on building work to the convent and one of the schools.[98] In Limerick in 1843, the Annals recorded a £100 bequest from a Mrs Baker of Catherine Street, given through Dr Ryan, their Superior.[99]

In addition to donations and bequests from various benefactors, the Thurles Annals record amounts given for specific projects. When the Sisters embarked on a new building for their Orphanage and Industrial School in 1874, the then Archbishop of Cashel and Emly, Dr Leahy, contributed £400 towards the costs.[100] A cloister joining the convent to the orphanage, a conservatory and a porch were built in 1875. The £200 that this work cost was given as a gift to Mother Stanislaus O'Shee by her uncle Matthew Quinlan.[101] As his first gift to the convent, Archbishop Croke enlarged the garden of the Thurles convent in 1877. He did this by donating land that lay within the grounds of the Archbishop's Palace, and by erecting a new wall at a cost of £100. A year later he gave the fields that adjoined the convent garden to the community.[102] The community in Wexford also benefited in this way in 1835 when, 'through the kindness and charity of the Rev Myles Murphy PP of the town the Sisters received the addition of a piece of ground to their enclosure extending from the centre of the garden to the house wall'.[103] Later, when recording the death of Murphy in 1856, the Annalist noted that he had introduced gas into the convent at his own expense.[104]

Whilst the Wexford Annals contain several references to various benefactors, special mention is given to Richard Devereux, who was described as 'the principal support of the house'.[105] Among the contributions received by the community between 1862 and 1867 were: the balance remaining on the building of the new school (1862); the entire cost of tiling the cloister that connected the convent and new school (1866); a £100 donation towards the new wing added to the convent, and a glass porch with windows above leading onto the garden at a cost of £50 (1867).[106] On the death of Devereux in 1883, the convent Annalist reflected that the community had 'lost its best earthly friend'.[107] His support of the Presentations continued after his death: in addition to contributions for specific projects, Devereux had allocated £50 per annum to the community for many years, and a £500 donation was invested for them in the National Bank.[108]

Over the nineteenth century, the convent communities also received practical gifts, such as furniture and school equipment. The communities in

Tralee, Doneraile, Wexford, Limerick and Clondalkin received useful items from the start. When Mother Joseph Curtayne and Sr Mary John Sheehy came to their first home in Tralee, there was no furniture for them to use until Mrs Egan gave them some chairs. The Doneraile Annals record the somewhat impractical gift of forty spinning wheels donated by the then Lord Doneraile; the well-meaning benefactor did not seem to know that there was no demand for spun flax in the area, and the spinning wheels went unused. The two Sisters who arrived in the first Wexford convent moved into a building that was in an unfinished state. They had brought two beds, two chairs and one stool with them from Kilkenny and improvised a table from some boards that were nailed together and placed on a stool. The first gift they received came from the Bishop, who gave them a Brussels carpet and six chairs for their chapel.[109]

Some years later, the Talbot sisters presented the convent with an Angelus Clock for the new chapel and the President of St Peter's College, Rev John Sinnott, gave a chandelier valued at thirty guineas. In the weeks after the convent in Limerick opened in 1837, the Sisters received gifts from relatives and members of the local community. Dr Murphy, Bishop of Cork, presented them with the new edition of *The Lives of the Saints*, *The History of the Christian Church*, *Homhold's Commandments*, *Sacraments Explained* and *Reeve's History of the Bible*. It was not uncommon for communities to be given gifts for their chapels, such as the chalice given to the Limerick community by a Mrs Carroll; her townswoman, Mrs Clement, presented a suite of vestments. Mrs Staunton, relative of one of the Sisters, provided the wherewithal to buy a missal, thurible, monstrance, large bell and other items for the chapel.[110]

More prosaic, but certainly very useful, was the gift that arrived in Clondalkin a year after the convent was founded: Sir Edward McDonnell gave the community a cow, which was the start of the Sisters' involvement with farming and which contributed to supplying the needs of the community until 1966. His equally practical sister bought furniture for the school.[111] The same kind of common sense may have directed Richard Devereux to donate a force pump to the Wexford convent, for conveying water to the kitchen and through the house.[112] Other men who provided practical help to the nuns included Humphrey O'Connor, remembered as a 'kind, generous benefactor and friend' to the Listowel community. He oversaw all their outdoor business, ensured that his men mowed the community's meadows, sent the turf up to the convent, and kept a cow or two for the Sisters every year.[113]

## Fundraising for Foundations: Convent Enterprise and External Support

Convents also derived income from other sources. Charity sermons provided consistent, if somewhat unpredictable, amounts of money to a number of the communities. Generally, these were an annual event although occasionally a special sermon was arranged to raise funds for a specific purpose. In his 1815 letter to the community in Kilkenny, Edmund Ffrench promised that the 'collection of the yearly Charity Sermon' would be used in the support of the Sisters that might establish a convent in the city of Galway.[114] While the convent received proceeds from the sermon of March 1823, it was also intended to supply the Female Orphan Asylum with money from the proceeds of this event.[115] A later notice in *The Connaught Journal* stated that the subscriptions from the sermon of 1832 were to benefit the 'poor female children, who receive a gratuitous education at the Presentation Convent'.[116]

In Limerick, the annual sermon took place at the beginning of December, on either the First or Second Sunday of Advent. In the 1830s and 1840s, the amount collected each year varied from £68 to £168.[117] The sermon in Clondalkin was held in August, and the proceeds 'paid in part for the cleaning of the School-rooms – for heating them in winter; for gifts of clothing to the poorest of the children as well as supplying books and stationery to those whose parents could not afford to pay'.[118] When the Sisters in George's Hill embarked on building a new Convent Chapel, one of the fundraising activities was a sermon held in the Church of the Dominican Fathers in nearby Dominick Street on 11 February 1877. After all expenses were paid, the sermon raised £300.[119] When the convent chapel was completed a year later, the sermon at the dedication Mass was given by the Rev T.N. Burke OP. The community sold tickets, with Reserved Seats in the Choir costing ten shillings each; tickets to the Transept that admitted three people, were priced at one pound, and single tickets to the Gallery were five shillings each. In Listowel, the first charity sermon preached by the newly appointed coadjutor bishop of the diocese, Bishop Moriarty, was given in September 1854 in the parish church, in aid of the new school the community was hoping to build. Moriarty's sermon raised £60 for the project.[120]

Sisters also appealed for financial support from the public, and from relatives and friends. When the community in South Presentation Cork employed a teacher for the newly opened Infant School in 1846, they had to raise the £30 annual salary through yearly subscriptions from a number of friends of the community.[121] The George's Hill accounts record amounts of £20.9s.10d and £12.11s.11¾d for Chapel Collections in 1854 and 1874.[122] In 1855, the community began a fundraising drive to build new schools by issuing a circular appealing for assistance.[123] When the Sisters in Wexford embarked on building a new Convent Chapel in 1820, they had raised some of the money for the venture through weekly collections in the town.[124] Over forty years later, in 1866, they began collecting once again to enlarge the convent and schools.[125] The community in Galway raised £505 to build their first new school in 1820 through private contributions.[126] However, in 1850, Sr Mary de Pazzi O'Donnel of the Galway community wrote directly to Count Douglas O'Donnel in Austria describing the difficult circumstances which pertained at that time and pleading for his interest 'to get relief from the faithful in Saxony in order to enable us to continue giving one meal a day to our poor afflicted and now greatly afflicted children'.[127]

Convents also ran bazaars and prize draws on a regular basis, the profits of which were applied to various purposes. On the advice of their supporters and friends, the Sisters in Listowel held a bazaar in October 1855 to raise funds to help them complete the addition to their school. After much planning, and some delays, the event took place over two days in the house of Mr D. Leonard, who removed a partition so that the space could be enlarged. The Sisters raised £300 and attributed the success of the venture to holding the bazaar at the same time as a Cattle Show, which brought many people to the town.[128] The Wexford community held bazaars in 1861 and 1862 to raise funds for the completion of their new schools and cloister; the 1862 bazaar held in the Town Hall raised £450 for the project.[129] The bazaar they ran over two days in 1868 realised £234.[130] In 1879, the Sisters in Limerick organised a bazaar and concert in the school to clear the balance due on the school they had built for infant boys. They raised more than the £270 that was needed, and could apply the excess to other school improvements.[131] The Clondalkin community held raffles and prize draws every year, generally after Christmas, though in some years bazaars were held between Easter and summer. The Annals record that amounts of between £30 and £125 were raised through raffles.[132] Between 1875 and 1890, the nuns embroidered vestments, banners and other items used in churches, selling them at home and abroad.[133] The Clondalkin community also raised money through baking altar breads between 1881 and 1892, and by occasionally taking in boarders.[134]

Until now, little has been known about the work of women religious who founded and funded convents in the late eighteenth and nineteenth centuries in Ireland. Analysis of archival information helps to construct an understanding of how Sisters set about making foundations, funding their convents and schools, and creating strong communities that would also make other foundations, at home and abroad. For many Irishwomen who entered Presentation convents in this period, there were opportunities to be educated in novitiates, and to develop their own experience as classroom teachers. Additionally, the spread of foundations meant that women had the opportunity to offer leadership in new convents, and to learn to manage finances, investments and property. Indeed, women religious were the only female cohort so deeply involved in the strategic management of land, property and personnel. Convent life may have made demands of women who entered religion, but it also offered some of them the chance to live out their vocations in enterprising and challenging environments. Further, many took the opportunity to go overseas, to be part of new nineteenth-century foundations in India, Tasmania, Australia, and North America.

The first call to the Irish Presentations to travel overseas was from Newfoundland, and it was the Galway community that rose to the challenge.

## CHAPTER 4

# The Presentations in Newfoundland: The First Foundation Outside Ireland

*If I could be of any service in saving souls in any part
of the globe, I would do all in [my] power.*

– Nano Nagle to Miss Fitzsimons, 17 July 1769.

In 1833, the Irish Presentations made their first overseas foundation, when they sent four Sisters from Galway to Newfoundland. They were the first Irish Order to make a foundation overseas, though many Irish-born women had entered congregations outside the country in the eighteenth and early nineteenth centuries.[1] The Newfoundland mission was ground-breaking in many ways: it afforded an Irish Order the opportunity to establish itself in an international context; it provided Newfoundland with Catholic schooling for girls, teacher training for women, and a novitiate into which many Newfoundland women would eventually enter; and it marked the start of a form of missionary chain-migration by Irish women religious, as they sent home for additional support and developed strong female kinship networks between Ireland and Newfoundland.[2]

During the nineteenth century, the Presentations opened fifteen convents in Newfoundland, with schools attached to all of them. In the twentieth century they continued to expand, opening a further thirty-four convents across the island, along with many schools.[3] Like other religious who would open missions in the nineteenth century, they were invited by a prominent churchman, in need of Catholic nuns to teach large numbers of Irish emigrants and their descendants. They therefore responded not only to the demands of bishops, but also to the needs of their compatriots. As will be seen, in Newfoundland and elsewhere, there was a strong sense of shared national identity amongst Irish-born Presentations overseas, and they were highly valued within Irish neighbourhoods and communities.

## The Irish in Newfoundland in the Eighteenth and Nineteenth Centuries

Irish migration to Newfoundland dates back to the seventeenth century, when small numbers of men made the 3,500-mile voyage to take up seasonal work cutting timber, and catching and curing cod. Although the long journey to Newfoundland was less attractive than seeking seasonal work within the British Isles, it was a journey made by Irish men from 1698, with numbers increasing from the 1730s.[4] Convoys of vessels sailed from Irish ports, sometimes having originated in England. Stopping in Irish ports, they took on salt provisions, linen and cloth. They also took on male passengers classed as 'servants', who had been 'recruited in Irish ports in response to a demand for labour in cod fishery'.[5] Women servants were also shipped to Newfoundland, and Captain James Story recorded, as early as 1681, that traders 'bring over a great many women passengers which they sell for servants and a little after their coming they marry among the fishermen that live there with the planters'.[6] This kind of settlement formation could not have a significant impact on the growth of the Catholic faith in eighteenth-century Newfoundland, however, as 'liberty of conscience [was] permitted to all persons, except Papists'.[7]

The Cork of Garrett Nagle, and his daughter Nano, would become important in the growth of a major migration corridor that spanned the Atlantic. While in 1698 only one Cork-owned ship sailed to Newfoundland, this number increased to five ships setting sail from Cork in 1715.[8] The increased cod production in Newfoundland meant that servants from the southeast of Ireland were to be found in 'most coves and harbours between St John's and Little Placentia by 1750'. The Catholic faith of the Irish migrants, and the threat they posed to law and order, was occasionally a concern of the English officials. Governor Samuel Gledhill reported in 1725 of the 'Irish papists … who yearly come out and settle here'.[9] However, most Irish servants worked for English planters, and there were few grounds for the perception of British officials that these Irish Catholics were 'felons' and 'scum', who were potentially disloyal and likely to collude with Catholic France.[10] In reality, Irish Catholics were a small minority amongst the English and French in eighteenth-century Newfoundland; each group tended to keep to themselves, and there was little intermingling or ethnic intermarriage.[11]

The greatest concentration of Irish migrants was to be found around St John's, and in Carbonear and Placentia. Between 1797 and 1836, when the first official census was taken, the Irish population in Newfoundland quintupled. The port at St John's was the principal point of disembarkation, and this city had some 14,000 Irish by 1836.[12] As many as 10,000 of these migrants arrived in Newfoundland between 1805 and 1815.[13] The majority came from southern Ireland, particularly Cork, Wexford, Waterford, Tipperary and Kilkenny. Dublin's contribution to early nineteenth-century population growth on Newfoundland was minimal, while the port of Waterford played a central role in labour recruitment in south-east Ireland.[14] Vessels from many English ports called in to Waterford harbour to collect provisions and passengers before commencing the voyage to Newfoundland. New Ross, in particular, contributed emigrants to the growing population of Placentia and St John's, where they found employment in the buoyant salt-fish trade.

By 1820, changes in the main shipping lanes of Atlantic commerce, and the growth of the timber market in North America, meant that Irish migration to Newfoundland went into decline; increasingly the Irish disembarked at the east coast ports of North America. The population of Newfoundland did not go into decline, however, rather it soared from 52,000 in 1822, to 144,386 in 1869, and by 1901 the population reached 217,307.[15] This population growth across the nineteenth century created a demand for some of the mainstays of community life: churches and school.

## The Catholic Church and Education in Newfoundland in the Eighteenth and Nineteenth Centuries

Religious freedom for Catholics in Newfoundland was established in 1784, and the Pope appointed an Irishman, the Rt Rev Dr O'Donel of Tipperary, as the first Prefect Apostolic to the island.[16] While this marked the start of the official history of the Catholic Church in Newfoundland, Catholicity was represented there from at least the fifteenth century. John (Giovanni) Cabot brought Augustinian friars to the island when he arrived from Bristol, commissioned by King Henry VII to annexe Newfoundland.[17] The French explorer, Jacques Cartier, also had chaplains with him who celebrated Mass on the island in 1534, and Sir George Calvert (later Lord Baltimore), who established the first English colony at Ferryland in 1623, brought Jesuit Fathers there in 1625. In 1689, Franciscan Friars were formally established in Placentia by the Bishop of Quebec, and the French became well established there until the Treaty of Utrecht in 1713, when Newfoundland was placed under English control.[18] With the withdrawal of the French from Placentia, there came an end to the embryonic Church. Indeed, the Irish 'papists' who settled in Newfoundland during the eighteenth century effectively exchanged one penal code for another. The practice of the Catholic religion was prohibited, individuals were fined for harbouring priests, and penalties were imposed on Fathers who 'publicly read mass, which [was] contrary to the law'.[19] In order to marry in church or have children baptised, Irish Catholics had to return to their homeland.[20]

In 1784, religious freedom was granted by the King to islanders 'providing they be contented with a quiet and peaceable enjoyment of the same, not giving offence or scandal to the Government'.[21] That year, the Rev James O'Donel arrived in Newfoundland. O'Donel, an intellectual and an Anglophone, became a good friend of successive governors, and was successful in securing land to build a church in St John's. He was also granted a pension by Governor Campbell. In 1795 he was appointed first Prefect Apostolic to the island, and in 1796 he was named Newfoundland's first Catholic Bishop, and went to Quebec to be consecrated.[22] His return to Newfoundland marked the start of a period of growth in the Catholic Church in Newfoundland. O'Donel was succeeded by the Rt Rev Patrick Lambert, whose short term was followed by the appointment of the Rt Rev Thomas Scallan. Like O'Donel, Scallan was 'no stranger at the dinner table in Government House', passing useful information to the General and cultivating the trust of Protestants.[23] Indeed, Scallan's gestures of ecumenism drew a reprimand from Rome.[24] None of the first three Catholic bishops in Newfoundland attempted to bring nuns to the island, or to attend to the education of Catholic girls. Instead, they were somewhat compliant with the *status quo*; during their benign terms of office, discrimination against Catholics went unchallenged, including taxes on marriages and burials. All of this would change in 1829, with the appointment of the Irish Franciscan, Michael Fleming. It was Bishop Fleming who would have discriminatory taxes abolished, and he would bring about a dramatic change in Catholic educational provision by inviting the Presentation Sisters to St John's.

Fleming was poor and friendless on arrival in Newfoundland, but this did not prevent him from an aggressive pursuit of land for the Catholic Church, which earned him a reputation for being determined, stubborn and even 'obnoxious'.[25] Records of his approach to the funding and erection of a cathedral in St John's suggest that he was eccentric and uncompromising; his relentless work – which included living in a hut beside the building works, and making daily use of a crowbar and pick to speed the progress of the workmen

– hint at a man whose zeal was excessive. Sr Mary Xaverius Lynch wrote of him in 1834, that he appeared 'not to care for anything in this world … he will not eat a bit … he takes no care of himself '.[26] Looking around him on his arrival in Newfoundland in 1829, Fleming was as unimpressed with Catholic educational provision as he was with the absence of places for worship.

Records of schooling on the island are scant for the eighteenth century, though there was a school in 1744 supported by the Society for the Propagation of the Gospel in Foreign Parts (SPG). It was established by the Rev Mr Peaseley, an Anglican clergyman, who was concerned that Protestant children were attending a 'Papist' school.[27] If there was a Catholic school in operation, it must have been managed with the kind of secrecy that surrounded the Irish hedge schools.[28] The school-going population of St John's had a Charity School, opened in 1785 by the Congregationalist parson John Jones, and connected to his Meeting House. In 1802, the St John's Society, organised by Governor Gambier, opened a Catholic and a Protestant school, and by 1809 the schools had become denominationally mixed.[29] There was also a school for the poor, founded in 1827 by the Benevolent Irish Society; while it was non-denominational, only Catholics attended.[30]

Some Protestant children attended a school founded by the North American School Society, which was a British Bible society. This amalgamated with the Charity School, once British government support was withdrawn at the end of the 1830s. Most of these schools in Newfoundland were poorly attended; when the country received Representative Government (1832–33), attention was given to the provision of a system of schooling, and non-denominational education was favoured.[31] Bishop Fleming, however, was emphatic in his determination that Catholic schools should be 'exclusively Catholic in their tone and management'.[32] He set about having Catholic schools built, with the same excessive attention to these projects as he showed with the cathedral, and he was to be found '… [n]ight and day … continually over the workmen … in the most severe weather and the snow coming down in flakes.'[33]

Unsurprisingly, when Fleming set his mind to bringing a community of nuns to Newfoundland to take charge of female schooling, he approached the task with determination. In subsequent years, on the many times when he recounted this project, he placed himself at the centre of the narrative, and erased the agency and initiative of the nuns who carried out the mission.[34] 'I resolved to found a community of nuns in order to make sure my plans would be fulfilled', he stated in a letter.[35] In his *Relatio*, written to place before the Cardinal Prefect of Propaganda in 1836, he recalled: 'I made up my mind and crossed the Atlantic in 1833 and was able to bring from Galway

in Ireland a little community of Nuns of the Presentation Order.'[36] The
pioneering Sisters appear in the *Relatio* as a diminutive group of anonymous
women, whose mission succeeded only because Fleming had made up his
mind that it should do so. The reality was very different.

## The Arrival of the Presentations in Newfoundland

Bishop Fleming visited Ireland several times during his episcopacy. In
1830, with only three active missionary priests to support his work, he set
out to get additional vocations.[37] He returned to Newfoundland early in
1831, having secured nine priests. He used his visit to Ireland to travel to
London and present a memorial to government on Catholic emancipation;
he successfully demanded that the terms of emancipation, gained by Daniel
O'Connell for Ireland, should be extended to Newfoundland. Returning to
Newfoundland, he was something of a hero for Catholics on the island, and
had their support as he began his campaign to found schools and build a
cathedral.

When he set sail once again for Ireland in 1833, Fleming had the
confidence of his flock. Indeed, they had become familiar with the righteous
anger that had motivated him to bring nuns to Newfoundland. Fleming
had witnessed young boys around the wharves and ports of Newfoundland,
drinking rum at an early age and developing crude habits.[38] He had also
despaired of the way in which these boys 'intermingled' with girls, in school
and outside, resulting in girls speaking a kind of coarse language that he
wanted to eradicate.[39] Girls, he believed, should not be exposed to 'the
dangerous associations which ordinary school intercourse with the other sex'
allowed.[40] He determined that the best way to improve the morals of future
generations of Catholic Newfoundlanders was via the education of girls,
who would become mothers capable of teaching their children integrity and
morality. Fleming believed that 'virtue and religion' should be 'instilled into
the little ones at their mother's knee.'[41] He later wrote of his motivation to
bring convent education to Newfoundland:

> I judged it of essential importance to fix the character of the female
> portion of our community in virtue and innocence ... when once
> the future mothers are impressed with the truths of religion ... once
> their young minds are enlarged and enlightened and strengthened by
> educational knowledge, the domestic fireside is immediately made the
> most powerful auxiliary to the school ...[42]

Fleming had seen the success of several religious congregations involved in education in Ireland, and decided to return there to find nuns willing to come to Newfoundland. His interest at this point was in providing instruction for the poor, and Nano Nagle's Sisters had been founded for this purpose. In Ireland in 1833, there was no other congregation suited to his ends, for although Catherine McAuley and two novices had made their novitiate with the Presentations and formed a community in 1831, the Rule and Constitutions of the Sisters of Mercy were not approved until 1835.[43] Later, when Bishop Fleming decided to develop education for the expanding Catholic middle class in Newfoundland, he would return to Ireland to ask Mother McAuley for some Sisters to found a 'pension' school for girls, as their Constitution allowed them to provide fee-charging private education. But in 1833, his focus was on educating the daughters of islanders who mainly worked in the fisheries. These girls traditionally started work at an early age, in the 'fish rooms' or picking, washing and packing blueberries.[44] They were likely to marry early, often to men who were much older, and have between five and eight children.[45] When their children were raised, they often resumed work in fish and berry processing, alongside sisters, mothers and aunts.[46] Bishop Fleming did not see female education as a route out of unskilled labour and early marriage. Far from challenging the demographic experience of Newfoundland women, Fleming promoted female education so that women would raise their children differently: in his critique of the coarseness and sinfulness of poor children, he placed the responsibility for remediation firmly on the shoulders of their mothers, with the help of the Presentation nuns that he would bring from Ireland.[47]

There are few surviving records of Bishop Fleming's visit to the Presentation Convent, Galway, in August 1833. It is therefore not clear why he chose this convent, above others such as the South Presentation Convent in Cork, or Presentation Convent, Kilkenny. It is possible that he had heard of the Galway convent indirectly, via those who knew Fr Charles Dominic Ffrench OP (1775–1852), whose mission to Canada included preaching in Newfoundland. Fr Ffrench was the brother of the former Warden of Galway, Dr Edmund Ffrench OP (1773–1851), who brought the Presentation Sisters to Galway. Equally, he may have chosen the Galway convent because the superior, Mother M. John Power, was a native of Waterford, a county with which Newfoundland had many ties of kinship and friendship.

The Galway convent was, at any rate, a good choice for Fleming. The convent annalist described the Galway community as having been blessed with 'holy, respectable and efficient subjects [which] in every way made it a flourishing convent'.[48] It had sufficient vocations that it could follow Presentation custom and allow the founding Superioress, Mother Angela Martin, to go back to her own Kilkenny convent in 1819.[49] In May 1833, the community were able to spare Sisters to establish a second Galway convent, and to make a new foundation in Limerick.[50] A few months later, Bishop Fleming arrived at the convent door carrying only a carpetbag. He begged for the attention of the Superioress, and laid his plans before her. Even though Fleming's request for nuns had the support of Bishop Browne of Galway, Mother Power had to consider its implications for her convent carefully, as she had only recently parted with eight Sisters.[51] One or two Sisters would not be sufficient to start a foundation in a country with no other nuns; she knew she needed to part with at least four women if the mission were to have a chance of success, but she also knew that this mission was not without dangers. No Presentation nuns had ever been sent out of the country before; once her Sisters left Ireland they were unlikely to return, and she had only Fleming's word that they would be safe. His zeal may have impressed the Superioress, but she was a pragmatist. She presented him with conditions: the Galway community retained the right to recall their Sisters from Newfoundland after six years, and the missionaries could return to Galway at any time if they so wished. She wrote to Fleming:

> ... this community will have it in their power to recall our Sisters any time after six years. Should the Convent at Newfoundland be sufficiently established, or should [the mission] ... not succeed, to their satisfaction, or for any other particular cause which they deem necessary ... your Lordship should have them safely conducted back to their own convent in Galway ... we the Sisters of this community deem it necessary to make this stipulation. I resign to your care our dear Sisters ...[52]

Mother Power was adamant that Bishop Fleming would have to agree to these conditions, and agree he did. The Sisters who offered to go with Bishop Fleming were M. Bernard Kirwin, M. Magdalen O'Shaughnessy, M. Xavier Malony, and M. Xaverius Lynch. Bishop Fleming went to Dublin and met with Archbishop Daniel Murray on 16 July 1833, to discuss his plans for the Presentation Convent in St John's, and to advise Murray that 'some ladies of the Presentation Convent of Galway [will] break asunder every worldly tie' to accompany him to Newfoundland to educate 'hundreds of poor children ... [who were] in danger of being lost to religion, to their parents, to themselves and to God.'[53] He advised Archbishop Murray that he had £1,500, left to him by his predecessor for the purpose of building a convent and schools. Murray 'pointed out the steps to be adopted for its better security, and kindly promised to do the needful' for Fleming, and even agreed to contribute to the convent. Fleming assured Murray that he would 'build a suitable dwelling house with a school ... and that until such an establishment would be ready ... a comfortable dwelling should be provided' for the Sisters.[54] Fleming further guaranteed that the Sisters would have an annuity of £100, until their 'own funds' became 'adequate to all their domestic wants'.[55]

Although Fleming made no mention of the dowries that the four pioneering Sisters would bring to Newfoundland, it was common practice that a dowry followed a Sister when she moved from one house to another; Fleming's oblique reference to the Sisters' 'own funds' probably included their dowries, and those that would come once additional women entered the convent at St John's. The Bishop was more direct in his hint to Mother M. John Power, that she might 'give every assistance to help us on in our infant establishment', no doubt aware that she had a substantial annual income from her brother, a wealthy businessman in the East Indies.[56] Fleming expected that the Sisters, in time, would 'awaken many a heart in their favour' and that donations from Newfoundlanders would be forthcoming once they saw 'the crowds of destitute female children rescued from crime and misery by the benefits of a Religious education'.[57]

Bishop Fleming struggled at first to make satisfactory travel arrangements for the four Galway nuns. He examined a vessel in Dublin, but found it was 'rather too small to make comfortable accommodation in her for the Ladies'.[58] He travelled to Liverpool at the end of July, and tried to arrange passage with several different ship owners, without success – perhaps because the Bishop 'would allow no [other] passenger on board'.[59] He knew that living on board ship included the risk of being with disease-infected passengers. It was not impossible to find a vessel bound for Newfoundland to collect timber which would take a small party of passengers, and he succeeded in arranging for them to sail from Waterford on 20 August. He called to the Galway convent to collect the nuns, and transport them to Dublin by mail-coach. Mother M. Magdalen O'Shaughnessy, the only member of the group to give an oral account of the full journey, recalled that 'there was great weeping and lamentation among the Sisters, as they knew they should never see us again in this world'.[60] With the Bishop seated beside the driver, the coach containing the four nuns travelled to Athlone; there the horses were changed, and the party continued on to Dublin. After a rest of several days, they continued on to Waterford; again they rested for some days before embarking the ship to sail to Newfoundland.

The Bishop was aware of the many risks attached to a long sea voyage, including fires on board that could prove fatal, storms that caused shipwrecks, and unseen icebergs that could sink ships even as they arrived at their destination. Earlier that summer, a brig from Ireland struck an iceberg and sank off the Newfoundland coast, with the loss of 265 passengers and crew.[61] The same year ships, such as the British *Emily*, were wrecked off the rocky coastline; other ships were simply reported as 'lost at sea', all on board presumed dead.[62] Fleming minimised risks by chartering the brig *Ariel*, which he deemed to be seaworthy, and by lavishing his 'paternal kindness' on the Sisters during the voyage.[63] The ship, with its two masts and seven sails, needed a large crew to sail it. Brigs were sturdy ships that could sail fast and manoeuvre easily, and were well suited to long voyages. The *Ariel* took over three weeks to reach Newfoundland, during which time it faced into a three-day storm, which broke one of the masts. The Sisters would have been terrified, had they not been too sick to care about their safety.[64] Mother M. Magdalen noted that 'the sailors were most respectful during the voyage', and the ship's cook 'was most attentive'.[65]

The crew managed to bring the ship safely into St John's harbour on Saturday, 21 September 1833. A large welcome party awaited them, including 'Protestants, Orangemen and all kinds of people', and the crowds followed the carriage as it transported the four women to the episcopal residence.[66] The next day the Sisters wrote letters to Galway to advise Mother Power of their safe arrival. However, these letters were delayed in Liverpool, and no word arrived to assure the Galway community that their Sisters were safe. As the months passed, they assumed the worst, and gave the Newfoundland pioneers up as lost. The Galway nuns carried out the usual obsequies in such a situation: copies of the nuns' vows were burned, following the solemn requiem Masses; a period of mourning was observed.[67] Four months would pass before the packet of missing letters arrived in Galway, to the astonishment and joy of the community.

## The First Convent at St John's, Newfoundland

Although the four Sisters had been promised both a convent and school, these were not ready upon their arrival in Newfoundland. Indeed, it would be almost a decade before a proper convent was built. The group stayed at the Bishop's residence for a month, but said that the elegant furniture and carpets were 'too comfortable' for them, and they longed for a simple convent where they would 'be happy together'.[68] Because the nuns were cloistered, they 'appeared to no one'[69] until their temporary convent was ready. It turned out to be a slaughterhouse known as 'The Rising Sun', renovated to serve as a convent, while a nearby house was to function as their school.[70] On 21 October the Sisters opened the doors to pupils, and some 450 children arrived to seek admission. The inadequacy of the temporary set-up prompted the Bishop to rent a larger building, to which he moved the Sisters in December.[71] It had a school for 800 pupils, and although this too was to be a temporary arrangement, the Sisters remained there for nine years, and the area became known locally as 'Nunnery Hill'. The hardships that the nuns suffered in their first Newfoundland winter were considerable. The severe weather was more punishing than the large classes and the lack of teaching equipment. Indeed, the cold was like nothing they had ever experienced yet they managed to sound optimistic in their letters to Ireland:

> … we cannot leave a drop of water in the basins or jugs … [and] our towels … after using them and putting them to dry, are frozen quite hard and stiff. As for the milk … we are obliged to cut it with a knife … While I am writing, the pen is frozen in my hand and the ink in the bottle … We all bear the cold very well and were never in better health …[72]

The Sisters were struck by the spiritual poverty of the children, and they were also surprised by their attachment to 'exterior things'.[73] The local children were 'very fond of dress-wear, necklaces, ear-rings', Sr Magdalen wrote, 'so that from their appearance you would scarcely think you are teaching in a poor school. No such thing as a barefoot child to be seen here, how great the contrast between them and the poor Irish!'[74]

There is no indication that the pioneering group wanted to abandon their mission at any point, even though this was one of the terms on which Mother Power had allowed Bishop Fleming to take them to Newfoundland. It may be that the women were content to stay, and happy with the progress of the school. Certainly Fleming very quickly received praise from Rome, for having 'accomplished so many things [including] the increase of religion', and for providing for 'the true instruction of girls'.[75] He was determined that his mission would succeed, and that the Sisters would continue their work. 'Dr Fleming tells us that we have given all up for Jesus Christ … and therefore it would be a breach of our Vow to look back on those things we have forsaken,' wrote Sr M. Xaverius. 'He is a very strict Superior ... the greatest stickler for rule and discipline.'[76] The nuns listened to his 'long exhortations' on themes such as 'self-denial [and] continual renunciation', though they needed little reminding about either practice.[77] They were motivated not by Fleming, but by their own faith. 'We have many trials and privations,' Sr M. Magdalen reflected. 'However, we have one consolation which sweetens all our trials – that it is for God we suffer.'[78]

## Presentation Expansion in Newfoundland in the Nineteenth Century

The success of the convent school in St John's was such that by 1840 there were 1,200 children enrolled there, and a daily attendance of 900. The teaching and management of the schools, and the running of the convent, still fell to the four women who had arrived from Galway over a decade earlier. The burden of work on the women was enormous. That same year, Bishop Fleming went once again to Ireland, questing for nuns. He had a new project, into which he threw himself with characteristic zeal: the education of young ladies. While it did not initially involve the Presentations, it would soon become connected with their mission.

Bishop Fleming had decided to establish the Irish Sisters of Mercy in Newfoundland, to run schools for the daughters of the growing Catholic middle class. In Ireland, the Sisters of Mercy and the Presentations did not provide élite education, rather they taught the daughters of the working classes and the poor. However, the Mercy Constitutions did not prevent them running fee-charging 'pension schools', and for this reason Bishop Fleming knew they could meet his needs. Further, the Sisters of Mercy were not cloistered, and their mission was not only in education: they also nursed the sick and visited the poor. By bringing them to Newfoundland, Fleming was not setting the Sisters of Mercy in direct competition with the Presentations. Indeed, this would not have been acceptable to the Mercy foundress, Catherine McAuley, who would not allow her 'nuns to open any school that could interfere with [a] school taught by the Presentation nuns.'[79] The annalist of the Mercy Motherhouse in Dublin wrote in 1840 that 'the holy foundress would never under any circumstances locate her convents near kindred institutions, or ... open any establishment or branch that could interfere with the prosperity of another convent.'[80] If anything, Fleming thought, a Mercy foundation in Newfoundland would complement the existing Presentation foundation.

To commence his plan Fleming sent a Newfoundlander, Mary Frances Creedon, to Ireland. She entered the Mercy novitiate in Dublin around 1840, in the expectation that she would return to St John's and help to make a foundation.[81] Fleming also hoped that his niece, Mary Justina Fleming, who was due to be professed as a Sister of Mercy in Dublin in 1841, might offer to go to Newfoundland. Indeed, at one point Mother Catherine McAuley had considered being part of the proposed pioneering group herself.[82] But by 1842, when Bishop Fleming arrived in Dublin to collect his little group of Sisters of Mercy, both Catherine McAuley and Justina Fleming had died from consumption.[83]

The arrival of the first group of Sisters of Mercy in Newfoundland gave the Presentations some companionship, but it was to be short-lived. The group was small, comprising Sr M. Frances Creedon, along with Mother M. Rose Lynch, Sr M. Joseph Nugent, and Sr M. Ursula Frayne. Within a year, both Frayne and Lynch returned to Ireland. Sr Joseph died of typhus in 1847. Newfoundlander Frances Creedon would have had to continue living alone in her convent, had she not offered shelter to the Presentations in 1846 when their own newly built convent was destroyed by a fire that raged through the city of St John's.[84]

The fire in St John's took place when Bishop Fleming was away on a trip to Europe that included yet another quest for nuns in Ireland. He had completed building the Presentations a fine new convent in 1844, and hoped that a phase of expansion was about to begin. Two Irish-born women had joined the original four in 1842, but more vocations were needed, as the school now had over a thousand pupils.[85] The pioneering group of nuns, therefore, appealed successfully to their mother house in Galway, starting a chain of female missionary migration that would continue for the rest of the century. Bishop Fleming travelled to the Presentation Convent in Galway to collect the nuns who volunteered to come to Newfoundland: Sr M. de Sales Lovelock, and Sr M. Josephine French.[86] Fleming received word of the fire when he was in Ireland, but the impact of the devastation was only fully realised when he arrived back in St John's. His health broke down, partly as a consequence of years of hard work and travel, and partly because of the shock at what he saw. After a protracted illness, he died in 1850, at the age of fifty-eight.

Bishop Fleming was succeeded by the Rt Rev John T Mullock, who embraced Fleming's education projects and immediately began building a large and gracious Presentation convent, in the Cathedral square of St John's. At last the congregation began to expand, attracting some vocations that allowed them to make new foundations around the island. There was a great demand for female schools, and the nuns opened convents in quick succession in Harbour Grace (1851), Carbonear (1852) and Harbour Main (1853). The group that founded the Harbour Grace convent was led by the experienced 'pioneer' Mother M. Xaverius Lynch.[87] Two more of the pioneering group were destined for leadership: Mother M. Xavier Maloney was sent to found the convent at Harbour Main, and Mother M. Bernard Kirwin was elected to make a new foundation in Fermeuse, in 1853.

In the decades that followed, careful succession planning was evident in the way that the nuns managed communities; Sisters who gained some experience in the role of Superioress were dispatched to make new foundations, and less experienced nuns were moved into positions of responsibility once they showed ability. Postulants who had been educated in Irish Presentation convents supported the Presentation legacy that had travelled from Nano Nagle's country with the pioneering group. For example, Mother M. Stanislaus Gealy had attended George's Hill, Dublin, before emigrating to Newfoundland, where she entered in St John's at the age of sixteen.[88]

The success of the convent schools depended on past pupils and local women joining the congregation. In this way, the Presentations succeeded in founding fifteen convents and schools by the end of the century, and a further thirty-one foundations would be made on the island in the twentieth century. The schools provided not only for children, but also for adults. In the Harbour Grace convent, for example, 'all the women of the town, both mistresses and servants' attended the convent Sunday School, where they learned to read and write, and were instructed in Catechism.[89] Sunday School was also popular with girls who had to work during the week, and would otherwise not have learned to read and write. Local families supported the nuns in return, supplying them with building materials and running fund-raising bazaars to help with projects. When a convent was built in Riverhead, 'a Bazaar was got up by the good ladies of the city which nearly liquidated [the] heavy debt of £3,000'.[90] Local people also provided practical gifts, to help the nuns survive. One family 'drove a beautiful cow with her calf into the convent yard, thus starting the domestic dairy' at Renews.[91] When the nuns opened a convent and school in Witless Bay in 1860, the gift of 'a cow and a field to graze her' was greeted with relief, as it provided milk for the nuns and pupils.[92]

The costs attached to Presentation expansion in the second half of the nineteenth century were also defrayed by nuns' dowries, and by gifts from nuns and their families. For example, Sr M. Ignatius Manwaring 'proved to be a great benefactress when the Convent had little financial means'.[93] She entered religious life at the age of fifty, bringing her wealth to the congregation. When Miss Johanna Murphy, a native of Newfoundland, entered the Harbour Main convent, she 'made a present of an altar for the chapel', while the local parish priest bequeathed the convent £210 in his Will.[94] Mother Patrick Walshe, and her brother who was the parish priest in Renews, benefited from financial gifts sent from their family in Ireland.[95] Other income was generated through property; for example, the convent at Harbour Grace received $200 from the Railway Company in 1898, when they needed to run track through the grounds, and in 1918 the same convent sold land 'for the purpose of making a runway from which the first trans-Atlantic air flight was made'.[96] Land was also gifted to the nuns: the Harbour Main community were given land to the value of over $300 by the Rev Edward O' Keefe in the 1860s.

Gifts and donations were, however, made with irregularity and, as the Presentations made foundations around the island, they more often than not had to live very modestly. While the 'heavy debt' of £3,000 recorded in Riverhead may seem excessive, the loan was needed so that the nuns could build a proper convent and school, having spent twenty-seven years living in 'a miserable, damp, uncomfortable dwelling, suffering much from the inclemency of the weather'.[97] The Riverhead community had slept in cells 'with the rain pouring in on them'.[98] Unsurprisingly, six of the Sisters died from consumption and pneumonia, in the early years.

## Presentation Schooling in Newfoundland: The Labour and the Legacy

The way in which local communities welcomed groups of Presentations who agreed to found convents and schools around the island, is an indicator of their enthusiasm for the educational opportunities that the nuns afforded. When a little group left their convent to make a new foundation, this was often the first and last time that they would leave their cloister.[99] The nuns were feted as they arrived at their new home. In 1853, a group left the convent in St John's to travel by steamer to Harbour Main to make a foundation. There was, perhaps, as much novelty in the sight of the steamer as there was in the arrival of four nuns, since this was the first time such a vessel had ever been seen in Harbour Main. Crowds gathered 'on every hill and rock', and once the steamer came in sight, guns were fired 'for eight miles along the coast [and] the hills and woods re-echoed with their sounds'.[100] A small boat was sent out to the steamer, to bring the nuns ashore. The Annalist recalled how, when the boat got to shore, 'men took it on their shoulders out of the water, and brought it to the convent door, amidst the firing of guns [and] cheers'.[101]

The party that left the Fermeuse convent, to make a foundation in Ferryland in 1858, was also warmly greeted. While there had been a Protestant school established at Ferryland in the 1840s, it had closed in 1856, as no suitable teacher could be found. The arrival of the nuns promised Sunday School for adults and children, in addition to a day school, and the locals welcomed the nuns by firing cannons in the harbour. Guns were fired and flags were flown in 1860, when the first Presentation nuns arrived in Witless Bay, and crowds gathered to accompany them to their convent. Once installed, the nuns rarely saw locals again, excepting those who attended Sunday School. Only in exceptional circumstances did the nuns appear in public. For instance, severe weather sometimes prevented the parish priest from getting to the convent at St Mary's, to say Mass. When this happened, the priest 'sent his horse and sleigh to carry the nuns to and from the church'.[102]

On moving into their convents, the nuns always began teaching immediately. Initially, the costs attached to running Presentation schooling were met by the Sisters and by Bishop Fleming. The passing of the first Education Act in 1836 brought about modest financial support for schools, including an annual grant of £100 to the Presentation convent school at St John's. But in the early decades conditions were often poor, and sometimes the nuns taught in makeshift schoolrooms while they waited for a school to be built. The numbers who turned out to register at the schools were large; a few days after they opened their school at Harbour Main, there were 180 pupils enrolled, 'and not one could read or write'. On Sundays, an additional 200 adults came to the school.[103] When the room became overcrowded, the nuns 'were obliged to teach classes in the yard'.[104]

While the Sisters were ambitious in their teaching, they were often hampered by a lack of equipment. When there were no textbooks or tablets, they improvised by cutting up 'advertisements and handbills, and forming them into words and syllables'.[105] They also created their own reading books, by copying extracts from encyclopaedias and illustrating them with well-executed line drawings.[106] It was recognised by education inspectors on the island that there was 'a great want of reading matter in most of the outposts'.[107] To deal with the shortage of teaching materials, Sisters wrote back to Ireland, to ask other Presentation communities to send them practical things, such as sheet music, copies of hymns, lace patterns, crucifixes and holy pictures, to use in the schools.

Despite privations suffered by the nuns, the schools went from strength to strength. In 1864, a national inspection of Catholic schools in Newfoundland singled out for particular praise the Presentation Convent in St John's, commenting that it provided 'an education equal to what [girls] would receive at boarding school in England or Ireland'.[108] By then, Presentation schools were providing education to 7,649 pupils, and the Inspector noted that a particular strength of the convent schools was that the nuns afforded great 'care, attention and skill', placing them 'above the other Catholic Schools of the island'.[109]

Although the congregation had established five schools by 1855, they had only twenty-nine professed religious to cover all of the teaching needs. Unsurprisingly, they adopted the monitorial system in their schools, to provide teaching support. It was a system developed in England, to meet the staffing demands in large schools in industrial cities.[110] School 'managers' trained older, capable pupils to become monitors; the monitors in turn supervised younger pupils and drilled them in spellings and arithmetic. In Ireland, both the Kildare Place Society and the National Board adopted the principles of the system.[111] The system was also used in Presentation convents that were affiliated to the National Board. Indeed, the Galway convent that provided Newfoundland with its first Presentation nuns was known for training monitors and teachers. As early as 1849, the Commissioners of National Education reported that the 'Presentation Convent School in Galway has educated and trained more teachers than any other institute in Ireland ... 80 of its pupils have charge of National or other schools'.[112] Many of the nuns who arrived from Ireland in the early decades were Presentation past-pupils. Others had attended National Schools, or schools run by other religious congregations in Ireland.

By adopting the monitorial system, and then developing formal teacher training for women in Newfoundland, the nuns opened up a new avenue of employment to girls.[113] Initially, the training was conducted at the mother house in St John's, and as other convents and schools were opened, they began training young women, who could then take up posts in district schools. By 1876, the nuns at Harbour Main sent out six teachers to other schools in the parish, who had completed their training in the convent school.[114] In 1862, the first *Report Upon the Inspection of Catholic Schools* examined some of the teachers who had trained with the Presentations. Concluding his inspection of the district of Placentia West, the inspector wrote: 'I found the schools in this district progressing favourably. Two trained female teachers from the Presentation Convent, St John's, had charge of the two schools ... and were conducting them very satisfactorily.'[115]

Two years later, the contribution of the nuns to the 'mental training' of teachers was noted in a survey of all of the school boards in Newfoundland, which commented that the 'nuns train free of expense any number of female teachers who present themselves'.[116] In 1880, the government announced that women 'pupil teachers are given permission by the Government to attend the Presentation Convent School, St John's, for the purpose of education and training'.[117] An Act of 1892 recognised the Presentation Convent as qualified to provide teacher training.[118]

Bishop Michael Fleming's impetus for inviting the Presentation Sisters from Ireland, and the way he managed them in their early years in Newfoundland, suggest that his main concern at the time was the rapid and successful expansion of his Church on the island. His haste in bringing them to a country where he had no convent to house them, meant that they lived in a variety of temporary dwellings, including a tavern and a barn. From the astonishment that they expressed at the severely cold winter weather on arrival, it seems unlikely that the Bishop had given them a realistic appraisal of the context of their new mission. His close oversight of the Sisters, and his insistence that they at all times remember that he was their Superior, added to the hardship felt by the four pioneering Irishwomen in Newfoundland. There is no evidence that the nuns considered abandoning the mission, even though the terms on which they had left Galway included the right to return there if they so wished. It is likely that they quickly agreed with Fleming, that there was a need for the civilising influence of convent schooling. They were warmly welcomed by the Catholic community, and were generally seen as a positive force in education. By 1861, *The Newfoundlander* reported on the 'value of conventual training', noting the pupils' proficiency at examinations; the report on the examination of pupils at the St John's convent was particularly enthusiastic about the 'thorough' nature of the teaching, and at the evidence of 'much progress and taste in music'.[119] The article continued its praise of Presentation convents:

> These institutions must truly be regarded as amongst the greatest blessings to society ... especially [for] the female poor, who if not taught at such establishments, would probably be denied all education ... Here they receive gratuitously an Education at once religious and secular ...[120]

The 1850s, a period when the Presentations expanded in Newfoundland, were characterised by a spirit of 'perfect religious freedom': the government divided the education grants *pro rata*, between all denominations.[121] This gave much-needed support to the convent schools, as the nuns did not charge any fees. Many of the nuns who arrived from Ireland in the early decades were Presentation past pupils. Others had attended National Schools, or schools run by other religious congregations in Ireland.[122] Though the Irish nuns who left Ireland for Newfoundland in 1833 had no official teacher training, evidence indicates that they were adept at teaching, and drew on their own education. The convents which they established made a significant – if largely forgotten – contribution to the development of teacher education for women in nineteenth-century Newfoundland. The Presentations also widened employment opportunities for working women who learned to read and write at Sunday School, and they prepared all of their pupils to be able to earn a living through fine needlework, lacework and dressmaking. By teaching music, singing, drawing and languages, the nuns also tried to cater to the needs of girls with artistic and literary abilities.[123]

The kind of education provided in Presentation schools was certainly constrained by gender expectations, but it significantly changed the career prospects of many Catholic girls who – prior to the arrival of the nuns – were confined to working in the fisheries and seasonal agricultural labour. Additionally, the convents presented nineteenth-century Newfoundland women with an alternative to early marriage and motherhood – an alternative that was simultaneously proving attractive to women in Ireland – they could become nuns, contribute to the expansion of schooling on the island, and live out their lives in female communities.[124]

## CHAPTER 5

# Presentation Education: Pupils and Pedagogy in the Nineteenth Century

*... the girls learn to read, and when they have
the Catechism by heart, they learn to work, they all
hear Mass every day, say their morning and night
prayers, say the Catechism in each school by
question and answer all together.*

– Nano Nagle to Miss Fitzsimons, 17 July 1769.

The programme of education that Nano Nagle outlined to Elizabeth Fitzsimons in 1769 was relatively simple. Her schools opened at eight in the morning; pupils paused for food at twelve, and the schools closed at five in the evening. The children were taught to read and learned their catechism by heart. Boys were taught to write, while girls learned to do needlework. They all heard Mass, said their morning and evening prayers, recited the catechism, and on Saturdays religious instruction was given to pupils who came to school to 'say their beads'. The daily routine outlined by Teresa Mulally in the *Rules Observed in the Schools for Poor Girls* describes a similar system of organisation in her school in George's Hill.[1]

When the *Rules and Constitutions* were drawn up by Laurence Callanan in 1793, the second chapter was devoted to the schools of the proposed new Order.[2] Perhaps unsurprisingly, the practices in the schools reflected the education theory and practice of the Ursulines, with some modifications. The Presentation model of schooling was well established by the time the non-denominational National System was established in 1831, and therefore did not rely on the State system in order to develop its *modus operandi*. Rather, it developed regulations and pedagogic practices, some of which eventually had to meld with those outlined by the National Board.

From an early stage, the recommendations for the running of Presentation schools had to be approached with flexibility. For instance, the Ursuline principle of shared responsibility was maintained, but the large numbers of children in attendance combined with the small numbers of Sisters available, particularly in the early stages, meant that adjustments were necessary.[3] In Ireland, in the early decades, it was not always possible to divide the children equally amongst the teaching Sisters, nor to order the classes by the age of the children. In countries where the Presentations made new foundations, such as America and Australia, there were challenges to the requirement to keep within a 'cloister', with the result that sometimes bishops provided the nuns with permission to teach outside the cloister. Other challenges, particularly when the congregation expanded overseas, included being able to clearly communicate the ethos of Presentation convent schooling.

In 1850, Mother de Pazzi Leahy finished writing the *Directory of the Religious of the Presentation Order*, copies of which could thereafter be sent to every new Presentation foundation, worldwide.[4] It was published at a time when the Order was experiencing very rapid growth, and communities were regularly writing back to Cork for guidance. In creating the *Directory*, Mother de Pazzi articulated the Presentation charism, and Presentation education principles, for each new generation of nuns. By the time it appeared, there were new pressures on Irish Presentation convents that had become affiliated to the National System, which had been established to afford 'a combined literary and separate religious education ... for the poorer classes of the community' and 'to unite in one system children of different creeds'.[5] A government-appointed Board of Commissioners ran the National System of schooling, and had control over the schools that it built, and those that became connected to the Board in order to benefit from financial support. In National Schools, religious instruction could not take place during the school day, and had to be provided separately, either after school or at the weekend. The Board had control over the books to be used in the schools, and the funds voted annually by parliament, and a system of inspection ensured that regulations were enforced.[6]

Some of the earliest applications for aid from the newly established National Board came from convent schools, with twenty-six of them connected to the system by April 1837.[7] The pressure for convent schools to conform to the regulations of a non-denominational system were not small, and it is perhaps not surprising that the *Presentation Directory* appeared in 1850. Three years later, the Annual Report of the Commissioners of National Education showed that ninety-nine convent schools had connected to the System. This rose to 111 in 1857, 132 in 1864, and 145 in 1870.[8] Among the earliest Presentation convents to connect their schools with the National Board were the houses in Galway, Killarney, Tralee and Dingle.

It is clear from the *Presentation Directory* that many of the principles of school management recommended by the National Board in the 1830s had been in operation in Presentation schools since at least 1790. For example, the nuns kept a record of the names of the children, their age on entrance, the names and occupations of their parents, their address and the exact date of reception into the school. The School Register kept by the community in the Presentation Convent, Doneraile, (1818) contains this data on the 398 children who enrolled during the first three months the school was in operation; similarly, the Sisters in the school at the Presentation Convent, Mitchelstown, (1853) recorded details for the 637 children who enrolled during their first four weeks of operation. In Doneraile, the ages of the children ranged from four to nineteen; in Mitchelstown the youngest pupil was three and the oldest was twenty, but the vast majority of the children in both schools were between seven and sixteen years of age. The occupations listed for their parents included Farmer, Shopkeeper, Labourer, Smith, Weaver, Servant, Butcher, Shoemaker, Carpenter and Saddler.[9]

The schools were to be situated as conveniently to the convents as could be allowed within the rules of the Institute, yet separated as much as possible from the convent house itself. Visitors were to be admitted to the schools only with the express permission of the Superioress, and only the members of the community who were engaged in instruction were allowed to be in the schools with the children. According to the *Constitutions*, schools were to open each day from 9.00 am until 12.00 noon, and 2.00 pm until 5.00 pm, however, the *Directory* altered these hours to 9.00 am until 3.15 pm. In addition to the periods of vacation that were set out in the *Constitutions*, the *Directory* suggested that holidays 'may also be granted on the feasts of the Conception, Nativity and Purification of our Blessed Lady'. It further recommended that the school should not be open when particular ceremonies took place in the convent, such as the reception, profession or burial of a member of the community.[10] A final suggestion was that a clock should be hung in each school to regulate the different exercises of the day. On the approval of the Superioress, the children were to discontinue their activities, bless themselves and 'devoutly recommend themselves to the

protection of the Holy Mother of God, saying a Hail Mary' whenever the clock struck.[11]

When the convents connected their schools with the National Board, they agreed to be bound by the conditions of the Commissioners regarding the general running of a school within the System.[12] These entailed keeping a register of the daily attendance of the children and the average attendance in each week and quarter; the conspicuous positioning of the inscription 'National School' on the school-house; the exhibition of the General Lesson in the school-room and the inculcation of its principles.[13] They also required that the school be open to receive children of all religious denominations; that the Commissioners be allowed to visit and examine the school, and that the public, of all persuasions, have access to visit the school, inspect the Register, witness the mode of teaching and see that the Regulations were observed.[14] In practice, when convent communities applied to join their schools with the Board their hours of opening were listed variously as between 9.00 am and 3.30 pm. Whilst the schools were assigned one roll number within the System, in the case of communities who were conducting infant and senior schools the Sisters were often operating two or three schools on the same campus.[15] The School Registers for Galway, Wexford and Clondalkin show that each of these communities was operating infant schools for girls and boys, and a senior school for girls only. Separate registers were kept for the infant girls and boys, with a third register dedicated to the senior girls. Children from three to seven years of age were accepted into the infant schools across the year and generally spent three years there before transferring to a senior school. Whilst the numbers fluctuated, at least half of the girls taken into the infant schools transferred to the senior schools three years later. In the senior schools, children of seven years and above were accepted for registration throughout the year also. Girls moving from other schools, or who had not attended any school before, were registered along with those who transferred from the infant schools.[16]

## The Curriculum at the Convent Schools

The secular subjects at the heart of the curriculum in Presentation schools were reflective of contemporary attitudes regarding the appropriate subjects for the education of girls. Describing Needlework as 'the most essential acquirement that the children could obtain', the *Directory* then outlined how other subjects were to be taught.[17] In reading lessons, the children were only allowed to read books that would inculcate the practice of virtue and

devotion, and reading books for amusement was forbidden.[18] When learning to write, children were first taught how to form the letters of the alphabet on a slate, then they learned how to hold a pen properly, before progressing to using ink and paper. They were not taught to write in 'small hand' until they could form a good 'bold large hand'. Finally, to write freely from dictation, children were taught to write in a running hand with speed and precision. Arithmetic was described as 'one of the most important branches of profane knowledge' and, when properly taught, was viewed as an excellent way of strengthening the mind and preparing it for the acquisition of any other kind of knowledge to which it may be applied. Children were taught to knit, hem, sew and how to mark out a garment on canvas or coarse linen. When they had advanced from this level they were taught to cut out and arrange the work for themselves, paying particular attention to finishing. Instruction in Needlework was given for the hour between twelve and one o'clock every day.[19]

For all schools operating in connection with the National Board, the syllabus for literary instruction was laid down in the Programmes of Instruction for Pupils in National Schools.[20] There were separate programmes for girls and boys, each describing the minimum level of proficiency required for pupils enrolled for at least one quarter in each class. The subject areas covered by these programmes were Reading, Writing, Spelling, Grammar, Arithmetic and Geography. Along with this basic curriculum, subjects such as Sewing, Knitting, Netting, Embroidery, Straw Plaiting and Cutting Out were taught to females. Beyond that, extra subjects including Mensuration, Geometry, Book-keeping, Agriculture, Music and Drawing could also be offered by schools.[21] Classes in National Schools were determined by the Lesson Books, and a pupil's progress was determined by the book she was using. Thus the First, Second, Sequel and Third Classes corresponded to the First, Second, Sequel and Third Books with Fourth and Fifth Classes equating to the Fourth Book and higher.[22]

These core subjects changed little with the advent of the 'payment-by-results' system in 1872, which introduced payments to teachers dependent on the examination performance of their pupils.[23] In addition to Needlework for girls and Agriculture for boys, the existing subjects of the basic curriculum became obligatory under the new system. Schools were encouraged to offer extra subjects and some began to offer Greek, Latin, French, Sewing Machine, Botany, Chemistry and Magnetism and Electricity.[24] After Infants, pupils progressed from First to Sixth Class, but there were 'stages' in Fifth and Sixth Class. To progress through the classes, pupils had to pass the examinations

in the compulsory subjects at the end of the results year. Failure in the examinations meant repeating the class until the pupil achieved a pass.[25]

As with all schools joining the National System, the Presentation Convent Schools undertook to follow the secular curriculum as it was defined by the Commissioners. In addition to the core subjects, the Presentation communities offered Vocal Music, Drawing and Embroidery as extra subjects. However, they met with varying degrees of success in these subject areas under the Commissioners. While the community in Thurles received a gratuity for teaching Vocal Music from 1863, and the Sisters in Clondalkin received a gratuity for teaching Music from 1860 and Drawing from 1863, the nuns in Wexford were denied theirs for Music in 1866 on the recommendation of the Inspector, Mr Dugan. In George's Hill there was a query in relation to the amount of time devoted to the subject and a request to District Inspector Sheahan to investigate.[26] South Presentation was one of a number of schools in Cork that was allowed to avail of the services of a Miss Ellen McKenna as a teacher of Vocal Music from 1 April 1862. They had already been involved in a similar arrangement in relation to Drawing where Mr Sheil, Second Master in the School of Design, taught Elementary Drawing from March 1856.[27] The Sisters in Limerick had introduced Embroidery to their school by 1852, hiring a teacher from the Limerick School of Ornamental Art.[28] Between 1850 and 1851, the convents in Galway, Thurles and Millstreet introduced Embroidery to their schools in a three-way arrangement between themselves, the Commissioners and a Glasgow company which paid a salary of 6s per week to four teachers of Embroidery in the Galway school from August 1850.[29]

Following the introduction of payment-by-results in 1872, all of the Presentation national schools were examined. In addition to the obligatory subjects, the Sisters continued to offer Vocal Music and Drawing as extra subjects. Presentation schools also variously offered extra subjects including 'the Sewing Machine', French, Book-keeping, Shorthand, Typewriting, Cookery and Drill.[30] In recording his observations on the first examination at Presentation Convent, Kilkenny, in October 1872, the District Inspector confined his comments to recommendations regarding the Sisters' display of the 'new programme', alterations to the timetable and promotion of infants who were turning eight years of age. In July 1873, his colleague W.R. Molloy recorded 210 pupils as presenting for examination and noted that, 'Though a full year has not elapsed since the previous inspection still the answering of the pupils … affords evidence of very satisfactory progress in the several classes.'[31]

The comments recorded by the inspectors in South Presentation for the same year were somewhat mixed. Whilst the Infant Department continued 'in a backward state, especially the 1st Book Class connected with that department', the '2nd Class and small drafts of 3rd and 4th in the room adjoining the Infants is in a very satisfactory state, and reflects much credit on the energy and skill of the Sister in charge'. In all classes, the performance in Arithmetic was described as low; however, the proficiency of the Fourth, Fifth and Sixth Classes in other subjects was considered to be 'very fair'. By 1881 the performance of the pupils in Cork had improved. The answering of the 148 Infants who were examined was recorded as being 'very good', with the proficiency and answering of other classes described as 'very fair'.[32] In recording the proficiency of the pupils in Kilkenny for 1885 as 'highly satisfactory', the Inspector, M. Keenan, noted an 8 per cent increase in the number of girls in the senior classes who presented for examination compared with 1883.[33] This was also borne out by the experience of both the Wexford and Clondalkin schools during the first ten years Results Examinations were carried out. In both cases, the numbers of girls in the Senior Schools who fulfilled the minimum attendance requirements increased, from 225 to 345 in Wexford and from 65 to 125 in Clondalkin. Their rates of success in the exams also rose, from 75.6 to 81.2 per cent in Wexford and from 42.6 to 96.8 per cent in Clondalkin.[34]

## Religious Instruction in Presentation Schools

While the secular curriculum taught by the Sisters conformed to general education standards of the National System, the programme of religious instruction was entirely that of the Presentation Order. The *Constitutions* nominated the education of poor girls in 'the principles of Religion and Christian Piety' as the central characteristic of the Institute, and over fifty years later the *Directory* detailed how this could be done in the day-to-day life of their schools.[35] The programme that was devised was based on *The Rudiments of Faith* by Cardinal Robert Bellarmine and the *Douai Catechism*, neither of which was entirely suited to the instruction of children.[36] Both the *Constitutions* and the *Directory* addressed this by clarifying that the Sisters were to explain the Catechism to the children with simplicity, prudence and caution 'lest anything be advanced extending beyond the capacities of the children'.[37] In practice, the Sisters were to devote a half an hour every day to teaching the Catechism exclusively, keeping simply to the text and without introducing any discussion or questions that would only serve to confuse the children. Curiosity on the part of the pupils was to be carefully repressed at this stage. Once the children were capable of reflection, they were instructed in the duties that attended conversion to God, which included morning prayer, honouring and respecting their parents and superiors, a daily examination of conscience and a thorough confession. Cleanliness was an important part of this process and it was to be insisted upon from an early age.[38]

Preparation for the sacraments of Confession and Communion began when the children were well versed in these aspects of Catechism. For Confession, instruction was in the three parts of penance: contrition, confession and satisfaction. The importance of a full confession was impressed upon the children. They were taught how to examine their consciences according to order, on the Commandments and on the seven deadly sins. They were also taught how to confess their sins properly, distinguishing three kinds of sins: sins against God, sins against the neighbour, and sins against the self in thoughts, words and works. They were instructed in reciting an act of contrition for their sins and the formation of resolutions of amendment. Those who were being prepared for first Communion received particular instruction every day, with frequent attendance at Confession included as part of the preparation. When the children were considered ready, a day was appointed and arrangements were made to hold the ceremony.[39] If sufficient funds were available, a breakfast was provided for the communicants and each child received a prayer book in which her name was inscribed and the date of her first communion.

Preparation for Confirmation followed the same routine as that for First Holy Communion. In addition to this the children were taught to recite specific prayers at various times of the day. At nine o'clock the children knelt for morning prayers led by the teacher. These included Acts of Adoration, Faith, Hope, Charity and Thanksgiving; a prayer offering and directing intentions; an invocation of the Blessed Virgin and Saints; the Pater, Ave, Gloria Patri, Credo and the Angelus Domini and adoration of the Blessed Sacrament, which was repeated three times. They were to bless themselves before and after the Catechism and at the striking of the clock when they were also to say a Hail Mary. From 11.45 am they were to make an examination of conscience since the evening before, while continuing to work. At noon they recited the Acts of Faith, Hope and Charity and the adoration of the Blessed Sacrament three times with the teacher. Evening prayers were said from 2.45 to 3.00 pm whilst the children were dressed for home, and included a lecture read by the Sister from *Challenor's Meditations* or another suitable book, and prayers. The Rosary was said at this time one day in the week.[40]

Apart from this regular instruction in Catechism and the sacraments, convents engaged in a variety of religious ceremonies that occurred on an occasional basis. Although the *Presentation Directory* recommended that the schools be closed for events that related directly to the life of the convent community, such as reception, profession and burial, other ceremonies took place that involved the schools, the children and the wider Catholic population of the district. The Annals of the Presentation Convent, Thurles, refer to a number of ceremonies that involved the pupils of the schools. When the foundation stone of the new convent was laid by Dr Laffan in May 1824, it was marked by a procession of the Religious and poor children.[41] Thirty-five years later, when preparing to expand in Thurles, a ceremony to take possession of the ground on which the schools were built took place. The children walked in procession, chanting with the Sisters; the Archbishop placed a banner of the Blessed Virgin at one end and St Joseph at the other; the *Te Deum* and *Magnificat* were sung and all returned to the chapel. The foundation stone was laid in place of the banner of St Joseph two years later, which involved the Archbishop and all the priests of the town. The nuns and the children, who were wearing white veils, entered in procession along with the clergy singing the Litany of the Blessed Virgin. Following the singing of the *Veni Sancte* by the Sisters, the stone was laid, a drum beaten and the *Te Deum* sung. Finally, on 23 June 1862 all the children assembled in the old school for the last time and along with the community walked in procession to the new school for the erection of a statue of the Blessed Virgin. The Annalist described this ceremony as 'most imposing. Hymns were sung, and the ceremony concluded by the *Magnificat* and *Te Deum*.'[42]

In Cahirciveen, the Annalist recorded a number of ceremonies during 1861 that involved the school children. On 29 January, Bishop Moriarty admitted several children into different sodalities giving each one a 'nice lecture'. This ceremony took place after the profession of Sr Stanislaus Roystan. 'A few of the Children of Mary of the Holy Angels, St Joseph and St Aloysius' were received into their sodalities by Fr O'Connor in June. Fr O'Connor was present again on 21 July when eighty of the school children dressed in white, along with boys from the Christian Brothers and confraternity, took part in a procession around the chapel yard. The school children 'subscribed to purchase two small banners for their procession'. When the Bishop arrived for the Confirmation ceremony a month later, ninety of the school girls wearing white with 'larger white veils', met him at the chapel gate 'in procession singing the Litany and some appropriate hymns'.[43] In recording the death of one of the convent's foundresses, Mother Joseph Mahony in

January 1885, the Annals include a press clipping containing her obituary and an account of the funeral ceremony that was held in the Convent Chapel. On the conclusion of the Requiem Mass and Office, 'a large number of the convent children in white dresses and crêpe sashes' followed the cross bearer and his acolytes in leading the funeral procession out of the Chapel.[44]

In 1863, the Fermoy community marked the Consecration of their new cemetery on 25 July with a procession led by forty school children dressed in white followed by the nuns, the priests and the bishop. They sang the Litany of the Saints and lit candles on three crosses. When the blessing was concluded the bishop said Mass in the Sisters' Chapel. The following October, when the community opened their new schools, 'the children walked in procession into them at 10 o'clock. At 11 o'clock the Bishop entered, the Sisters sang the *Te Deum* after the Litany of the Blessed Virgin; at the conclusion his Lordship made a short prayer.'[45] The Sisters in Crosshaven moved into their new convent on 25 April 1878. They marked the occasion with a procession from the old building to the new one. Leading the procession was 'A band from the Green Mount Industrial School Cork, playing Sacred music … next followed the children of the Convent School dressed in white, who sang at intervals, the *Tantum Ergo* &c – after the children came the nuns, and then the Priests followed.' Fr Joseph O'Keeffe celebrated Mass and Benediction in the new convent and when the religious ceremonies were over everyone 'sat down to breakfast, which was laid out in one of the School-rooms'. To celebrate the 1 May 1881, the children 'walked in procession around the enclosure, sang the Litany of the Blessed Virgin, and had a Lecture given them by Revd Father Carey PP. … A Carpet was spread on the field, and a platform for the Preacher.'[46] An entry in the Limerick Convent Annals for 2 September 1888 recorded the formal visit to the school of Monsignor Persico, the Papal Envoy. Accompanied by local Bishop Dwyer, Monsignor Gualdi and local clergy, Persico visited the boys' room first where he was greeted with three cheers for Rome, a song of welcome and presented with a Kindergarten basket of flowers. He then visited the Upper Room where the different classes were arranged to meet him. All the girls knelt to receive his blessing and sang a song of welcome composed by Sr Columba, one of the Sisters in the community.[47]

## Zealous and Generous Teaching: The Model for the Nineteenth-Century Nun

The role of the Presentation nun in classroom management was highlighted in the Chapter of the *Presentation Directory* devoted to the method of instruction. The 'holy and excellent function of instructing the poor' required great zeal on the part of the individual Sister which was to permeate all aspects of her work in the school. She was to be animated with a mild and gentle zeal, to win the hearts of 'the little ones'. Her zeal was to be generous, allowing her to renounce all the conveniences and enjoyments of life that could afford her pleasure; it was to be wise, prudent and cautious, informing her dealings with others. She was to be patient, even in the most trying and difficult of circumstances; her zeal was to be disinterested, seeking only the salvation of souls and the Glory of God. Finally, she was to be persevering and enlightened, and never to feel sad or dejected when there was little success from her labours.[48] In correcting the pupils, the Sister was cautioned to suppress whatever emotions of passion that arose, taking care not to give way to anger. She was never to hurt or strike them, as this form of chastisement – if found necessary – was only to be inflicted on the children at home. As different children responded to different approaches, the 'Mistress of each school … was to … study their natural dispositions, inclinations, and capacities, in order to treat them accordingly, and to conduct them prudently'.[49]

The Programme of Instruction devised by the Commissioners of National Education promoted explanation, interrogation and repetition as the three great means of instruction to be employed in their schools.[50] This was also the approach of the Sisters in Presentation schools, who were trained to use a process of instruction, questioning and repetition. For example, the Catechism was to be taught by reciting, repetition and questioning. When the chapter for the day had been recited two or three times through the class, and the questioning process completed, the Sister in charge would ask the questions in a different format to ascertain whether the children fully understood the content. In the event they did not, she was to explain it again in an easy and simple manner. During the lessons children were encouraged to ask one or two questions of their own relating to the content, provided they were relevant and not frivolous.[51] While methods for the teaching of Reading receive little attention in the *Directory*, the Annals of the Presentation Convent, Clondalkin, note that the children were taught to read by reading out loud in drafts of ten or twelve. Until the alterations to the Senior School in 1874 this was done in a circle around the teacher's desk. After the alteration work was completed, the children stood in a line in front of the new raised platform and had 'to give out their voices and read distinctly'.[52]

The *Presentation Directory* gave some general advice on how to teach children to write. It advised the nuns to pay close attention to the pupils when they first learnt to write, as this was the phase during which habits were formed. To teach writing effectively, the nun needed to move between the children constantly. She was to model the writing of any words or sentences given to the child to transcribe, wait for the child to complete the exercise and correct the work then so that any mistakes in formation or spacing could be addressed. Those pupils who were weak at writing would require more particular attention, most effective of which was to hold their hand to help them to control the pen.[53]

The importance in life of a good knowledge of Arithmetic meant that it was necessary to adopt a good method of teaching it. Accuracy and speed were the two essential characteristics of a good 'arithmetician', neither of which could be obtained without a knowledge of the principles and rules, and continuous practice in their application. The teaching of arithmetic began with instruction in the nine figures along with zero or nought. Having mastered these, the pupils were arranged into groups of ten or twenty and were instructed in addition, as numeration could be combined with it.[54] Needlework was to be taught by imitation and constant practice. The Sister was to practice great patience and forbearance in the annoyances the pupils might cause her, and encourage them to be attentive and to learn well by every means at her disposal. The girls were to be taught how to hem and sew at first, then to mark out on canvas or coarse linen. Once these skills were mastered, they were to advance to more difficult areas.[55] Work was to be examined often and, when necessary, was to be ripped to be done again – more than once if required. Those children who were having difficulty were to be instructed on an individual basis, which was considered to be the most successful method of helping them.[56]

## Developing Teaching Skills

Conscious that good teaching methods were essential to any success the children might attain, Presentation nuns made use of tried and tested methods in presenting these subjects. But they also showed an openness to new methods of instruction.[57] Mother Baptist Frayne, in the Presentation Convent, Wexford, was particularly curious about new ideas, and carried on an enthusiastic correspondence with Mrs Julia Campbell, of the Protestant Kildare Place Society (KPS), concerning school management and pedagogy.[58] Early in 1832, Campbell sent KPS teaching equipment to Mother Baptist, and said she was 'delighted to learn that [the] school prospers'.[59] Later that year, she told Frayne about a book the KPS were about to publish containing directions for needlework, and said she would send it to the Wexford convent.[60] In a long letter in 1834, Mrs Campbell explained the motivational value of the Merit Ticket system that was in use in National Schools, and compared it to the merit system operated by the KPS. The correspondence between Mrs Campbell and Mother Baptist, which also ranged over needlework specimens and irregular desk heights, hints at a shared joy in teaching that crossed denominational boundaries.[61] It is not known whether Mother Baptist ever shared the contents of these letters with her bishop, who may not have seen the value of nuns corresponding with Protestant teachers.

From the 1850s, convent communities availed themselves of the services of the 'Organising Mistresses' who supplied expertise in all aspects of school organisation for schools within the National System. Organising Mistresses and Masters were selected from the best National School teachers, and were classified separately at a higher grade.[62] They travelled around the country, spending a few weeks with schools to which they had been assigned. The Presentation communities in South Presentation, Galway and Maryborough each availed of the services of an Organising Mistress. In 1853, Miss Doyle was appointed as Organising Mistress in the Presentation school in Galway, and was sanctioned from June until November.[63] In the Register for Maryborough, the entry for 27 February 1857 noted the appointment of Mary Hargaden to organise the school for three months from 1 March. A Miss Cleary went as Organising Mistress to the Presentations in Thurles, and the Presentations in Cashel in 1859.[64] While their salaries were paid by the National Board, the Organisers were given board and lodgings by the nuns.

The willingness of the nuns to apply for an Organising Mistress was a measure of their wish to succeed within the National System, and the support of a Miss Ryan was greatly appreciated. The nuns in Tralee were keen to get her help in 1869, as they found that the requirements of the National System 'required much toil'.[65] Miss Ryan also visited Bandon in 1869, where she introduced 'many useful changes in the School discipline'. In addition, she encouraged a practice of calling out 'the most deserving children in every class' on Fridays, which the Sisters found to be very effective especially when any priests of the parish were present for the ceremony.[66] In March 1872, the nuns in Wexford were delighted with Miss Ryan's work, noting that 'She fulfilled her duties perfectly and her system promises the most favourable results.'[67] Ryan then went on to the Presentation school in Thurles, and to Limerick where the inspector later noted that 'The good effects of Miss Ryan's organisation are already quite apparent and a marked improvement may be anticipated in the proficiency of the pupils and in the various details of school keeping.'[68]

## Inspectors and Inspections at the Presentation Schools

The inspectors who were appointed by the National Board acted as its officers, and their duties included visiting and inspecting the ordinary, convent, model, workhouse and industrial schools in their districts; reporting on new applicants to the system; investigating queries and complaints; examining teachers and paid monitors and completing all the necessary correspondence with the Board and the schools.[69] A *District Inspector's Observation Book* was kept in every school, and the inspectors entered their comments and observations about each visit they made. An *Observation Book* survives for both the South Presentation and the Kilkenny convent, covering the years 1856–1936 and 1856–98 respectively. In the period between June 1856 and June 1896, eleven different inspectors made entries in the book for the South Presentation School.[70] The nature of the comments for South Presentation varied over the years. John E. Sheridan's Report for April 1856 was positive, ranging from 'fair' in some areas to 'excellent' in others.[71] Edward Sheehy's report for October 1860 pointed out that 'Owing to the length of time the School was closed, on account of vacation and improvements made in some of the rooms, the answering of the pupils, as recorded above, was not so good as under other circumstances.'[72]

In 1868, the District Inspector noted that 'The School is in a highly effective state, and has made very satisfactory progress since last inspection.'[73] However, by 1883, the Head Inspector commented on the exceptionally high number of pupils assigned to each teaching Sister, noting that he had 'found 34 girls 27 Monrs. [Monitors] & 7 others with their one Teacher. –Ten at a time is about enough for one to teach or examine in any real working sense. Thirty or so become a mob'.[74] The nuns were, by this time, using some of the school management principles of the Lancasterian system, whereby older pupils were trained as monitors to help with the instruction of younger pupils. Even then, the monitors needed to be directed and supervised, and the Inspector did not consider that one nun could possibly manage the work of a group totalling sixty-eight youths.

The teacher–pupil ratio continued to be a challenge in many convent schools; in part this was because each Presentation convent was an independent community and relied on attracting vocations in order to increase the number of teaching Sisters. However, when a convent sent a group of nuns overseas to make a new foundation, they usually lost a few of their best teaching Sisters; similarly, when they made a filiation in Ireland, their numbers were depleted. Communities very rarely sent nuns to swell the teaching ranks in neighbouring houses, unless in exceptional circumstances, so teaching Sisters needed to train monitors to support the growing numbers of children in their schools.

In 1864, the Commissioners completed a *Special Report on Convent Schools*, in which convent education nationally was surveyed. The *Report* provides a useful snapshot of Presentation schooling, as it covered staffing levels, teacher proficiency, the quality of instruction across all subject areas, adequacy and quality of school accommodation and equipment, the impact of convent schools on ordinary female schools and the overall impact and effect of convent schools on an area.[75] The school inspectors visited the convent schools during the months of May and June 1864 and their reports offer a range of views. The Wexford, Limerick and Millstreet schools were considered under staffed, though other convents such as Bagenalstown, Carlow, Doneraile and Fermoy were assessed favourably in this regard. Thomas Stronge, the Inspector in Millstreet, explained that of the seven nuns that formed the community only four were available to teach in the school, the others being incapacitated through age and poor health.[76] The Sisters in Cahirciveen were 'effective' in organising their school, whilst the organising skill of the community in Bandon was assessed as 'tolerable'. For the Dingle community, the inspector noted that the 'method of teaching and organising skill are defective'. The views relating to the quality of instruction in the various subjects, both core and extra, were also varied. The assessment of instruction in Galway was excellent; in Mountmellick and Maryborough it was good and very fair respectively. However, in Limerick it was considered to be very unsatisfactory in every branch except Reading and Spelling.

While literary instruction was uneven across Presentation schools in the nineteenth century, the quality of industrial instruction was considered high by all inspectors. In Kilina, the inspector described it as 'superior'. Denis O'Driscoll stated that the standard of industrial instruction given in Castleisland was 'superior to that given in any lay female school of the district'. In Youghal, L.G. Fitzgerald observed that 'This branch is taught with more than ordinary success' and for Mountmellick, Mr Graham noted that 'Since 1859, upwards of 200 pupils have left school fully competent to earn their bread by their needle; 100 became servants, and 45 emigrated.'[77]

Even though Presentation schools were often over-subscribed, inspectors generally viewed the popularity of convent schools as a way of raising education standards more generally, in a locality. In Limerick, the school could only cater for 347 pupils, yet it had an average attendance of 449. In South Presentation, the inspector noted that 'The seven school-rooms can accommodate 720 pupils, which is much larger than the average attendance, but not so large as the attendance on some days.' The supply of equipment and requisites was considered very satisfactory overall.[78] Visiting the Clane convent, the inspector noted that the impact of convent education was to encourage 'a healthy spirit of competition' resulting in greater efficiency in the neighbouring schools; similarly, Inspector MacDermott reported that the success of George's Hill forced 'good schools to increase their exertions to keep up a sufficient average attendance' whilst simultaneously relieving weak schools of pupils whose instruction was neglected.[79] Mr McNamara, who visited Killarney, stated that 'No ordinary female national school or schools, if established in the town for the same time, could possibly have dispensed education to so many.'[80]

The *Special Report on Convent Schools* investigated whether or not there were pupils attending the schools who were so destitute that they would not have been able to attend an 'ordinary' national school. Fully half of the children attending the school in Galway would not have attended an ordinary school, according to Mr Simpson. The nuns' practice of feeding poor pupils was noted, and indeed the inspector in Limerick said that of the fifty children who were fed daily, thirty would not have been sent to school but for the food.[81]

Generally, the commissioners recognised the 'civilizing influence' of convent schools and remarked favourably on the devotion, meekness and gentleness of the Sisters who worked in them. However, they were critical of some aspects of teaching, particularly the teaching of arithmetic.[82] It was argued that the areas where convent national schools were superior to ordinary national schools were 'manners and discipline, organisation, cleanliness, ventilation, sprightliness, and cheerfulness'. The Powis Commission concluded in favour of convent national schools in 1878, noting that 'All branches of hand-work, such as sewing, drawing, penmanship, and, particularly, exercise-books, &c, are carried out on the most correct plan, and with the most gratifying proficiency.'[83]

## The Sisters in their Schools

How Sisters behaved in their schools was determined by both the demands of their Order, and the regulations of the National Board. Occasionally, these demands were in conflict, particularly when the non-denominational system required the Sisters to modify religious expression in the schools. But the general novitiate training of a Presentation nun was otherwise designed to make her a patient and responsible teacher.

The *Presentation Directory* described the instruction of poor children as a divine function in which all members of a community must be employed according to their abilities and outlined the duties for the Superioress and Sisters with regard to the schools.[84] The Superioress was charged with daily superintendence of the schools to ensure their smooth running. She also supervised all the teaching Sisters – known as Mistresses – and oversaw school discipline, the appointment and direction of the monitresses and the regulation of equipment and supplies.[85] Regulations for the Mistresses stated that they were to show great respect for and deference to the Mother Superior, following any orders she gave. They were also to support and assist one another in their work. Each Mistress had to take her turn in charge of the care of the school for a week at a time. This mainly involved opening the door at a particular hour each morning to let the children in; saying the morning and evening prayers; reading the evening lectures; signalling the changes in duties throughout the day and dismissing the children when all the devotions were concluded.

Punctuality was considered essential, and when engaged in their work in school they were not to allow their attention to be distracted by useless conversations or work that was not directly pertinent to the act of instructing the children. Sisters were not to converse with one another in school, and any necessary communication regarding the improvement of the children was to be postponed until a more appropriate time. They were not to engage in worldly news or idle conversation with the children, neither were they to receive any presents from them. On occasion, they were to meet with the parents or guardians of the children to discuss their progress and behaviour in school and at home. The overall conduct of the teaching Sisters with the children was to be characterised by sweetness, prudence and maternal indulgence.[86] Unless they were unable to do so through ill health or infirmity, all of the Sisters in the convent communities worked in the schools.

The ethos of the Presentation schools was clearly defined by the time the National System was established in 1831, and was well known in many towns in Ireland. As a Catholic Order of nuns dedicated to the education of poor children, the Presentations had their own set of customs and practices, and these were what the Sisters brought with them when they connected their schools with the National Board. The convent annalist at Doneraile pointed out: 'none of us entered religion to become schoolmistresses, but rather to make the dear little ones of Jesus useful active members of society and prepare each one of them for the battle of life.'[87] However, in connecting their schools with the non-denominational National System, convent communities had to agree that religious instruction would not interfere with secular instruction. They were not always successful in obeying this requirement. At the Presentation Convent, Maryborough, the school was struck off in 1834 'as the rule for Religious Instruction [was] not observed' and some classrooms were in the 'precincts' of the convent.[88] Other convents fell foul of the inspectors at intervals; in 1855, an inspector visiting the school in Galway was displeased to see that the school was closed as a result of the death of the Roman Catholic Bishop. In 1858 and 1862 the attention of management in Galway, Wexford and Maryborough was drawn to the rule regarding the correct number of hours per day that should be devoted to literary or secular instruction, four hours daily on five days of the week. Some Sisters clearly decided that religious instruction could be introduced during literary instruction, with the result that the inspector reported on the use of 'Denominational Headlines in copybooks'. He was mollified by the Superioress, who said she 'was unaware of their being written and promised it should not again occur'.[89]

While the daily routine of convent schools normally included regular prayer, this was not acceptable to the National Board. In 1858, a Board Order was made stating that pupils were to discontinue making the sign of the cross when they heard the clock strike. But inspectors were regularly frustrated by nuns who continued to say the Angelus and prayers during school time.[90] Religious iconography was not to be displayed in schools supported by the National Board; again, the Sisters seem to have generally ignored this regulation, and indeed one inspector noted wearily that he could not get 'a statue of a nun placed on the staircase' removed.[91] But inspectors generally adopted a somewhat benign approach to the enforcing of rules concerning prayers and iconography, and many admired the cloistered Catholic women that they saw running large convents and schools.

In addition to teaching, many nuns had the opportunity for leadership in Presentation convents and schools, though this sometimes took its toll. The model of governance outlined in the *Constitutions* prescribed the way in which individual communities were to be organised and how they were to operate. It also clarified the traits that were desirable in the women who filled the positions of leadership in the communities.[92] The Sisters who formed the founding groups of new convents needed to be capable, adaptable and courageous. Indeed, the groups that went to Tralee, Galway, Thurles and Crosshaven took several years to secure suitable accommodation for themselves and their schools. Once they found the right location, nuns concentrated on developing their convents and schools into secure, successful institutions.

In their dealings with the National Board and its officers, Sisters displayed a desire to manage their own affairs whenever possible. They wrote letters of application to become affiliated to the National System, and they assumed the title of School Manager where possible, although bishops and priests sometimes challenged this, removing the nuns and reinstating clergymen in the role of Manager. The Superioresses of the convents in Galway and Wexford made the initial applications, and, along with their successors, were listed as the school managers throughout the century.[93] In February 1853, the records of the Commissioners for Maryborough note their agreement to a request from Mary C. Duff, Superioress, to be appointed Manager. However, she resigned the position in favour of Rev Dr Taylor shortly after.[94] In Waterford, Bishop John Power proposed the Superioress as Manager of the school in the initial Application to join the System in 1879. But his successor changed this, appointing the parish priest as Manager in January 1894.[95]

Women religious were not sanguine about the appointment of priests as Managers of their convent schools. Writing from the South Presentation Convent, Mother de Sales White told the Resident Commissioner, Sir Patrick Keenan, of the unhappiness of her community with the fact that a clergyman was listed as Manager, between 1889 and 1890.[96] Mother de Sales outlined the circumstances under which the Commissioners could recognise her as Manager, and how the position could then be retained by the Sisters. Her views went unheeded, and Keenan advised her that Fr O'Keefe, temporarily appointed as Manager, was to be regarded as the official signatory for all Board documents until more permanent arrangements were in place.[97]

In each convent community, the first fifty years were typically characterised by the struggle for economic security, the challenges of establishing a successful school, and the need to attract more vocations in order to survive. The rapid spread of Presentation convent schooling in the nineteenth century belies the grimness of the early decades, and indeed the efforts involved in the drive for security took its toll on many pioneering Sisters. In Galway, the community lost their first Superioress, Mother Angela Martin, when she died in January 1820, at the age of thirty-eight. Other members of the community also died in their thirties, depriving the convent of crucial support.[98] In the Presentation Convent, Thurles, there were also many who died young. Sisters

Joseph Kenny, Magdalen Griffin, Joseph Bradshaw, John Aherne, Magdalen Hely and Magdalen Fitzharris were all in their twenties when they died.[99] Infectious diseases, and especially tuberculosis, caused most of the deaths; convent registers and annals frequently indicate the prevalence of TB, and hint at the pain felt by communities when newly professed young women died before ever fulfilling their vocations.

Despite challenges – including poverty, sickness and intransigent bishops – the Presentation order grew, and its schools became interwoven with 'official' National education in nineteenth-century Ireland. Even though many Presentation schools were affiliated to the National System, they provided a legitimate and popular alternative to wholly non-denominational education, such as was available at the Model Schools, run by the Board. There was a clear religious inflection to education at Presentation National Schools, which made them important for Catholics who sought both the dignity of a basic schooling, and the right to confessional freedom.

## CHAPTER 6

# Schools for the Starving: Presentation Education Before and After the Great Famine

*… we must prefer the schools to all others.*

–Nano Nagle to Miss Mulally, 30 October 1779.

Nano Nagle opened her first school in a rented mud cabin and Teresa Mulally's first school was a rented back room on the top floor of a three-storey house in Mary's Lane.[1] The humble beginnings of Nagle and Mulally foreshadowed what was ahead for other nuns, and served as a reminder that temporal needs were not important. In the first half of the nineteenth century, most of the schools went from being poorly furnished little rooms to properly equipped buildings. To improve their schools, the nuns relied on charity, economy, and eventually some schools were granted an income from the National Board. Nano's own first schools had provided food and clothing to poor pupils; perhaps unsurprisingly, the Presentation schools continued to be a source of unofficial poor relief during the Great Famine and afterwards. Records of individual convents, together with the Annual Reports of the National Board, help to construct a picture of what the schools were like, before and after the Famine, and indicate the conditions in which the nuns and children worked.

For the first three years of their time in Tralee, the Presentations had one room in an old house beside the milk market at Black Pool that they used for 'teaching, recreation, and refectory'. They also taught in a church, until they finally secured enough funding to build a school.[2] On their arrival in Galway, the Sisters used a room in their house on Kirwan's Lane as their school – a practice they continued when they moved to the house on the Green. In the first years after their move to the larger Charter School building, they continued to use rooms within the convent.[3] The early situation in Thurles was hardly better, and the first house in Stradavoher that acted as both convent and school proved entirely unsuitable.[4] The purchase by the Sisters of the Christian Brothers' house and schools both improved their living conditions and provided them with spacious accommodation for their school. Although the foundation at Wexford opened in a purpose-built convent, the community conducted their school in a ground-floor room within the convent too.[5] The community in Maryborough conducted their first school in a space beneath the church that was poorly lit and badly ventilated. Without doubt, the sparse and damp conditions in which nuns lived and taught in the early Presentation foundations took a heavy toll on their health.

What is clear, from an examination of how convents flourished, is that early communities showed resilience by managing to either improve the buildings they used, or by moving – often several times – until they found a suitable convent and a decent school. This way of working dated back to Nagle, who started her work in the small cabin in Cove Lane. Having founded her new congregation in 1775, she and the three members of her fledgling Institute continued to work in the rented cabins on Douglas Street, only moving to a new convent building in July 1780. Between 1777 and 1780, classes for the children were conducted in this building.[6] After the transfer, the community continued to use the various cabins as their schools in addition to Nano's cottage that had now become available.[7] Having gained final papal recognition in 1805, the community began to attract new members, and the growth in numbers resulted in the completion of a second new convent in 1810, leaving the 1780 building free to be used by the school.[8] By the 1830s the pioneering convent was thriving, and the *Second Report of the Commissioners of Irish Education Inquiry* listed four separate schools run by the South Presentation community, two in the parish of St Dominick and two in St John of Jerusalem. One of the former was described as 'a very excellent building' with 120 pupils in attendance, whilst the second was described as 'two large and two small rooms' with 126 pupils. One of the St John of Jerusalem schools was described as 'a substantial building: cost 350*l*' and catering for 100 pupils. The second of these schools was 'a room in the last mentioned house' with 157 pupils.[9]

The final move by the South Presentation community was made possible by the transfer of the Ursuline Convent from Douglas Street to Blackrock, also in Cork. In spite of a number of additions to their convent and schools on the Douglas Street campus, the expansion of the Ursuline community and its various educational enterprises outgrew the space that was available. They sold their site to the Presentation community and moved in October 1825.[10] This move allowed the community to consolidate and develop their educational activities in the larger area. In October 1846, the Sisters first established their Infant School and employed Miss Mary Anne Mahon, a 'finished teacher in the art of Infant training', as its teacher.[11] When the community applied to connect their school with the National System in the summer of 1850, the District Inspector, M. Coyle, noted that the school was in excellent condition, made of stone with a slate roof.[12] The South Presentation Convent School became known as Saint Nicholas Female National School.[13] The opening of their new chapel in 1865 enabled the Sisters to incorporate the ground floor of one of their buildings, which had until then been used as the chapel, into the schools. When the inmates of Nano Nagle's Almshouse were transferred to the care of the Little Sisters of the Poor in Montenotte in 1887, the building that had been their home was converted into a school for senior pupils.[14]

The Galway community similarly made several moves, and gradually expanded their mission. Having moved to a former Charter School in 1819, the nuns realised that they needed a better arrangement for their school. In 1820, Dr Ffrench wrote to Cardinal Fontana in Rome, outlining the work of the Sisters, in which he explained that the community operated two schools, 'One school has thirty pupils who are fed and clothed. They are given instruction in crafts. The other school has 500 girls who are educated in accordance with religious principles.'[15] In 1820 also, the Sisters began to build a new school beside the convent. The *Second Report of the Commissioners of Inquiry* described this new building as 'a large slated house, two stories high: cost 505*l*', which had been built with charitable contributions. Between 272 and 395 pupils attended the school, and books were provided by the collections at an annual Charity Sermon and by private subscriptions.[16] At the time the school became affiliated to the National System in August 1832, it had two rooms, both measuring seventy feet long by twenty-six feet wide. The rooms had large windows, and wooden desks, and it was named Rahoon Female National School.[17] In 1837, the Sisters received £100 from the National Board to defray the cost of setting up a lace school to give girls a skill with which to earn a living.[18]

As the only school in Wexford run by religious, the Presentation Convent School attracted large numbers of children and adults when it opened in

1818. In addition to the children of the town, it also catered for the children from the orphanage that had been opened by the Talbot family.[19] The *Second Report of the Commissioners of Inquiry* describes the schoolroom used by the community as 'a good room attached to the convent: cost 200*l*', which catered for between 120 and 180 pupils.[20] Like the nuns in Galway, the community in Wexford joined the National System relatively early in its operation, in January 1834.[21] The application from Mother Baptist Frayne, Superioress at the time, described the school as a lime and stone building located under the Convent chapel, which had been built using the private donations of an individual. It consisted of three rooms and the building was in good repair, with twenty desks and forms that accommodated ten children in each.[22] Mother Baptist wrote to the National Board, referring to the condition of the furniture:

> The desks and forms [are] all out of repair and of a condition unsuited to the school. It would be very requisite to be furnished [with] desks on metal supports and forms on the same plan – as used in all the well supplied public schools – these and stools (?) are the greatest want at present necessary to be supplied.[23]

Mother Baptist's successor as Superioress was Mother Evangelist Butler, who bought the interest in the adjoining field to build a new school in 1855. Construction began four years later, when funding had been gathered from 'friends and benefactors' and through fundraising activities. The new school was opened in 1866, allowing the Sisters to admit more pupils to their classes.[24] In 1867, the stock of school furniture was augmented to the value of more than thirty pounds when a Miss Byrne from Dublin presented several items to the Convent, and in 1869 the Community opened their new Infant School. Steadily, the community kept making small improvements, when they could afford them. For example, the Sisters built a lavatory adjoining the school with a bequest of £100.[25] In August 1876, two new schoolrooms were opened by the Bishop of Ferns, Michael Warren: St Patrick's to cater for the infant boys and St Anne's to serve as a workroom for Industrial training.[26]

In Clondalkin, the Presentation National School was a two-storey, neo-gothic building, in excellent repair, constructed from limestone and mortar with a slate roof. It was connected to the convent by means of a corridor. There three rooms had open fires; there were seats for eighty pupils, and desks for forty. Over the course of the first year they fully furnished all the rooms. The finance for this came from two sources, a donation from a wealthy lady and a collection. This was supplemented by the proceeds of the collection, which was organised by the Sisters and to which the other Presentation convents contributed 'with great good will and generosity'.[27] The supply of school furniture was replaced and augmented again in 1876, with the proceeds of a raffle held at Christmas of that year.[28]

Some alterations to the schoolrooms were necessary to accommodate the growing number of children attending the school. In 1864, Mother Joseph Cosslett decided to increase the length of each room by eight feet. This was done by moving the school stairs into a section of the room occupied by the original Benefit School of the convent. A new music room with a fireplace and a much-needed cloakroom were also part of this alteration work. The work on the school cost a 'very moderate' £150, which the convent arranged to pay off in instalments. However, the profits from a 'Drawing of Prizes' the following December, combined with some private donations, enabled the Sisters to discharge the debt earlier than expected.[29] Ten years later, during the summer vacation, the gallery in the Senior School was replaced by a raised platform, two steps higher than the floor. Blackboards were attached to the walls of both rooms and the old cumbersome teachers' desks were also replaced. Though the improvements to Presentation schools were piecemeal, they were sufficiently regular that the nuns could steadily increase their pupil numbers.

## Pupil attendance at Nineteenth-Century Presentation Schools

By the time the National System began operating in 1832, the Presentation Order already had a network of twenty-eight schools. The reaction of individual convents to the System was mixed. Whilst some communities such as Killarney, Tralee, Dingle, Galway and Wexford connected their schools relatively early, others remained outside its influence until the middle of the century and later.[30] However, the connection of the Millstreet, Listowel and Clondalkin schools from the time they opened bears out the observation that almost all of the foundations made between 1834 and 1871 were placed in connection with the Board.[31] The swift association with the National System by the two women in charge of the Galway and Wexford Convents indicates their interest in, and enthusiasm for, the project and stands in contrast to the approach taken by their counterparts in South Presentation, George's Hill, Waterford, North Presentation and Thurles.[32] Although John Murphy, Bishop of Cork, was a supporter of the System, he made no attempt to put pressure on the community in South Presentation to join.[33] The situation was different in Dublin, where Archbishop Daniel Murray, the prominent Catholic Commissioner on the Board, was anxious that the schools in his diocese would connect with it. The Superiors in George's Hill, used to their autonomy, were initially unwilling to participate. Indeed, Dr Murray was 'a little pained at the Nuns' tardiness in falling in with his generally expressed wish'.[34] As a result relations, whilst remaining friendly, cooled a little during the period that the school remained outside the System.[35] The application submitted by Rev T. O'Malley on 22 December 1849 was the second application to be entered for the George's Hill school by a clergyman. The first was put forward by Rev Coleman in early December 1832, and although it was accepted by the Commissioners, it was withdrawn before a grant was paid or Roll Number assigned.[36] The second application was successful, and the school finally received a grant by the end of the year.[37]

Irrespective of whether or not a convent school was affiliated to the National Board, a Register and a Daily Attendance Book were kept. The Register noted enrolments, while the Attendance Book recorded each pupil's attendance across the days, weeks and months of the year.[38] These are valuable sources to give an indication of how many children were enrolled in schools, and how many attended. Additionally, the reports of various inquiries into Irish education during the nineteenth century help to track pupil attendance in the convent schools both in and outside the National System (see Table 6.1).[39]

**Table 6.1.   Presentation Convent Schools' Attendance Figures, 1826–70**

|  | 1826 | 1854 | 1864 | 1870 |
|---|---|---|---|---|
| **South Presentation** | 503 | 802 | 830 | 794 |
| **Killarney** | 350 | 245 | 231 | 301 |
| **George's Hill** | 175 | 306 | 624 | 511 |
| **Waterford** | 430 | | | 318 |
| **North Presentation** | 570 | | | 546 |
| **Kilkenny** | 200 | 447 | 346 | 390 |
| **Richmond/Terenure** | 90 | 149 | 173 | 166 |
| **Tralee** | 180 | 485 | 434 | 344 |
| **Dungarvan** | 300 | | | 294 |
| **Carlow** | 300 | 243 | 371 | 340 |

|  | **1826** | **1854** | **1864** | **1870** |
|---|---|---|---|---|
| **Carrick-on-Suir** | 130 | | | 134 |
| **Drogheda** | 240 | 593 | 486 | 502 |
| **Clonmel** | 300 | | | 441 |
| **Galway** | 395 | 305 | 352 | 444 |
| **Thurles** | 300 | 274 | 255 | 270 |
| **Rahan** | 36 | 66 | 79 | 80 |
| **Doneraile** | 220 | 335 | 273 | 257 |
| **Wexford** | 180 | 304 | 300 | 431 |
| **Maryborough** | 207 | 198 | 145 | 271 |
| **Maynooth** | | 156 | 117 | 121 |
| **Mullingar** | | 265 | 343 | 336 |
| **Kildare** | | 140 | 132 | 61 |
| **Kildare 2** | | | | 17 |
| **Bandon** | | 432 | 394 | 237 |
| **Castlecomer** | | | | 240 |
| **Enniscorthy** | | 182 | 173 | 222 |
| **Dingle** | | 366 | 249 | 257 |
| **Mooncoin** | | 146 | 139 | 173 |
| **Cashel** | | 151 | 364 | 419 |
| **Youghal** | | 369 | 278 | 405 |
| **Midleton** | | 487 | 460 | 630 |
| **Tuam** | | | | 138 |
| **Lismore** | | | | 118 |
| **Limerick** | | 500 | 546 | 580 |
| **Milltown** | | 231 | 215 | 212 |
| **Bagenalstown** | | 197 | 196 | 234 |
| **Fermoy** | | 407 | 335 | 371 |
| **Clane** | | 85 | 88 | 76 |
| **Millstreet** | | 339 | 157 | 272 |
| **Cahirciveen** | | 216 | 245 | 226 |
| **Listowel** | | 353 | 423 | 349 |
| **Castleisland** | | 294 | 304 | 335 |
| **Stradbally** | | 188 | 196 | 152 |
| **Mitchelstown** | | | | 435 |

|                | 1826 | 1854 | 1864 | 1870 |
|----------------|------|------|------|------|
| Mountmellick   |      |      | 187  | 115  |
| Portarlington  |      |      | 151  | 112  |
| Clondalkin     |      |      | 131  | 170  |
| Oranmore       |      |      | 169  | 208  |
| Fethard        |      |      | 255  | 293  |
| Lucan          |      |      |      | 13   |

Source: *Special Reports of Educational Inquiry, 1826–70.*

Of the nineteen schools that were included in the Returns of the *Second Report of the Commissioners of Inquiry*, nine recorded a significant increase in Daily Average Attendance in 1854.[40] The figures recorded in the Educational Census published as part of the Powis Commission (1870) show the numbers of pupils present on the day of the Census in all schools, whether or not they had joined the System. Eight of the original nineteen schools show an increase in the numbers of pupils in attendance over the 1854 figure, seven of which represented an increase on the figure for 1826 also. Two of the five schools not in connection with the Board also show an increase in the numbers reported on their behalf in 1826. The *Special Report on Convent Schools* included the figures for the total number of pupils enrolled in the schools for the year 1863.[41] The difference between these numbers and the Average Daily Attendance is stark (see Table 6.2). In twenty-nine of the schools, under half of the pupils who were registered attended school, with the lowest showing under a quarter.[42] For ten of the schools, at least half of the pupils who registered attended, with the highest Daily Average for any of the schools recorded in Fethard at 75 per cent. However, these convent schools compare favourably when placed within the context of daily attendance figures in National Schools countrywide, with figures of 32 per cent in 1860, 35 per cent in 1870 and 43 per cent in 1880.[43] By 1864, thirty-six of the schools had surpassed the 1870 national average, and twenty-one the 1880 average. Indeed, by this year also, nineteen had exceeded the raw figure for average attendance in convent national schools, given by Powis as 243.5.[44]

## The Convent Schools and the Great Famine

During the years of the Great Famine (1845–9) the numbers of poor children coming to the convent schools increased. Whilst Ireland experienced a number

### Table 6.2. Attendance Figures as a Percentage of the Total of Pupils Enrolled 1863

| | Total on Rolls for the year 1863 | Average Daily Attendance for year 1863 | Average Daily Attendance % of Total |
|---|---|---|---|
| South Presentation | 2575 | 603 | 23.4 |
| Killarney | 626 | 264 | 42.2 |
| George's Hill | 1128 | 529 | 46.9 |
| Kilkenny | 690 | 318 | 46.1 |
| Richmond/Terenure | 354 | 169 | 47.7 |
| Tralee | 735 | 443 | 60.3 |
| Carlow | 728 | 292 | 40.1 |
| Drogheda | 1113 | 411 | 36.9 |
| Galway | 644 | 380 | 59.0 |
| Rahan | 154 | 62 | 40.3 |
| Thurles | 512 | 262 | 51.2 |
| Doneraile | 405 | 196 | 48.4 |
| Wexford | 725 | 270 | 37.2 |
| Maryborough | 422 | 182 | 43.1 |
| Maynooth | 266 | 129 | 48.5 |
| Mullingar | 693 | 224 | 32.3 |
| Kildare | 260 | 108 | 41.5 |
| Bandon | 612 | 374 | 61.1 |
| Enniscorthy | 405 | 169 | 41.7 |
| Dingle | 568 | 230 | 40.5 |
| Mooncoin | 288 | 140 | 48.6 |
| Cashel | 644 | 366 | 56.8 |
| Youghal | 715 | 293 | 41.0 |
| Midleton | 834 | 502 | 60.2 |
| Limerick | 1222 | 449 | 36.7 |
| Milltown | 374 | 140 | 37.4 |
| Bagenalstown | 297 | 150 | 50.5 |
| Fermoy | 572 | 274 | 47.9 |
| Clane | 184 | 84 | 45.7 |
| Millstreet | 446 | 201 | 45.1 |

|              | Total on Rolls for the year 1863 | Average Daily Attendance for year 1863 | Average Daily Attendance % of Total |
|--------------|:---:|:---:|:---:|
| Cahirciveen   | 602 | 228 | 37.9 |
| Listowel      | 818 | 295 | 36.1 |
| Castleisland  | 579 | 252 | 43.5 |
| Stradbally    | 368 | 184 | 50.0 |
| Mountmellick  | 360 | 144 | 40.0 |
| Portarlington | 277 | 108 | 39.0 |
| Clondalkin    | 413 | 130 | 31.5 |
| Oranmore      | 283 | 189 | 66.8 |
| Fethard       | 359 | 271 | 75.5 |

Source: *Special Reports on Convent Schools, 1864.*

of food crises during the early decades of the nineteenth century, most of them were caused by adverse weather conditions. The relatively modest loss of life resulting from these crises and the country's ability to export food, in addition to producing enough to feed its own population, gave little cause to anticipate the disaster that was to happen. The rural poor were vulnerable, however, and in 1845 the arrival of potato blight (*Phytophthora infestans*), an incurable fungal disease, decimated their staple food, the potato crop. Having already affected the crop in the south of England in August, blight was observed in Waterford and Wexford in September. Because of the wet harvest season it spread rapidly and destroyed approximately 40 per cent of that year's crop. Between 1846 and 1849 blight affected the potato crop three times, and when relief from private and official sources proved inadequate, tens of thousands died annually from malnutrition and epidemic disease, such as typhus, relapsing fever, dysentery and hunger oedema.[45] Accounts of the Famine are contained in many of the convent Annals. In 1847, the North Presentation Annalist recorded 'the fearful ravages' caused by the 1846 failure stating 'we daily witness sad traces of them in the pale countenances and emaciated forms of the wretched little beings who now throng our schools, not so much for instruction as to have their hunger relieved and to escape for a time from the misery of home.' In an effort to alleviate the distress, the Sisters distributed soup and bread to the 1,000–1,100 who attended daily.[46] Also in 1847 the Tralee Annals explain that the potato crop, which appeared to be flourishing, failed over two nights, with the stalks turning black as if they were burnt. The Annalist notes that thousands died as a result of 'a frightful dysentery'. The community used the donations they were given to provide breakfast for 200–300 children every day, baking bread in the convent.[47] The letter to Dr Murray from Sister M. O'Donel in Presentation Galway stated:

> I am happy to inform your Grace that the Annual Charity Sermon preached for our poor children's breakfast by Dr Cahill was very successful we got £50 at the collection & never did we require it so much as now as every effort is making in these trying times to bribe our poor little charges to renounce the faith. Our school is full thank God we have upwards of 600 each day. The Work Houses are all I may say supplied with teachers from the National School of Rahoon.[48]

In Thurles in 1846 and 1847, 'famished people came in crowds to the Convent certain of obtaining relief … like spectres'.[49] Following the outbreak of cholera in Wexford, the nuns gave 'relief as far as their limited means allowed'.[50] In Maryborough, the Presentation community fed their pupils, many of whom were clearly starving,[51] and in Dingle, the nuns baked bread and made soup which they gave out to several hundred daily.[52]

In Listowel, the Presentation Sisters entered an agreement in 1846 with the Mistress of the Workhouse to make 'inside garments' for the men and women in the Workhouse, which gave an income to the girls who were making them. This arrangement was short-lived, however, after complaints from the Poor Law Guardians resulted in the work being given over to women in the town. In 1847, the community used donations and contributions from various sources to provide breakfast consisting of bread, which they baked, and a mug of boiled rice with a little milk to 250 children every day. The convent Refectory was given over to the enterprise whilst the Sisters used a cell for their meals. By the time they had exhausted their own resources, in February 1848, they had supplied 31,000 breakfasts.[53] The Annals for the Presentation Convent in Limerick state that: 'The suffering occasioned by starvation and disease were very great yet nothing could exceed the efforts made by all ranks to give relief to the Sufferers. Over eight hundred poor children frequented the Schools.'[54]

For those convents that had not already connected to the National System by this time, the drain that was placed on their resources tipped the scales: it was imperative to get funding not just to run the schools, but to buy food for the children. In Doneraile, the Annals record the connection of their schools with the Commissioners in 1845. Whilst approving of the plans of imparting knowledge; the books, maps and writing materials, the Annalist says that not least important was 'the salary of £40 per annum useful for supplying books to the poor children, keeping the schools in repair and the overplus is disposed of in charity to the destitute children, of which the number is great'.[55]

## Funding the Schools: Local Sources

The records of the convents and schools show a ceaseless effort to somehow piece together the means to run schools, feed and clothe children, and expand the schools wherever possible. Typical sources of support were bequests from individuals, and the proceeds of annual charity sermons. At the Presentation Convent in Galway, income to maintain the school came from 'an Annual Charity Sermon producing with private subscriptions from £60 to one hundred hitherto'.[56] In Cashel, the school '[had] not any income but the gratuitous donations of the Parish Priest of Cashel at whose expense it is entirely'.[57] In Limerick, the charity sermon provided £75 a year towards the school. The convent in Millstreet recorded £27 yearly in local funding in addition to an annual bequest of £40 for the dispersal of Rt Rev Egan.[58] The Inspector's Report on Thurles noted that the amount in respect of local funding was 'None … the Ladies keep the house in repairs'.[59] In all cases the scholars were recorded as paying nothing as they were admitted gratuitously. In the case of Limerick they were clothed and fed also.[60] In the Commissioners' Annual Reports, the local aid received by schools was listed under two headings, school fees and endowments. The experience in Presentation Clondalkin gives an indication of how convents fared in this area. The Report for 1858 recorded that the convent received £2.4s.8d in local contributions in aid of salaries, which came in the form of school fees.[61] In the years between 1858 and 1885, the amounts for local aid ranged from nothing in the years 1859, 1861, 1867 and 1869, to £51.8s.3d in 1880.[62]

Up to 1874, this aid was listed under school fees only. Apart from the four years for which the amount recorded was nothing, amounts returned in school fees ranged from 3s.5d in 1864 to £36.4s.11d in 1868. The 1868 figure was an exception during these years, as the next highest amount cited was £6.2s.4d for 1874.[63] From the mid-1870s onwards, endowments are recorded as a significant source of income with £31 received in 1877 and 1880, and £36 in 1883.[64] Valuable as these sums may have been in their own right, they fell a long way short of what was necessary to maintain the schools. The Sisters depended on their capacity to generate finance through all means available to them.

The multi-layered system of financial support that the members of the Order developed to maintain their convents and communities, also provided funding for the convent schools. From the beginning, working in schools was central to the identity of the Order, and the connection between each convent and its school was elemental. Many volumes of Convent Annals highlight some of the details in relation to the donations, bequests, gifts, dowries or fundraising that took place. In 1830, the Tralee Annals record that the new school, along with some new cells, were built by subscription, with Dr Egan and Dr McEnery contributing £50 each. The convent paid out £100 on this project and some other repairs. Between 1830 and 1835 'an annual subscription was made for repairing the school and furniture and for clothing the children'. Twenty years later, the Sisters raised £133 of the £259 it cost to build their new school and cells from subscriptions. The amount far exceeded their expectations given the 'distressed state of society' at the time.[65] When the community in South Presentation appointed Mary Anne Mahon as lay teacher for their new Infant School, the Annalist explained that:

> Her salary was at the rate of £30 a year; and as there are no means of defraying the expenses necessarily incurred by this most desirable undertaking, we have been obliged to solicit the aid of many friends of the Community who have kindly given an annual subscription of a few shillings each, for the purpose of enabling us to carry on a work of such advantage to the poor.[66]

The Sisters in Listowel began work on enlarging their school by building a new Infant School, Workroom and Classrooms in May 1853. Among the contributors to the work was Fr Mahony, who gave £100, and Lord Listowel, who gave £50 towards the roof.[67] The new school that the Sisters in Thurles opened in June 1862 cost £1,950, £300 of which came from a contribution made by Sr Peter Magan on her profession in 1825, a further £300 was paid by Dr Leahy, Archbishop of Cashel, as repayment of a loan made by the community to the College and £200 was made up of subscriptions. The balance was paid out of convent funds with 'Furnishing and all other school matters, painting, etc. gradually done, were defrayed from the yearly allowances, granted by the Board of Education'. Leahy also contributed £400 towards the building of the Orphanage and new Industrial School, for which he laid the foundation stone in late 1874.[68] Charity sermons in Limerick generated £168, £97 and £68 in 1839, 1840 and 1843 respectively – all of it designated for the poor schools.[69]

In Clondalkin, bequests amounting to £1,800 followed the deaths of members of the community in 1869 and 1871. The money was used to defray the costs of providing a proper schoolhouse for the Benefit School, completed in 1870. In addition to the fees paid by the pupils of the Benefit School, which offered a regular form of income for the convent, less regular sources came from the fees paid by women who boarded in the convent at different times. The Annals note that in 1862 the fees paid by Mrs Shields, a wealthy widow who wished to enter the novitiate, proved 'a means of helping the community, as yet poor and struggling'. A similar situation arose in 1875 when another widow, Mrs Keenan, boarded with them for nine months, for which time she paid a total of £45.[70]

## Public Funding: Salaries, Supplies, Premiums and Gratuities

The only source of public funding for these convent schools throughout the nineteenth century was the Commissioners of National Education. For those convents that had operated outside the National System for any length of time their connection to the Board opened a new vein of financial support. Under the rules of the Commissioners, convent schools were only entitled to financial assistance towards teachers' salaries, books and supplies. They did not get grants towards school buildings or land for new schools, or towards any kind of infrastructural developments. The grant was paid to the Sisters, who could discharge the office of teachers with or without the help of others. However, the salaries of any assistants they employed were paid by the Sisters.[71] Up until the change in Rules in 1885, the Commissioners granted aid to only one school in connection with the same convent. This meant that although some of the convent Annals refer to the Infant and Girls' Schools, their two schools were treated as one within the system. From the establishment of the National System until 1885, the salary for convent schools was paid on a capitation basis, the amount depending on the average number of children in daily attendance.[72] However, in 1874 the Annals of both the Tralee and Killarney houses record that sixteen Sisters, eleven from Tralee and five from Killarney, were examined for classification by Inspectors of the National System. The Dingle Annalist noted that this change was described by the public Press as 'teeming with difficulties and dangers, so that for forty-three years it was never before accepted, or attempted in the case of Convent Schools connected with the National Board'. The Annalist added her own comment: 'God knows how to protect His own.'[73]

From 1885, nuns could choose whether or not to be tested and classified for basic salary purposes. Those who did adopt the system of classification were paid the same class salaries as teachers in ordinary national schools. For female teachers, this ranged from £58 a year for First Class, First Division to £12 a year for Workmistresses.[74] Nuns who stayed outside the system of classification were paid on the basis of average attendance in lieu of class salary; they received a 'merit' capitation grant of twelve shillings a head when the results examination was entirely satisfactory and ten shillings when it was only fair or passable.[75] The year was divided into quarters which ended on 31 March, 30 June, 30 September and 31 December.[76] An average attendance was recorded for each quarter, and part payment of the annual salary was generally made during the month following the last day of a quarter. This meant that the convent schools had an income over the course of the year. The salaries of the paid monitors ratified by the Board were also paid on a quarterly basis. The combined salaries of both the nuns and monitors were recorded in the Annual Reports of the Commissioners as a separate total until 1865. From 1866 onwards the salaries, premiums and gratuities were recorded together in a single total.[77]

Financial assistance was also given towards books and supplies. This took the form of free stock, which consisted of books and requisites, and books and supplies at reduced rates. In addition to the grants towards salary, books and supplies, the Commissioners established a system of financial rewards, referred to as Premiums and Gratuities in the Annual Reports. These payments served to augment the amount of public money that was paid to teachers in the national schools. They were awarded for order, neatness and cleanliness in teachers, pupils and school premises; to teachers of Workhouse National Schools; for training students to be National Teachers; for training pupil teachers for Model Schools; for instructing paid and unpaid monitors; for good service and for teaching Vocal Music, Drawing and Navigation. Having connected their schools with the System in 1833, the Sisters in Killarney and Tralee received £20 and £15 respectively as the first year's payment from the Commissioners. The community in Tralee was granted £16, which was used to buy desks. Just over a year later the Killarney community received £37.7s.6d for repairs.[78] For the ten-year period 1833–43, the convents in Galway, Cashel, Kildare and Maynooth received amounts ranging from £3 to £40 in payments annually, and the amounts were dictated by the numbers of children who were in attendance. Whilst not paid every year, amounts received for Free Stock and Requisites went from one shilling to £16.14s.10d, paid to the community in Galway. Each of the communities was paid for training monitors, teaching Vocal Music and order and cleanliness.[79]

The interaction of the school in Clondalkin with the Board shows how the financial support of the Commissioners operated on an individual school basis. From 1858 to 1885 the salary paid to the convent ranged from £20 to £30 in fourteen years, £30 to £35 in thirteen years and £73 in one year.[80] The lowest amount was £20, paid for 1858, the first year the school was in the system; the highest was £73.16s, paid for 1885.[81] As the school had been organised in 1861, the nuns received payments for training both paid and unpaid monitors. The amount paid for training two Junior Monitors in 1860 was £2, £1 for each Monitor. Grants for training unpaid monitors were recorded for only two years, £4 in 1862 and £2.10s in 1864.[82] Although the system of classifying monitors changed in 1872, and again in 1881, the amount of the gratuity for their training did not vary greatly. Between 1860 and 1871 the Sisters in Clondalkin received payments for teaching Vocal Music. With the exception of 1868, they were also paid for teaching Drawing from 1863 to 1871. In general, payment of these monies was made in the year following their award; however, payment could also be delayed up to eighteen months. The nuns also received grants for order and cleanliness six times between 1861 and 1868, with the amounts varying from £1 to £4.[83] This grant was limited to a total of £22.10s for each school district, divided into thirteen awards of £1 to £4 per year.[84] The introduction of the payment-by-results system in 1872 signalled an end to gratuities for Music, Drawing and order and cleanliness. From that year the convent only received grants for the instruction of monitors.

## Presentation Schools and Payment-by-Results

The introduction of the payment-by-results system occurred two years after its recommendation by the Powis Commission. Under the system, 'results fees' were paid to teachers, in addition to their basic salary. The size of the fee was determined by the performance of pupils in examinations based on a defined programme of instruction for each class. The programme, taught during school hours, consisted of a core set of obligatory subjects: Reading, Writing, Spelling, Grammar, Geography and Arithmetic for each class. From Fourth to Sixth Class, Needlework was obligatory for girls in all schools.

Book-keeping and Vocal Music could also be taught during school hours as optional subjects. To earn additional fees, a wide range of extra subjects could be taught within and after school hours and included Drawing, Geometry, Navigation, Physical Geography, Latin, Greek, French, Sewing Machine, Cookery and Poultry Management.[85] A fixed sum was paid for each child who passed in each subject, provided that the child had made a given number of attendances during the year preceding the exams. Initially the required number of days was ninety or above, but this was raised to 100 or above from 1 March 1877.[86] The scale of the fees ranged from sixpence to three shillings for obligatory subjects, and one shilling and sixpence to ten shillings for the extra subjects.[87]

As all schools operating within the National System were required to undergo the examinations, all of the convent communities whose schools were connected with it received payments under the scheme. The Annalist in Tralee recorded that they received £87.10s as Results fees for 1872, which was 'a great boon to this straitened community'. They received £106.7s the following year. Indeed, up to 1880 the amounts paid to the community increased to £226.10s. The Crosshaven community's experience was similar, with the amounts paid to them rising from £29.14s in 1877 to £173 in 1886, the first ten years that the school was open.[88] In Dingle, the community received 'nearly £50 – not including music or drawing'. The nuns noted: 'This was higher than any of the Convents we heard of, though we labour under many difficulties unknown to them, such as Irish being entirely spoken in the homes of many of our poor children: distance from the school and in many cases – poverty.'[89] In addition to Vocal Music and Drawing, Sisters expanded the range of extra subjects they taught including Sewing Machine, Book keeping and French, from as early as 1873.[90]

The entries in the South Presentation and Waterford *Daily Report Books* for 1880–91 track the Commissioners' payments from the viewpoint of the school.[91] While the first payments in each year were made in January, they related to monies owed for the previous three-month period. The Sisters in Waterford received £11.8s in 'Salaries for Quarter & gratuities for monitors' in January 1882; South Presentation received £35.3s.4d a year later. Both were the capitation grants due on the average attendance for October to December 1881 and 1882 respectively. Sums of £10 in Waterford and £50.0s.8d in South Presentation for those quarters were disbursed to the monitresses by the Sisters.

Very occasionally, the income from the Commissioners was supplemented by a gift or bequest towards the running of the school. For example, the South Presentation account for 1884 notes a donation of £25 given by a lady. But by and large, the nuns depended on the income from the Commissioners in order to run their schools, and to pay salaries to the monitresses. In 1883, the Sisters in South Presentation were paid an overall total of £653.11s.3d of which they passed on £187.0s.11d in salaries to the monitresses, leaving them with a little over £466 to run the school and support the Sisters. Five years later, with the increased success of the pupils, the income from the Commissioners was £1,292.4s.7d of which £238.0s.1d was paid out to monitresses, leaving them with £1,054.4s.6d – just over twice the amount they received in 1883.[92] By training older schoolgirls to become monitresses, the nuns gave young women the opportunity to earn a living in a respectable job, which held out the possibility of further training, employment, and even emigration. Additionally, monitresses who decided to enter religious life – with the Presentations or with other congregations – were well-prepared for their vocation to education, and were ideally placed to serve in convents overseas.

The nineteenth century saw the Presentations expand across Ireland at a rapid rate. They attracted vocations, and they attracted those in need of a free education. Indeed, the century saw the congregation become a significant provider of free Catholic schooling, as Presentation convents became a feature of Irish towns, particularly in Leinster and Munster. The impetus for founding convents was always to provide free schooling for the poor, and the Sisters in new foundations relied on the support of benefactors and on their own ability to generate funds to run their schools. Charity sermons, interest on nuns' dowries, and legacies to nuns were the main forms of financial support, while many convents had small farms attached to supply food for the nuns and their pupils.

During the Great Famine, the convents became a form of unofficial public support, and nuns drew on their own resources to provide food for thousands of children and adults who were destitute. In the South of Ireland, particularly, Presentation convents fed hundreds daily. When the National System of education was established in 1831, it became possible for the nuns to affiliate some of their schools to the Board, so that the schools could benefit from grants. They began to avail of this support at a time when the impact of famine, and the need for education by those who would eventually emigrate, were making serious demands on the women who ran convents. Even then, nuns were disadvantaged by the State system, as many were not able to become 'classified' teachers. Nonetheless, evidence indicates that women religious who were convent bursars were adept at stretching funds to cover costs such as replacing school roofs, building new classrooms, and paying salaries to secular teachers. The nuns made a particular, and heretofore unexamined, contribution to teacher education, by training many young women to become monitresses. Their own education, often attained in other Presentation convents, prepared them somewhat to become teacher-educators, but early generations of teaching Sisters learned their profession by going into classrooms and getting on with the business of education. Presentation convents often found their own past pupils entering religious life, and becoming teaching Sisters.

The rise in female vocations to religious life in the nineteenth and early twentieth centuries meant that not only were Irish convent schools well supplied with teaching nuns, but there was also an ample supply for the global mission field. There, the Presentations would expand at a rate that was dramatic: they would become one of the largest congregations of teaching Sisters in history.

CHAPTER 7

# The Presentation Sisters and Education in England

*When the Catholics saw what service it did, they begged I*
*would set up schools at the other end of the town …*

–Nano Nagle to Miss Fitzsimons, 17 July 1769.

England in the nineteenth century was a hostile mission ground for Irish Catholic nuns, even when they only wanted to run schools for their own people: migrant Irish Catholics who sought work in Manchester, Liverpool and parts of London. Therefore, it took courage for the Presentations to become the first indigenous Irish Order of nuns to establish a mission in England, when they sent a little group of nuns to Manchester in 1836.[1] Three Sisters from the Presentation community in Clonmel, Co. Tipperary, made the foundation in the densely populated Irish immigrant centre of Salford, in Manchester. It was a town where no convents whatsoever had been founded since the Reformation, and where Catholic education was poorly served.[2]

In the decades that followed, the work of the Presentations in England would primarily be concerned with the provision of free elementary schooling and, to a lesser degree, private second-level education. However, the Sisters also undertook other work including running orphanages, Sunday Schools, and night schools for adults who wanted an education.[3] In time, the establishment of novitiates in Liverpool (1919) and Matlock (1927) would provide the English foundations with international ties, particularly with the Madras region of India.[4]

When the Presentations left Ireland to make their first English foundation, the National System had been in existence for a mere five years, but already convents had become affiliated to the system, providing an attractive model for elementary schooling that was lacking in England. Indeed, many historians have viewed the National System as an 'education experiment' which would be adopted in England four decades after its inception in Ireland.[5] The economic expediency of having free convent school buildings, and a supply of teaching Sisters with which to fulfil the education aims of a National System, would have had a distinct appeal in other jurisdictions. This relied on attracting teaching congregations into parts of English cities where there were concentrations of Catholics, and where there were Protestants who had no objection to free Catholic schooling. The Presentations were well suited to providing this kind of elementary education, and were optimistic when they arrived in Manchester in 1836.

However, for various reasons the growth of the Order in England during the nineteenth century was slow, and by 1900 only two convents had been founded: Presentation Convent, Livesey Street, and Presentation Convent, Buxton.[6] The twentieth century brought new opportunities for expansion, and by 1958 seventeen convents had been established, all of which were involved in Catholic schooling.[7] While invitations from local priests and bishops provided the impetus for most of these new foundations, in some instances the nuns responded to an appeal to assume responsibility for a pre-existing educational institution.[8] The frequency of such appeals throughout the nineteenth and twentieth centuries suggests that the Presentations had become a highly regarded congregation of teaching Sisters. Moreover, in answering such appeals the Presentation Sisters were fulfilling the true call of their foundress: 'we must prefer the schools to all others'.[9]

## The Irish in England in the Nineteenth Century

The necessity for Irish men and women to emigrate to England during the nineteenth century is not difficult to understand. The impoverished state of the Irish economy, coupled with the change from tillage to graze farming, and the impact of the Great Famine, left many people with little choice but to seek a living elsewhere. In contrast, the English economy was experiencing a period of rapid industrialisation and Irish migrants sought employment in the mines, ports and factories scattered throughout England's urban districts. The passage to England was relatively accessible to the Irish, compared with the expensive long-haul voyage to other parts of the British Empire, such as Australasia and North America. The tradition of Irish migration to Great Britain had been well established long before the potato failure of 1845, and while emigration to England intensified during the Great Famine, it would remain a feature of Irish life in the decades that followed.

During the nineteenth century, the Irish tended to settle in the industrial areas of north-east and north-west England. The largest concentration of Irish could be found in the counties of Yorkshire, Cheshire and Lancashire, where industrial productivity attracted large numbers of immigrants from around the globe.[10] The scale of Irish migration is evident in the records of thousands of people who settled in the country in the first half of the nineteenth century. In the 1830s for example, the Irish population of the city of Manchester stood at approximately 22,000.[11] By 1841, the number of Irish immigrants living in Liverpool was almost 50,000 and accounted for 17 per cent of the total population there.[12] Although many Irish went to England in the hope of a better standard of living, the reality was that employment opportunities were limited and generally confined to unskilled, low-waged, manual labour jobs. Irish immigrants worked as brick layers, lodge-house keepers, factory workers, petty traders and domestic servants.[13]

The types of low-paying employment obtained by the Irish contributed to the poor living conditions which were characteristic of the Irish diasporic centres of English towns and cities during the nineteenth century. Writing about the Irish slums in Manchester in 1845, Friedrich Engels noted:

> The cottages are very small, old and dirty, while the streets are uneven, partly unpaved, not properly drained and full of ruts. Heaps of refuse, offal and sickening filth are everywhere interspersed with pools of stagnant liquid. The atmosphere is polluted by the stench and is darkened by the thick smoke of a dozen factory chimneys. A horde of ragged women and children swarm about the streets and they are just as dirty as the pigs which wallow happily on the heaps of garbage and in the pools of filth.[14]

Unsurprisingly, the health of poor Irish immigrants was affected by the level of squalor in which they had to live. The 1832 cholera epidemic claimed the lives of 674 people across the working-class districts of greater Manchester, many of whom were Irish.[15] Moreover, during the 1840s there were reports of widespread fever in Irish districts such as Little Ireland, where victims were described as 'utterly helpless from the disease'.[16]

The Irish were seen as separate not only on economic and social grounds but also because of their religious and cultural practices, which distinguished them from most English. Any effort at assimilation into British society was resisted by the Irish, and a strong sense of Catholicism and devotion to their religious heritage became a unique factor of their separateness.[17] According to Fitzpatrick, 'the Irish clustered defensively in certain districts and ... settled apart from other birthplace groups'.[18] In the city of Manchester for example, two distinct areas, New Town and Little Ireland, became community hubs for the Irish Catholic diaspora.[19] The Catholic faith served as a unifying bond among these communities, and Irish immigrants were particularly devout. Indeed, during a trip to England in 1835, Alexis de Tocqueville noted that 'few but Catholics go to church'.[20] The church was seen as the pillar of community life and 'the Catholic chapels are kept open during the evenings and form a species of asylums'.[21]

During the 1830s, the Irish population in Manchester swelled to such a degree that the Catholic hierarchy resolved to establish a new parish in the city.[22] On 31 August 1830, a site of three-and-a-half acres was purchased near St George's Road in New Town, Manchester.[23] A large church was built on the site and completed in 1832.[24] An Irish priest, Rev Fr Daniel Hearne, was appointed the first Rector of St Patrick's parish and became an influential figure among the Irish.[25] The Catholic devotional tradition contributed to the isolation of the Irish immigrant and in Liverpool, in particular, anti-Catholic sentiment was strong among the Protestant English labouring class.[26] Competition for employment at Liverpool's docks and factories also heightened tensions between the working-class Catholic and Protestant populations.[27]

Anti-Irish and anti-Catholic prejudices were compounded in the apparent lack of order and governance in the Irish slums. Drunken and disorderly behaviour was common, particularly on Saturday nights when 'the streets of Manchester, Liverpool and other manufacturing towns were taken over by hundreds of drunken and brawling Irishmen'.[28] There was a marked disrespect shown by the Irish towards the police and it seems that the only figure who could demand obedience from the unruly masses was the Catholic priest. Indeed, Fr Hearne was noted for his numerous successes in subduing the boisterous Irish of St Patrick's parish in Manchester.[29] Defending his congregation during an investigation into the condition of the Irish poor in Great Britain in 1836, Fr Hearne claimed that, 'There is not much legal crime among the Irish of my flock; nor is there much pilfering.'[30]

As was the case in Ireland, the Catholic Church in England experienced a period of growth in power and influence during the nineteenth century. The high levels of Irish migration to England greatly increased the need for a strong, unified Catholic Church presence. Safeguarding the moral and religious principles of the men, women and children who populated the many Irish centres of a largely Protestant country became a major driving force behind the movements of the Catholic Church in England at this time.

## The Catholic Church in England in the Nineteenth Century

The migration of Irish Catholics to various countries throughout the world became a major concern for the Catholic Church in Ireland during the nineteenth century. In the 1830s, an Irish missionary movement evolved and developed into two distinct areas: missionary evangelisation and pastoral evangelisation. While the former movement was concerned with bringing the light of faith to 'the poor abandoned souls still plunged in the darkness of idolatry' in countries in Africa and Asia, the latter centred on a desire by the Irish Catholic hierarchy to 'sustain the faith of their compatriots at risk through lack of pastoral care' in the many Irish diasporic centres of America, Canada, Australia, and Great Britain.[31] For the greater part of the nineteenth century, pastoral evangelisation was the dominant feature of the Irish missionary movement and between 1840 and 1900 approximately 1,500 priests were sent abroad to minister specifically to Irish immigrant communities.[32] In the nineteenth century, nowhere was the threat to the Irish diaspora and Catholicism more evident than in England.

Anti-Catholic sentiment had been an almost universal trait of Protestant England since the Reformation. Although the passing of Catholic Emancipation in 1829 removed many of the established barriers that had restricted the practice of Roman Catholicism and penalised anyone who was seen to exercise the popish faith, anti-Catholic fever remained a constant feature of nineteenth-century England. Vilification of Catholicism was promoted through the popular 'No popery' literature of the Victorian age.[33] In such works, the Catholic priest was commonly depicted as a rapist and murderer while Catholic convents were viewed with suspicion, with many believing that such institutions were 'no better than brothels of the worst description'.[34] Satirical publications such as *Punch*, which were popular among the middle class during the Victorian era, also reinforced notions of Catholic ignorance and the guile of the Catholic hierarchy. These anti-Catholic publications promoted ideas surrounding the inferiority of Irish Catholics and suggested reasons as to why they should be suppressed and controlled. In political circles, Catholicism was greeted with similar prejudices. At Westminster, many MPs despised Irish Catholics because of their increased demands for denominational education, and the abolition of oaths following the removal of the Penal Laws. There was also a constant fear of rebellion in Ireland and many doubted Irish Catholic loyalty to the crown. Sectarian riots among the working classes were common, though there was often little distinction between anti-Catholic and anti-Irish prejudices and generally, within this grouping, tensions mounted as a result of competition for labour and employment and not because of religious issues.[35]

Despite hostilities towards Catholicism, thousands of Irish men and women left for England every year during the nineteenth century. In 1841, there were approximately 400,000 Irish immigrants living in Great Britain. By 1861, the total Irish-born population residing in England and Wales alone had risen to 600,000.[36] The influx from Ireland undoubtedly contributed to the overall growth of the Catholic population in England, which according to the 1851 religious census was between 610,000 and 700,000.[37] The Catholic hierarchy were increasingly anxious to safeguard the moral interests of the Irish diaspora and to protect their congregation from the dangers and vices of Protestant English life. They acknowledged that 'in order to build a strong, unified constituency, [they] needed to instil religious piety and develop religious practice in [an] ever-growing but very wayward flock.'[38] However, the Catholic clergy were aware that such grand designs could not be achieved by a handful of priests and bishops. They knew that a ready and plentiful supply of female religious congregations was necessary for the pastoral evangelisation movement and the renewal of the Catholic Church in England.

In 1800, there were just twenty-four Catholic religious communities in operation in England.[39] Following the restoration of the Catholic hierarchy in 1850, this number had increased to more than fifty. At the time of publication of the 1880 *Catholic Directory* the figure stood in excess of 300.[40] The development and expansion of Catholic religious houses was not a phenomenon unique to England but followed a more general pattern of Catholic revival that was having an impact across the globe.[41] During the nineteenth century, communities of women religious became valued for their philanthropic and evangelical efforts, which commonly responded to societal needs in areas such as education, welfare, and health. It was recognised that nuns 'were effective, needed little managing and were a source of cheap labour.'[42] Throughout the nineteenth century, the Catholic clergy in England regularly invited female religious congregations to assist in ministering to the needs of their communities and to assume responsibility for vital services such as education and health. The main source of supply initially was France, Belgium and Germany. As the century progressed, and new congregations emerged, native Irish and English congregations became important in the pastoral care of the Catholic population of England.[43]

In post-Emancipation England, education became the core instrument of the Catholic revival mission. The hierarchy believed that education would 'transform working-class Irish into loyal English subjects, sober members of the working class and above all, devout Catholics'.[44] The centrality of education to the restoration of the Catholic Church in England was highlighted in the first Synod of the reinstated English Catholic bishops in 1852:

> The first necessity ... is a sufficient provision of education adequate to the wants of our poor. It must become universal ... to prefer the establishment of good schools to every other work. Indeed, wherever there may seem to be an opening for a new mission, we would prefer the erection of a school, so arranged as to serve temporarily for a chapel, to that of a church without one.[45]

Leading members of the Catholic hierarchy, including Cardinal Nicholas Wiseman, Prelate of England and Wales and Archbishop of the diocese of Westminster (1850–65), and his successor Cardinal Manning (1865–92), were keen advocates of a sound Catholic education at all levels of English society. They promoted the introduction of congregations of teaching Sisters across England.[46] The Presentation and Mercy Sisters became involved in the provision of education to the poor at elementary level, while the Society of the Sacred Heart and the Daughters of Charity of St Vincent de Paul provided education for middle-class girls. The Sisters of St Paul the Apostle also operated select, middle-class boarding schools. Teacher training colleges, which were recognised by the State, were established by the Sisters of Notre Dame de Namur and the Faithful Companions of Jesus. Other educational institutions operated by female religious included industrial and reform schools, orphanages, blind and deaf asylums, Sunday and night schools, and crèches for infants. In England, therefore, a network of educational institutions, run by female religious and providing instruction from the cradle to the grave, evolved and developed during the nineteenth century.

For the most part, convent schools were voluntary and operated independently of any governing body. State involvement was limited and there existed no statutory obligation to provide education. Although parliament introduced grant aid for voluntary schools in 1833, the funds awarded were usually insufficient and the religious congregations who operated these institutions had to depend largely on charitable subscriptions and donations or, in the case of private schools, a consistent enrolment of affluent middle-class pupils whose parents could afford to pay tuition and boarding school fees.[47] The passing of the Elementary Education Act in 1870, which introduced a scheme of universal education for all children aged 5–13 years, brought increased demands for Catholic schooling. Anxious to meet these demands and to ensure that Catholic education remained on an equal footing with that provided by the Church of England and other denominations, Cardinal Manning suggested entering into negotiation with the government in the hope of winning favourable terms in the provision of grant aid for Catholic schools.[48]

While some members of the Catholic hierarchy were concerned that acceptance of grant aid would increase the secularisation of elementary schooling, Manning believed that all children were entitled to receive help from the State regardless of their denomination or religious affiliation.[49] Nonetheless, in a letter to the British Prime Minister, William Gladstone, in 1870 Manning indicated that, 'The integrity of our schools as to (i) Doctrine, (ii) religious management, and the responsibility of the Bishops in these respects, cannot be touched without opening a multitude of contentions and vexations.'[50] The Catholic hierarchy's stance in relation to the independent operation of their schools was accepted by the government and from 1870 onwards an increasing number of Catholic schools came into operation, without an obvious increase in State involvement in the organisation and delivery of that education.[51]

The agenda of the Catholic hierarchy in nineteenth-century England was clear: to create a strong, unified, Catholic Church with a devout and loyal Catholic following. Priests and bishops believed that the surest way to secure this end was to gain a stronghold in Catholic education. For this reason, female religious teaching orders became integral in the restoration of the Catholic Church in England. However, until recently there existed a lacuna in our knowledge of the significance of such women's congregations to life in Victorian Britain. What is possibly more surprising is that in the growing number of publications surrounding female religious, education, and convent life in Britain, the narrative concerning the Presentation Sisters remains largely underdeveloped. In most instances, their contribution has been diminished to a single point of reference concerning their initial arrival in England and even these occurrences are often replete with factual errors.[52] While the Presentation Sisters may not have expanded as rapidly throughout England as other communities of female religious during the nineteenth century, their arrival in the immediate post-Emancipation era predates the influx of numerous other Catholic religious orders, many of whom did not establish convents prior to the restoration of the Catholic Church in 1850. Moreover, their contribution to society in one of Manchester's largest Irish Catholic immigrant districts during a period of strong anti-Catholic and anti-Irish prejudice merits greater attention.

## Arrival of the Presentation Order in England

> From the beginning, the history of the Parish has been bound up with the presence of the Presentation Sisters. Their great influence on the development and formation of the parish is well known and held in great esteem.[53]

The history of the Presentation Sisters in Manchester predates their actual arrival in England by more than a decade. Moreover, had it not been for the resolute determination of a wealthy Irish merchant the foundation might never have come to fruition. Mr Patrick Lavery was an Irish immigrant who had come to England and made a prosperous life for himself through the silk industry. In 1820, Lavery had retired and was anxious to pay tribute to the many Irish men and women who had worked in his silk factories in Lancashire and to whom he felt he owed his wealth and prosperity. To this end, Lavery decided to bequeath a sum of £2,000 for the establishment of a Presentation convent and girls' school in his home town of Navan, Co. Meath.[54] However, Fr Thomas Lupton of St Mary's parish, Manchester persuaded Lavery to reconsider investing the money in a local foundation in England. Lavery consented, but only on the condition that the foundation be offered to a branch of the Presentation Order.[55] The funds were subsequently given to Rev Charles Lupton, brother of Fr Thomas Lupton, to be invested until such time as a group of the Presentation Sisters could be secured and brought to Manchester.[56] Mr Lavery died in 1821 and plans for founding a Presentation convent in Manchester were abandoned for the next eleven years.[57]

By 1832, the interest on Mr Lavery's donation had been growing for more than a decade and Fr Thomas Lupton had become anxious to see the benefactor's wishes for a Presentation convent in Manchester fulfilled. Fr Lupton sought the advice and counsel of the bishop, the Rt Rev Doctor Penswick, who subsequently appointed the parish priest of St Patrick's, Fr Hearne, to oversee the project of constructing a convent and acquiring a group of Presentation Sisters for the mission.[58] The Catholic hierarchy decided that a portion of the grounds which had been obtained for St Patrick's church and cemetery should be given over to the convent foundation.[59] However, there was some controversy surrounding which religious congregation would best meet the needs of the Catholic population in Manchester. According to the Annals of the Presentation convent, Livesey Street, the local hierarchy 'were most desirous to have Sisters of Mercy or Sisters of Charity instead of the Presentation Nuns'.[60] It is likely that the Catholic clergy in Manchester were aware of the limitations of the Presentation Rule and Constitutions, which prevented them from charging fees or from going outside their cloister. For this reason, the clergy may have favoured a congregation of female religious who could be self-supporting and flexible in their apostolic work.[61] Nonetheless, Mr Lavery's bequest was conditional, and if a branch of the Presentation Order could not be secured for Manchester then the money was to be used for the benefit of a Presentation convent in Navan. With such restrictions, the Catholic hierarchy had little choice but to consent to a Presentation foundation.

Although the sum of £2,000, and the interest which had been gained on it during the intervening years between 1820 and 1832, was considerable for the time, Fr Hearne was aware that more would be needed in order to provide for an adequate school and convent.[62] As a result, the parish priest embarked upon a fundraising expedition throughout England which proved successful.[63] He also obtained permission from the Catholic Church in Manchester to 'place a debt of £500 on St Patrick's Church' to secure additional finances for the building of the convent.[64] On 22 May 1834, the foundation stone of the convent was laid by Fr Thomas Lupton.[65] Sometime in 1833, Fr Hearne travelled to Ireland to seek Sisters for the new foundation and, while he made appeals to several houses of the Order, none were either willing or able to offer recruits. Finally, at the Presentation Convent, Clonmel, Co. Tipperary, three Sisters were put forward for the mission: Sr M. Magdalen Sargent, Sr M. Francis d'Assi Mulcahy and Sr M. Baptist Murphy.[66] The Clonmel community, together with their local bishop, the Rt Rev William Abraham d'Assi, and Fr Hearne, agreed to undertake the foundation at Manchester on condition that a suitable house and schools would be provided; additionally, it was required that the Sisters could attend Mass daily at St Patrick's Church; they would be exempt from rent and taxes; and Fr Hearne should give £30 per year per Sister for their support.[67] According to the Annals of the Presentation Convent, Livesey Street, 'This was a verbal agreement, not a word of it was written at the time.'[68]

Fr Hearne, having secured an assurance from the Sisters in Clonmel, returned to Manchester to oversee the building of the convent and schools. As construction continued and the building began to take shape, the architect, whom Fr Hearne had appointed to carry out the work, died. The parish priest was thus obliged at 'a considerable increase in the expenses' to hire another architect to complete the work.[69] The Sisters in Clonmel were informed of all progress, alterations and the mounting expense of the project at regular intervals. Fr Hearne and the Sisters in Clonmel frequently spoke about the 'arrangement for their support' and the 'difference of expense in Ireland and England'.[70] While the community were assured by the parish priest that there was 'plenty of money to do all that was promised', no written agreements were ever produced to support Fr Hearne's arrangements for the Sisters.[71]

During one of Fr Hearne's visits to the Clonmel community in 1835, the Sisters were advised of the extensive expenses, particularly in relation to the building of the schools. The convent Annalist wrote of Fr Hearne that he had:

> ... expended a hundred pounds more than he expected on the school and he proposed to them that the children should pay a penny a week school wages until the hundred pounds would be made up. He stated that the parents would set a higher value on what they had to pay for, than on what they might receive gratis, and he wished the Community to consider this his proposition.[72]

Fr Hearne's proposal raised a very obvious difficulty for the Presentation Sisters in Clonmel. According to the constitutions of the Presentation Order, the Sisters were not permitted to 'receive money, or any other temporal emolument' for the instruction that they gave in their schools.[73] The Sisters were bound to observe every rule outlined in their constitution and Fr Hearne's suggestion that they charge a penny fee presented a very real obstacle to the Sisters assuming responsibility for the school in Manchester. Rev Mother Joseph Sullivan, Superioress of the Presentation convent, Clonmel, assembled her council to discuss the matter and it was decided that the Sisters should be permitted to collect the weekly fee but only on condition that the money obtained be used strictly for the benefit of the school.[74]

Once the question of charging a fee to the pupils who attended the Presentation school in Manchester was resolved, Fr Hearne set about preparing the convent for the Sisters' arrival. Shortly after Christmas 1835, he travelled to Clonmel to accompany the three pioneering Sisters to their new home in Manchester. On arrival at the convent, Fr Hearne informed the Sisters that he had been obliged to borrow a sum of £100 from Fr Thomas Lupton to defray the cost of their journey to Manchester.[75] While the Sisters were surprised at this revelation, they concluded that funds were undoubtedly low as a result of the cost of the building of the convent and schools but felt sure that their support and the income of the house was still secure.[76] Before the Sisters left Clonmel they were provided with beds and bedding, clothes, books and £30 to be divided equally among them for any particulars they may require for the house or schools on arrival in Manchester.[77] The Sisters, accompanied by Fr Hearne, left Clonmel in early January 1836 and travelled, for most of their journey, by post chaise to Dublin.[78] The group rested *en route* at various Presentation convents and spent some time with Br Ignatius Rice, founder of the Christian Brothers.[79] On arrival in Dublin they stayed with the Presentation Sisters in George's Hill before setting sail for Liverpool on 15 January 1836.[80]

There is no surviving account of the Sisters' crossing to England. In any case, the voyage was short and they landed in Liverpool on 16 January.[81] After Mass at St Nicholas, Copper's Hill they travelled to Newton, a small market town midway between Liverpool and Manchester.[82] The Sisters rested overnight in Newton and the following morning, Monday 17 January, they were received by the Vicar Apostolic of the Northern District, the Rt Rev Dr Thomas Penswick.[83] Dr Penswick appointed Sr M. Magdalen Sargent as Superioress of the Presentation convent, Manchester, with Rev Fr Hearne as Superior.[84] After receiving the bishop's solemn blessing, the pioneering Sisters continued their journey to the village of Garswood where they were received by Rev Thomas Lupton.[85] The following morning, after breakfast with Fr Lupton, the Sisters embarked on the final stage of their journey to their new home and the site of their future labours in England.[86]

## Livesey Street: The Convent and the School

The Presentation Sisters arrived in St Patrick's parish on Tuesday, 18 January 1836. It is not clear if the Sisters had any indication of what to expect on arrival, but an extract taken from the Annals suggests that they had little knowledge of the depth of poverty and squalor which characterised this newly formed city parish:

The neighbourhood was the most wretched part of Manchester. The district of St Patrick's extended many miles and contained the poorest, and most abandoned and immoral people, very few decent persons lived in it. Frequent and very dreadful fights took place close to the convent, children and even grown-up people were often to be seen shamefully naked, horrid language was on the lips of the dear [?] and everything relating to children ... [87]

Despite the apparent deprivation of the city's inhabitants, the Sisters were not deterred from fulfilling their charge. The following day, they were taken to Livesey Street where they finally took possession of their new convent and school.[88] It was a large, red-brick building, adjacent to St Patrick's parish church, and appeared to have been built with the utmost consideration for the conventual life of a congregation of female religious governed by solemn vows and enclosure:

> On the ground floor there was an entrance hall, parlour for visitors, community room next to it, a larger one for a refectory. On the right of the entrance hall was a large schoolroom with folding doors that opened into the Convent hall near the foot of the large staircase. At the top of the staircase to the left was a schoolroom the same size as the one downstairs and a small staircase at the further end of the school conducted from one room to the other for the children, etc. Opposite the large staircase was a room intended for a Chapel and to the right hand was a corridor with five rooms, three of them fitted for cells. There was also a room for our infirmary and a water-closet. A small staircase conducted to the kitchen, pantry and scullery.[89]

Although it seemed that Fr Hearne had spared no expense in constructing a building that was entirely fit for purpose, the Sisters on examination of the convent and school were 'well reminded of poverty, want and cold'.[90] According to the Annalist, the convent was extremely damp as a result of 'the new brickwork and the Winter season'.[91] Moreover, 'there was very little furniture in the house and not a fire grate upstairs, neither was there a cupboard or shelf in the whole place'.[92] There were no adequate toilet facilities for the children in the school, and the Sisters had to make temporary out-houses in a section of the cellar.[93] Despite the inadequate conditions, the Sisters assumed their duties and immediately set about preparing for the opening of their school.

The date selected by Fr Hearne for the commencement of their teaching duties in the school was 2 February.[94] The Sisters had much to do to ensure that the property was ready to receive its pupils and were assisted in their labours by the Brothers of the Christian schools. The Sisters were especially indebted to Br Francis Phelan, who had spent many years working with poor boys in Manchester, and also Br Joseph Maher, who assisted in the early days with the admittance of the pupils.[95] It is recorded that 100 pupils attended on the first day.[96]

Shortly after their arrival in Livesey Street, Fr Hearne came to Mother Magdalen and asked for the money which the Sisters had received as a gift when leaving Clonmel.[97] £10 had already been spent on necessities for the convent but the Superioress obliged Fr Hearne by giving him the balance of £20.[98] It is not clear what Fr Hearne intended to do with this sum and neither is it clear if it was ever used for the benefit of the Sisters, the Presentation convent or their school. In Clonmel, the Sisters were accustomed to having a servant to assist in the upkeep of the convent and also a regular income of support for the Sisters. However, when Mother Magdalen inquired about such provisions, Fr Hearne responded: 'the ways in England are so different from those at home'.[99] As Fr Hearne had been appointed by the bishop as Superior, and in light of the Presentation constitutions which indicated that 'The priest thus appointed shall duly attend to the government and good order of the Community in Spirituals and Temporals', there was little that the nuns could do. Additionally, the Presentation constitutions stated that 'nothing of moment' could be attempted by the Superioress without consulting Fr Hearne, in his capacity as Superior; Rev Mother Magdalen was obliged to obey his decisions.[100] Nonetheless, the relationship between the Presentation Sisters and their Superior was continuously strained.

The Annalist recorded that in 1837 there 'was an evident change in the manner of the Rev. D. Hearne' and life became increasingly difficult for the Sisters.[101] The Livesey Street community felt that they were frequently 'tried by the marked disrespect shown them, and the many annoyances they had to bear in the trying regulations the Rev. D. Hearne made for them, and sometimes given to them in a most thoughtless way, before his servants in the school, or with seculars'. The nuns were particularly uneasy about 'remarks that the Rev. D. Hearne used to make about money and expenses'.[102] Moreover, the Sisters soon discovered that it was not just Fr Hearne who had altered his attitude towards them. In general, 'there was less interest shown by those who had been kind in coming to the convent' and the Sisters recorded that 'there was not a priest in Manchester who showed the slightest interest or kindness' to them.[103] They also had to contend with the 'extreme roughness' of the parents of the pupils who attended their school, who constantly complained that their children were 'not learning anything'.[104]

A condition which had been agreed to when accepting the mission in Manchester was that the Sisters could be permitted to return home if 'they did not find things as they wished, or they could not succeed'.[105] While it is apparent that the early years in Manchester proved extremely trying for the pioneering Sisters, they did not abandon their mission. Certainly, the Sisters considered on a number of occasions returning home, 'but then they thought of the great work they had undertaken and renewing their good purposes they continued to endure the trials that surrounded them'.[106]

Despite the patently difficult circumstances in which the first Sisters attempted to build up their new foundation, they 'went on day by day hoping that the good work might succeed' and it was not long before the fruits of their labours showed signs for optimism.[107] In addition to their day elementary school, a Sunday School was commenced in May 1836.[108] The Papal Brief for the establishment of the Order in England was also granted in May 1836 by Pope Gregory XVI.[109] In 1837, the first postulant, Miss Lupton, entered in Livesey Street and was professed, Sr Mary Austin, in 1839.[110] An extract taken from the *Catholic Directory* in 1838, just two years following the establishment of the Presentation Convent, Livesey Street, undoubtedly gave the first Sisters a sense of achievement and provided them with encouragement to continue in the difficult work they had undertaken in Manchester:

> The youthful mind is brought into contact with everything that is pure and attractive in religion ... the obedient child, the modest virgin, the discreet matron, and the virtuous wife are formed in the nursery of piety, and become useful members, nay, ornaments of society; whilst but for [the] existence of this institution, they might become prey to the deplorable consequences of ignorance and vice.[111]

In 1842, a night school was opened for poor women and in 1845 the Sisters commenced an orphanage for Catholic orphan girls.[112] The numbers of pupils attending the Presentation school also continued to increase and by 1886, 1,000 students were listed on the rolls.[113]

The first Sisters who came to Manchester endured much hardship and adversity. Not only did they face anti-Catholic sentiment, but they were also tried by the difficult relationship which developed between them and their Superior. Nonetheless, they persisted in their apostolic work to provide education for the Catholic population of Manchester and their mission was revolutionary in many ways. The lack of support and compassion from male clergy made it difficult for the community to progress and expand, in the way that the pioneering Presentations in Ireland and in Newfoundland were expanding at the very same time. Indeed, the Presentation Convent, Livesey Street, remained the only active branch of the Order in England between 1836 and 1898.

## Vows, Rules and the Difficulty of Presentation Expansion in Nineteenth-Century England

The second half of the nineteenth century witnessed a dramatic increase in the number of Catholic female religious houses being established in England and Wales.[114] While religious communities from the continent such as the Sisters of Charity of St Paul the Apostle, from France, and Notre Dame de Namur, from Belgium, had founded ninety and twenty-four convents respectively, it was the Sisters of Mercy from Ireland who dominated the Catholic revival movement in England.[115] By 1900, this congregation of Irish female religious had established no fewer than 119 convents throughout England and Wales.[116] The Presentation Sisters' formative years in Ireland had led to fifty-nine foundations being established before the end of the nineteenth century, while their first oversees mission in Newfoundland had succeeded in opening a total of fifteen convents and schools prior to 1900. Presentation expansion in England, however, was altogether less impressive. Despite numerous attempts at expansion during the Victorian period, the Presentation Convent, Livesey Street, remained the only active branch of the Order in England for more than fifty years.

In 1851, for example, the Bishop-elect of Salford, Rt Rev Dr Turner, applied to the Presentation community in Manchester for three Sisters to establish a new foundation and assume responsibility for a girls' school near St John's Cathedral in Salford.[117] The Bishop-elect offered the Sisters a house adjoining the school rent free for use as a convent until such time as the convent proper could be established.[118] Although the proposed house was small, and had no adjoining grounds or gardens in which the Sisters could walk, the Manchester community consented to form the new mission in Salford.[119] Dr Turner informed the Sisters that 'should health fail or any other unforeseen circumstance occur, the Sisters might be at liberty to leave by giving the Committee six months' notice'.[120] Moreover, Dr Turner promised to provide a sum of £30 per annum per Sister which was to be paid quarterly.[121] Sr de Sales Dempsey, Sr Agnes Taylor and Sr Agnes Meynell were selected to commence the foundation in Salford, which they accordingly did on 1 August 1851.[122] However, within six weeks Dr Turner had contacted the Sisters in Manchester and advised them that he did not have the required funds to support the mission and that it should be abandoned by the Presentation Order.[123] It also emerged that the clergy in the Salford district were of the opinion that a group of female religious who observed simple vows, as opposed to the solemn vows adopted by the Presentation Sisters, would better suit the needs of the locality.[124] The priests also desired to employ a congregation of women who were not bound by their Rule to serve only the poor but also persons of respectable means thus providing them with a basis to support themselves.[125]

It seems unlikely that Dr Turner, after just six weeks, suddenly realised that he could no longer support the Presentation Sisters in Salford and it is more probable that the objections of the local clergy ultimately forced the Bishop-elect to retract his initial offer. Susan O'Brien has suggested that during the immediate aftermath of Catholic Emancipation, the hierarchy believed that the revival of the Catholic Church in England could not be dependent on the efforts of newly established and largely inexperienced Irish congregations. Instead, many priests and bishops favoured obtaining orders of female religious from France where there was an abundant 'supply of properly formed and trained religious sisters who came from a culture which ... educated English people admired and was certainly preferred to that of Ireland'.[126] However, as many French congregations relied on Irish women for vocations, and as other native Irish religious orders such as the Mercy Sisters were growing rapidly throughout England and Wales, it seems unlikely that anti-Irish prejudice was the reason for Turner's *volte face*.[127] It is more likely that he was concerned about the costs attached to having the nuns in Salford.

One of the many attractions of female religious congregations was that they provided a cheap source of labour. Additionally, they usually earned an income from their teaching.[128] However, the Presentation Sisters provided free education to the poor and could not exact any income for their services; the clergy arguably felt that this kind of congregation was not a sound financial 'investment' for a parish. It seems probable that the reluctant stance of the clergy in Salford had more to do with practical objections than any prejudice towards an Irish institute of female religious. The Sisters in Salford were disappointed to hear of Dr Turner's decision but were resolved to continue their work in the school until Easter 1852.[129] Dr Turner consented to this request and the Sisters remained until 7 April when the foundation in Salford was finally dissolved.[130]

A similar situation unfolded in 1894. In August that year, Fr John Lathouwers, from Rishton near Blackburn, wrote to the Reverend Mother of Livesey Street, stating that he 'would dearly like to have nuns' to provide instruction in his school.[131] While the Sisters were not unwilling to undertake this new charge, they were concerned about Fr Lathouwers' poor health. According to the Annalist of the Presentation convent, Livesey, 'Some nuns were very exacting … about daily mass … [and … Father Lathouwers] being delicate he could not promise daily mass.'[132] However, Lathouwers assured the Sisters that 'whenever he had a Curate the Sisters would have mass daily and if that obstacle could be overcome he would go at once to the bishop [for permission].'[133] With this guarantee, the Reverend Mother immediately contacted the bishop and informed him of the community's willingness to establish a new foundation in Rishton 'if your Lordship thinks it a suitable place for us.'[134]

After several weeks of negotiations, it was finally agreed that the Manchester community would provide Sisters for a mission in Rishton. Sr M. Xavier was subsequently selected as Superioress of Rishton and Sr Magdalen and Sr Alphonsus were appointed to go with her.[135] There is no further account of how the Sisters settled into their new home in Rishton, or what trials and difficulties they experienced during their first weeks and months there. However, in June 1896, the Annals of the Presentation Convent, Manchester, recorded that affairs in Rishton 'seemed doubtful.'[136] It is not clear why the community in Manchester came to this conclusion regarding the foundation in Rishton. It is possible that a lack of adequate financial support, or failure to secure government recognition and grant aid for the school, may have meant that the Sisters did not consider it feasible to continue the mission. Insufficient pupil enrolments may also have had a negative impact on the work being done by the community in Rishton. It is also possible that anti-Catholic sentiment was strong in Rishton and the Sisters may not have felt welcome in the locality.

A brief hope of a new mission emerged when the nuns received a request from Fr W. Palmer, for a group of Sisters to assume responsibility for his schools in West Houghton.[137] As the foundation in Rishton was not prospering, Rev Mother Elizabeth had suggested that those Sisters respond to Fr Palmer's appeal and transfer their foundation to West Houghton.[138] However, on reflection, the consensus was that they 'felt themselves unable to work up another school after all their hard work [in Rishton] … so all idea of changing was given up'.[139] On 31 July 1896, Mother Elizabeth wrote to Fr Lathouwer and informed him that she wished to recall her Sisters from his mission.[140] The Rishton community returned to Livesey Street on 24 August 1896 just two years after commencing the foundation.[141] Although the Sisters had lived and worked in Rishton for almost two years, their mission ultimately did not succeed and thus marked the second failed attempt at expanding the Presentation Order in England.

The Sisters' decision to return to Livesey Street had less to do with Church interference and more with the community's own decision regarding the practicability of continuing the foundation or starting another one in West Houghton. Indeed, one of the most common misconceptions surrounding female religious, is that they were reliant on invitations and help from priests and bishops. This idea of tiered hierarchical decision-making around foundations is 'convent myth' and masks the true agency and influence of female religious themselves who generally based their decisions for expansion on calculated choices concerning their financial circumstances and manpower resources.[142] While religious congregations required the consent of the local bishop before establishing a foundation in a particular diocese, 'this legal reality disguised the agency of women religious as they discerned which requests for convent foundations to accept or reject'.[143]

In England, the Presentation Sisters' decision to accept or reject an invitation for the development of a new foundation was largely based on whether the proposed establishment conformed to the needs of their Sisters, and the conditions of their constitutions. For example, on 1 July 1886, Father Brewer visited the Presentation convent in Livesey Street to see if the community there would be willing to provide Sisters for a new foundation in St Joseph's, Halliwell near Bolton. According to the Annals of the Manchester Convent, 'The community were willing to send three Sisters, providing the necessary conditions for a foundation would be made.'[144] Having obtained permission from the bishop, Rev Mother Elizabeth, Mother de Sales, and Mother Philomena visited the site of the proposed foundation in Halliwell.[145] However, upon arrival the Sisters found that 'The distance from the house to the school was too great, and [there was] no boundary wall to shield them from the public, and Fr Brewer said he would never be able to assist in building a convent. Of course, that put an end to all ideas of making the foundation.'[146] The Manchester community's decision not to accept the new foundation in Halliwell was directly concerned with upholding the requirements of their constitutions and observance of their rule of enclosure.[147]

The Sisters in Manchester were approached again in August 1889, when Mrs Longueville petitioned Fr Ryder to intercede on her behalf and apply to the Presentation community at Livesey Street 'for three Sisters to take charge of a school on her husband's estate' in Oswestry.[148] The building of a convent on the estate had already commenced and the Sisters were invited to see its progress and to consider whether a foundation would be possible. Fr Forbes subsequently accompanied Rev Mother de Sales Dempsey, Mother M. Elizabeth Boosey and Mother M. Joseph [?] to Oswestry. It was noted in the Annals of the Presentation Convent, Livesey Street, that the group, were much pleased with their visit and all seemed on the point of being satisfactorily settled when a letter came to say that neither now, nor at any time could Mr Longueville hold out hopes of enlarging the small house built for three, and with this all further communication on the subject ceased because there could be no foundation.[149] It is possible that the restrictions imposed on the Presentation Sisters by the small size of the convent made the venture impractical. While the Presentations regularly established new foundations with a limited number of Sisters, it was always expected that communities would grow. As the house in Oswestry would never be able to accommodate more than three Sisters, it is not surprising that the Manchester community decided to proceed no further with plans for the foundation.

It is clear that during the nineteenth century, development and expansion of the Presentation Order in England was slow and oftentimes challenging. While the Sisters responded to invitations from various clergy to establish new houses, such ventures were often fraught with difficulties. The Rules and Constitutions adopted by the Presentation Sisters determined what they could do, and this sometimes conflicted with the wishes of the local clergy. The decision to respond to a new appeal to open a convent and school had to be carefully considered by the nuns, and they were not willing to undertake foundations which seemed unlikely to succeed. By retaining this kind of decision-making power, the Presentation Sisters challenged the tiered system of hierarchical control which has too often been seen as a hallmark of female religious expansion during the nineteenth century.

## CHAPTER 8

# The Presentation Sisters and Second-Level Education in Ireland, 1800–1958

*… all my children are brought up to be fond of instructing*
*as I think it lies in the power of the poor to be of service*
*that way …*

–Nano Nagle to Miss Fitzsimons, 1770.

Prior to the implementation of the Intermediate Education (Ireland) Act, 1878, there had been no formal secondary school system in Ireland.[1] The restrictions placed on Irish Catholics as a result of the Penal Laws meant that education in general was limited and the provision of secondary schooling was practically non-existent. For the greater part of the eighteenth century, Irish Catholics wishing to avail of second-level education had to travel to continental Europe, to schools and colleges in Paris, Louvain and Rome.[2] Following the introduction of the Relief Act, 1782, educational provision for Catholics in Ireland improved, and Catholic religious orders began to found 'superior' or intermediate schools that provided secondary education to young people between the ages of twelve and seventeen. These institutions were largely denominational, single-sex, private and voluntary. By 1820, a total of nine Catholic intermediate schools had been established in Ireland.[3] Progress was slow and unbalanced, however, particularly with regard to the provision of secondary schooling for girls.

Paul Cullen was appointed Archbishop of Dublin in 1852.[4] As Primate of Ireland, Cullen's ambition was to create a Catholic ascendancy, whereby the religion and culture would be dominant throughout the country.[5] In order to achieve this end, Cullen became highly influential in political, social and religious developments from the mid-nineteenth century, and he was particularly concerned with Catholic education. Although Cullen welcomed the establishment of Catholic secondary schools, he viewed it as a distinctly gendered sphere. In particular, Cullen's attitude towards female education was that it prepared her for a domestic role, and he wrote:

> Teach the young women to be wise, to love their husbands, to love their children, to be discreet, chaste, sober, having a care of the house, gentle, obedient to their husbands, that the word of God be not blasphemed.[6]

The Catholic Church in general believed that young women should be educated to be 'holy women and accomplished ladies'.[7] In convent secondary schools there developed a specific emphasis on female morality, deportment and accomplishment.[8] Politeness, order, regularity, good conduct and application were valued, and girls were taught 'feminine' subjects such as needlework, singing, reading and cooking. Most importantly, they were encouraged to be modest and submissive.[9]

Until the end of the nineteenth century, female intermediate education was dominated by continental religious orders such as the Society of the Sacred Heart, the Faithful Companions of Jesus, the Dominicans, and the Ursulines.[10] Even the Loreto order, founded in Ireland with its roots in the Institute of the Blessed Virgin Mary, York, had a continental inflection, concentrating girls' attention on the study of French, Art, and European composers. By 1900, there were sixty-two convent secondary schools in Ireland, a mere six of which had been founded by indigenous congregations.[11] The majority of these were boarding schools, which catered for Catholic middle-class girls.[12] Fees ranged from £20 to £40 per year, a fee which few Irish families could comfortably afford to pay.[13] In any case, the consensus was that primary education was sufficient for the majority, and secondary education was wasted on girls who were destined for marriage.[14] The novelist and poet, Katherine Tynan, who attended the Dominican convent boarding school in Drogheda between 1872 and 1874, noted: 'I left school at the mature age of fourteen. I could have gone back if I liked, but no one troubled to make me go.'[15]

Two religious orders that pushed hard against the widespread apathy around education for working-class girls were the Presentations and the Mercy Sisters. They developed 'day pension' or 'benefit' schools for less affluent Irish Catholics.[16] The fees that they charged were relatively low, at between £2 and £4 per annum, making intermediate education possible for those who could never have afforded the élite boarding schools.[17] Among the first Presentation communities to establish benefit schools were those in Tuam (1852) and Bagenalstown (1852).[18] In 1857, the Presentation Sisters in Listowel, Co. Kerry, 'projected making one of [their] rooms a select pay school ... [where] some children would pay extra for lessons in music and French etc.'[19] A year later, in 1858, the Clondalkin community commenced a benefit school in the convent parlour.[20] According to the Clondalkin Annals, 'The necessity for opening a day school for young ladies, being obvious from the fact of not having one of the kind in the entire neighbourhood, our Holy Rules made provision for this necessity to permit it.'[21]

By 1869, the convent parlour had become unsuitable for the purposes of the benefit school and a new schoolhouse was built to meet the needs of the pupils and Sisters. The new school, St Catherine's, opened in January 1870 and provided girls from 'the more respectable families of the parish' with instruction in 'French, Music (piano) and other accomplishments suitable to their station in life'.[22] In 1866, the Presentation Sisters in Mountmellick, Co. Laois established a benefit school; branches of the order in Castleisland and Lucan were successfully running pay schools by 1875.[23] In 1877, the Presentation Sisters in Tralee opened a 'select school'. According to the Tralee Annals, 'Under the special protection of the Sacred Heart and with the permission and approbation of the late Bishop Moriarty (he died October 1, 1877), a select school was opened to cater for those pupils who desired some extras in education and accomplishments and were willing to pay for them.'[24] A benefit boarding school was also established by the Presentation Sisters in Ballingarry, Co. Tipperary in 1887.[25]

Despite these advancements, progress was slow and the general organisation of the system left much to be desired. There was no centralised management body, so schools conducted their own affairs privately. Lack of funding, the geographical imbalance in the location of schools, the relatively few pupils, and the uneven abilities of the teachers were all weaknesses within Irish second-level education.[26] These limitations came to the fore during the 1870s. Following the establishment of the National Board of Education in 1831, and the subsequent introduction of payment-by-results in 1872, it became clear that some form of intermediate education needed to follow from primary schooling.[27] The Intermediate Education (Ireland) Act was passed in 1878, and under the terms of the Act, a board of commissioners and assistant commissioners was made responsible for a system of public examinations in intermediate schools.[28] The intermediate examinations were subsequently divided into three grades, junior, middle and senior, and included subjects such as English, Latin, Greek, modern languages, natural sciences, mathematics, drawing and music.[29] Schools were awarded fees based on the success of their pupils at public examinations. Furthermore, students who performed well in the examinations received prizes and certificates.[30]

Wealthy convent schools run by the Dominican and Loreto nuns were well placed to succeed in the new intermediate examinations, and it was to be expected that they would be able to enter their girls for examinations and exhibitions from the outset. More surprising is the willingness with which some of the Presentation Convents responded, given their modest incomes and resources. Presentation annalist Sr M. Anselm wrote: 'In this year [1878] the Intermediate Board of Education was set up in Ireland and the Presentation Sisters Tralee began to teach under that board almost immediately.'[31] Three years later, the school had prepared 'eleven of the grown children' to go to an examination centre in Killarney, 'to undergo the Intermediate Examination'.[32] The Presentation Sisters in Killarney were among the first of the congregation to implement the formal system of second-level education in their school.[33]

Presentation schools were well placed to respond to the growth in career opportunities for women that opened up in the period 1880–1910. Clerical work in the post office and in the civil service, together with the opening of university education to females, gave Catholic girls opportunities from which they had traditionally been debarred. As early as 1882, a past pupil of the Presentation Convent in Enniscorthy competed successfully in the examinations for both the Irish and the UK postal service.[34] In 1908, the Presentation Sisters in Bandon commenced their 'intermediate school', in an attempt to increase employment opportunities for local girls:

> As some of the people of the town were anxious their children should qualify for Civil Service and other positions we felt it was incumbent on us to give them an opportunity of preparing for them, and thus keep them longer under our care. We therefore resolved to open intermediate classes. This we did in the month of October and by very strenuous effort on the part of the teachers ten children were presented for examination. Considering the very short time they had to prepare, and that some of the subjects were quite new to them, the results were far more successful than we had anticipated …[35]

The Intermediate Education (Ireland) Act, 1878, was non-denominational in its terms of reference, awarding fees and prizes directly to school managers and pupils based solely on their performance in examinations.[36] However, in practice, the Act supported the growth of a denominational system of secondary schooling. School authorities were free to organise their institutions along denominational lines, without any impact on the fees they were awarded.[37] In fact, a spirit of competition between Protestant and Catholic schools soon developed, and was encouraged in popular publications such as the *Freeman's Journal*.[38] In 1919–20, efforts were made to reform intermediate education via the MacPherson Education Bill.[39] However, the Bill was defeated, having failed to win the support of either the Catholic Church or any leading political party.[40] The system of intermediate education thus remained largely unchanged from its inception in 1878 through to the establishment of the Irish Department of Education in 1924.

## Second-Level Education in the Irish Free State, 1922–58

In 1922, administration for educational services was transferred from the British government to the Irish Free State.[41] Two years later, in June 1924, the Irish Department of Education formally came into being.[42] The newly formed government body moved quickly to assert its position regarding intermediate education, which was outlined in the first *Annual Report* of the Department of Education, published in 1926:

> The State at present inspects these schools regularly and exercises a certain amount of supervision through its powers to make grants to schools as a result of these inspections, but it neither founds secondary schools, nor finances the building of them, nor appoints teachers or managers, nor exercises any power or veto over the appointment or dismissal of such teachers or the management of schools.[43]

The government's role in the provision and management of secondary education was clearly extremely limited. This subsidiary role was solidified through the implementation of a programme entitled *Rules and Programmes for Secondary Schools*, first published in 1925, which was to act as a blueprint for secondary education in Ireland for the next four decades.[44]

One of the main objectives outlined in *Rules and Programmes* was the implementation of a system of co-operation between national and intermediate schools.[45] The classification of examinations into three distinct levels under the Intermediate Education Act, 1878, had led to the development of a number of separate junior and senior centres.[46] In some cases, junior schools evolved as an extension of the national school.[47] By 1924, approximately forty-two national schools were already offering instruction to junior intermediate level.[48] The Department of Education decided to devise a process of formal recognition for primary schools that provided instruction at intermediate level. From 1924/25 onwards, national schools wishing to provide secondary education had to comply with conditions as set out by the Department of Education in *Rules and Programmes*. The terms demanded that the ordinary primary work of the school is 'highly efficient'. Additionally, there had to be 'adequate' numbers of qualified staff, suitable accommodation, and the courses of instruction had to be approved by the Department. Importantly, a national school could not be approved as a provider of intermediate education in a locality if there was an existing secondary school 'within the reach and within the means of the pupils'.[49]

National schools that were awarded recognition for the provision of intermediate education became known as 'secondary tops'. As national schooling was free, secondary tops became an attractive option for pupils who could not otherwise afford to attend second-level education.[50] By 1940/41 a total of fifty-six secondary tops had been recognised by the Department of Education, of which six offered secondary education to boys and fifty to girls.[51] The Presentation Sisters managed fourteen of these schools (see Table 8.1).

Secondary tops remained a feature of Irish second-level provision until the early 1970s. They were a cost-effective way of supplying education beyond primary level, requiring little more than a few classrooms and a couple of teachers. Additionally, they suited Presentation pupils who could simply stay on at their local convent primary school for a couple of additional years. When a secondary top was established by the Sisters in Milltown in 1942, the innovation was described with little fuss:

> Pupils from sixth class remained in school and were taught French etc. After two years in secondary top they sat for Inter Cert. As we had no centre they had to sit exams in Tralee. Two rooms were provided for secondary top. One was just a passageway, the other was a good room. It was also used on Saturdays and afternoons as an art room. On finishing at secondary top pupils went to Tralee to prepare for Leaving Cert; some went to Killarney to do the same.[52]

**Table 8.1.   Recognised Presentation Secondary Tops, 1940/41
According to Location and Year of Establishment**

| Location | Year of establishment |
| --- | --- |
| Athenry | 1920 |
| Castleisland | 1925 |
| Limerick | 1928 |
| Cahirciveen | 1933 |
| Mitchelstown | 1934 |
| Castlecomer | 1937 |
| North Presentation | 1938 |
| Terenure | 1938 |
| Kildare | 1939 |
| Portarlington | 1939 |
| Wexford | 1940 |
| Carrick-on-Suir | NA |
| Dungarvan | NA |
| Portlaoise | NA |

Source: Annals of individual Presentation communities, DE, *Annual Report*, 1925–38 and Catholic Education and Irish Schools Trust (CEIST), http://www.ceist.ie/ceist_schools/index.cfm?loadref=13, 1928–55 (accessed 13/06/2016).

*NA denotes information not available.

Presentation secondary top schools also prepared girls for county council scholarships and civil service examinations, responding in a practical way to the changing needs of their pupils.[53] Unsurprisingly, the enterprise of the nuns did not go without scrutiny from their bishops, and the Galway convent struggled at first to get permission from Michael Browne, Bishop of Galway and Kilmacduagh, to open a secondary top in August 1946.[54] When he finally gave them permission, it was both provisional and limited. The Sisters were not permitted to enrol external pupils and were to provide instruction only to intermediate level. Browne clearly indicated his intention to review the situation before allowing the Sisters to extend the curriculum to leaving certificate level. This condition ensured that Browne maintained his status as an authority figure and further reinforced his level of control over the congregation and their activities. Nonetheless, on Tuesday 27 August 1946, the secondary top was formally opened by Canon Glynn. Thirty-five pupils, all from the senior class of the primary school, were enrolled on the first day.[55] A new uniform was created for the secondary top pupils which consisted of 'a kilted skirt in Foxford tweed of a pretty shade of blue with white shirt blouse and blue tie, a white cap and brown shoes and stockings'.[56]

Another feature of *Rules and Programmes* was the introduction of an official process of recognition for secondary schools. In order to achieve this, managers of existing second-level institutions had to apply in writing to the Department of Education before 1 September in that school year.[57] Recognition would only be awarded to schools that complied with the requirements outlined in the programme for secondary education. These conditions included a suitable school premises, a sufficient number of staff and pupils, provision of 'the necessary subjects' outlined in the school curriculum, permission for the visitation of school inspectors to ascertain 'if the Department's regulations are being observed' and the furnishing of school records to the Department of Education such as examination results and school timetables.[58] This process allowed the government to regulate, to a limited extent, the organisation of secondary schools in Ireland. Once again, the Presentations embraced the possibilities that secondary schooling held out to Irish girls who could not afford to attend fee-charging boarding schools.

While *Rules and Programmes* provided a clear outline for secondary education the Department of Education did not make these regulations compulsory, and compliance with the rules was entirely at the discretion of individual school managers. By 1940, there were 352 recognised secondary schools in Ireland; 160 boys' schools, 160 girls' schools, and 32 mixed sex schools.[59] The Presentation Sisters accounted for fourteen of the total number of recognised girls' secondary schools (see Table 8.2).

According to the Annals of the Presentation Convent, Waterford:

> In accordance with modern trends when secondary education has become the right of every citizen, Reverend Mother Philomena Bergin opened an intermediate school in 1938 so that the pupils might have every advantage that modern education can give.[60]

With the introduction of a formal system of recognition for secondary schools, many secondary tops applied to the Department of Education to change their status. Planning for this kind of change, implied training nuns to teach girls right up to Leaving Certificate level. Nuns moved from one convent to another, if needed; others were sent to study for degrees. For

Presentation Convent, St John's, Newfoundland. Community and pupils, with Bishop Fleming and two priests (1853). By kind permission of the Presentation Convent Archives, Newfoundland.

Presentation Convent, Crosshaven. Mother M. Teresa Tynan and First Holy Communion Class. (c. 1880s). By kind permission of the Presentation Sisters Congregational Archives.

Presentation Convent, New York. Pioneering community from Ireland (1874). By kind permission of the Presentation Convent Archives, Fermoy.

Presentation Convent, Waterford. Community and pupils (1906). By kind permission of George's Hill Archives, Dublin.

Mother John Byrne, Presentation Convent, Wagga Wagga, (*c.* 1890). By kind permission of George's Hill Archives, Dublin.

Sister M. Canice O'Shea and pupils, after the 1906 earthquake and fire, Presentation Sisters 'Refugee School', San Francisco. By kind permission of the Presentation Archives San Francisco. Photographer, Hugo Weitz.

Presentation Convent, Galway. Community (1908–9). By kind permission of the Presentation Convent Archives, Galway.

South Presentation Convent, Cork. First Holy Communion procession (*c*. 1920s). By kind permission of the Presentation Sisters Congregational Archives.

Presentation Convent, Bandon. Community (*c*. 1950s). By kind permission of the Presentation Convent Archives, Bandon.

Presentation Convent, Listowel Community (1944). By kind permission of the Presentation Sisters Congregational Archives.

Presentation Convent, Pickering, England. Sr Augustine with pupils (*c.* 1960). By kind permission of the Presentation Convent Archives, Galway.

Presentation Convent, Egmore, India (1960). By kind permission of the Presentation Sisters Congregational Archives.

Irish Presentation Sisters in Rawalpindi, Pakistan (1961). By kind permission of the Presentation Sisters Congregational Archives.

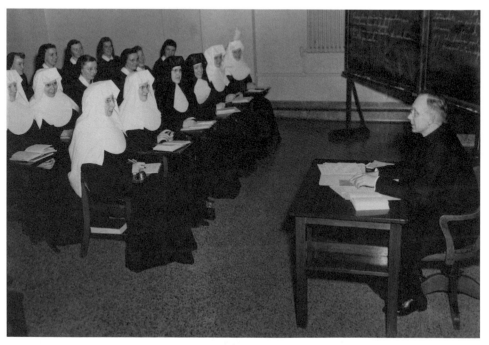

Presentation Convent, Aberdeen, South Dakota. Postulants, Novices and Sisters, attending a lecture on logic by Fr Jung SJ (*c.* late 1950s/early 1960s). By kind permission of the Presentation Sisters Congregational Archives.

Presentation Novitiate, Mt St Anne's, Portarlington (*c.* 1950). By kind permission of the Presentation Sisters Congregational Archives, Cork.

Presentation Convent, Lucan. By kind permission of George's Hill Archives, Dublin.

Presentation Convent, Tralee. By kind permission of George's Hill Archives, Dublin.

Presentation Convent, Thurles. By kind permission of George's Hill Archives, Dublin.

✓ 2    Cork april 29 y[e] 1770

Dear Miss

I had y[e] pleasure of receiving
y[r] kind favor, and hope my last letter, has convinc'd
y[u] y[t] it was now neglect on my part, not answer=
ing y[u] soon'r, as nothing can give me more real plea=
sure y[n] hearing often, from y[u] dore. bett I have that
of seeing y[u], and y[t] long'd for sight, I hope is not at
such a distance as I sometime a goe imagin'd it to be; I cant
to much admire y[r] zeal, and great trust in y[e] divine
providence, w[ch] I always look'd on as y[e] most solid
beginning any foundation, of this kind cou'd have, &
I build more on y[e] success of it from y[e] poor way
it first took its rise y[n] any means, it has plain'd
god to give me at present to carry it on: I cant
express how much I suffer to think of all y[e] severe
trials y[u] have gone true, and am sensible its
more painfull to meet y[u] where shou'd I expect

MS Letter, Nano Nagle to Miss Fitzsimons, 29 April 1770. By kind permission of the Presentation Sisters Congregational Archives, Cork.

Nano Nagle. Oil on canvas. (James Barry RA, attrib.) By kind permission of the Presentation Sisters Congregational Archives, Cork.

Table 8.2.   Recognised Presentation Secondary Schools According to Location and Year of Recognition, 1940/41*

| Location | Year of recognition |
| --- | --- |
| Tuam | 1912 |
| Bagenalstown | 1921 |
| Cashel | 1921 |
| Fethard | 1921 |
| Tralee | 1921 |
| Hospital | 1921 |
| Midleton | 1921 |
| Mountmellick | 1922 |
| Clonmel | 1925 |
| Drogheda | 1925 |
| Lismore | 1925 |
| Ballingarry | 1934 |
| Dingle | 1937 |
| Waterford | 1938 |

Source: Waldron, *Out of the Shadows*, p. 57; *Report of the Intermediate Education Commissioners* (Dublin, 1921–3); DE, *Annual Report*, 1925–40.

* Statistical information regarding the recognition of secondary schools prior to 1921 is unavailable. Where the exact date of recognition is unknown but the school is included in the 1921 report, 1921 is given as date of recognition.

example, when the Presentation Convent, Cahirciveen, made the transition from secondary top to full secondary school in 1943, a nun who had a BA degree 'was borrowed from the Dingle Convent' to teach there, and an unqualified Sister 'was sent to the Cork University to qualify there – a four-year course'.[61]

Prior to 1950, pupils who attended the secondary top in Athenry were required to sleep at the Presentation Convent, Tuam, for two weeks in order to complete their intermediate examinations at the Tuam centre. In 1947, Athenry secondary top was awarded full secondary status and from 1950, following the construction of a new school building, the intermediate and leaving certificate examinations were held in Athenry convent school.[62] One pupil remembered the way nuns had to somehow patch together everything necessary in time for the first September intake of pupils:

I left Craughwell National School in July 1947 and went to the Convent School in Athenry and entered 7th class. There was also 8th class (all in one room in the National School). Then in September of that year the Sisters decided to start off Secondary Education and acquired two rooms in the Canton Hall, upstairs – one big room for 1st years and 2nd years and a smaller one for Inter Certs. There were no Leaving Certs yet. Thus began Secondary Education. We had two nuns only ... After a year or so we had a lay teacher ... The nuns taught all subjects. The uniform consisted of a dark green dress with a beige collar and buttons.[63]

In Galway, the Presentations also 'decided to have the secondary top to [the] primary school recognised as a secondary school proper.'[64] As was the case with the establishment of secondary tops, Presentation communities wishing to apply to the Department for recognition of their secondary schools had first to obtain permission from their First Superior. While the Sisters in Galway were successful, those in Terenure were not so fortunate, and the Archbishop of Dublin, John Charles McQuaid, refused them permission to form a secondary school. McQuaid's main objection was that the provision of secondary education could have a detrimental impact on the primary schooling provided by the Sisters. McQuaid, in announcing his decision, was also reinforcing his position as First Superior and all that position entailed: 'nothing of moment shall be attempted ... without consent from the bishop.'[65]

A similar event occurred in December 1947, when the Mother Superior of the Presentation Convent, Clondalkin, wrote to Archbishop McQuaid requesting permission to establish a fully recognised secondary school.[66] At the time there was no secondary school for girls in Clondalkin and many pupils were 'obliged to take buses daily at half past eight ... to city secondary schools and return home at five o' clock or five thirty.'[67] According to the Mother Superior, 'many parents consider the day too long and regret there is no secondary school in Clondalkin.'[68] The Superior's request was rejected. McQuaid wrote to her on 29 January 1948, stating: 'I consider that it would be more advisable for your Institute to concentrate on its proper work of primary education of girls.'[69]

Not all bishops confined Presentation nuns and their pupils to primary schooling. For example, Dr Jeremiah Kinane, Bishop of Cashel and Emly, did not prevent any of the Presentation schools in his diocese from developing secondary schools. Indeed, although the transfer from secondary top to secondary school was often a difficult affair, the number of Presentation

**Table 8.3.   Recognised Presentation Secondary Schools According to Location and Year of Recognition, 1940–58**

| Year | Province of Armagh | Province of Cashel | Province of Dublin | Province of Tuam | Total |
|------|------|------|------|------|------|
| 1940–41 | 1 | 10 | 2 | 1 | 14 |
| 1941–42 | 1 | 11 | 2 | 1 | 15 |
| 1942–43 | 1 | 12 | 2 | 2 | 17 |
| 1943–44 | 1 | 12 | 3 | 2 | 18 |
| 1944–45 | 1 | 13 | 3 | 2 | 19 |
| 1945–46 | 1 | 14 | 3 | 2 | 20 |
| 1946–47 | 2 | 17 | 3 | 3 | 25 |
| 1947–48 | 2 | 17 | 3 | 4 | 26 |
| 1948–49 | 2 | 18 | 3 | 4 | 27 |
| 1949–50 | 2 | 18 | 3 | 4 | 27 |
| 1950–51 | 2 | 18 | 3 | 4 | 27 |
| 1951–52 | 1 | 18 | 3 | 4 | 26 |
| 1952–53 | 1 | 18 | 3 | 4 | 26 |
| 1953–57 | NA | NA | NA | NA | NA |
| 1957–58 | 1 | 25 | 3 | 5 | 34 |

Source: DE, *Annual Report, 1940–58.*

secondary schools increased annually. By 1958, the Presentation Sisters had thirty-four fully recognised secondary schools (see Table 8.3).

These figures, however, are not a reflection of the total number of intermediate schools managed and owned by the Presentations during this period. As late as 1951, South Presentation, Cork city, was providing second-level education to 411 pupils, but was not formally recognised by the Department of Education.[70] Other Presentation schools in a similar position included Lucan, Bandon, and Dungarvan.[71] This would indicate that a number of benefit schools continued to operate independently of the Department of Education. Nonetheless, the process of recognition for both secondary tops and secondary schools proper provided a structure that had not been evident in Irish second-level education before. While such advancements were a welcome development within the educational sector, there remained a number of inherent issues with the system, not least the lack of adequate funding.

## Supporting Presentation Second-Level Education

In 1924, the Irish government passed the Intermediate Education (Amendment) Act which abolished the existing payment-by-results system.[72] Under the new Act, the intermediate and leaving certificate examinations were established and financial aid from the government was henceforth to be provided by means of a capitation grant per pupil.[73] Until the late 1950s, the capitation grant awarded to school managers did not exceed £16 for each recognised senior pupil and £11 for each recognised junior pupil.[74] In addition to the capitation grants, the Department of Education also provided incremental salaries for recognised secondary school teachers which amounted to £200 per annum.[75] Under the terms of *Rules for the Payment of Grants to Secondary Schools*, only recognised secondary schools could avail of the capitation grant and incremental salaries.[76] By 1958, the Sisters had thirty-four recognised secondary schools, all of which were in receipt of the capitation grant and incremental salary.

In addition to the capitation grant and incremental salary, the Department of Education offered a further financial incentive for secondary schools that promoted the use of the Irish language. This took the form of a three-tiered classification system, dependent on the use of Irish in the school. Irish was the primary medium of instruction in 'A' schools, and they were awarded an extra 25 per cent on their grant each year. Schools classed as 'B1' used Irish 'on an equal, or greater, level than English', and were awarded an additional 10 per cent; schools where Irish was 'efficiently taught and … used as the medium of instruction in at least two other classes', were classed as 'B2' schools, and could be awarded anything from 2.5 to 10 per cent onto their grant.[77] In the school year 1940/41, twelve of the fourteen recognised Presentation secondary schools were in receipt of Irish and bilingual school grants (see Table 8.4).

Only two of the fourteen recognised Presentation secondary schools were not in receipt of the Irish and bilingual school grants during the school year 1940/41: Bagenalstown, Co. Carlow, and Midleton, Co. Cork. In these schools Irish was taught at a curricular level only and was not promoted beyond what was required for the certificate examinations.

As the number of Presentation secondary schools increased, so too did the number applying for the Irish and bilingual grants. Between 1940 and 1958 many Presentation schools were awarded 'A' status including Headford and Thurles in 1943, Lixnaw in 1944, Cahirciveen and Crosshaven in 1946, Millstreet and Oranmore in 1947, and Athenry in 1948.[78] The Irish

Table 8.4.   Number of Presentation Secondary Schools Promoting
Use of Irish as Teaching Medium and Number of Pupils in
each Category, 1940/41

| Category of school | Number of schools | Number of pupils |
| --- | --- | --- |
| A | 8 | 796 |
| B1 | 4 | 336 |
| B2 | - | - |
| - | 2 | 120 |

Source: DE, *Annual Report, 1940/41.*

classification of secondary schools was reviewed by the Department of Education annually, and sometimes schools dropped their status. Retaining the status of an 'A' school was no easy task. Only the Presentation secondary schools in the west of Ireland and larger schools such as Mountmellick, Co. Laois, and Thurles, Co. Tipperary, appear to have retained their 'A' status throughout the 1940s and 1950s. These schools were situated in areas where Irish was more widely spoken. Although many Presentation schools achieved some form of Irish or bilingual status during the period 1940–58, the progress at national level was not maintained. By 1958, schools classed as Irish and/or bilingual catered for just 50 per cent of the total number of secondary pupils.[79]

The financing of secondary schools was no easy task. While the Department of Education offered capitation, incremental salaries and Irish and bilingual school grants, the reality was that in many cases this kind of support did not meet the basic needs of the school. Convent accounts from the Presentation Ballingarry provide an example of the typical yearly expenses accumulated in a rural, secondary boarding school in Co. Tipperary (see Table 8.5).

The total expenses for the Presentation Ballingarry in 1940 were approximately £1,866. The total received from incremental salaries and capitation was £623.10s.0d. To manage the shortfall, Presentation Sisters had to rely on other forms of income in order to support their schools. To some degree, the balance was met by parents and guardians and the amount paid by pupils varied from school to school. The average annual tuition fee paid by a day pupil was £13. However, in some areas £13 would have been too high a fee for parents, and so the convents either provided free tuition, or

**Table 8.5.   Expenses for the Presentation Secondary School,
Ballingarry, County Tipperary, 1940**

| Expenses | Amount | | |
|---|---|---|---|
| | £. | s. | d. |
| Fish and meat | 217 | 9 | 8 |
| Butter and eggs | 158 | 16 | 8 |
| Clothing | 59 | 10 | 0 |
| Furniture and repairs | 163 | 12 | 6 |
| Bread and potatoes | 71 | 5 | 9 |
| Fuel and lights | 144 | 8 | 2 |
| Laundry and maids | 65 | 13 | 11 |
| Farm, feeding stuffs and hire | 199 | 3 | 2 |
| Groceries | 176 | 4 | 7 |
| Stationery and stamps | 26 | 4 | 6 |
| Chapel and retreats | 98 | 12 | 11 |
| Doctors and infirmary | 145 | 12 | 4 |
| Rent, rates, insurance | 33 | 5 | 7 |
| Charity | 3 | 7 | 0 |
| Day school | 52 | 12 | 7 |
| Building repairs out-offices | 25 | 0 | 0 |
| **Total expenses** | 1,866 | (approx) | |

Source: MS Accounts, Presentation Convent, Ballingarry, 1940.

charged low fees. Boarding fees were, naturally enough, higher than fees in day schools. In 1930, the Presentations in Ballingarry charged £34 a year to pupils who attended their select boarding school.[80] Yet as late as 1962/63 their school in George's Hill, Dublin, was charging less than £3 per annum.[81] Where a boarding school and day school ran on one campus, the income from the boarding school was used to support the secondary day school; this was a common practice for many teaching Orders in Ireland.

Interest from investments was a major source of income, which the Presentation Sisters relied on for financing their schools. For example, in George's Hill the community received interest on shares in various public, corporate and government-backed stock, private estates and industries. Many Orders bought shares and stock with dowry income, as they could not spend the principal during the lifetime of the dowered nun. In 1951, for example, George's Hill investments yielded an income of £769.1s.5d. The Sisters' total income for the same period did not exceed £988, thus highlighting the importance of interest from investments as a form of income. George's Hill was neither a secondary top nor a recognised secondary school, and was not in receipt of any financial support from the Department of Education. It was not until 1954 that the school was officially recognised by the Department of Education as a secondary top.[82] Other sources of income came from more traditional industries which the Sisters developed within their enclosure. For example, rural communities such as Ballingarry, Co. Tipperary, managed farms and sold milk, vegetables, fruit and butter.[83] In 1940, the Sisters earned a total of £255 from the sale of the produce on their farm.[84] During the summer months, the Sisters in Oranmore regularly rented out their boarding school to other female religious. In 1949, for example, the Sisters of La Sainte Union des Sacrés Coeurs, Athlone, and the Holy Family Sisters, Newbridge, were expected to stay in the boarding school in Oranmore during the month of July.[85] The leasing of the convent boarding school during the summer months provided some additional support for the Sisters in Oranmore.[86] Nuns were frugal in their spending, and were early adopters of the idea of recycling. The convents at George's Hill and Oranmore sold off old lead piping,[87] and the Oranmore Sisters earned £5 from the sale of two doors and £60 from the sale of stones from an old mill.[88]

The poverty of many Presentation pupils meant that the Sisters needed to be innovative in how they would generate money to feed and clothe pupils. Charitable donations were also an occasional source of income for twentieth-century Presentation communities, and usually were given with stipulations. For example, in 1943, the Ballingarry nuns were bequeathed £200 by the Very Rev Canon Thomas O' Meara, parish priest of Mullinahone, Co. Tipperary.[89] It was stipulated in O'Meara's will that the sum was to be given 'to the Superioress of the Presentation Convent, Ballingarry for the clothing of poor children in their schools'.[90] Occasionally, nuns were left something in the will of a relative, and this automatically became the property of the convent. In 1946, a Sister in the Galway Presentation was bequeathed a sum of £700 in the will of her brother.[91] It was used by the nuns for the provision of clothes and food for poor girls attending their schools.[92]

Concerts and raffles were a direct way to generate additional income for the support of the schools, and were commonly run for one-off, large-scale school projects. In 1947, the Sisters in Oranmore requested permission from the bishop to organise a play, the proceeds of which were intended to carry out repairs on their school.[93] Similarly, in 1950 the Galway Sisters were granted permission by the bishop to organise a gift sale, a sale of work and three raffles to help raise finances to build a new school in Shantalla.[94] In March 1958, the Sisters in Ballingarry held a number of draws to raise funds for the establishment of a concert hall in the secondary school.[95] Within a month, the Sisters had raised over £1,000 for this building.[96] The accounts of the Presentation Sisters in Ballingarry and Oranmore are replete with examples of revenue received from concerts, plays and raffles. In 1940, the Presentation Sisters in Ballingarry secured £25 from a concert held in their school.[97] A further £100 was raised in this way in 1944.[98] Similarly, in 1948, the Oranmore Sisters raised £61 from the proceeds of a play, £84 from other entertainments, and £143 from a sweepstake.[99] These sums, often modest, were always deployed in the completion of building projects and school repairs.

## Staffing the Convent Secondary School

Official teacher training for Sisters generally did not commence until after they had completed their novitiate, and the Presentations observed the tradition of spiritual formation followed by academic training. Indeed, their bishops were insistent on this. For example, in September 1949 the Reverend Mother of the Presentation Convent, Galway, requested permission from Bishop Michael Browne to send a novice in the community to University College Galway to begin her degree.[100] The Sister had completed her spiritual year a few days earlier, on 28 August 1949, and the Reverend Mother needed her to begin her teaching training at once.[101] Bishop Browne, however, declined the request, on the basis that the nun's 'full and complete' spiritual formation was more important than university qualifications.[102]

Upon completion of their religious formation, the newly professed Sisters were assigned by the Superioress to the schools in accordance with the particular needs and demands of individual schools. The Superioress often consulted her Council or the managers of the schools when deciding where Sisters would be sent. However, it was ultimately the Superioress who was responsible for all appointments in the schools. The Sisters themselves were not privy to the process regarding their appointments, nor did they decide what subjects they would be trained to teach. In the early days of their novitiate, young Sisters learned that 'they are to obey the Mother Superior …

whether agreeable or disagreeable, they must never give way to murmuring or discontent'.[103]

Within the schools, a manager and a principal were responsible for its governance and administration, and these were appointed by the Rev Mother. Only senior Sisters were appointed to managerial roles in the school, once they had attained experience within the schools. There were very few lay staff employed in denominational secondary schools until the 1960s, and as late as 1964/65 members of religious congregations outnumbered lay staff by 58 per cent to 42 per cent in denominational secondary schools.[104] As the nuns owned the schools and comprised the greater part of the teaching staff, it is not surprising that only Sisters were appointed to positions of authority. Indeed, the Presentations were not unique in this regard, and this was the pattern in all denominational schools. Parents and the wider public tended not to interfere in how denominational schools were run, and viewed the religious as suited to being in charge of schools, because of their 'religious commitment, their total devotion to their work and the fact that they were not distracted by family demands and problems'.[105] Further, the bishop did not welcome public interference in how the schools in his diocese were run. The control which the Church extended over secondary education did not only limit outside involvement, it also limited the type of curriculum that was offered in the secondary schools – particularly the schools for girls.

## Nuns and the Gendered Curriculum

During the period 1924–58, the Department of Education set the curriculum, though by and large, school authorities decided what would be taught. As noted in the Report of the Council of Education, *The Curriculum of the secondary school*, until the 1960s secondary schooling in Ireland was conducted on the lines of the traditional grammar school.[106] Secondary schools typically provided a general academic education whereby there was a strong emphasis on the arts and classical languages such as Latin.[107] The 'official' curriculum included Irish, English, history and geography, mathematics, another language or science, commerce or domestic science for girls.[108] But not all schools had the classrooms, equipment and teachers to teach every subject, and convent schools were expected to prepare girls for the limited – and largely domestic – role accorded to women in Irish society.

A woman's role in Irish life was reinforced in the 1937 Constitution, article 41.2, which emphasised that her place lay 'within the home'.[109] This directly affected the curricular provision for girls attending convent secondary schools. The Conference of Convent Secondary Schools continually stressed that the correct place for the woman was in the home and that the curriculum provided in convent secondary schools should prepare young girls to be good mothers and wives.[110] Catholic theologians in Ireland advised that girls should study subjects 'in a different way and for another purpose' than boys, and their schoolwork 'should lack the competitive note'. The main focus should be 'the practical arts and accomplishments called into play in the management of the home'.[111] Despite these constraints, the Presentations were remarkably successful in pushing out the limits of what their pupils might achieve. They did not have the resources of convents that attracted the fee-paying families of the middle and upper-class Catholics, such as Loreto Abbey and the Ursuline Convents in Cork and Thurles, yet they added subjects that would increase the employability of young women, and give them options other than 'the management of the home'. The *Cork Examiner* in 1940 indicated that the Presentation secondary school, Crosshaven, Co. Cork, 'prepared [pupils] for the secondary board certificates, for matriculation and civil service examinations, also for examinations in the Royal Irish Academy of Music. Instruction is given in domestic economy.'[112] The same year, the *Irish Press* reminded readers that girls in Co. Tipperary were prepared by the Presentations 'for civil service, intermediate, leaving certificate, matriculation, and music, etc.'[113] The Sisters in Thurles prepared girls 'for all public examinations, including Dublin Corporation, all branches of civil service, Aer Lingus, ESB and bank, special classes for teachers' training colleges'.[114] And in Waterford, the Presentations could boast that many of the girls who attended their school 'passed into the civil service, post office, or qualified for commercial positions in the business houses in the city, while others have qualified for teaching or nursing.'[115]

The nuns also had to accommodate changes in regulations concerning the teaching of Irish in their schools. The language became compulsory at national school level in 1922, intermediate level in 1928 and leaving certificate level in 1934.[116] The introduction of the Irish and Bilingual grant scheme in 1924 also acted as an incentive among school managers and teachers. From the start, Sisters were expected to embrace any opportunities to improve their Irish, and in the summer of 1922 many nuns packed their bags and headed to a language course. Three Sisters from the Rahan community completed a two-month Irish language course in the Presentation Convent, Mullingar,[117] and twelve Sisters from Portlaoise were ordered by their bishop to 'attend Irish courses of six weeks duration in Abbeyleix (elementary) and Carlow/ Stradbally (intermediate)'.[118] The Clondalkin Sisters went to Irish courses in

Maynooth that summer, and 'lodged in a house nearby [where they] had to bring everything they needed with them – including, of course, a cow'.[119]

Down in Cork in 1923, nine nuns from South Presentation 'were obliged ... at the desire of our bishop to follow a higher course of Irish lessons which was held in our convent of Crosshaven'. They left the convent with reluctance, and the annals record that 'their exit was more like a funeral than a pleasant drive ... They were very glad at the end of two months to return notwithstanding the great kindness of our dear Sisters in Crosshaven'.[120] Throughout the 1920s, Presentations also attended Irish courses at Carysfort College[121] and at Mary Immaculate College,[122] with the result that convent annalists heralded the summer months with the somewhat plaintive lament, 'Irish courses as usual'.[123] Reluctance on the part of the nuns was less to do with having to study Irish, and more to do with the fact that they did not wish to leave their cloister. In July 1931, for example, eight Sisters from South Presentation Cork 'were sent to Ring Irish College to study and improve themselves in the correct pronunciation of the Irish language'.[124] The nuns knew that having to leave the convent to go to Ring was 'a great departure from our old customs which is to be regretted but cannot be helped owing to the demands made by the Board of Education ... and inspectors are very exacting'.[125] To ameliorate the situation for enclosed Orders, the Department of Education reserved the college 'for nuns alone, of whom there were over a hundred of different Orders, so there was no unnecessary intercourse with seculars'.[126] Some nuns even benefited from the change of scenery, 'and returned home on the 30th July looking well as if the sea breezes and Irish atmosphere ... had done them good physically as well as intellectually'.[127]

The advantages of leaving the convent enclosure for summer school were not lost on Superiors, and the community in Cahirciveen decided in 1939 to 'build a house at the seaside to which the Sisters of the whole diocese may go for the summer holidays'.[128] The Reverend Mother in Cahirciveen, having obtained permission from Bishop O'Brien, chose a site at Ballinskelligs because it was an Irish-speaking district and the Sisters would have facilities there for learning Irish, which was by then a compulsory subject in all schools. The Reverend Mother announced with satisfaction that 'Professors at the College are to come and hold Irish classes for the Sisters at the seaside house ... His Lordship ... also gave permission for bathing and long walks through the country roads in the afternoons when the Sisters may speak to the natives in Irish but to no other.'[129]

Irish was not the only subject for which nuns required training. In 1918, the Department of Education had introduced a system of registration to

### Table 8.6. Number of Registered Teachers

| Number of recognised pupils | Number of registered teachers |
|---|:---:|
| Less than 50 | 1 |
| More than 49 but not more than 80 | 2 |
| More than 80 but not more than 110 | 3 |
| More than 110 but not more than 140 | 4 |
| More than 140 but not more than 170 | 5 |
| 'And so on' | 'And so on' |

Source: DE, *Rules for the payment of grants to secondary schools*, 1946.

regulate the qualification of teachers employed in secondary schools.[130] A qualified teacher had to have a university degree, a recognised postgraduate qualification in teaching, a year of experience in a recognised secondary school, and the required Irish language competence.[131] For a Presentation school to be recognised by the Department of Education, it had to comply with the pupil–teacher ratio (see Table 8.6). For the Sisters to adhere to all these requirements, they had to leave their own convent, sometimes for several years. In 1936, for example, Sr M. Joseph Fox went from the Presentation Convent, Rahan, to the Brigidine Convent in Goresbridge to complete a year's training in domestic science, after which she went on to the Presentation Convent in Dundrum, Co. Tipperary, for another course. She secured a Teacher's Diploma in Domestic Science.[132]

In convent schools where there were shortages of qualified nuns, untrained Sisters stepped in. Though this contravened the regulations that 'the staff of teachers … must be qualified to give instruction in those subjects of the programme which they teach', the Department of Education allowed a certain amount of flexibility depending on the circumstances of the schools.[133] While convents were waiting for Sisters to complete university and teacher training, they could improvise by drawing on young nuns who had recently completed their novitiate, or older Sisters who had decades of experience but no official training. But this was a temporary situation; the day when nuns ran their schools independent of state interference was over, and the requirements for professional credentials forced Sisters out of the enclosure and into universities, colleges, and halls of residence where daily routines were adapted to suit undergraduate student life.[134] Throughout the mid-twentieth century, the Sisters attended universities, completed their teacher education, and often gained experience by doing some teaching practice in different Presentation schools. Their engagement with Irish education involved being prepared to go out into the wider world of learning.

For Presentations in Ireland, profound changes in their education mission took place between the mid-nineteenth and mid-twentieth centuries. During the very same period, the nuns overseas had to meet the demands of diverse and challenging education environments; this was particularly so among the 'impoverished Catholic minority in Britain'.[135] A Jesuit priest who gave a talk to pupils in Ballingarry in 1958, impressed them with his missionary rhetoric. While stressing the importance of Presentation example to English girls, he said: 'The faith is to be found *only* among the Irish people in England, so let us not remove the *only* spark that is there'.[136]

CHAPTER 9

# 'Service to the kingdom':
# Expansion in Britain

*Though you nor I should not live to see it prosper in our
time, yet I hope it may hereafter, and be of universal
service to the kingdom.*

– Nano Nagle to Miss Mulally, 31 January 1783.

Despite the apparent slow growth of the Presentation order in England
during the nineteenth century, the first half of the twentieth century
brought increased opportunities for expansion and development. The Sisters
in Livesey Street were responsible for the initial progress, but Presentations
in Ireland and India also became central to developments in Britain. In
new British foundations, the Sisters continued to work mainly in teaching.
However, parliamentary reform in education, and the impact of two world
wars, would bring new challenges to the role of the Presentations. Throughout
the twentieth century, the Order continued to grow in Britain, and while their
expansion could never be described as rapid, new foundations were made
regularly. Between 1919 and 1958 fifteen new foundations were established
in England (see Table 9.1). The ways in which the nuns adapted to the needs
of their time made a significant contribution to the enduring legacy of the
Presentation order and its foundress, Nano Nagle.

## Presentation Expansion in the Twentieth Century

Expansion of the Presentations in England in the early twentieth century
fell to the community of Sisters in Livesey Street. The congregation had
grown internationally during the nineteenth century, with new foundations

Table 9.1.   Foundations of the Presentation Order in England
According to Year of Establishment, Location and Founding
House, 1836–1958

| Year | Foundation | Founded from |
|------|-----------|--------------|
| 1836 | Livesey Street, Manchester | Clonmel, Ireland |
| 1851 | Salford | Manchester |
| 1894 | Rishton | Manchester |
| 1898 | Buxton | Manchester |
| 1904 | Glossop | Buxton |
| *1919 | Liverpool | Madras, India |
| 1919 | Pickering | Galway, Ireland |
| *1927 | Matlock | Madras, India |
| *1933 | South Kirkby | Matlock |
| 1935 | Crowle | Buxton |
| 1938 | New Moston | Manchester |
| *1945 | Castleconnell (Ireland) | Matlock |
| 1946 | Penzance | Rawalpindi, Pakistan |
| 1949 | Ryde | South Kirkby/Matlock |
| 1951 | Scunthorpe | Buxton |
| 1953 | Bicester | Portarlington/Mountmellick Ireland |
| 1954 | Stapenhill | Buxton |
| 1954 | Market Harborough | Buxton |
| ^1957 | Elswick | Manchester |
| *1958 | Chaddesdon | Buxton |
| 1958 | Mansfield | Buxton |

*denotes novitiate

^denotes holiday house/retreat centre

Sources: Presentation Convent Ryde Annals, 1948–70, and *60th Anniversary of the Presentation Sisters in Bicester, 1953–2013* (n.d., n.p.), p. 2.

in Newfoundland (1833), India (1842), America (1854), Australia (1866) and Pakistan (1895), with the result that few Presentation communities, either at home in Ireland or globally, were in a position to help develop the Order in England. Indeed, there is no evidence that Presentation communities, outside of that at Livesey Street, were approached to make foundations elsewhere in

England. When the opportunity for expansion eventually came, it was the result of a chance meeting between the Livesey Street community and a local parish priest in Buxton in the summer of 1896.

Two Sisters from the Livesey Street community, Mother Elizabeth Boosey and Sr M. Aquinas Clarke, spent some time in Buxton during the summer of 1896.[1] During their stay, the nuns became acquainted with the local parish priest, Canon Hoeben, who would become a regular visitor to the convent in Livesey Street.[2] Hoeben was so impressed by the foundation in Manchester that he became determined to have some Sisters manage his school in Buxton. In November 1896, he appealed to Reverend Mother Elizabeth for assistance.[3] The Manchester community were willing to consent to the new foundation, but 'obstacles arising from some members of the congregation' delayed progress.[4] It is not clear what objections were raised; however, it is possible that some Sisters may have been concerned about assuming responsibility for a school that depended largely on private and voluntary subscriptions. Although the British government had provided grant aid for schools controlled by voluntary bodies since 1833, Canon Hoeben's numerous attempts over a twelve-year period had failed to secure a grant for his school in Buxton.[5]

Early in 1898, Canon Hoeben made one final appeal to the Sisters in Manchester. In a persuasive letter, he wrote that the school managers wished to know on what terms the Presentation Sisters would consider coming to Buxton.[6] He offered a school, convent and garden rent free, and advised that £80 per annum could be obtained on voluntary subscriptions until such time as the school was awarded grant aid.[7] Mother Elizabeth put the proposal to the Discreets in Livesey Street and informed Canon Hoeben that they would require 'three days for prayer and consideration'.[8] In the meantime, Canon Hoeben contacted the Catholic Poor School Committee and the Education Department and applied once more for grant aid.[9]

On the day that the Presentation Sisters assembled to give their views on the matter of the new foundation in Buxton, Mother Elizabeth received a letter from Canon Hoeben, marked 'victory'.[10] According to the convent Annals, the determined Canon 'had obtained the victory over the school board, his school was recognised by the Education Department as "necessary" and would from that date be certified to earn the various grants paid by government for the maintenance of elementary schools'.[11] The nuns took this as a 'good omen for the new foundation' and unanimously agreed to undertake the charge.[12] However, before giving full consent to Canon Hoeben, the Sisters were required to obtain permission from their local bishop. Rather than see Buxton as a new foundation, the Sisters had decided that it should be a 'branch house' of the Manchester community 'where delicate Sisters might go to for change of air when necessary'.[13] The Rule and Constitutions did not permit the establishment of branch houses; however, as the local bishop had 'power to exempt from Rule or not', the Sisters applied to him for permission.[14] The bishop consented, but suggested that the foundation should initially be undertaken for a period of just three years after which time the continued viability of the institution, or not, would be assessed.[15]

On 7 February 1898, a small group of four nuns left for Buxton: Rev Mother Elizabeth, Mother Austin, Mother Calasanctius and Mother Joseph.[16] The Sisters were pleased with their visit and the following day they presented a report of their findings to the Vocals in Manchester.[17] A form of agreement was subsequently drawn up which outlined the regulations of the school and community life for the new foundation in Buxton. The foundation would be undertaken as a branch house for three years, and the Sisters would run the elementary school, teaching 'the syllabus of the Nottingham diocese and the requirements of the education code', and they would be paid £100 per annum.[18] While the nuns were required to assist in Sunday school and sodality work, it was agreed that the Superioress should be free when necessary for 'household and business matters'. Finally, it was agreed that if the Sisters gave a loan to pay for furnishings or repairs, the Canon would pay interest at 4 per cent per annum, until he could pay off the principal.[19] The three Sisters chosen to lead the foundation were Mother M. Calasanctius, Sr M. Margaret and Sr M. Stanislaus.[20] The pioneering group left Manchester on Friday 22 April 1898, and by the following Monday (25 April) they were running their new school, with forty-eight children present. From the start, the school had a denominational mix, with twenty-three Catholic and twenty-five Protestant children.[21] As the convent was not yet ready, the Sisters lived in temporary accommodation.[22]

In 1904, another opportunity to expand in England emerged. The Sisters of Charity of St Paul had run a school in Glossop, on Lord Howard's estate, for almost half a century. When the nuns were recalled to staff one of their larger convent schools, the parish priest, Fr Scully, together with Lord Howard, decided to look for another congregation of female religious to run the Glossop school.[23] Fr Scully successfully applied to the Presentation community in Buxton for Sisters.[24] On 28 December 1903, Reverend Mother Stanislaus and Sr Joseph travelled to Glossop to prepare the school and convent.[25] Upon arrival, they discovered that the convent was not ready and the repairs which had been undertaken by Lord Howard were still ongoing.[26] The Sisters were offered the coachman's cottage as a temporary dwelling, until the convent was completed.[27] The delay in refurbishments did not deter the Sisters from opening the school, and on 2 January 1904, Sr Mary Catherine Jones and Sr Mary Aloysius Redmond arrived to commence their teaching duties.[28] The school flourished in the decade that followed, and the community became settled. But at the end of that decade, irreversible change was on the horizon: Britain was going to war.

## The Presentation Sisters in England during the First World War

The Presentation Sisters had been in Buxton for approximately sixteen years when the First World War broke out in July 1914. Shortly after the war commenced, Catholic refugees from Belgium arrived in Buxton. The Belgian children attended the convent school, and 'several youths and grownups came at night to the convent to learn English'.[29] The nuns tried to maintain a sense of normality in their daily lives, but they could not escape the wartime measures which had been implemented throughout the country. The Buxton Sisters noted that the winter of 1914–15 was a particularly 'hard one. War prices were demanded for everything and owing to [the] danger of submarines, our imports were considerably lessened'.[30] In Glossop, the Sisters teaching in the school were frequently granted 'war bonuses' and salary increases on account of the 'high price of living'.[31]

In addition to the influx of Belgian refugees, thousands of soldiers were billeted in Buxton and 'brought the war very near'.[32] At Easter 1915, the nuns were asked to give up one of their properties in Buxton, for use as a 'study house' for English officers, and for six months their High Croft property was occupied by between two and ten lieutenants.[33] In 1917, the nuns offered to take in Sisters from other religious congregations for respite. These were nuns who 'were suffering from nerve strain caused by dreadful "Air Raids" that they had been in'.[34] The community found themselves caring for nuns who 'had witnessed some awful sights and had experiences that seldom fall to creature's lot'.[35] The Presentation Annalist recorded regretfully 'several of them after improving here went back home to face [the] same again perhaps [on the] first or second night of return'.[36]

The Presentation Sisters in Glossop also provided accommodation for those who needed it during the War.[37] In 1917 for example, a sister of Sr Aloysius, Mrs Stuart, was granted permission to stay in the convent in

Glossop as 'her husband had joined the army' and as a result she had been living alone in Manchester.[38] Mrs Stuart remained with the Presentation community in Glossop until early spring 1918, when her health improved and she found suitable lodgings which enabled her to return to Manchester.[39] While the First World War officially came to an end in November 1918, food shortages and an increase in the cost of living meant that rationing remained in place for much of 1919.

## Expansion in England after the First World War

Though the War had exhausted the efforts of civilians and nuns alike, it did not stop convent expansion. A Presentation foundation, greatly influenced by the work of Fr Albert Power SJ, was established in Pickering, in 1919. In 1918, he had produced several widely circulated leaflets, marking the bicentenary of the birth of Nano Nagle.[40] One of the leaflets came to the attention of a London man, Mr Edward Eyre. He was a close friend of Fr Edward Bryan, parish priest of a struggling Catholic mission in Pickering, North Yorkshire.[41] According to the Annals of the Presentation Convent, Pickering, Fr Bryan had been for some time 'vainly striving to introduce a small community of nuns into his parish to take charge of a small day school and a proposed orphanage'.[42] Edward Eyre suggested to Bryan to bring a group of Presentation Sisters to assist on his mission in Pickering, and offered to contact a friend at the Presentation Convent, Galway. The Galway Sisters welcomed the invitation to go to Pickering. As usual, the final decision of how to live their lives was not in the women's own hands: the proposal was laid before their First Superior, Bishop of Galway, Most Rev Thomas O'Dea. Negotiations ensued between the Bishop of Galway, the Bishop of Middlesbrough, Most Rev Dr Lacey and Rev Fr Bryan. An agreement was reached that £200 per annum be granted to the Sisters in the proposed Pickering foundation, as well as a workable school and convent with spacious grounds.[43] Mother Stanislaus Downing, Sr M. Augustine Maume and Sr Gerard O'Connor, were selected to take charge of the foundation.[44]

On 16 March 1919, Mother Stanislaus, Sr M. Augustine and Sr Gerard left Galway and made their way to 'alien soil'.[45] They sailed from Dun Laoghaire, travelling through North Wales and 'past the great industrial centres of Lancashire' before arriving in Leeds where they rested overnight in the convent of the Sisters of the Immaculate Conception. The following day, Mother Stanislaus and her two companions completed the final phase of their journey and arrived in Pickering. A grim situation awaited them in the little Yorkshire town:

> A pipe had burst that day – the weather was intensely cold and a plank provided a dry crossing over a stream of water in the hall … as preparation for their coming, a tray laid on an up-turned box on which were three cups and saucers and plates, three hard boiled eggs and three apples. Very desolate and uninviting everything looked …[46]

The nuns, however, had brought some food supplies from Ireland, recognising that 'rationing was still in force in England'.[47] Rationing was the least of their worries; they needed to ready themselves to start running a mission that was new for Presentations: a war orphanage. Fr Bryan had asked them to run a home for daughters of soldiers who were killed in the War.[48] However, the nuns quickly discovered that the orphanage 'did not exist – except in name'.[49] Four months would pass before the first orphan children were placed in their care. On 2 July 1919, three young girls, Ivy, Lily and Nellie Fisher, arrived from London.[50] Three days later they were joined by another young girl, Maeve Scott-Allen, and in September 1919 'Mrs Fisher came bringing her fourth and eldest child, Daisy'.[51] The number of orphan children had grown to six by the end of January 1920, when a little girl from Derbyshire, Margaret Gibbons, was left with the nuns. In May 1921, three more girls arrived: Lily and Annie Wilkes from Hammersmith and Mary Shephard from Newcastle.[52] During the early days, the orphanage was supported by the Duchess of Norfolk, Lady Sykes and Lady Mary Saville. An additional allowance was provided by the government for the direct care of the orphans.[52] The Sisters were required to provide monthly accounts and statements concerning the upkeep of the home to the War Charity organisation for inspection.[54]

Although the convent and the orphanage were running smoothly, tensions soon emerged between the Sisters and their superior, Fr Bryan. The priest was parsimonious in his support of the nuns and the children, complaining about the costs of feeding them. He refused to admit two sets of orphan children to the home and had complained to the London Committee that he had been required to 'sell his furniture to feed the nuns'.[55] The nuns accounted for Fr Bryan's poor behaviour as a form of 'mental aberration', but continued to struggle to survive on his support, which never exceeded £5 – an amount which he expected 'to go a long way'.[56] Bryan claimed he had 'fed 40 boys on a shilling', but the nuns dismissed this, saying that the meals he gave the children must have been 'of the Oliver Twist variety'.[57] In

1920, Fr Bryan decided to take matters into his own hands and, unknown to the Sisters, transferred guardianship of the orphan children to himself.[58] He was required to have the signature of one Presentation Sister in order to complete the transfer, but instead 'brought the pension papers to the master of the non-Catholic Grammar School' and managed to get the necessary authorisation.[59]

On 23 June 1920, the Sisters were visited by the chairman of the London Committee, Mr George Coldwell. Mr Coldwell had been appointed to travel to Pickering, investigate the claims made by Fr Bryan, and to examine the day-to-day operation and governance of the orphanage, including its funds. In the course of his investigations, Mr Coldwell found that Fr Bryan had been 'very unreasonable', and concluded that the nuns were like 'three poor children in a penitentiary'.[60] The difficulties were put before the Vicar General and other sympathetic Catholic clergy, including Canon O'Connell and Fr McKenna, but there was little practical advice offered other than to give up the foundation and orphanage in its entirety.[61] This, however, was rejected by the Sisters. Unsurprisingly, the relationship between Fr Bryan and the Presentation Sisters further deteriorated. The Annals note that the priest 'had got rather tired of the Sisters as they could not carry out his impractical schemes – which often bordered on proselytising. He made several covert plans to get them out of the parish but with Irish grit they determined to stay'.[62]

The three nuns remained in the house which had been provided for them by Fr Bryan on their arrival in 1919 until May 1931. By then, the First World War had been over for more than a decade and the war orphanage had become a 'thing of the past'.[63] The Sisters left in order to take possession of Westgate House, a property granted to them by a non-Catholic, Mr E. Cossins.[64] Even though the new house was small, the women were grateful to have their 'own property at last'.[65]

During the inter-war years, the Presentation Sisters in Britain tried to return to some level of normality, continuing in their mission of providing education. New foundations were established in Matlock (1927), South Kirkby (1933), Crowle (1935) and New Moston (1938). Matlock, the first of these foundations, had an unusual genesis: it was founded to supply missionaries to India. The Presentation mission in India had been established in 1842, and throughout the nineteenth century the community of Presentation Sisters in India evolved and flourished. By the turn of the twentieth century there were fifteen active houses of the Order. The success of the Presentation Sisters in India depended on a continuous flow of young, female postulants from

Ireland and England. Some of the largest supporters of the Indian missions were the communities in Rahan and Limerick.[66] However, the outbreak of the First World War had a considerable impact on the recruitment and training of Sisters for the Indian missions. Travel restrictions disrupted the usual crossings between Ireland and England, and the supply of new Sisters to India suffered.

When the War ended in 1918, the Presentation Sisters in India decided to establish a novitiate in Ireland, for the sole purpose of providing a direct supply of postulants to the Indian missions. However, owing to the unsettled political climate which persisted in Ireland from 1916 to 1923 it was decided that the novitiate would be better situated in England.[67] On 18 May 1919, Rev Mother Berchmans Murphy accompanied by Sr M. Teresa Anderson, left India aboard the SS *Rewa* and sailed for London, England.[68] Shortly after their arrival, Mother Berchmans was approached by an old friend, Rev Fr Rawcliffe, who had previously spent some time in Madras and was anxious that a branch of the Order be established in his diocese in Liverpool.[69] Permission was sought from the Archbishop of Liverpool, Most Rev Dr Whiteside, to found the proposed novitiate in Wavertree. Dr Whiteside consented but only on condition that the Sisters would not attempt to open a school in addition to the novitiate.[70] The proposal was subsequently put before the Sisters in Madras, who approved the foundation and promised to offer assistance wherever they could.[71] Mother Berchmans then set about trying to locate a house which could serve as a convent and novitiate. A property close to the Redemptorist monastery in Wavertree became available some time in 1919. The house, known as Etonfield, was large and could accommodate the needs of the Presentation Sisters, but the asking price was £6,000, a significant sum for any potential buyer in post-war England. Negotiations ensued and the property was eventually obtained by the nuns at the considerably reduced price of £3,250.[72] On 21 November 1919, Mother Berchmans took up her new position as Mistress of Novices in Etonfield.[73] Eight postulants from Ireland, and one from Liverpool, entered on this date.[74]

The early days of the novitiate in Liverpool were difficult. Almost all of the money which the Sisters had raised was put towards buying Etonfield, so there was nothing left to buy furniture or other necessities. The novitiate had no school, and the nuns were obliged to depend on whatever funds could be sent from India.[75] A small knitting industry was established in the novitiate where the postulants regularly mended socks for the Redemptorist fathers at just two pence a pair.[76] The financial situation had improved little by the time the Rev Mother General of the recently amalgamated houses of South India and Liverpool, Mother Xavier Murphy, arrived on her first visitation in 1926.[77] Mother Xavier decided that the novitiate could not continue in Liverpool and should be transferred to another location in England. Her preference was that the novitiate be moved to an area where the community could support themselves through work in schools. She also wanted novices to be close to a university where they could get higher education and teacher training.[78]

While she was in Etonfield, Mother Xavier received numerous requests to found convents, from various parts of England. They included an appeal from Fr Cossins, parish priest of Matlock, Derbyshire, who wanted a group of Presentations to run a school in his locality.[79] At the time, there was no Catholic school in Matlock and Catholic children were required to attend non-Catholic schools or enrol in Catholic boarding schools.[80] Mother Xavier recognised that this invitation might be the answer to her prayers. In March 1927, she and Mother Berchmans travelled to Matlock, to look at some potential properties for the new novitiate. Fr Cossins showed them a house which he believed could serve as both convent and novitiate, but Mother Xavier disagreed. Finally, she settled on an alternative property, Chesterfield House, for the convent, novitiate and school. Chesterfield House was an ex-hydro situated on approximately twelve acres.[81] It was well furnished and consisted of 120 rooms.[82] The property in Matlock was purchased for £12,000 on 19 March 1927.[83] Etonfield was later sold for £6,750, and £5,850 was put towards the debt on Chesterfield House.[84] On 24 May 1927, the novitiate was transferred from Liverpool to Matlock.[85] The new community consisted of eleven Sisters, postulants and novices.[86] Mother Cecilia Murphy was appointed Superioress, and Mother Berchmans continued as Mistress of Novices.[87]

One of the reasons for transferring the novitiate from Liverpool to Matlock was that the Sisters would have the space to operate a fee-charging school so that they could be self-supporting, and they were given permission to do this. So, while the Sisters continued in their founding mission to provide education to the poor in Matlock, they also opened a boarding school for the daughters of prosperous families.[88] Mount St Joseph's was the first Presentation boarding school in England.[89] It opened on 18 September 1927, with approximately thirty pupils (boarders and day students) enrolled.[90]

It was expected that the boarding school would also supply vocations and thus help support the novitiate. But the number of pupils entering the novitiate was small: between 1927 and 1939, only six past pupils became

Presentations.[91] The nuns realised that the success of the school spoiled the success of the novitiate: 'the convent became a scene of absorbing activity which was out of harmony with the recollection that a preparation for the religious life requires'.[92] Not only was the school absorbed by worldly interests, but the novitiate was not sufficiently secluded, and by 1933 this had become a concern for Mother Xavier.

Fr McNiff, parish priest of South Kirkby in Yorkshire, provided a solution. He invited the Presentation Sisters in Matlock to establish a foundation in South Kirkby, where the Sisters would have a convent and would go out to provide instruction in the local parish school.[93] The priest had also promised that the Sisters would assume complete control of the school upon the death or resignation of the current headmistress.[94] This invitation suited the nuns, as it meant that they could move their novitiate from the Matlock convent to the new Yorkshire convent, which was located in an environment conducive to preparation for religious life. In August 1933, negotiations commenced for the purchase of a site, known as 'the Grove', to serve as convent and novitiate in South Kirkby.[95] In the meantime, Mother Xavier applied to Rome for permission to once again transfer the novitiate.[96] In August, the Grove was purchased for £1,800.[97] Sanction to transfer the novitiate was granted by the Holy See and in September 1933 the new convent in South Kirkby was finally opened.[98] Mother Berchmans was again appointed Mistress of Novices, and had the care of eight postulants.[99] A period of stability and growth was established, though the routine and regularity of convent and school life was disrupted when, from September 1939, the country was at war once again.

## English Presentation Convents during the Second World War

With the onset of the Second World War, the nuns at all of the convents adapted to wartime measures. Blackouts were imposed across England and air-raid and bomb shelters were constructed in the event of an attack. The Sisters in Matlock recorded that they were required to fit out all the windows in the convent and school with blackout blinds, the cost of which amounted to more than £100.[100] In October of the same year, an 'underground reinforced concrete air-raid shelter was constructed … and was fully equipped with electric light, central heating, sleeping bunks, etc.' at a total cost of £1,400.[101] In February 1940, the Matlock community were obliged to make further wartime provisions with the erection of a 'covered entrance from the main school building to the air-raid shelter' which cost them an additional £100.[102]

For many of the Presentation communities in England at this time, the reality of the war was inescapable. The Buxton Annals record the Sisters' reactions to the first air raid that they experienced:

On ... the early morning of June 25 [1940] the Sisters were awakened at 1 am by the ... moaning of an air-raid signal. They all repaired to the cellar of the convent and spent their time saying the rosary and other prayers until [the] 'All Clear' siren was sounded at 2:15 am. This was the first touch of war we had experienced apart from the food rationing. It was a dreadful experience ...[103]

Similarly, the Sisters in Pickering 'had many alerts and alarms but the only bomb fell in Middleton, a mile away and did no damage in Pickering though the noise was terrifying'.[104]

Numerous fund-raising activities were organised to help support the war effort in England, and the nuns became involved whenever possible, staging little dramatic productions to raise money, and encouraging the children to save towards War Weapons Week. According to the Annals of the Presentation Sisters in Buxton, 1941, 'This war is requiring a great amount of money and the towns and villages in England are doing their best to supply as much as possible'.[105] Local fund-raising campaigns such as Warship Week and War Weapons Week were organised to help generate large sums for specific wartime activities, personnel and equipment. For example, the town of Benfleet held a War Weapons Week between 31 May and 6 June 1941 with the hope of realising £40,000 for 'two bombers'.[106] A leaflet advertising the campaign contained the slogan: 'Better cash in than crash in'.[107] The Presentation communities throughout England regularly participated in such fund-raising campaigns. For example, in March 1941, the Presentation Sisters in Matlock organised that the children attending their school would perform a variety show, the proceeds of which were to go to 'Matlock's War Weapons Week fund'.[108] A War Weapons Week was also organised in Buxton from 1 to 10 May 1941 and according to the Buxton Sisters 'all the schools are taking part in encouraging themselves to put all they possibly can into the war savings'.[109] The Presentation elementary school, which at the time of the War Weapons Week had 150 pupils enrolled, raised a total of £1,777.[110] The Annalist noted that they raised more funds than any of the other schools in Buxton but 'it meant a great deal of labour for the Sisters engaged in the school'.[111] The Presentation school in Glossop also participated in the War Weapons Week between 21 and 31 May 1941.[112]

During the War, children were regularly evacuated from areas of danger, usually from the larger cities such as London and Liverpool, and transferred to locations where the threat of bombing and air raids was less immediate. Anyone who had the means to provide accommodation for evacuee children was required to assist in this wartime measure. The Presentations in Pickering were 'obliged to take six little evacuee children from Hull – three sets of two cousins each – good Catholics and no trouble'.[113] They also took in a brother and sister, Arthur and Angela Watson.[114] As the Sisters had already operated an orphanage, it is not surprising that evacuee children were put in their care. However, in 1943 the Sisters were presented with a request of a different kind when their dentist, Mr Walker, petitioned them to take his two young girls and teach them. Mr Walker's daughters had been attending a convent day school in Scarborough but, owing to the dangers and unpredictability of the war, he had become concerned for their safety.[115] At this time the nuns in Pickering had neither the facilities, equipment nor accommodation in their present property at Westgate House to start a school. Walker persisted with his appeal and 'asked for nothing' except what the Sisters 'could do for the girls'.[116] The nuns finally consented, slowly building a little school:

> Only the one room – our parlour. As younger children came we had to use our small refectory/community room as a classroom clearing away for our meals. Then the only other available room at the back was taken into use and eventually we had to rent a large room which was part of the Church Hall for the older girls. There were many inconveniences and no place for the children to play.[117]

In Buxton, the community took in nuns from other congregations who required respite, just as they had done during the First World War. In the summer of 1941, ten Sisters of Mercy from Derby, two Franciscan Sisters from Belper and one Sister of Mercy from Oldham stayed at the convent for varying periods between one, two and three weeks: 'They were mostly suffering from the effects of the war the Sisters of Mercy having experienced a few bombing raids.'[118]

The First and Second World Wars certainly had an impact on the lives of the Presentation Sisters in Britain. General wartime measures, such as having to construct air-raid shelters and hang blackouts, as well as coping with food rationing and inflation, all had an effect on the communities of Presentations. However, the nuns were also facing new challenges and responsibilities from a very different part of the world: India.

## Britain, Ireland, and the Presentation Mission to India

The Presentation foundation at South Kirkby initially served the needs of the Presentation Order in recruiting and training Sisters for the Indian missions. However, following the outbreak of the Second World War, the viability of South Kirkby as the central novitiate for the amalgamated houses of South India came into question. As had been the case during the First World War, it became increasingly difficult to recruit postulants and send them to the Presentation missions of Madras and George Town. The novitiate was heavily reliant on Irish women entering in order to then go to India, but this practice had become unsustainable during the War. According to the Annals of the Presentation Convent, Castleconnell, the difficulty was twofold. Firstly, 'it was impossible for Sisters from England to come to Éire in quest of postulants' and secondly, 'no communities wished to bring young girls from the safety of neutral Éire to war-ridden England'.[119] The Presentation Sisters in India could see that the number of postulants entering the novitiate in South Kirkby was gradually declining and there would soon be a shortage of trained Sisters ready and able to assist them in their schools.[120]

In 1943, Mother Teresa Moore, Mother General of the amalgamated houses of South India and England, wrote to the superiors of South Kirkby and Matlock and asked them to investigate acquiring a new location for the novitiate in Ireland.[121] Even though invitations from Catholic clergy had been a regular feature in the development of many Presentation convents throughout Ireland and England, when the Sisters tried to find a suitable location for their novitiate they were met with 'polite refusal[s]'.[122] Many bishops objected on the grounds that in 'recent years so many religious foundations had been made in their diocese that they could not admit another'.[123] A failed attempt at securing a suitable property in the diocese of Kilmore in Autumn 1944 caused the Presentation Sisters to abandon all hope of relocating the novitiate to the east or broader midlands of the country.[124] In February 1945, the petition was forwarded to five further bishops in Ireland, including the Bishop of Killaloe, Most Reverend Dr Fogarty.[125]

On 2 March 1945, the Presentation community in Matlock received the following reply from the Bishop of Killaloe, telling them that he fully sympathised with their 'desire to secure a collecting house in Ireland in the hope of thus getting more postulants … to meet the big demands of [the] mission in India.'[126] He agreed to allow them to establish a convent but limited the role of the novitiate to a 'collecting house' where they would gather aspirants and postulants together. They could not run a full novitiate, with training towards profession. Dr Fogarty suggested that a suitable property might be found in Castleconnell, Co. Limerick, and recommended a property known as 'The Island'. In May 1945, Rev Mother Michael Lawlor arrived in Ireland to inspect various properties.[127] All proved unsuitable and Mother Michael decided to travel to Castleconnell to inspect The Island for herself. On her journey she noticed a large house with spacious grounds which she believed would suit the needs of the Sisters. On discovering that the house had been recently sold to an Englishman, Captain Dixon, she had an offer made to the captain.[128] He accepted the offer, and the house, known as Woodlands, was bought for £3,000 in June 1945.[129]

Now that a house had been secured, all the Sisters had to do was convince the Bishop to extend his original offer of a 'collecting house', or aspirancy, to a full novitiate. In a letter to Mother Liguori, dated 24 July 1945, Dr Fogarty finally consented to the establishment of a novitiate in Castleconnell.[130] Mother Victoire Carroll and Mother Michael Lawlor were appointed to lead the new foundation in Castleconnell. On 21 September 1945, they left England via Holyhead; on arrival in Ireland they spent a number of weeks travelling the country securing vocations for the new novitiate.[131] The Sisters finally arrived in Castleconnell on 29 October 1945 and the novitiate was formally opened on 21 November.[132] Mother Michael was appointed Superior and Mother Victoire, Mistress of Novices.[133] The new novitiate would connect the British Presentation convents with both Ireland and India in new ways in the decades that followed.

## The Legacy of the Presentation Sisters in England

Though the Presentations, like other Catholic congregations, managed to run schools in nineteenth and twentieth-century England, they did so against hostility and occasional direct resistance. For example, the 'no popery' publications which were widely circulated during the nineteenth century did much to sway popular opinion against Catholic religious and institutions. This movement was particularly critical of female religious and their convent schools. Pamphlets and information leaflets, which sought to caution against the threat of convent education in English society, were regularly disseminated. Protestant parents were warned against convent schools: 'You may be compelling your children to practise that polluted form of worship at which you yourself shudder. You may be leading them to the very brow of the precipice which overhangs the gulf of hell.'[134] The 'no popery' movement was emotive and it is, therefore, not surprising that when the Presentation Sisters first arrived in Livesey Street in 1836, they were received with suspicion. As the Annalist recorded, they were the 'objects of a vast amount of curiosity and many droll remarks were made about them'.[135] The only way that the nuns could dispel any misconceptions was by leaving the convent and school open for anyone who wished to see 'that a convent was not really what the world said it was'.[136]

Discourses of anti-Catholic prejudice remained a constant feature of the lives of the Sisters in England. When the Presentation Sisters from Manchester first assumed responsibility for their new foundation in Buxton in 1898 it was noted that, 'The spirit of the town was supposed to be anti-Catholic and many of the best Catholics and their friends thought the nuns would never succeed on that account'.[137] However, despite any existing prejudice, the Presentations experienced the support of many non-Catholics. Soon after the Sisters arrived in Buxton, they were greeted by a Protestant woman who was extremely anxious that her children, and those of her sister, would be permitted entry to their school. She had heard a rumour that the Sisters 'would not receive Protestant children into the school' and came to see 'if this was correct' as she and her sister had seven children between them, 'and they were most anxious for them to be with the nuns'.[138] Similarly, when the Galway Sisters established the foundation in Pickering they were received by 'friendly Protestants'.[139] Miss Riley, a non-Catholic, was noted for being 'extremely kind and helpful' towards the community in Pickering.[140]

Women religious were recognised by the Catholic clergy in England for their important contribution to evangelisation during the restoration of the church. The Catholic hierarchy believed that nuns, through teaching and instruction, could promote a strong religious devotion. However, it was precisely this evangelical role that evoked anti-Catholic prejudice from the Protestant population. The authors of 'no popery' publications argued that the works of charity carried out by nuns were merely cover for proselytism. The Protestant poor were deemed particularly susceptible to the influence of Catholic female religious; one writer claimed that 'by the gift of free dinners, gifts of clothes, in addition to free schooling, the Protestant poor are bribed to send their children to RC schools'.[141]

What won the confidence of many non-Catholics was the way that Presentation nuns alleviated the lot of the poor. In Manchester, the Presentation Sisters recorded that 1842 was a particularly difficult year for the inhabitants of the city as 'thousands of men were out of work'. The Presentation Sisters noted that their 'poor children frequently fainted at school from want and weakness' and consequently they decided to feed them 'at dinner hour and there was never a morsel left. They were only too glad to get anything to eat.'[142] Again, in December 1878, 'between thirty and forty poor children received dinner every day for seven–eight weeks at the expense of the community.'[143] In Buxton, the children attending the Presentation convent school were presented with prayer books and rosary beads 'in memory of their first day under the care of the nuns.'[144] The Sisters initially intended to give the gifts to the Catholic pupils only. However, they recorded that 'the Protestant children looked so disappointed that they too received them' but only on condition that they return the objects of devotion should their parents object.[145] At the school, the Protestant pupil intake surpassed that of the Catholic children attending the Presentation school. On the first day of school in April 1898 it was recorded that forty-eight children were enrolled: twenty-three Catholics and twenty-five Protestants. In April 1908, the Annalist noted: 'During that time some 568 children had passed through the school, half of them Protestants, but many are leading good edifying lives and often come to see the Sisters and some may in time become Catholics.'[146] While the Presentation Sisters were happy when some of their former pupils converted to Catholicism, this was not central to their mission in Buxton.

The Victorian convent school was religious in character, and instruction reflected traditional ideals of femininity, and reinforced notions of how to be a good wife and mother. Young girls were taught to be 'Good Catholic women, strong in faith, faithful in virtue.'[147] Consequently, the curriculum offered in convent schools generally included basic instruction in the 'three Rs', religion and some form of practical training such as sewing or knitting. From 1890, for example, the young women and girls attending the Presentation night school in Manchester, in addition to religious and secular instruction, received education in cooking and laundry.[148] While this type of convent school curriculum was undoubtedly limited, the general consensus was that it was considered sufficient for the time.[149] In any case, convent schools were voluntary and were often the only form of schooling available to the public in an otherwise largely inadequate education system.

From the 1830s, voluntary schools had been accepted by parliament as a recognised instrument in the provision and delivery of elementary education.[150] Grant aid was awarded to voluntary school bodies in 1833 and from 1839 those in receipt of the funding were subject to council inspection. However, State involvement in education outside the remit of direct funding was limited and there was no universal system of elementary education. Moreover, there existed no single government agency or specifically appointed personnel to oversee educational practices, ensure efficient standards of instruction or implement a common, core curriculum and syllabus. Between 1833 and 1870, piecemeal reforms were implemented by the government in order to address some of the inherent practical and financial difficulties associated with the English education system.[151] Despite the fear among the Catholic hierarchy of the growing secularisation of schooling in England, the Presentation Sisters regularly adapted to and implemented changes in accordance with official regulations. For example, in July 1849 the community at Livesey Street recorded 'a great change being made in the plans of the education of the poor. The government was paying great attention to it and various methods had been adopted to obtain a quick and attractive way of conveying knowledge to the children; plan of teaching in the school was changed and improved a little.'[152]

In 1850, the Presentation school in Livesey Street was placed under government inspection. According to the community Annals, 'A grant for books and maps was accepted from the government for the schools and pupil teachers were appointed to assist the Sisters in teaching the poor children.'[153] Thereafter, the Presentation school in Livesey Street was to be subject to an annual inspection by an appointed government official and 'classes of school to be examined by him also.'[154] Under this grant-aid system, the Presentation convent school was expected to conform to a more secularised curriculum and extend subjects to include history, geography, grammar, art, science and political economy.[155] From the time the Sisters assumed responsibility for the provision of education in Buxton in 1898, the school was listed for government inspection. During the twentieth century, this trend of becoming 'recognised as efficient' by the British government was adopted by subsequent Presentation foundations including Pickering (1928), Matlock (1937), and Ryde (1964).

Following the passing of the Education Act 1870, government inspections of state-aided schools were conducted by School Boards and from 1902 by Local Education Authorities. The reports produced by these committees provide evidence of the specific educational work undertaken by the Presentation Sisters while also highlighting their interest in offering a broader curriculum and more efficient instruction. In 1901, for example, the inspector's review of the instruction provided by the Presentation Sisters in Buxton indicated that 'The children are in excellent order and have been carefully taught.'[156] Similarly, in 1902, the inspector recorded that 'The attainments in the various subjects of instruction are quite satisfactory. Needlework is marked good' while in 1903 order, discipline and instruction were described 'for the most part' as 'highly creditable.'[157] By the 1920s, the inspections undertaken by the local education committees had become increasingly detailed. The report on the Presentation convent school, Livesey Street, in 1925 concluded:

> The girls in this school are mannerly and responsive. Their clean and tidy appearance calls for special attention … the work as a whole is commendable … Reading and articulation are remarkably good throughout the school … Their written composition gives evidence of careful and thorough teaching … Writing and spelling are good … Their singing is first rate.[158]

Throughout the nineteenth century, the Catholic Church in England was committed to retaining uncontested responsibility for the education of Catholic children. When the Presentation Sisters in Livesey Street first submitted to government inspection in 1850, 'It was decided by the Catholic bishops that the gentleman appointed to inspect Catholic schools must be one approved by the Poor School Committee and a Catholic of course.'[159] Despite, the increasing secularisation of elementary education, the Catholic hierarchy were determined to slow down the process. To this end, in 1856, during a synod of Catholic bishops, it was decided that 'each diocese should have an ecclesiastical inspector to test the advancement of religious training in each school, in order that it might keep pace with the increase of secular knowledge required by government.'[160] According to the Annals of the Presentation community in Livesey Street, not all of the clergy agreed with this movement and 'there were some who endeavoured to persuade the nuns that "to have an inspection of the religious teaching in their schools would be to submit themselves to great insult and infringe their rights".'[161] Nonetheless, the Sisters submitted to the annual religious inspection.

The religious inspection reports provide further evidence of the competence of the Sisters in providing instruction. Though the Presentation Sisters had only been in Buxton since late April 1898, the pupils attending the school were examined for the first time in November of that year. According to the religious inspection report carried out by Rev Fr French:

> This school has made the most wonderful progress. The greatest credit is due to the manager and teachers. The children are bright and seem to take a great interest in their religion. I have never seen a school that has made such progress in so short a time. The new teachers (nuns) have only been here six months. An excellent and most satisfactory report.[162]

Similar reports were made on the Presentation school in Livesey Street. In December 1915 for example, the chief religious inspector reported that 'The examination of this large girls' school proved that the children are being conscientiously taught the knowledge and trained in the practice of our Holy Religion. The other inspectors who assisted me with the examination expressed themselves as highly pleased with the children's answers. Evidently the school is in good hands.'[163] Five years later, in July 1920, the religious inspector claimed that 'All the standards were excellent', while the assistant examiner noted that 'the juniors were a credit to their teacher'.[164]

A further indication of the proficiency of the Presentations in education was evidenced in the rapid growth of their schools. When the Presentation Sisters commenced their school in Manchester in 1836 approximately 100 girls were admitted on the first day.[165] By May 1912, the average daily attendance stood at 555 while by 1935 the number of registered pupils had decreased only slightly to 525. In Buxton, forty-eight children were present on the first day of school in April 1898. With the arrival of Belgian refugees during the First World War the number increased to 149 and by 1958 there were 180 on the roll.[166] In March 1904, the nuns in the Glossop community recorded that in spite of the early difficulties of their foundation, they were consoled by the fact that 'the people and the children seemed to appreciate their labours and the attendance at school kept up'.[167] The Presentation boarding school in Matlock, which opened in 1927 with approximately thirty pupils, also thrived. Owing to the continuous rise in the number of boarders attending the school, extensions and improvements were carried out on the grounds in 1934 and again in 1937.[168] On the opening of the Presentation school in Ryde, Isle of Wight in September 1948, forty-eight pupils were present and within three years there were 150 pupils attending the school.[169]

In addition to teaching children, the nuns also prepared their pupils to become monitors and pupil teachers. The monitorial system emerged in England in the nineteenth century to provide mass education. The system included training older pupils to teach those 'who knew less', through drilling, and rote learning. This type of instruction was adopted by many Presentation communities, not just in England, but in their international schools. In an effort to promote a more unified and higher standard of instruction among school monitors, the British government introduced funding in 1847. Thereafter, pupil teachers or apprentices were appointed to replace the traditional school monitor. The Presentation Sisters in Livesey Street responded to this change, and from 1850 they appointed pupil teachers 'to assist the Sisters in teaching the poor children'. According to the Annals, 'pupil teachers were to receive a salary and a higher degree of education than [what was] formerly' available to them.[170] Similarly, in 1905 the Presentation Sisters in Buxton were permitted by their local bishop to take 'boarders desirous of becoming teachers' and to prepare them for 'government examinations'.[171]

The nuns developed a reputation for being skilled teachers, and they adapted to educational demands. Their success in teaching was partly due to the schooling that many of them had received in Presentation schools in Ireland, before entering for the English foundations. Furthermore, many of the nuns received formal training in England's teaching universities. Teacher training colleges were first established by Catholic religious in England in 1856, when the Notre Dame de Namur Sisters opened their institution in Liverpool. Other State-recognised teacher training colleges were founded by the Faithful Companions of Jesus, the Religious of the Sacred Heart, and La Sainte Union des Sacrés Coeurs. During the nineteenth and early twentieth centuries, these women's religious congregations were the main providers of Catholic female third-level education in England and the Presentation Order routinely enrolled their Sisters in these teacher training colleges. As early as 1863, the convent Annalist in Livesey Street recorded: 'We had the pleasure of a visit from Sr Mary of Saint Paul, principal of the Training College Liverpool. Ever since our teachers had gone to college to complete their educational training, a friendship sprang up between the two convents.'[172]

By the early twentieth century, it seems that holding a recognised teacher qualification was paramount for the work of the Order. When the Presentation Sisters first made their foundation in Glossop in 1904 they had not enough trained Sisters to staff the school. It was, therefore, decided that just two Sisters could be spared from the Buxton community and that a secular mistress would be engaged until 'one of the Sisters obtained a certificate'.[173] The Buxton community Annals noted that a new government regulation had been introduced in 1909 which required that every school have 'at least one trained teacher on the staff'.[174] There is no doubt that this regulation led to an increase in the number of Presentation Sisters attending college. Immediately following the announcement, the community in Buxton decided to send Sr Dominic to the Faithful Companions of Jesus' training college at Sedgley Park, Prestwich, to earn her teaching certificate.[175] On completion of her training in 1911, Sr Dominic was sent to Glossop, where she took up duty as headmistress, and Sr Mary Aloysius was subsequently enrolled in Sedgley Park so that she too could undertake her formal teacher training.[176] By operating this way, the convent could ensure that steady planning for the training of nuns would continue.

Following the commencement of the foundation in Matlock in 1927, Presentation Sisters regularly enrolled members of their community for degrees and for teacher-training programmes. In July 1931, Sr Mary Victoire O'Carroll completed her degree in history at Manchester University. A year later, she was awarded an MA honours degree from the same university. In 1933, Sr Mary Patrick was sent to Croydon Montessori College to complete her training in the teachers' handicraft diploma. Similarly, in January 1937, Sr Mary Perpetua undertook a Montessori course in London, and 'in July of the same year she was awarded a First Class Honours Teacher's Diploma for Montessori'.[177] Despite the outbreak of the Second World War in 1939, the Sisters continued to train for their teaching qualifications. In 1940, Sr Mary Regis was admitted to Sedgley Park for her two years' teacher training. In 1942, 'Sr Mary Liguori was awarded the Oxford Teacher's Diploma by the University of Oxford' and in 1944, Sr Mary Christine completed her MA in Sheffield University.[178]

Despite facing anti-Catholic prejudice when they arrived in Manchester in 1836, the pioneering Sisters built a reputation as skilled and capable teachers. While expansion during the nineteenth century was slow, the twentieth century brought new opportunities for development. Notwithstanding the challenges of the First and Second World Wars, and continuous reform within the English education system, the Presentations continued to flourish in Britain, so that by the late 1950s, they had seventeen branches operating throughout the country.

CHAPTER 10

# The Global Reach of Presentation Education

*… my schools are beginning to be of service to a great many parts of the world.*

–Nano Nagle to Miss Fitzsimons, 17 July 1769.

## Entering to Leave: Mission Contexts in America, Australia and India

Nineteenth-century Ireland witnessed a dramatic growth in the power of the Catholic Church, while also witnessing famine, large-scale emigration, and political and agrarian unrest. Many historians have researched the histories of Irish women, in an attempt not only to understand their experiences but also to place them within the wider narratives of Irish history, and women's history. But much work still needs to be done to interrogate ways in which Irish women engaged with their faith during this period, including their participation in vowed religious life, in Catholic schooling, and in the rapidly expanding global mission field. The Presentation Sisters were playing a central role in the development of female education in Ireland by the second half of the nineteenth century, while also expanding their network of convents and providing women with an alternative to marriage and motherhood.

Presentations were also part of the landscape of education in countries to which Irish Catholics emigrated, and countries which had been identified as mission territories by Propaganda Fide.[1] Though the Presentations were not a 'missionary' order founded for the purpose of evangelisation, they often worked with non-Catholic communities. However, their explicit mission was the education of the poor, and as they began to make foundations outside

Ireland they frequently found themselves serving the Irish Catholic diaspora. Some Sisters went overseas, having gained many years of experience in Ireland; for example, Sr M. Aloysius Neville, who led a group to Madras (Chennai) from Presentation Convent, Maynooth, in 1844, was in her early forties and had twenty years of experience.[2] On the other hand, Margaret McCarthy, who entered the congregation at the unusually young age of fourteen, was professed Sr M. Angela two years later in the Cathedral in Madras; her mission began at once, and she spent thirty-four years in Presentation education in Madras, and served two terms as Superior.[3]

In nineteenth-century Ireland, single or widowed women who had either modest means or an education that made them suitable to work as teaching Sisters, could consider entering religious life in one of the growing number of convents, and live out their lives in Ireland. These are the women whose lives can be traced – albeit faintly – in the registers, annals and necrologies of the convents where they worked. Less is known about nuns who served the Irish overseas, by following their migration routes and setting up schools in towns and cities in America and Australia. Many women who entered religious life in Ireland left their home country almost at once, with no expectation of ever returning. During the nineteenth century, emigration would become so commonplace that the destiny of missionary nuns was probably more secure than that of women who had to turn to emigration societies to find a job or a husband. Emigration schemes sent between 250,000 and 300,000 Irish to America in the nineteenth century, and close to a quarter of a million Irish to Australia between 1836 and 1919.[4]

These schemes were developed in part as a response to famine, and also to 'remove the surplus population' that had resulted in unemployment, overcrowded homesteads and agrarian lawlessness.[5] For example, Nano Nagle's homeland, the Blackwater area of Munster, had the Peter Robinson Scheme, which was assisted by landowners such as Lords Doneraile, Mountcashel and Kingston.[6] To clear their estates of tenants, landlords helped in the recruitment and selection of applicants, whose passage and settlement they funded. Women often availed of female emigration schemes and public funding, such as Vere Foster's Irish Pioneer Immigration Fund, and the Women's Protective Immigration Society.[7] Other Irishwomen emigrated having scraped their passage together, or having been sent passage money by a relative, with the result that over three million Irishwomen left the country in the nineteenth century.[8]

Single women and female orphans were vulnerable from the moment they stepped on board ship, and many did not know what awaited them in their adoptive countries.[9] On the other hand nuns, along with single women who left the country to enter religious orders overseas, usually travelled in groups, and often had the protection of one or two priests. They were almost penniless, but had either contacts meeting them on arrival, or relatives in the convent communities that awaited them.[10] In many ways, their future was more promising than that of many single women emigrants. Although these nuns were viewed as missionaries rather than 'emigrants', they were nonetheless part of the mass exodus of Irish during the nineteenth century. It was in this context that Presentation nuns left Ireland to become teachers of Ireland's diaspora and the Catholic emigrant poor.

The Irish had been leaving Ireland in a steady stream from Nano Nagle's lifetime: over a million made their way to the United States and Canada between 1780 and 1845.[11] During and after the Famine, emigration increased dramatically, and patterns of emigration changed, with the number of women emigrants exceeding the number of men by the end of the century. Ireland was unique in this regard: 'no other major group of immigrants in American history contained so many women.'[12] Studies of female emigration from Ireland show that it was Nagle's homeland, Munster, which sent out the greatest number of women.[13] Between 1851 and 1910, a total of 713,905 women emigrated from Munster, out of a total female emigrant population of 2,011,802.[14] Some American cities, including New York, had more immigrant Irish women than Irish men. For example, Dubuque, Iowa, had 183 single Irish men and 317 single Irish women in 1860, and it had a further 98 Irish-born widows. Female-dominated Irish communities were not uncommon, not only because of the high number of Irish women immigrants, but because of the extremely high rate of fatal accidents amongst Irish men in hard labour and industrial work.[15] New York and Dubuque were just two cities in which Irish Presentation convents would flourish in the second half of the century, as Irish-born nuns taught the daughters of Irish immigrants, and fitted into 'female-dominated communities' with an ease that they had not always experienced at home.

The Presentations who arrived in San Francisco in 1854 also served the growing population of Irish Catholics. The gold discoveries of 1848–49 drew English, Italian, German and Irish immigrants across from the east coast, as well as from the mid-west. By 1880, the Irish-born were the most numerous of the immigrant population in San Francisco, accounting for 30,721 people, and there was an additional 43,000 second-generation Irish. The Catholic hierarchy knew that 'the most important institution acting to maintain the homogeneous Irish community was the Catholic Church.'[16] The provision of Catholic schooling, as an alternative to public schooling, was crucial, and it was also of major importance that Catholic religious were available to provide separate religious instruction for Catholics who attended non-denominational public schools. Though Catholic schools would never outnumber public schools, enrolments in schools run by the Sisters of Mercy, the Sisters of Notre Dame, and the Presentation Sisters reached several thousand in the 1880s, and they would expand significantly in the first half of the next century.

The nuns who went to Australia in the nineteenth century served a similar constituency as those who missioned in North America. While early migrants to the Australian colonies had been convicts shipped at a rate of about 1,000 a year in the 1820s and 1830s, by the second half of the nineteenth century most Irish arriving in Australia arrived either through assisted migration or they were attracted by the gold rush; in 1851–60, over 100,000 Irish arrived, and in the decades that followed the number of Irish immigrants remained high.[17] This did not come close to the number that had gone to America, but it nonetheless established a strong Irish presence and with that came the presence of the Catholic Church, with powerful Irish-born churchmen such as Bishop James Quinn of Brisbane, and Bishop Daniel Murphy of Hobart.

A Catholic school system in Australia was established from the 1860s, run by religious teaching orders from Ireland. The Catholic Church in Australia was not just the locus of power and influence for Catholics, it was also their social centre, and the source of organisational ability, financial support, and education. Bishops wrested control of schooling for their flock, by negotiating conditions. For example, in Hobart, Tasmania, where Presentations made their first foundation on the Australian continent in 1866, Bishop Willson negotiated a compromise with the colonial authorities that replicated the situation in National Schools in Ireland: pupils at government-funded schools could receive religious instruction for one hour per day.[18] However, religious at Catholic free schools could manage their own affairs where denominational instruction was concerned, and this made the need for more religious teaching orders pressing. The Presentations were approached with a view to running schools not only in Hobart, but also in Victoria from 1873 and New South Wales from 1874. By the time the Presentations arrived in Hobart, it had ceased being a convict establishment, and government-sponsored free settlement was attracting migrants to a colony with rich and fertile land.

Presentation schools would make a substantial contribution to the education and employment prospects of girls, and to teacher training for women. Like the nuns who went to Newfoundland in 1833, and England in 1836, those who went to America and Australia mainly settled amongst Christians, where English was widely spoken, and the food – though rarely plentiful – was familiar. But the small group of nuns who went to India in 1842 found themselves in an alien world. In India, the nuns faced many challenges; they needed to learn Tamil, to understand the Indian caste system, to manage bishops and negotiate with priests, to build schools and orphanages in poor environs, and to adapt to the climate. The heat and humidity had a damaging effect on the health of many of the pioneering Sisters; some contracted diseases, others suffered from heat exhaustion, and many died young.[19]

India was a different mission from America, involving the education of both 'native' and migrant groups. They set up schools and orphanages for Indians and Anglo-Indians, including Irish-born soldiers and administrators who were part of the imperial project. The nuns bound for Madras in 1842 knew almost nothing about the country to which they were going, even though Ireland and India had been connected by 'an intricate series of networks of military recruitment, intellectual exchange and political interdependence'[20] that dated back to Nano Nagle's own lifetime. In the nineteenth century, many Irish men and women were involved in administration, medicine, education and missionary work, within the imperial system. Because scholarship has traditionally viewed the history of the British Empire 'almost exclusively from the perspective of England', the history of the Irish in India is still poorly understood.[21] More recently, historians have begun to 'pluralise the imperial experience', moving Irish, Welsh and Scottish history in from the margins, and recognising the 'complex multilateral relationships' that constituted overseas expansion.[22] Within that revised and complex narrative, the history of Irish nuns in India has received almost no attention at all, and their experiences tend to be absorbed within the record – such as it is – of the Catholic Church hierarchy in colonial India.[23] It is important and timely to raise questions about how Irish nuns engaged with the 'empire overseas', not only by serving the Irish in India, but by their engagement with Indian families, in schools and communities.

How teaching Sisters participated in a two-way exchange of ideas and practices, and filtered their experiences back to Ireland, is just one compelling area of transnational historical research.[24] A starting point to transnational research on Presentation Sisters is to understand the contexts into which pioneering groups of Presentations arrived, in the various countries to which they were invited.

## Pioneering Sisters: Voyaging and Arriving

Given the rate of Catholic population expansion in India, America and Australia, it is not surprising to find that bishops, tasked with educating and strengthening their Church, reached out to women religious to found schools. The Presentation Convents in Maynooth and Rahan supplied the pioneering Sisters for India. Unsurprisingly, the nuns were invited to India by a Catholic bishop, whose networks brought him to the Maynooth convent in 1842. Bishop John Fennelly was the third of a succession of Irish secular priests appointed by Propaganda Fide to the role of Vicar Apostolic of Madras (1841–68).

The Madras mission had struggled under Fennelly's predecessors; Church members under Bishop Daniel O'Connor (1834–40) had commented on the 'particular type of Catholicism that the Irish introduced into Madras in the 1830s', viewing it as too informal.[25] High-caste Indian Catholics criticised Irish missionaries for being unable to speak Tamil, and for 'trying to treat Indian Catholics as if they were Irish'.[26] When John Fennelly was appointed to replace O'Connor in 1839, he was requested by Propaganda Fide to address the problems in Madras. Fennelly's arrival was slightly delayed, during which time Dr Patrick Carew served as O'Connor's coadjutor, and it was Carew who reported to Propaganda in 1840, on the neglect of the children of Catholic troops, and the need for priests and nuns.[27] He sent a deputation to Ireland in early 1841, seeking teaching Sisters. Mother Teresa Ball, Superior of the Loreto Convent, Rathfarnham, agreed to send a small group of Sisters, and they left for Calcutta in August of that year.[28] It is possible that Dr Carew also enquired at the Presentation Convent in Maynooth at that point, though the annals of Presentation Convent, Madras, attribute the arrival of the pioneering group of nuns to Bishop Fennelly.[29]

John Fennelly arrived in Madras in 1842, and was soon joined by his younger brother Stephen, who would succeed him as Bishop in 1868. Fennelly had been bursar at Maynooth College, and a number of Irish priests and students from Maynooth College followed him to Madras. He also quickly secured more priests through his contacts at All Hallows College, which had been established the year he left Ireland. Fennelly wrote to Fr David Moriarty, President of All Hallows, that 'the natives have hitherto been considerably neglected in our mission'.[30] He was determined that Irish priests would show 'respect and sensitivity to Indian customs and traditions', even going so far as to encourage his priests to wear the traditional clothing of the region.[31] He also wanted to construct a parochial system modelled on that which operated in Ireland, and knew that Sisters were crucial for the catechetical and literary instruction of Indian children. There was also an urgent demand to provide education for the children of Irish soldiers: the numbers of Irish recruits grew significantly in the nineteenth century; by 1871 there were some 16,000 Irish-born in India, accounting for 21 per cent of the Anglo-Indian population. Almost immediately, Fennelly turned to the Presentation Convent, Maynooth, to seek nuns to support the Madras mission by establishing schools and orphanages. Like many bishops before him, he made his appeal for nuns where he was known, and where he was likely to be heeded.

At the Maynooth convent, there were three volunteers for Madras: Sr M. Ignatius Healy, Sr M. Regis Kelly, Sr Martha Kelly; there was also a postulant from the Presentation Convent in Kilkenny. An experienced Superior to lead the group was required, and the Presentation Convent in Rahan sent Mother M. Francis Xavier Curran. Curran was eleven years professed, and had 'a most ardent desire for the foreign missions'.[32] The group journeyed first to London, and then set sail for Madras on the *Lady Flora*, on 17 September 1841, arriving at their destination on 13 January 1842 to found the first Catholic school in British India.

The Sisters assumed responsibility for an orphanage with about thirty-six children, and commenced a mission that included gradual expansion, with additional convents, schools and orphanages, in Vepery, Kodaikanal, and Royapuram. Their boarding schools, such as Church Park in George Town, were fee-charging, and attracted 'the well-to-do suburban residents and upper classes',[33] and the fees were used to fund the free school and orphanages. The Sisters provided for the Indian poor, including the children of railway workers,[34] and for Eurasian children of soldiers and administration officials who had either been killed, or had returned to Europe.

Though convent annals are silent on the circumstances which left so many Eurasian children orphaned, scholarship provides the contexts in which religious congregations and secular missionaries were needed to run orphanages. The marriages of European men and Indian women had been encouraged by the East India Company as early as the mid-seventeenth century; additionally, Company officials often lived with Indian mistresses. This 'offered new licence to men', who were 'away from the moral scrutiny of white women' and the Church.[35] Many relationships were long-lasting: some 30 per cent of all European wills, drawn up in Bengal in the 1780s, included large bequests made to Indian female companions.[36] By 1786, the East India Company had begun to harden its attitude towards Eurasians, reducing prospects for the sons of mixed-race relationships; by the turn of the century they could not be employed in European branches of the civil and marine services, or the army.[37] Eurasian 'orphan' children, male and female, could no longer travel to England to further their education.

The fate of the orphans of soldiers was particularly precarious. These were children born to European soldiers who often lived temporarily with their mistresses in cantonments, and 'if they were not killed, they were often redeployed elsewhere in India … [or] other parts of the empire'.[38] Often homeless, and unable to belong to Indian communities, orphans relied on the literacy attained in orphanages and asylums in order to help them find basic jobs, and girls were prepared to go into service. The Presentation annals record the hope of the pioneering groups, who went out from Maynooth, Rahan and Mullingar, to labour 'among the poor and underprivileged of Madras City, giving them an education that would enable them to make their way in life, and free them from the burdens that held them in bondage'.[39] The early interventions of the Presentations in India kept them remarkably close to their roots: they were working with children, just as Nano Nagle had in the streets of Cork.

The Presentations who arrived in Tasmania, in 1866, were also brought out at the invitation of a Bishop, Daniel Murphy, newly appointed to Hobart and keen to do something about schooling. Murphy knew the Presentation charism; he was a Cork-man, and his youngest sister was Mother M. Xavier Murphy, Superior of the Presentation Convent in Fermoy, Co. Cork. She had been educated by the Ursulines in Thurles, and later in the Ursuline Convent in Cork that Nano Nagle had established. It was she who agreed to go to Tasmania, as first Superior to a little group of pioneers from Cork that included her niece, Ellen Beechinor. The Bishop and his sister had other family support for the mission: their nephews, Fr Daniel Beechinor and Fr Michael Beechinor travelled to Tasmania with them, and more Beechinor nieces would follow to enter in Tasmania. Bishop Murphy had been Vicar Apostolic in Hyderabad, India, and had a strong network of influential contacts. He was focused on developing an educated Catholic élite in Hobart, and made sure to secure a Papal Indult before the group departed, that permitted the nuns to educate the wealthy, and to run a boarding school.

The Sisters departed for Tasmania on 20 July 1866, sailing from Cork on board the *Empress*. The group that gathered on the quay at Queenstown was representative of many parties of missionaries that left Ireland in the second half of the nineteenth century. Amid 'trunks, boxes, beds and bedding', onlookers had a view of Dr Matthew Quinn, Bishop of Bathurst and Dr

James Murray of Maitland – both newly appointed and commencing their own missions. There were also 'Sisters of Mercy from Charleville bound for Bathurst, Sisters of Mercy from Athy for Brisbane, and Sisters of Mercy from Baggot Street, for Geelong.' And there was the impressive figure of Mother Xavier Murphy, with seven of Nano Nagle's daughters bound for Tasmania; only one of them would ever see Ireland again.[40]

Mother Xavier Murphy may have struggled to reconcile her own mission to the poor with the comforts that the Catholics of Hobart seemed determined to lavish on the Sisters. She had entered the Presentations against her parents' wishes; they were wealthy Catholics who had hoped their daughter would marry, or – if determined to be a religious – enter the Ursuline congregation. Her decision to become a Presentation was born out of a wish to serve the poor and she may have been dismayed with the relative luxury that the parish prepared for her little community. While no convent was ready on their arrival, a very fine one was erected quite quickly, and was known as St Mary's Convent. The *Catholic Standard* described the elegant neo-Gothic building, with its command of the harbour, 'richly moulded openings, and gables surmounted by floriated stone crosses.'[41] The nuns developed free schools, supported by the fees of the boarding school and day school pupils, but the life that Mother Xavier experienced was not like that of Presentation nuns who missioned in poorer parts of the world; the over-weaning ambition of the Church hierarchy in Tasmania, and later in both Wagga Wagga and Melbourne, meant that catering to the rising middle-classes and the upper echelons of society was a priority. Presentation nuns had to obey their bishops, who were – in fact – their Superiors.

Presentation schools in Hobart developed a distinctly European, classic curriculum: Greek, Astronomy, Italian, French, and Music, were taught along with algebra, arithmetic, history, reading and writing. Exhibitions, prize days and concerts were part of the convent school routine. Mother Xavier's Ursuline education, and the education that other Presentation nuns had received from the Faithful Companions of Jesus and the Society of the Sacred Heart,[42] provided them with a template, attracting boarders from all over Tasmania, Victoria, New South Wales, and Queensland.

Unsurprisingly, the success of Presentation schooling in Tasmania recommended it to other bishops who watched and waited for an opportunity to bring Presentation groups to Victoria and New South Wales. Similar means were used to secure nuns, with clergymen turning to Irish convents in which they had relatives and friends. In St Kilda, Melbourne, the Rev James Corbett of St Mary's parish made a successful appeal to the nuns that he knew in the Presentation Convent in Sexton Street, Limerick. A group travelled to Melbourne to found a 'select day school', a free school, and a boarding school.[43] In Wagga Wagga, New South Wales, Fr Patrick Bermingham had relatives at the Presentation Convent, Kildare, from which a group of nuns would depart in 1874 bound for the Wagga district, with its growing Catholic population.[44] There, the prosperous Catholic network became thoroughly involved in funding and building a splendid convent, on a site that was gifted to the project. Fr Bermingham seemed to lack the ability – or will – to take control of the elaborate building plans, and watched with some alarm as 'a magnificent structure in Tudor style' was erected on forty acres of prime land.[45] Bishop Lanigan, who had complained at the cost being 'extravagant in every way', benefited from the status and visibility of the new convent.

The convent site was known as Mount Erin, and there the new community flourished, attracting vocations and developing boarding, day and poor schools. A novitiate and teacher training school added to the success of Mount Erin. The foundation benefited from the experience of one of the founding group, Sr Paul Fay, who had been a pupil in George's Hill and trained as a monitor there; she had then trained as a teacher in Dublin, working for a while at the Dublin Model School, before entering the Presentation Convent, Kildare. Another source of knowledge and strength was the first Superior at the Wagga convent, Mother John Byrne. She went on to make several more foundations and approached the building of convents and schools with remarkable enthusiasm and ability. She was known widely as 'a great builder', and the best-known image of this Dublin woman appropriately shows her holding architectural drawings for one of her several convent projects. Her foundation in the Brighton–Elsternwick part of Melbourne, had a boarding school which grew into a 'Ladies College' that not only had significant academic success but also quickly generated many well-educated postulants who went on to teach in Presentation schools in Perth, Melbourne and Wagga.[46]

## Surviving and Expanding: Presentations and the American Frontier

Nothing could provide a greater contrast with the Australian Presentation experience than the experience of the Irish nuns who went to Dubuque, Iowa (1874) and the Dakota Territories (1882). These missions saw Irish nuns at the heart of the American 'frontier' experience, as migrant Catholic populations moved Westward, settled in newly emerging states, and started to build churches and schools.[47] Even before these foundations were made, Irish nuns had established Presentation convents in California, travelling as far west as Catholic migrants could be found. Other Catholic religious were also running parochial schools, in Colorado, New Mexico, parts of Texas, and Arizona.[48] Indeed, it is now recognised that Catholic women religious played an 'important role in settlement and development of the West', though it has been overlooked until very recently.[49]

Nuns who journeyed into the American West as migrants, would live a life that was very different from the monastic one they had left behind.[50] There was rugged travel on steamboats and wagons, and great distances that had to be covered. On arrival, they had to accustom themselves to 'social interactions … daily hardships, human intimacy and personal danger', and to the regional isolation and extremes of weather.[51] What nuns soon learned was that the 'life of monastic stability was more or less useless in the nineteenth-century West'.[52] It was only by being adaptable that the Presentations would survive, and eventually thrive on this continent. Indeed, it has been argued that the West, 'with its oddly different environment, offered nuns … a chance to think about submission, its benefits, and its costs'.[53] Sisters frequently decided to exert their energies against the kind of domination that they were used to in Europe, whether from 'local bishops, priestly spiritual directors, congregational leaders, local superiors, or each other'.[54] America offered a very different landscape to the first Presentations who arrived there, and for some of them it provided exactly the kinds of challenges and opportunities on which these Irishwomen would thrive.

The first Presentation foundation in America was made in San Francisco, in 1854. It was not uncommon for priests and bishops to quest for nuns while visiting Ireland,[55] and this is how Fr Hugh Gallagher secured a group of five Sisters to return with him to California. They were from the Presentation Convent, Midleton, in Nano Nagle's home county. As the annals record, 'California in 1854 was regarded as the end of the earth and very little was known of it', so the women who left their enclosure in Co. Cork had to place their trust in Fr Gallaghar. When one of the group, who had been singled out for leadership, became ill, it was necessary to find a replacement. Sr M. Teresa Comerford, from the Presentation Convent, Kilkenny, volunteered and a reluctant Bishop Walsh finally gave her permission to go to America. Illness and hardship made the first year of the mission almost unbearable, and most of the pioneering group returned to Ireland in 1855, at which time Archbishop Alemany begged Comerford to stay, in the role of Superior.

Reluctantly, she agreed, with the result that while she was not initially chosen as the first Presentation foundress in America, that is what she became, and she is recorded as such in Presentation archival records.[56]

Teresa Comerford would prove to be an outstanding leader, and was described by the Bishop of Salford as 'the most persevering and determined nun [he] ever met.'[57] She brought about the successful expansion of the congregation in California through calm and purposeful stewardship, and showed great clarity in communicating the Presentation mission to religious and the public alike. One of the earliest tests of her mettle took place within her first year in San Francisco. She had been requested by the Superintendent of Public Schools to present her nuns at the City Hall for examination, to demonstrate their ability to conduct schools. Comerford refused to take her community out of the cloister. A priest intervened and ordered her to comply with the demand to attend City Hall. Teresa Comerford calmly advised him: 'I do not consider your authority sufficient, and cannot act according to your directions', insisting that she would only leave the cloister with 'due dispensation from the Holy See.'[58]

Mother Comerford and her group were not the first Irish teaching Sisters to arrive in America. In 1834, Bishop John England of Charleston, South Carolina had turned to his native Cork to find four Ursulines to establish a school. This group were part of the 'first wave' of Irish religious to leave Ireland after the Catholic Emancipation Act of 1829, to follow the Irish diaspora.[59] Another Cork-born Bishop, Michael O'Connor, invited the Sisters of Mercy from Carlow to Pittsburgh in 1843, and three years later a group of Sisters of Mercy went from Dublin to New York, at the invitation of another Irish Bishop, Dr John Hughes. Eight Sisters of Mercy, including a cousin of Teresa Comerford, were also part of the group that included the Presentations and three priests, who boarded the *Canada* on 21 September 1854. The journey, documented by Comerford in a series of cartoon drawings, included a second ship passage to Panama, after which they crossed the Isthmus on mules. The group then journeyed by train and steamer to San Francisco. Thirteen days after arriving in America, the nuns moved into their temporary home, a 'shantie' which had 'a small yard twenty feet square.'[60] There they began a school, though it would be over a year before a proper convent and school building would be completed. Late in 1855, the first Presentation convent in America was ready, and Mass was celebrated in the convent chapel on 4 December.

Very quickly, Comerford realised that she needed more Sisters from Ireland. Indeed, over the next two decades the expansion of the Presentations in California relied heavily on Irish-born nuns.[61] Comerford secured support from the Presentation Convent in Kilkenny, and her own sister who had entered the Presentation Convent in Midleton also came out to San Francisco. On at least two occasions she returned to Ireland to secure more vocations for California. The *Kilkenny Journal* followed her visit in 1867, advising readers that Mother Teresa Comerford and her Irish sisters in San Francisco were trying to provide education to 1,100 children. The publicity no doubt helped: Comerford returned to America with 'eight accomplished ladies'.[62] The second half of the nineteenth century saw many Irish missionary nuns, bishops and priests return home, questing for vocations. Local bishops complained that the practice was draining the country of women who were needed to teach at home, but they could do little to prevent it. Comerford faced competition from other congregations, such as the Sisters of Mercy, the Sisters of the Holy Cross, and the Sisters of St Joseph, all of whom sought Irish nuns for American and Australian convents.

Back in San Francisco, filiations had been made at Taylor Street, and in Berkeley. The demand for Presentation schooling was huge. Comerford's greatest problem was a lack of American vocations and 'the impossibility of getting suitable subjects from among the educated classes'.[63] As an enclosed order, which ran free schools, the Presentations in California had 'no staple means of support'.[64] Comerford wrote to Rome to describe the parlous state of her community, arguing that 'the necessity of establishing a Noviciate in Europe is indispensable, to provide our Convents with Sisters trained in the same spirit'.[65] An Irish novitiate, she proposed, would attract 'ladies of independent rank', whose dowries would help support the Californian mission.[66] Her staunch ally, Bishop Vaughan, wrote to Rome in support of her plan, saying that 'there are no vocations to religious life in California'.[67] The plan went ahead with remarkable speed and efficiency, and Teresa Comerford's cousin, the Rev Thomas Geoghegan, made the generous gesture of building a convent, novitiate and school in Kilcock, financed by inheritances and gifts. The purpose of the Presentation Convent in Kilcock was to educate young girls who thought they might have a vocation, and then prepare them in the novitiate; it was a model later adopted very successfully by the Sisters of Mercy who established an aspirancy and novitiate in Callan, Co. Kilkenny, in 1884.[68] Unlike seminaries for Irishmen, such as All Hallows Missionary College (1842), female aspirancies did not receive financial support from Propaganda Fide and were supported by the nuns who founded them.

The Presentation Convent, Kilcock, opened in 1879 and by 1880 it had 150 pupils and six novices. Teresa Comerford, who had travelled to Ireland to see the project through, returned to California, where – to the shock of her community – she died in 1881. Her Irish novitiate supplied fifteen Sisters for San Francisco, but it did not continue; once Patrick William Riordan was appointed archbishop of the San Francisco diocese he made it clear that American convents could not continue to rely on overseas Sisters, and that they should promote vocations amongst girls born in America. Riordan was not wrong: the expansion of Presentation education in California in the twentieth century was mainly the work of American Sisters.[69]

Records of the Presentations in California show that the next wave of entrants were the American-born daughters of immigrants who had come to America from Italy, Ireland, France, Portugal, Spain, Scotland and England. There was also a little mobility between independent Presentation foundations in nineteenth and early twentieth-century America. Sometimes this was because volunteers from two or more houses came together to make a new foundation. Mobility was also a consequence of Superiors 'questing' for vocations and, occasionally, movement between independent houses was due to the need for a young nun to find the 'right' mission. The peregrinations of Sr M. Clare Browne offer an example of all three kinds of mobility: when Mother John of Fargo, North Dakota, went questing in Ireland in 1885, Sr Clare agreed to leave George's Hill Convent and return to North Dakota with Mother John, and three other Irish recruits.[70] Finding life on the frontier too difficult, Sr Clare asked to be received into the Presentation Convent in New York. The first New York foundation of the Presentations had been established from Presentation Convent, Terenure, in 1874. The New York foundation quickly made other foundations, including one on Staten Island (1884), and one in Fitchburg, Massachusetts (1886). In 1890, Sisters from Fitchburg joined with some from San Francisco, and went to Gilroy, California to make a new foundation; Sr Clare asked to be received there, and she remained in Gilroy until her death in 1907.[71]

While Sr Clare chose to leave the unforgiving conditions in the Dakotas in 1885, others battled on with one of the hardest missions in nineteenth-century Presentation history. Though the first foundation in the Dakotas dates from 1882, the Presentations arrived in 1880 and had two years of struggle before establishing a successful convent in Fargo. The initial invitation to the community in George's Hill came from Bishop Martin Marty, shortly after he was appointed Vicar Apostolic of Dakota Territory in 1879.[72] Marty, a Benedictine, had missioned amongst the Sioux since 1876. He was keenly aware that Catholics were not only a minority but were viewed as second-class citizens by their Protestant neighbours, whose community life was more organised. Additionally, it was the Episcopalians and Presbyterians that ran almost all of the large 'Indian missions', funded by the federal government.[73] Marty's handful of mission territories struggled; anti-Catholic bigotry flared from time to time, and he was plagued by lack of finances and lack of support.

However, in the year of Martin Marty's appointment to Dakota Territory, he secured 50,000 acres through the Northern Pacific Railroad in order to build a Catholic settlement, and he needed to find a community of nuns to run a Catholic school. Following a visit to Rome in September 1879, he travelled to Dublin and visited the George's Hill convent, where he persuaded Mother M. John Hughes to return to America with him. Mother John had a sister in the Presentation Convent in Doneraile, Mother M. Agnes Hughes, who agreed to be part of the mission, and she recruited two other Sisters and a novice. The group was joined by Sr Teresa Challoner, of Manchester, and they set sail for New York. They visited with the Presentations in Newburgh, learning a bit about teaching in American schools, before continuing their journey by train 'to Chicago, then to Omaha, to Sioux City and finally to Yankton'.[74] The final part of their journey took them up the Missouri River by steamboat, to the town of Wheeler. The dwelling that awaited them was a small stone-and-sod building, far from the nearest railroad station. It had no furniture, beyond a few log benches for pupils to sit on; upstairs they had five unfurnished cubicles in which to sleep, and a solitary wood-burning stove heated the entire building.

The accommodation that awaited the nuns was typical of the houses that were thrown up outside the railway towns, as vast swathes of the American frontier were occupied by 'homesteaders', who claimed land under the Homestead Act of 1862, which they then tried to farm.[75] The Act encouraged Western migration, by providing a settler with 160 acres of land on payment of a filing fee. The settler then had to farm the land for five years, before claiming full ownership. Homesteaders also had the option of buying the land outright, after six months of occupancy, at $1.25 per acre. In 1862, only about a thousand people lived in what is now South Dakota; by 1890, 329,000 people had arrived to settle on the land, and build the towns. When the Presentations arrived in 1880, 'homesteading' was booming; that year the *Fargo Times* had distributed forty thousand copies of a special issue promoting the beautiful farmland, direct rail routes for easy sale of crops, and perfect climate. Posters advertised 'God's country' and promoters promised land that 'laughs with abundance when tickled by the plough'.[76] The railroads determined expansion, 'dropping down towns upon a map of raw land'.[77] Once a town was laid out, lots were sold, and railway companies also gave away plots of land to people like Bishop Marty, to encourage large settlements. In the decade that followed the arrival of the nuns, homesteaders paid filing fees for more than 41 million acres in Dakota Territory. But God's country was not always kind to its people, and Mother John's little community were poorly prepared for prairie life.

It is unlikely that Mother John had been told about the severe droughts and the freezing winters that made life gruelling for farmers. Word would not have reached George's Hill convent in 1875 that a plague of locusts had swarmed from Saskatchewan to Texas, devouring everything from crops to the wool on the backs of sheep. Some 3.5 trillion insects had covered about 198,000 square miles, in a dense swarm that was 110 miles wide and 1,800 miles long. The plague caused widespread starvation and many homesteaders abandoned their farms and moved back East, while others who were too poor to move away scratched out an existence. Arriving in Wheeler, in September 1880, the Presentations were about to witness another exceptional natural phenomenon that would make history: a severe snowfall that commenced in October and continued right through May. Mother John wrote of how they survived:

> We have got no milk direct from the cow since October ... Those who can afford may kill a fat cow, cut it up in suitable pieces and hang it out of doors and use it as required, we have done so already and at present we have a large antelope in this way ... We had a great number of fowl but nearly all have frozen to death – we shall be more experienced next year.[78]

No trains reached Yankton that winter, and months of blizzards made any kind of work impossible. When food supplies ran out, people survived by eating the seed that had been stored to sow the next season's wheat crop.

On 1 April, after four gruelling months, the Sisters watched as the thaw started. Their house started to collapse, just as many sod-and-stone houses did, when the freeze ended and heavy rain started to fall. The neighbouring towns of Vermillion and Fort Pierre were washed away, and the nuns saw the wreckage, including people's furniture, flowing down the river.[79] Bishop Marty advised the Sisters to move to Deadwood, where a new school was needed and a priest would be able to help them. Though the nuns explored that possibility, they knew they would have to leave their convent cloister to attend Mass in Deadwood, and this was not acceptable. They turned instead to other Irishwomen, the Sisters of Mercy in Yankton, and stayed with them until June 1882, when they left for Fargo. There a parish school was needed, and the nuns set about fundraising to build classrooms. The school soon succeeded to the point that more Sisters were needed, and in 1885 Mother John went to Ireland to seek support from George's Hill Convent. On her return to Fargo with four Sisters, she was in a position to accept an invitation to establish a convent and school in Aberdeen. She brought two of the newly arrived Irish nuns with her to make the foundation, and in October 1886 they opened a school to fifty pupils.

By adapting to circumstances, the communities at Fargo and Aberdeen were able to survive and grow. For example, they accepted an official dispensation from Bishop Marty to leave their cloister, so that they could beg for money when it was needed, and they also accepted tuition fees from pupils who boarded at the schools. In 1887, they opened the Sacred Heart Academy, Fargo, providing a progressive academic education to Catholics and non-Catholics, and added teacher training to their remit.[80] Fargo made a further ten foundations by the middle of the twentieth century, while the foundation at Aberdeen also expanded, making nineteen new foundations in South Dakota in the same period.

Meanwhile, in other parts of America, Presentations similarly had to adapt quickly to their circumstances, which could change very suddenly. In San Francisco in the 1870s, the nuns witnessed strong anti-Catholic agitation, and the effects of the depression that followed 'Black Friday', 27 August 1875, and the closing of the Bank of California. Like the Presentations in the Dakotas, the San Francisco community was reduced to begging.[81] They had to adapt to new challenges after the 1906 earthquake, and the fires that ravaged the city of San Francisco and completely destroyed their convent on Powell Street. Within days, the Sisters started to run a relief camp, and as refugees gathered in makeshift shelters and tents, they doled out food and blankets. Approximately ten days after the earthquake, the Sisters set up the first temporary school established for refugees, in a building on the corner of Montgomery Avenue and Union Street.

Adaptability was the hallmark of the Sisters who commenced new foundations in the nineteenth century. It was also characteristic of the Sisters who, in the first half of the twentieth century, responded to calls to run schools in Northern India (Pakistan) and Southern Rhodesia (Zimbabwe). These became part of a vastly extended Presentation network that reached around the world by the 1960s. Each Presentation house had autonomy, yet the historical evidence shows that different convents were remarkably connected, even at a time when communication was complicated and costly.

The Presentation Order is a compelling example of how female networks have operated in the past, and only detailed work in the archives of their worldwide convents will reveal the myriad ways in which this kind of networking operated, connecting women, convents, and continents. For example, the Sisters in Madras made a foundation in Vepery in 1884, which in turn established a convent in Rawalpindi; there the foundress was Mother Ignatius McDermot, a Roscommon woman who had entered the Presentation Convent in San Francisco in 1873.[82] From Rawalpindi, a multiplicity of foundations were made, in places as far apart as Delhi, Cornwall, Kashmir, and Cavan. To support the expanding Indian network, the English novitiate in Etonfield was founded, to prepare Irish and English novices. Meanwhile, the foundation at Church Park, Madras, sent out Sisters to Southern Rhodesia (1949), and African foundations multiplied. As the Order spread and Sisters made new foundations, they had to challenge their own thinking and make demands of their bodies. Like other congregations whose apostolic mission took them around the globe, they were often faced with circumstances that forced them to reassess the boundaries of their abilities. Arguably, the Sisters drew some of their resilience from their history and from their founding Mother, for although the Order had multiple independent houses it was rooted in a single convent in eighteenth-century Cork.

On the ever-expanding Presentation family tree, twentieth-century Pakistani and Rhodesian foundations can trace their history back to nineteenth-century Madras, thence to Rahan, and finally to George's Hill, founded in 1794. All other global foundations can similarly reach back through time to one of the other five eighteenth-century Irish foundations. From New Zealand to North America, there were convents rooted in Presentation Convent, Killarney (1793); houses from Derbyshire to Co. Tipperary could trace themselves to the first Waterford foundation (1798); dozens of Presentation schools, from New Mexico to Midleton, were all linked back to North Presentation (1799); the Kilkenny foundation (1800) had a vast legacy that included Newfoundland and New South Wales. And all the Presentation communities worldwide can trace their heritage to the South Presentation Convent (1775), and to one woman: Nano Nagle.

# Endnotes

## CHAPTER 1

1   Standard histories of Irish education are almost without reference to Presentation schools, including those that operated within the State 'national system'. They are absent from Donald Akenson, *The Irish Education Experiment: The National System of Education in the Nineteenth Century* (London: Routledge & Kegan Paul, 1970), though the Christian Brothers are included; nor are they examined in Akenson's *A Mirror to Kathleen's Face: Education in Independent Ireland, 1922–1960* (Montreal and London: McGill-Queen's University Press, 1973). A handful of women religious, including Nano Nagle, are mentioned in John Coolahan, *Irish Education: Its History and Structure* (Dublin: Institute of Public Administration, 1981). In placing all of their attention on the involvement of the institutional Catholic Church, and on Church–State relations and the actions of bishops, these scholars – however unintentionally – rendered almost invisible the thousands of Irish women religious involved in teaching. Nuns as educators in Ireland get some mention in Deirdre Raftery and Susan M. Parkes, *Female Education in Ireland, 1700–1900: Minerva or Madonna* (Dublin: Irish Academic Press, 2007), and they are examined in Catherine Nowlan-Roebuck, 'The Presentation Order and National Education in Nineteenth Century Ireland' in Deirdre Raftery and Karin Fischer (eds), *Educating Ireland: Schooling and Social Change, 1700–2000* (Dublin: Irish Academic Press, 2014). Growth in the area of women's history and the history of women religious, has meant that scholars have begun to research the history of religious orders involved in philanthropy and teaching. See for example, Maria Luddy, *Women and Philanthropy in Nineteenth-Century Ireland* (Cambridge: Cambridge University Press, 1995); Caitríona Clear, *Nuns in Nineteenth-Century Ireland* (Dublin: Gill & Macmillan, 1987); Mary Peckham Magray, *The Transforming Power of the Nuns: Women, Religion and Cultural Change in Ireland, 1750–1900* (New York and Oxford: Oxford University Press, 1998), and Deirdre Raftery, '"Je suis d'aucune Nation": The recruitment and identity of Irish women religious in the international mission field, c. 1840–1940', *Paedagogica Historica*, 49, 4 (2013), pp. 513–30.

2   Members of the Presentation leadership recognise that it is currently impossible to establish the exact number of Presentation schools and colleges that have existed, worldwide, since the foundation of the Order in 1775. Over time, many convents and schools closed, and some schools amalgamated with neighbouring (non-

Presentation) schools. To map every Presentation house in the world would be a major research project, and certainly a worthwhile one.

3   See for example [M. McCarthy] *Edmund Ignatius Rice and the Christian Brothers* (Dublin: Gill and Son, 1926); M.C. Normoyle, *A Tree is Planted: The Life and Times of Edmund Rice* (Dublin: privately published, 1976); D. Rushe, *Edmund Rice: The Man and His Times* (Dublin: Macmillan 1982); Barry M. Coldrey, *Faith and Fatherland: The Christian Brothers and the Development of Irish Nationalism, 1838–1921* (Dublin: Gill and Macmillan, 1988); Dáire Keogh, *Edmund Rice and the First Christian Brothers* (Dublin: Four Courts Press, 2008).

4   The Sisters of St Joseph originated in France, in 1650, and made foundations around the world, giving rise to new branches, and administrative federations, that all trace their origin to the original French foundation. Their schools were particularly numerous in America and Canada; today the congregation numbers about 14,000, half of whom are located in the US. They are examined in work including Evangeline Thomas, *Footprints on the Frontier: A History of the Sisters of St Joseph, Concordia, Kansas* (Westminster, MD: Newman Press, 1948); *The Sisters of St Joseph of Carondolet* (n.n.; St Louis, MO: B. Herder Books, 1966); Marguerite Vacher, *Nuns Without Cloister: Sisters of St Joseph in the Seventeenth and Eighteenth Centuries* (Lanham, MD: University Press of America, 2010); Jo Ann Kay McNamara, *Sisters in Arms: Catholic Nuns Through Two Millennia* (Cambridge, MA: Harvard University Press, 1996); Elizabeth M. Smyth (ed.), *Changing Habits: Women's Religious Orders in Canada* (Ottawa: Novalis, 2007), and Anne M. Butler, *Across God's Frontiers: Catholic Sisters in the American West, 1850–1920* (Chapel Hill, NC: University of North Carolina Press, 2012). The Society of the Sacred Heart (RSCJ) was founded in France in 1800. Their foundress, St Madeleine Sophie Barat, has been the subject of scholarship, and the history of the congregation has been explored in many studies. See for example Louise Callan, *The Society of the Sacred Heart in North America* (New York: Longmans, Green & Co., 1937); and *Philippine Duchesne: Frontier Missionary of the Sacred Heart, 1769–1852* (Westminster, MD: Newman Press, 1957); V.V. Harrison, *Changing Habits: A Memoir of the Society of the Sacred Heart* (New York and London: Doubleday, 1988); Phil Kilroy, *Madeleine Sophie Barat: A Life* (Cork: Cork University Press, 2000); Christine Trimingham Jack, *Growing Good Catholic Girls: Education and Convent Life in Australia* (Melbourne: Melbourne University Press, 2003); Sarah A. Curtis, *Civilizing Habits: Women Missionaries and the Revival of French Empire* (Oxford and New York: Oxford University Press, 2010); Phil Kilroy, *The Society of the Sacred Heart in Nineteenth-Century France, 1800–1865* (Cork: Cork University Press, 2012).

5   For a recent comprehensive study of Protestant women, education, and poor relief in Ireland see Eilís O'Sullivan, *Ascendancy Women and Elementary Education in Ireland: Educational Provision for Poor Children, 1788–1848* (Basingstoke: Palgrave Macmillan, 2017). See also Maria Luddy, 'Religion, philanthropy and the state in late eighteenth and early nineteenth-century Ireland' in H. Cunningham and J.

Innes (eds), *Charity, Philanthropy and Reform from the 1690s to 1850* (London: Macmillan Press, 1998), pp. 148–67; and Eilís O'Sullivan, 'Irish women and elementary education for the poor in early nineteenth-century Ireland' in Raftery and Fischer (eds), *Educating Ireland*, pp. 61–90.

6 See for example Noela M. Fox, *An Acorn Grows among the Gums: The Presentation Sisters in Tasmania, 1866-2006* (Tasmania: Presentation Sisters Property Association, 2006); Mary Margaret Mooney, *Doing What Needs to Be Done: Sisters of the Presentation of the Blessed Virgin Mary, Fargo, 1882-1997* (Published by the Sisters of the Presentation of the Blessed Virgin Mary, Fargo, 1997); Bernard Dowd and Sheila Tearle (eds), *Centenary History of the Presentation of the Blessed Virgin Mary, Wagga Wagga, New South Wales, 1874-1974* (Published by the Sisters of the Presentation of the Blessed Virgin Mary, Wagga Wagga, NSW, 1973); Roger C. Paavola, *Upon the Rock: A Centennial History of the Presentation Sisters of the Blessed Virgin Mary, Aberdeen, South Dakota, 1886-1986* (Privately published, 1986); Ruth Marchant James, *Cork to Capricorn: A History of the Presentation Sisters in Western Australia, 1891-1991* (Published by the Congregation of the Presentation Sisters of Western Australia, 1996); Mariam Murphy, *Pakistan Presentation Story* (Privately published by the Army Press, Rawalpindi, 1986); Mary Rose Forest, *With Hearts of Oak: The Story of the Sisters of the Presentation of the Blessed Virgin Mary in California, 1854-1907* (Privately published by the Sisters of the Presentation of the Blessed Virgin Mary, San Francisco, 2004).

7 Rev T.J. Walsh, *Nano Nagle and the Presentation Sisters* (Dublin: Gill and Son Ltd., 1959); Camillus Galvin, *From Acorn to Oak: A Study of Presentation Foundations, 1775-1968* (Published by the Sisters of the Presentation of the Blessed Virgin Mary, Fargo, North Dakota, 1968); Raphael Consedine, *Listening Journey: A Study of the Spirit and Ideals of Nano Nagle and the Presentation Sisters* (Published by the Congregation of Presentation Sisters, Victoria, 1983); Pius O'Farrell, *Nano Nagle: Woman of the Gospel* (Cork: Cork Publishing, 1996). Most recently, a volume edited by three Presentation Sisters has been published, though it is not a historical study: Bernadette Flanagan, Mary T. O'Brien and Anne M. O'Leary (eds), *Nano Nagle and an Evolving Charism: A Guide for Educators, Leaders and Care Providers* (Dublin: Veritas, 2017).

8 William Coppinger, 'The Life of Miss Nano Nagle' (1794), reprinted in Walsh, *Nano Nagle*, pp. 384–95, *passim*.

9 Ibid.

10 Ibid., p. 389.

11 Ibid., p. 385.

12 Ibid.

13 Mother Clare Callaghan to Bishop Coppinger, n.d. [1800–1804], Presentation Sisters Congregational Archives (hereafter PSCA), IE PBVM [SPC] 1/1/4. Mother Callaghan drew her authority in this matter from Mother Angela Collins, Nano Nagle's closest confidante, who read and corrected this letter to Coppinger. Collins succeeded Nagle as Superior of South Presentation Convent.

14  Ibid., p. 392.

15  Rev William Hutch, *Nano Nagle: Her Life, her Labours and their Fruits* (Dublin: McGlashan & Gill, 1875).

16  See 'Conspectus of the Presentation Order from its foundation in 1777 to the year 1875' in Hutch, *Nano Nagle*, p. xvii.

17  O'Rahilly Box, PSCA, IE PBVM [SPC] 1/1/3/1–1/1/3/4.

18  T.J. Walsh to Sister Lucy, 18 September 1980, PSCA, IE PBVM [SPC] 1/1/4/1.

19  Other researchers who had some interest in writing about Nano Nagle include Fr Louis Nolan OP, Sr Patrick Rupert, and Fr Aloysius OFM Cap., although they did not continue their work once the official biography by Walsh was under way.

20  Sr Catherine Condon was secretary to the book project, carrying out a significant amount of research for T.J. Walsh. PSCA, IE PBVM [SPC] 1/1/4/11.

21  While Walsh's book made no mention of Sr Catherine Condon's work, letters to Condon indicate that other Presentation Sisters knew of the extent of her involvement in the book. A Sister in Presentation Convent, George's Hill, wrote to Condon on 14 December 1959, to say: 'Congratulations to you in a very special way for your share in the new and very beautiful Life of Nano Nagle ... I was longing to see how your labour of love, the genealogical map, would be reproduced ... it is a work of art.' PSCA, IE PBVM [SPC] 1/1/4/7.

22  Sr M. Pius O'Farrell's *Nano Nagle: Woman of the Gospel* provides a survey of Nagle's life, but is not referenced and is of limited use to researchers. O'Farrell also edited a privately published volume of documents related to Presentation history, entitled *Breaking of Morn: Nano Nagle (1718–1784) and Francis Moylan (1735–1815)* (Cork: Cork Publishing, 2001); many of the documents in the book were included in the *Positio*.

23  *Cause of Beatification and Canonisation of the Servant of God, Nano Nagle (1718–1784). Positio Super Virtutibus*, Books 1–3. PROT. N. 1494 (Rome, 1994). Cited with permission of the Sisters of the Presentation of the Blessed Virgin Mary.

24  O'Farrell, *Breaking of Morn*.

25  David Dickson, *Old World Colony: Cork and Munster, 1630–1830* (Cork: Cork University Press, 2005); Ian McBride, *Eighteenth Century Ireland* (Dublin: Gill Books, 2009); Michael Brown, *The Irish Enlightenment* (Cambridge, MA: Harvard University Press, 2016); Jane Ohlmeyer, *Making Ireland English: The Irish Aristocracy in the Seventeenth Century* (New Haven, CT and London: Yale University Press, 2012); Thomas O'Connor and Mary Ann Lyons (eds), *Irish Communities in Early Modern Europe* (Dublin: Four Courts Press, 2006).

26  The potential for using congregational archives in research in medical history is discussed in Deirdre Raftery, 'The "third wave" is digital: researching histories of women religious in the twenty-first century', *American Catholic Studies*, 128, 2 (2017), pp. 29–50.

27  See for example Gary McCulloch and William Richardson, *Historical Research in Education Settings* (Maidenhead: Open University Press, 2000); Peter Cunningham and Philip Gardner, *Becoming Teachers: Texts and Testimonies, 1907–1950* (London:

Woburn Press, 2004); Ian Grosvenor, Martin Lawn, and Kate Rousmaniere (eds), *Silences and Images: The Social History of the Classroom* (New York: Peter Lang, 1999); Christine Trimingham Jack, 'Sacred Symbols, School Ideology and the Construction of Subjectivity', *Paedagogica Historica*, 34, 3 (1998), pp. 771–94; Christine Lei, 'The Material Culture of the Loretto School for Girls in Hamilton, Ontario 1865–1971', *Canadian Catholic Historical Association Historical Studies*, 66 (2000), pp. 92–113; Catherine Burke and Ian Grosvenor, *School* (London: Reaktion Books, 2008).

28  See Bart Hellinckx, Frank Simon and Marc Depaepe, *The Forgotten Contribution of the Teaching Sisters* (Leuven: Leuven University Press, 2009).

29  See Presentation Convent Youghal Annals (1838–1941), IE PBVM YOU; *Rules of the Youghal Co-operative Lace Society Limited* (Dublin: Sealy, Bryers and Walker, 1897); *The Youghal Lace Industry* (n.n., Dublin: Browne and Nolan, 1898).

30  Margaret MacCurtain, 'Late in the field: Catholic Sisters in twentieth-century Ireland and the New Religious History', in Mary O'Dowd and Sabine Wichert (eds), *Chattel, Servant or Citizen: Women's Status in Church, State and Society* (Belfast: Institute of Irish Studies, QUB, 1995), p. 43.

31  Ibid.

32  Clear, *Nuns in Nineteenth Century Ireland*; Rosemary Raughter (ed.), *Religious Women and their History* (Dublin: Irish Academic Press, 2005); Peckham Magray, *The Transforming Power of the Nuns*; Máire M. Kealy, *Dominican Education in Ireland, 1820–1930* (Dublin: Irish Academic Press, 2007); Stephanie Burley, 'Engagement with Empires: Irish Catholic Female Religious Teachers in Colonial South Australia, 1868–1901', *Irish Educational Studies*, 31, 2 (2012), pp. 175–90; Maria Luddy, '"Possessed of Fine Properties": Power, Authority, and the Funding of Convents in Ireland, 1780–1900', in Maarten Van Dijck, Jan De Maeyer, Jeffrey Tyssens and Jimmy Koppen (eds), *The Economics of Providence* (Leuven: Leuven University Press, 2012); Deirdre Raftery, 'The "Mission" of Nuns in Female Education', *Paedagogica Historica*, 48, 2 (2012): pp. 299–313; and '"Je suis d'aucune Nation"'.

33  *A Directory of the Religious of the Presentation Order, According to the Practices of the Parent House, Founded in the Year 1775* (Cork: Wm. Hurley, 1850).

34  *Presentation Directory*, p. 183.

35  Ibid., p. 184.

36  Ibid., p. 183.

37  Ibid., p. 70.

38  Ibid., p. 72; p. 73.

39  *Constitutions* (1935), pp. 22–5.

40  Ibid., p. 22.

41  Ibid., p. 30.

42  *Presentation Directory*, p. 255.

43  Ibid., p. 246.

44  Ibid., p. 256.

45 For example, in the early stages of the foundation at Rahan, several of the Sisters died; the records indicate they died from tuberculosis, and from unspecified illnesses. Presentation Convent Rahan, Notebook A2, Registry of the Foregoing Acts, IE PBVM RAH, uncatalogued.

46 Presentation Convent Killarney Annals. IE PBVM KLY, uncatalogued.

47 *Constitutions* (1935), p. 35.

48 Rev Fintan Geser, *Canon Law Governing Communities of Sisters* (St Louis, MO and London: B. Herder Book Co., 1950), p. 220.

49 Louise O'Reilly, *The Impact of Vatican II on Women Religious: A Case Study of the Union of Irish Presentation Sisters* (Newcastle upon Tyne: Cambridge Scholars Publishing, 2013), p. 33.

50 The two-tiered system of membership in teaching orders is discussed in Christine Trimingham Jack, 'The Lay Sister in Educational History and Memory', *History of Education*, 29, 3 (2000), pp. 181–94.

51 In the Middle Ages, the *conversi* were the uneducated or illiterate, who entered monasteries late in life.

52 *Presentation Directory*, p. 256.

53 It is possible to get some idea of the role of Lay Sisters by examining the Rule and Constitutions of an Order, and any 'house rules' that exist in archives.

54 Occasionally, registers indicated that entrants were Lay Sisters; generally it was only possible to deduce that a woman was a Lay Sister because she was not given 'Mary' as one of her names in religion; Choir Sisters were give the name Mary followed by the name of a Saint.

55 Mother M. Teresa Comerford to Mother Josephine Hagarty [?], 28 March 1880. Mother M. Teresa Comerford's Kilcock Correspondence, PASF.

56 This point is discussed in Raftery, '"*Je suis d'aucune Nation*"'.

57 *Presentation Directory*, p. 242.

58 Mother M. Teresa Comerford to Mother Josephine Hagarty [?], 28 March 1880.

59 Mother M. Teresa Comerford to Cardinal Simeoni, 25 January 1878. Mother M. Teresa Comerford's Kilcock Correspondence.

60 *Presentation Directory*, p. 264.

61 Ibid., p. 265.

62 Mooney, *Doing What Needs to be Done*, p. 16.

63 Sr M. de Sales Carrrick to Bishop O'Connor, 25 January 1878, Omaha Chancery Office Archives. Cited in Mooney, *Doing What Needs to be Done*, p. 16.

64 Bandon Annals, Vol. 1 (1829–1938), p. 152, IE PBVM BAN, uncatalogued.

## CHAPTER 2

1 James Kelly, 'The Emergence of Scientific and Institutional Medical Practice in Ireland, 1650–1800', in Elizabeth Malcolm and Greta Jones (eds), *Medicine, Disease and the State in Ireland, 1650–1940* (Cork: Cork University Press, 1999), p. 27.

2  Between 1717 and 1746, smallpox (the *variola* virus) was responsible for the premature deaths of one third of all children in Ireland. This was extremely high, by international standards. See Gabrielle Ashford, 'Children's Smallpox and Inoculation Procedures in Eighteenth-Century Ireland', in Anne MacLellan and Alice Mauger (eds), *Growing Pains: Childhood Illness in Ireland, 1750–1950* (Dublin: Irish Academic Press, 2016), p. 19.

3  Ian McBride, 'The Edge of Enlightenment: Ireland and Scotland in the Eighteenth Century', *Modern Intellectual History*, 10, 1 (2013), p. 136.

4  For a discussion of agrarian unrest see for example Sean J. Connolly, *Priests and People in Pre-Famine Ireland, 1780–1845* (Dublin: Four Courts Press, 2001); famines in the eighteenth century, and the emergence of foundling hospitals and orphan asylums, are discussed in Joseph Robins, *The Lost Children: A Study of Charity Children in Ireland, 1700–1900* (Dublin: Institute of Public Administration, 1980).

5  For an outline of the penal code and Catholic Ireland, see Richard Bourke, *Empire and Revolution: The Political Life of Edmund Burke* (Princeton, NJ and Woodstock, Oxon.: Princeton University Press, 2015).

6  There are many detailed genealogical studies of the Nagles, including those published in Walsh, *Nano Nagle*, and in the *Positio*. I am grateful for information gleaned from Sr Una Burke, Presentation Convent, Midleton.

7  McBride, *Eighteenth Century Ireland*, p. 256.

8  See Dickson, *Old World Colony*, p. 187 & p. 253.

9  Ibid., p. 174.

10  The Popery Act (Ann 2., c. 6), an 'Act to prevent the further growth of popery'. This Act, passed in 1704, exempted Catholic property from primogeniture; a gavelling clause in the act meant that estates were reduced in size as they passed down through generations. See Bourke, *Empire and Revolution*, p. 216.

11  Joseph Nagle was admitted to Gray's Inn in 1696. Penal legislation disqualified Catholics from becoming barristers or attorneys, and effectively lawyers were 'squeezed out of the judicial bench'. See McBride, *Eighteenth Century Ireland*, p. 131.

12  *A report from the committee appointed to inspect the original papers seized in the houses or lodgings of one MccCarthy [sic] alias Rabah, a reputed titular bishop, and Joseph Nagle, a reputed popish solicitor, both of the city of Corke* (Dublin: 1733), p. c, cited in McBride, *Eighteenth Century Ireland*, p. 455.

13  Dickson, *Old World Colony*, p. 272.

14  David Dickson states that the Nagles, the Coppingers and the Kenmares did not conform. See Dickson, *Old World Colony*, p. 273.

15  See M. Romero-Maroto and J.M. Sáez-Gómez, 'Mouth ulcers: A deadly disease for children from the sixteenth to eighteenth centuries', *Irish Journal of Medical Science*, 182, 2 (2013) pp. 297–300.

16  Ibid., p. 299.

17  See Dickson, *Old World Colony*, p. 271.

18 Nano's great-grandfather was James Nagle of Annakissey, and his son was Pierce Nagle of Annakissey. Pierce's brother, David Nagle of Ballygriffin, was father to Garrett Nagle of Ballygriffin, and grandfather to Nano. The Annakissey and Ballygriffin branches of the family were always closely connected.

19 Sir Richard Nagle (1636–1699) left Ireland with his wife and twelve of their thirteen children after the defeat of James II; they lived at the Château Vieux, Saint-Germain-en-Laye, which had been given to James II by King Louis XIV. Saint-Germain-en-Laye was the site of the Jacobite court in exile, and provided the Nagles with the kind of social milieu and economic contacts desired by status-conscious élite Catholics. His brother, Pierce Nagle (dates unknown), settled at Cambrai. Richard and Pierce were married to sisters, Mary and Jane Kearney.

20 In 1717, Jacques Nagle was empowered by Garrett Nagle to administer his property in France. Typescript, entitled 'Nagles of Saint Germain-en-Laye', Presentation Archives Midleton, citing MS letter, 30 December 1719, empowering Jacques Nagle to act as administrator to the property in France of Garrett Nagle of Ballygriffin, Ireland (Document LXV1 373, National Archives Paris).

21 Mary Burke to Mrs Hennessy, 25 October 1766. In *Positio*, p. 262.

22 See McBride, *Eighteenth Century Ireland*, pp. 236–7.

23 This point is made by McBride, in *Eighteenth Century Ireland*, p. 237.

24 Typescript entitled 'Problems arising from Nano Nagle's will', Presentation Archives Midleton, IE PBVM MID, uncatalogued; see also *Positio*.

25 Copy of the Will of Nano Nagle, in *Positio*, pp. 421–2.

26 Nano left Elizabeth £1,500 sterl., and a sum of £500 sterl. to her niece, Mary Ann Ffrench. She left nothing to her nephew, Robert Ffrench, perhaps because she knew he would inherit the estate in Rahasane, Co. Galway. See copy of the Will of Nano Nagle, in *Positio*, p. 421.

27 Dickson, *Old World Colony*, p. 95.

28 Ibid.

29 Toby Barnard, 'Reading in eighteenth-century Ireland: public and private pleasures', in Bernadette Cunningham and Máire Kennedy (eds), *The Experience of Reading: Irish Historical Perspectives* (Dublin: Economic and Social History Society of Ireland, 1999), shows how lawyers and the clergy had book collections in their homes.

30 Barnard, 'Reading in eighteenth-century Ireland', p. 68.

31 Máire Kennedy, 'Reading the Enlightenment in Eighteenth-Century Ireland', *Eighteenth-Century Studies*, 45, 3 (2012), pp. 356–7.

32 Antonia McManus, *The Irish Hedge School and its Books, 1695–1831* (Dublin: Four Courts Press, 2002), p. 75.

33 See L.M. Cullen, 'Patrons, Teachers and Literacy in Irish: 1700–1850', in Mary Daly and David Dickson (eds), *The Origins of Popular Literacy in Ireland: Language Change and Educational Development, 1700–1920* (Dublin: Trinity College Dublin and University College Dublin, 1990), p. 18.

34 Ibid., p. 16.

35  Ibid., p. 17. For a study of Cork scribes, see Breandán O Conchúir, *Scríobhaithe Chorcaí 1700–1850* (Dublin: An Clóchomhar, 1974).

36  Kennedy, 'Reading the Enlightenment', p. 357. Though some writers have speculated that Nano Nagle attended the same hedge school attended by Edmund Burke, this is unlikely. It is more likely that she was educated by a visiting hedge-school master/tutor. Girls of her social rank were usually educated at home, until they reached the age when they could travel to the continent to attend a convent. For the provision and use of hedge schools see McManus, *The Irish Hedge School*.

37  McManus, *The Irish Hedge School*, pp. 170–1.

38  See Deirdre Raftery, *Women and Learning in English Writing, 1600–1900* (Dublin: Four Courts Press, 1997).

39  Dolan indicates that there was a much more robust trade in publications for Catholic women than has, heretofore, been understood. See Frances E. Dolan, 'Reading, Work and Catholic Women's Biographies' in Karen Raber (ed.), *Ashgate Critical Essays on Women Writers in England, 1550–1700*, Vol. 6 (Abingdon, Oxon.: Routledge, 2009).

40  See Dolan, 'Reading, Work and Catholic Women's Biographies'.

41  Mita Choudhury, *Convents and Nuns in Eighteenth-Century French Politics and Culture* (Ithaca, NY and London: Cornell University Press, 2004), p. 130.

42  See Dickson, *Old World Colony*, p. 268.

43  Research for this book included examining the possibility that Nano Nagle was educated with the Dames de St Maur, in Paris. Their records for the pre-revolutionary period are at the National Archives, Paris, and contain no relevant surviving evidence; similarly, at the archives at Kylemore Abbey, there are no surviving records from the monastery at Ypres, which was destroyed in the early days of the First World War. The only relevant record is a deposition made by Dame Bernard Stewart OSB, Abbess at Kylemore in 1916, in which she states that oral tradition within the community always held that Nano Nagle was educated by the Benedictines at Ypres, between 1728 and 1734.

44  The Benedictine monastery at Ypres was established in 1665, by the Benedictines of Ghent; they had been established from the Brussels monastery founded by Lady Mary Percy in 1598. The Ypres community moved to Ireland in 1920, as the Abbey at Ypres was destroyed in the First World War. They settled at Kylemore Abbey, Connemara.

45  Nano Nagle to Miss Fitzsimons, 29 April 1770, PSCA, IE PBVM NN 1/1/3.

46  S.J. Connolly, 'Family, Love and Marriage: Some Evidence from the Early Eighteenth Century', in Margaret MacCurtain and Mary O'Dowd (eds), *Women in Early Modern Ireland* (Dublin: Wolfhound Press, 1991), p. 278.

47  This is discussed in Connolly, 'Family, Love and Marriage', p. 280.

48  Ibid. The sum of £500 was a generous dowry, and was the same sum that Nano left her niece in 1784. Connolly calculated that an annuity of £100 per annum in the mid-eighteenth century would have allowed a gentlewoman to live independently

if modestly; see S.J. Connolly, 'A woman's life in mid-eighteenth-century Ireland: the case of Letitia Bushe', *The Historical Journal*, 43, 2 (2000), p. 441.

49  James Kelly, 'The abduction of women of fortune in eighteenth century Ireland', *Eighteenth Century Ireland*, 9 (1994), pp. 7–43.

50  Connolly, 'Family, Love and Marriage', p. 279.

51  Sometimes spelled Malpas. See Basil O'Connell, *The Nagles of Mount Nagle and Later of Jamestown and Downower, Barts, (with notes on the families of Rice, O'Riordan, FitzGerald and Mapas or Malpas)*, NLI, Pamphlet P 1912/P 2170 (http://catalogue.nli.ie/Record/vtls000482357).

52  See Connolly, 'Family, Love and Marriage', p. 284.

53  Kieran Hickey and Robert Devoy, 'Weather and Natural Disasters', in *Atlas of Cork City* (Cork: Cork University Press, 2005), p. 21.

54  Mother Clare Callaghan wrote that Nano 'retired to a convent in France'. Mother Clare Callaghan to Bishop Coppinger [1800–1804], PSCA, IE PBVM [SPC] 1/1/4. See also *Positio*, vii, which indicates that 'the religious house of Nano's choice is unknown'. A letter written by Bishop Butler of Cork, in 1772, indicates that Nano had taken a vow to enter religion; there are no references whatsoever to Nano making her novitiate in Ireland; it is presumed she was a novice in Paris.

55  For a study of many aspects of monastic and convent economics and management, see Van Dijck et al., *The Economics of Providence*.

56  See Elizabeth Rapley, *The Dévotes: Women and Church in Seventeenth-Century France* (Montreal and London: McGill-Queen's University Press, 1990), pp. 115–17.

57  Rapley, *The Dévotes*, p. 117.

58  See Anon., *The Charitable Mistresses of the Holy Infant Jesus, Known as the Dames de St Maur, 1662* (Dornach: Braun and Co., 1925).

59  See *The Charitable Mistresses*, and see also Rapley, *The Dévotes*, p. 127.

60  *The Charitable Mistresses*, p. 61.

61  Though the pre-Revolutionary records of the Dames de St Maur are at the National Archives, Paris, no novitiate registers have survived. By the time Nano Nagle made her foundation, she had determined that a cloistered life would not suit women who needed to go out amongst the poor to find children to catechise and teach. Her initial attempts involved bringing the Ursulines to Cork, but their rule of enclosure defeated Nano's aims. When Nano made her own foundation in Ireland, she referred to it as the Sisters of the Charitable Instruction of the Sacred Heart of Jesus. The title was temporary, while a rule and constitutions were being determined; in 1791, the apostolic brief of Pope Pius VI gave approval to the foundation; the congregation was given the title, The Presentation of the Blessed Virgin Mary, by Fr Callanan, a Franciscan friar and confessor to Nano Nagle, who had been asked by the Bishop of Cork to draw up the rule and constitutions.

62  See Harvey Chisick, 'French Charity Schools in the Seventeenth and Eighteenth Centuries – with Special Reference to the Case of Amiens', *Social History*, 16, 32 (1983), pp. 241–77.

63   Chisick, 'French Charity Schools', p. 244.

64   Ibid., p. 246.

65   Nano Nagle to Miss Fitzsimons, 17 July 1769, PSCA, IE PBVM NN 1/1/1.

66   Ibid.

67   Ibid.

68   These are discussed in Connolly, 'A woman's life in mid-eighteenth-century Ireland', pp. 433–51.

69   Connolly, 'A woman's life in mid-eighteenth-century Ireland', p. 437.

70   Ibid., p. 438.

71   See Kennedy, 'Reading the Enlightenment in Eighteenth-Century Ireland', p. 355. Kennedy notes that 'Irish readers of the eighteenth century had access to a large pool of ... texts' on subjects such as philosophy, literature, political science, history, exploration, botany, architecture, the law, education and astronomy.'

72   Brown, *The Irish Enlightenment*, p. 287.

73   Mary Nagle and Pierce Nagle had seven children: Stephen, Patrick, Margaret, Sarah, Theresa, James, and Pierce.

74   Elizabeth Nagle and Robert Ffrench had six children: Francis, Christina, Maryann, Mary, Honora, and Robert. The family homestead at Ballygriffin passed from David Nagle to the Nagle Ffrench side of the family, as David's only child died in 1753. It was inherited by Joseph Chichester Nagle, the son of Honora Nagle Ffrench and her English husband, Charles Chichester.

75   Mother Clare Callaghan to Bishop Coppinger [c.1800–1804], PSCA, IE PBVM [SPC] 1/1/4.

76   See Kenneth Milne, *The Irish Charter Schools, 1730–1830* (Dublin: Four Courts Press, 1997).

77   Seán O Comdealbáin, 'The Charter Schools of Cork County', *Journal of Cork Historical and Archaeological Society*, 39 (1944), p. 95.

78   O Comdealbáin, 'The Charter Schools', p. 93.

79   Ibid., p. 94; see also Milne, *The Irish Charter Schools*.

80   See Áine Hyland and Kenneth Milne (eds), *Irish Educational Documents Vol. 1* (Dublin: CICE, 1987), pp. 51–4 *passim*.

81   Ibid.

82   Ibid.

83   Nano Nagle to Miss Fitzsimons, 17 July 1769.

84   Ibid.

85   Ibid.

86   'Wicked' in the eighteenth century was a term that was used to refer to the absence of religious faith, rather than bad behaviour. Mother Clare Callaghan to Bishop Coppinger [1800–1894], PSCA, IE PBVM [SPC] 1/1/4.

87   Nano Nagle to Miss Fitzsimons, 17 July 1769.

88   Ibid.

89   Ibid.

90   Ibid.

91  *Positio*, p. 108.

92  Deed of Trust, Ballyglunin Papers, reproduced in Pius O'Farrell, *Breaking of Morn*, p. 41.

93  Ibid.

94  Nano Nagle to Miss Fitzsimons, 17 July 1769.

95  Margaret Butler (Sr Francis of Assisi) was born in Mophin, Co. Wexford, in 1718; she entered the Ursuline Convent on 4 October 1763, and was professed on 19 December 1765.

96  Annals of the Ursuline Convent, Saint Denis, cited by Assumpta O'Neill, in 'Nano Nagle's Ursuline Friends' (n.p., n.d), p. 5. Nano later referred to her inability to write in French.

97  Ibid.

98  Ibid.

99  Charles Smith, *The Ancient and Present State of the County and City of Cork*, two volumes (Cork: John Connor, 1750), pp. 401–2, cited in Jessie Castle and Gillian O'Brien, '"I am building a house": Nano Nagle's Georgian convents', *Irish Architectural and Decorative Studies*, 19 (2016), pp. 57–8.

100  See Castle and O'Brien, 'I am building a house', p. 60.

101  Ursuline Convent Blackrock, MS 04293, cited in Castle and O'Brien, 'I am building a house', p. 66.

102  Nano Nagle to Miss Fitzsimons, 28 Sept 1770, PSCA, IE PBVM NN 1/1/6.

103  Castle and O'Brien, 'I am building a house', p. 65.

104  Nano Nagle to Miss Fitzsimons, 17 December 1770, PASF.

105  *Freeman's Journal*, 18 February 1772.

106  See Ursula Clarke OSU, *The Ursulines in Cork Since 1771* (Cork: Privately published by the Ursuline Convent, Blackrock, 1996).

107  Novitiate Account Book, Ursuline Convent Cork, UCB/00678.

108  Nano Nagle to Teresa Mulally, 24 August 1778, GHAD, IE PBVM [GHD] 3/1/1/1/4.

109  Ursuline Convent Annals, 18 September 1771, reconstituted in Annals of South Presentation Convent Cork, 1771–1892, PSCA, IE PBVM [SPC] 1/1. The early years of the Ursuline Annals were copied faithfully by the Presentation Annalist, to ensure that a full record of Nano Nagle's foundations was kept at South Presentation Convent; the Annals of South Presentation Convent were reconstituted after Nano's death, and are clearly not contemporaneous. An inscription on the Annals indicates that they were reconstituted by Sr M. de Pazzi Leahy, who entered the PBVMs in 1832.

110  South Presentation Convent Annals, p. 12, PSCA, IE PBVM [SPC] 1/1.

111  Abbess Lynch to Teresa Mulally, 24 February 1784, GHAD, IE PBVM [GHD] 3, A. I (i) FD/12.

112  Abbess Lynch to Teresa Mulally, 13 August 1784, GHAD, IE PBVM [GHD] 3, A. I (i) FD/13.

113  The number of boarding schools for Catholic girls quickly increased in the nineteenth century. Convent education for girls, similar to that of the Ursulines,

was provided by the Loreto Sisters (1822), the Society of the Sacred Heart (1842), the Faithful Companions of Jesus (1844), the St Louis (1859), and the Sisters of St Joseph of Cluny (1860).

114 South Presentation Convent Annals, p. 19.

115 Ibid., p. 20.

116 Nano Nagle considered the rule and constitutions of three societies: the Hospitallers of the Third Order of St Francis (Grey Sisters), the Hospitallers of St Thomas of Villanova, and the Sisters of the Charitable Schools of the Holy Child Jesus (Dames de St Maur). Nagle died before final decisions were made. An apostolic brief of Pius VI (3 September 1791), gave approval of Nagle's foundation, but an instruction required the Bishop of Cork to draw up new rules and constitutions that would be modelled closely on those of the Ursulines.

117 See Clear, *Nuns in Nineteenth-Century Ireland*, pp. 36–9.

118 Nano Nagle, to Miss Mulally, 31 January 1783, GHAD, IE PBVM [GHD] 3/1/1/1/9.

119 'Annual report of the asylum for aged and destitute women, Douglas Street, Cork for the year ending the 31st of December, 1863' (*Cork Examiner*, 20 February 1864).

120 Dickson, *Old World Colony*, p. 454.

121 Sr Francis Tobin to Teresa Mulally, 28 February 1795. Reproduced in O'Farrell, *Breaking of Morn*, pp. 191–6.

122 South Presentation Convent Annals, p. 20.

123 Sr Angela Fitzsimons to Teresa Mulally, 21 May 1784, GHAD, IE PBVM [GHD] 3/1/1/2/1.

124 Ibid. Sr Angela Fitzsimons and Sr Francis Tobin both wrote of Nano Nagle's illness, and self-mortification.

125 South Presentation Convent Annals, p. 11.

126 The disease is spread more easily in small, poorly ventilated rooms where air does not circulate properly, such as the cabins and cottages that Nagle visited constantly. German microbiologist Robert Koch published his findings that *Mycobacterium tuberculosis* caused TB in 1882.

127 Nicole Fogel, 'Tuberculosis: a disease without boundaries', *Tuberculosis*, 95 (2015), pp. 527–31. See also Thomas M. Daniel, 'The history of tuberculosis.' *Respiratory Medicine*, 100, 11 (2006), pp. 1862–70. Available at: https://doi.org/10.1016/j.rmed.2006.08.006 (downloaded 12 February 2018).

128 Nano Nagle to Miss Fitzsimons, 17 July 1769.

129 Sr Angela Fitzsimons to Teresa Mulally, 21 May 1784.

130 Ibid.

## CHAPTER 3

1 Copy of the Will of Nano Nagle, in *Positio*, pp. 421–2; O'Farrell, *Woman of the Gospel*, 175; Mother Angela Collins to Joseph Nagle, 12 June 1800, cited in Walsh, *Nano Nagle*, pp. 376–8.

2   Mother Clare Callaghan to Charles Chichester, 21 December 1814, in O'Farrell, *Breaking of Morn*, pp. 327–8.

3   South Presentation Convent Annals, 1771–1892.

4   Walsh, *Nano Nagle*, p. 179.

5   'Conspectus', in Hutch, *Nano Nagle*; Presentation Foundation Chart, in Walsh, *Nano Nagle*; Raphael Consedine, *Nano Nagle Seminars July–August 1984* (Cork: Nano Nagle House, Douglas Street, 1984), pp. 37–41. This was also the period just prior to Catholic Emancipation in 1829.

6   Hutch, *Nano Nagle*, pp. 161–7; Roland Burke Savage, *A Valiant Dublin Woman: The Story of George's Hill, 1766–1940* (Dublin: M.H. Gill and Son, Ltd., 1940), p. 221.

7   Burke Savage, *A Valiant Dublin Woman*, pp. 221–2; Consedine, *Listening Journey*, p. 216. The move to Richmond was facilitated by the financial assistance of a Miss Brown, a friend of Sr Francis de Sales Knowd who was a member of the George's Hill community at the time.

8   Burke Savage, *A Valiant Dublin Woman*, pp. 225–32. Miss O'Brien of Rahan Lodge, a sister-in-law of Anna Maria O'Brien, built a convent and school for the Sisters, endowed the community with three acres and a yearly income and subsequently joined the community. Anna Maria O'Brien was the sister of Frances Ball, who later founded the Loreto Sisters.

9   'Conspectus', in Hutch, *Nano Nagle*; Presentation Foundation Chart, in Walsh, *Nano Nagle*; Burke Savage, *A Valiant Dublin Woman*, p. 222. When Xavier Doyle left Mullingar there were fourteen sisters in the new community.

10  Hutch, *Nano Nagle*, pp. 167–9; Presentation Foundation Chart, in Walsh, *Nano Nagle*.

11  Hutch, *Nano Nagle*, pp. 172–80; Presentation Foundation Chart, in Walsh, *Nano Nagle*.

12  Hutch, *Nano Nagle*, pp. 326–33.

13  Presentation Foundation Chart, in Walsh, *Nano Nagle*.

14  Hutch, *Nano Nagle*, pp. 188–98.

15  This bears out the findings, concerning Irish convents more generally, in Clear, *Nuns in Nineteenth-Century Ireland*, p. 38. With the exception of Presentation Convent Galway, all of the convents were located in dioceses within these two provinces.

16  Presentation Convent Galway Annals, pp.1–4, IE PBVM GAL, uncatalogued.

17  Edmund Ffrench, Warden of Galway and its District, to Mrs McLoughlin, Presentation Convent Kilkenny, 17 October 1815, quoted in Hutch, *Nano Nagle*, pp. 180–2. See also Margaret C. Scully, 'Galway Schooling and the Presentation Sisters: An Account of the Work of a Religious Body in the Practice of Education, 1815–1873', (unpublished MEd thesis, University College Cork, 1973), pp. 4–5.

18  This school had been established in 1808 under the patronage of Warden Valentine Bodkin. Also known as the Female Orphan Asylum, it was established by means of subscriptions. See Scully, 'Galway Schooling', p. 8.

19　Edmund Ffrench, Warden of Galway and its District, to Mrs McLoughlin, Presentation Convent Kilkenny, 17 October 1815, quoted in Hutch, *Nano Nagle*, pp. 180–2; Scully, 'Galway Schooling', pp. 4–5. In 1809–10, the Rev Bartholomew Burke, Parish Priest of St Nicholas East, Galway, collected £4,800 for the purpose of establishing a community of nuns that was devoted exclusively to the instruction of poor female children. On his death in 1813, he bequeathed £6,000 for the foundation of such an establishment. See Hutch, *Nano Nagle*, p.180; Scully, 'Galway Schooling', p. 10.

20　Hutch, *Nano Nagle*, p. 180; Scully, 'Galway Schooling', p. 10.

21　Presentation Convent Galway Annals, pp. 3–4.

22　Presentation Convent Thurles Annals, pp. 1–2, IE PBVM THU, uncatalogued.

23　Ibid., p. 2. In her work commemorating the bicentenary of the Ursulines in Thurles, Sr Mercedes Lillis suggests that in 1816 the first two Presentation nuns who came to Thurles taught with the Ursulines in Saint Anne's Free School, which was then housed in three rooms of the Ursuline Convent, until their own apostolate started. See Sr Mercedes Lillis, *Two Hundred Years A-growing: The Story of the Ursulines in Thurles, 1787–1987* (privately published: A Bicentenary Commemorative Publication, 1987), pp. 52–3.

24　Presentation Convent Thurles Annals, pp. 2–3. See also Maria Luddy, 'Presentation Convents in County Tipperary 1806–1900', in *Tipperary Historical Journal* (1992), p. 85. As they were not in a position to organise a chaplain, the Sisters could not have Mass daily or at a regular hour. Luddy describes the house in Stradavoher as a thatched cottage.

25　Presentation Convent Wexford Annals (1818), IE PBVM WEX, uncatalogued. The Annals of the Wexford Convent are not paginated, but the entries are given under years. See also Hutch, *Nano Nagle*, p. 198.

26　Presentation Convent Wexford Annals (1818). The special sanction of the Metropolitan Dr Troy was necessary for the foundation as Dr Ryan was suffering from 'mental infirmity' at that time.

27　Ibid.

28　'Conspectus', in Hutch, *Nano Nagle*. Although Hutch gives the year as 1836 in his 'Conspectus', the Annals of the Presentation Convent Limerick, record the year as 1837.

29　M. Moloney, 'Limerick in Emancipation Days', in *Presentation Convent, Limerick Centenary 1837–1937* (Limerick: City Printing Company, 1937), pp. 37–9.

30　Presentation Convent (Sexton Street) Limerick Annals, p. 1, IE PBVM SSL, uncatalogued.

31　Ibid. See also Paula Coonerty, 'The Presentation Sisters and the Education of "Poor Female Children" in Limerick, 1837–1870', *The Old Limerick Journal*, 33 (Winter 1996), p. 38.

32　Presentation Convent (Sexton Street) Limerick Annals, pp. 2–3.

33　Patrick Hogan was also a friend and advisor to King. In addition to the failed attempts at establishing a convent of teaching sisters in the city, the Christian

Brothers were introduced to the area in 1816. Ten years later they opened their new schools at Sexton Street. In an effort to address the problem in relation to girls' schools, Hogan leased property in Sexton Street and superintended the building of a school. See Moloney, 'Limerick in Emancipation Days', p. 38.

34  Presentation Convent (Sexton Street) Limerick Annals, p. 3. See also Hutch, *Nano Nagle*, p. 347. Fr Pat Hogan gave a lease of the convent to Catherine King and Honoria Harnett at the yearly rent of £50. The rent was to commence in 1840 with the specific date left blank. See Presentation Convent (Sexton Street) Limerick Register (8 May 1837).

35  Presentation Convent (Sexton Street) Limerick Annals, pp. 4–6. Harnett was appointed first Superioress of the new convent.

36  Ibid., pp. 15–23 and p. 34.

37  'Conspectus', in Hutch, *Nano Nagle.*

38  Presentation Convent Clondalkin Annals, Vol. 1, pp. 1–12, IE PBVM CDN, uncatalogued. And see *Reportorium Novum*: Dublin Diocesan Historical Record, Vol. II, No. 1 (1958), pp. 215–16.

39  Presentation Convent Clondalkin Annals, Vol. 1, pp. 1–12. *Bicentenary Vista: Presentation Convents, Dublin* (n.n., Drogheda: Drogheda Printers, 1976) pp. 23–30. Fr John Moore was a curate in the parish of Clondalkin from 1840 and the Parish Priest from 1855–93. The convent and parish church are still interlinked.

40  Having resigned as Superioress of the Carlow community, Sr Joseph Cosslett became the first Superioress of the Clondalkin Convent, a position she held for more than one term of office. In 1867 she accompanied the group of Sisters that founded the Presentation Convent in Lucan. When the Lucan house was established she returned to Clondalkin. She died on the 6 January 1872, aged seventy years. Sr Regis Cosslett, a sister of Mother Joseph's, became the Assistant Superior and taught in the school. Sr Stanislaus Mulcahy became the Mistress of Novices and was named by Rev John Moore as being chiefly responsible for the school in the application to the Commissioners. Presentation Convent Carlow Annals (1857), pp. 25–6, PSCA, IE PBVM CAR; Presentation Convent Clondalkin Annals, Vol. 1, pp. 1–12; Vol. 2, pp. 20–1. Applications, ED 1 / 29, MS No. 174, National Archives of Ireland (hereafter NAI). Hutch, *Nano Nagle*, p. 425.

41  Presentation Convent Clondalkin Annals, Vol. 1, pp. 1–12.

42  Presentation Convent Milltown Annals, IE PBVM MLT, uncatalogued.

43  Presentation Convent Tralee Annals, Vol. 1 (1809–12), IE PBVM TRA, uncatalogued.

44  Presentation Convent Galway Annals, pp. 3–7. The Green is now known as Eyre Square.

45  Ibid. Built sometime after December 1749, the building was used as an artillery barrack after the closure of the Charter School. It continued as such until 1814 after which it was left without tenants until the arrival of the Presentation Sisters.

46  Presentation Convent Thurles Annals, pp. 3–5. The Christian Brothers had opened a school for the boys of the town near the Cathedral a year before the arrival of the

Sisters. After the move to their smaller quarters the Archbishop paid the rent of £17 per annum in favour of the nuns.

47  Ibid., p. 5.

48  Ibid., p. 10. Dr Blake had come to the convent to preach at the reception of Sr M. Peter Magan in January 1821. Blake was concerned at the cramped conditions under which the nuns were living and, on hearing of their failure to come to an agreement with the owner, decided to work on their behalf. After considerable difficulty, he persuaded the old gentleman who owned the property to sell.

49  Ibid., pp. 10–12.

50  In May 1833, a group of five went from Presentation Galway to Blackrock, also in Galway, to open a new convent. This attempt did not succeed, however, and in June 1835 the Sisters were recalled, 'the poor children not attending the school there, it being so near this Convent'. In April 1836, the Galway Annals recorded the return of a group of Sisters who attempted to open a convent in Limerick. The group was recalled 'not having got any encouragement to remain in Limerick as no subjects joined them – the situation of the Convent being very bad'. See Presentation Convent Galway Annals, pp. 8–11. Consedine noted that a foundation in Sneem, Co. Kerry, opened in 1881 from the Castleisland convent, 'met with obstacles which could not be overcome' and the three founding Sisters returned to Castleisland. She also refers to a Limerick attempt to open a house in Kenmare that ended because the Sisters could not 'harmonize the school hours demanded there with the demands of their Rule'. See Consedine, *Listening Journey*, p. 283.

51  'Rules and Constitutions of The Sisters of the Congregation of the Charitable Instruction 1793', in Consedine, *Listening Journey*, pp. 406–17.

52  Presentation Convent George's Hill Annals, p. 117.

53  Burke Savage, *A Valiant Dublin Woman*, p. 153. This first house cost her £870.17s.5d and was rented by Fr James Mulcaile, Mulally's friend, advisor and benefactor, who moved out of his house in Pill Lane.

54  Teresa Mulally to Sir Edward Bellew, 24 June 1802, quoted in Burke Savage, *A Valiant Dublin Woman*, pp. 165–6.

55  Ibid., p. 165. Owing to a legal bar on Catholic school endowments the terms of the bequests could not be specific.

56  Ibid., p. 166. In 1788 Patrick Bellew had arranged to give a bond of £1,200 at 5 per cent and to pay the remainder of the principal of £800 in instalments as convenient. Between 1789 and 1801, Teresa had received £825. Although Burke Savage noted that payments from this source appeared to cease in 1832, an entry on the Account Sheet for Cash Received between January and December 1854 records the sum of £55.7s.8d as 'Lord Bellew's Yrs Int'. Expenditure Account Sheets, GHAD, IE PBVM [GHD] 3 AD/1 (2).

57  Mother Xavier Doyle to Mrs George Butler, n.d., quoted in Burke Savage, *A Valiant Dublin Woman*, p. 167.

58  Ibid., p. 167.

59 'The Last Will and Testament of Maria Teresa Mulally', quoted in Ibid., pp. 185–7.

60 Presentation Convent Doneraile Annals, PSCA IE PBVM DON/1 (2). Yearly Accompt Book, October 1ˢᵗ 1818, PSCA IE PBVM DON/38 (1).

61 Hutch, *Nano Nagle*, p. 347.

62 Presentation Convent (Sexton Street) Limerick Register, 8 May 1837, IE PBVM SSL. The entry also recorded that 'Miss King handed to Sister Mary Francis Cantillon, Bursar £60.0.0.'

63 Presentation Convent (Sexton Street) Limerick Annals, pp. 21–3.

64 Edmund Ffrench, Warden of Galway and its District, to Mrs McLoughlin, Presentation Convent Kilkenny, 17 October 1815. Quoted in Hutch, *Nano Nagle*, pp. 180–2.

65 Ibid. The funds referred to the annual return on the £1,000 invested in Government Five Per Cent Debentures.

66 Hutch, *Nano Nagle*, pp. 373–4, NAI, ED 1 / 13, MS No. 168, Applications.

67 Presentation Convent Clondalkin Annals, Vol. II, pp. 21–2.

68 Ibid., p. 21.

69 Clear, *Nuns in Nineteenth-Century Ireland*, p. 70.

70 Barbara Walsh, *Roman Catholic Nuns in England and Wales 1800–1937: A Social History*, (Dublin: Irish Academic Press, 2002), p. 103.

71 Peckham Magray, *The Transforming Power of the Nuns*, p. 38; Clear, *Nuns in Nineteenth-Century Ireland*, p. 79.

72 Presentation Convent Wexford, Names of Sisters Professed in Wexford 1817–1968, p. 1. Presentation Convent Wexford Annals (1871).

73 See Peckham Magray, *The Transforming Power of the Nuns*, p. 36.

74 Clear, *Nuns in Nineteenth-Century Ireland*, p. 87. In addition to Angelina Gould's entrance to Presentation Doneraile, Clear refers to the entrance of one of the Arthurs, a Limerick business family, who brought with her a dowry of £35,000 on her admission to the Loreto Convent in Rathfarnham. This amount freed the convent funds to build a Pugin-designed chapel adjacent to the convent. See Hutch, *Nano Nagle*, pp. 190–5; Peckham Magray, *The Transforming Power of the Nuns*, p. 14.

75 Peckham Magray, *The Transforming Power of the Nuns*, p. 37.

76 'Rules and Constitutions of The Sisters of the Congregation of the Charitable Instruction 1793', in Consedine, *Listening Journey*, p. 410.

77 Consedine, *Listening Journey*, pp. 124–50. In the case of the Killarney foundation the first postulant, Lucy Curtayne, was the daughter of a widow and feared that the 'smallness of her fortune' would prevent her from joining a religious institute. This was resolved when Lord Kenmare agreed to pay a pension on her behalf. Margaret Tobin, one of the three sisters who came to South Presentation with the intention of making the earlier foundation in Thurles, also came from more modest circumstances. It is likely that her parents had died before her entrance to the convent leaving her with no great family support after she entered. In addition, the small amount of money returned to her two older sisters when they left the Cork house reflected the amount that they had brought with them.

78   South Presentation Convent, Funds of the Convent Income 1824–1974, 26 April 1824, PSCA, IE PBVM [SPC], uncatalogued. The Sisters X. and J. Harnett were the two sisters, Hanoria and Jane, who had entered Cork for the intended Limerick foundation in 1823.

79   Presentation Convent Doneraile Yearly Accompt Book, PSCA, IE PBVM DON/38 (1).

80   Presentation Convent Fermoy Convent's Receipts and Expenditures 1838–1888, IE PBVM FER, uncatalogued. The women were named as Sr Cahill, Sr Murphy, Sr Martha (?) Miss O'Gorman, Miss Peyton and Miss Coughlan.

81   Presentation Convent Killarney, Yearly Accounts, IE PBVM KLY, uncatalogued. Presentation Convent Bandon, Yearly Accounts, IE PBVM BAN, uncatalogued. Presentation Convent Mitchelstown, Yearly Accounts, PSCA, IE PBVM MTN, uncatalogued. Presentation Convent Crosshaven, Receipts and Expenditure Book, PSCA, IE PBVM CRO, uncatalogued.

82   North Presentation Convent, Early Financial Matters and Record of Professions, pp. 1–50, PSCA, IE PBVM NPC.

83   South Presentation Convent, Funds of the Convent Income 1824–1974, PSCA, IE PBVM [SPC], uncatalogued.

84   South Presentation Convent Annals, pp. 276–7.

85   Ibid., p. 304 and p. 310.

86   Presentation Convent Clondalkin Annals, p. 107.

87   Ibid., p. 95.

88   South Presentation Convent Annals, pp. 195–202.

89   Ibid., pp. 202–3. He also bequeathed a trust of £1,500 invested in French Funds to the community, directing that the interest be spent on food and clothing for the poor children with whom they worked.

90   George's Hill Convent Annals, p. 11, pp. 25–6. After the death of Daniel Murray in 1852, Paul Cullen became Archbishop of Dublin. He was elevated to the position of Cardinal in 1866.

91   Ibid., p. 524.

92   Ibid., pp. 481–2. Robert Healy was a brother of Mother M. Francis.

93   Ibid., pp. 496–8.

94   Presentation Convent Tralee Annals, Vol. 1 (1812–30).

95   George's Hill Convent Annals, p. 11.

96   Presentation Convent Wexford Annals (1868). James Beehan, who died in the United States, left a bequest of £1,000. The Bishop of Virginia requested of Roche that some portion of it be given to the charitable institutions in the town.

97   Ibid., 1869 and 1870. Mr d'Arcy was part of a group who visited the Presentation Schools on 29 September 1869. Other members of the visiting party were Cardinal Cullen, Dr Furlong Bishop of Ferns, Canon Roche PP, the Earl and Countess of Granard, Sir John Grey and several clergy.

98   Presentation Convent Clondalkin Annals, Vol. 2, p. 111.

99   Presentation Convent (Sexton Street) Limerick Annals, p. 35.

100 Presentation Convent Thurles Annals, p. 52.

101 Ibid., pp. 55–6.

102 Ibid., pp. 59–60. In Thurles the Presentation Convent is located beside the Cathedral and Archbishop's Palace.

103 Presentation Convent Wexford Annals, 1835. This entry in the Annals describes how the workmen, who were knocking the existing wall to extend the space, detached the wall at each end to let it fall. Without giving warning of the danger attached, they went to breakfast and allowed the wall to fall in their absence.

104 Ibid., 1856. Dr Myles Murphy was consecrated Bishop of Ferns on 10 March 1850.

105 Ibid., 1883. Devereux, a wealthy businessman from South Main Street, was also a benefactor to other religious houses in the town including the Christian Brothers.

106 Ibid., 1862–7.

107 Ibid., 1883. Included in these were more than £500 towards the enlargement of the convent and an enclosure wall for the outer garden; the building of an Infant Girls' School; £350 towards the boys' school St Patrick's and playgrounds; an additional classroom attached to St Joseph's School at a cost of £300 and two additional classrooms to Our Lady's School.

108 Ibid., 1883.

109 Presentation Convent Tralee Annals, Vol. 1 (1809); Presentation Convent Doneraile Annals (1818); Presentation Convent Wexford Annals (1818).

110 Presentation Convent (Sexton Street) Limerick Annals, pp. 6–7. Miss Harnett donated £10 and Mrs Staunton £23.

111 Ibid., pp. 26–9.

112 Presentation Convent Wexford Annals (1867). The Annalist commented, 'This is of immense advantage, and calls for our deepest gratitude, as heretofore the water required for drinking and cooking purposes had to be brought from Summerhill, and the consequent difficulty of procuring it makes the gift of our Benefactor all the more estimable.'

113 Presentation Convent Listowel Annals, p. 37, PSCA, IE PBVM LTL, uncatalogued.

114 Edmund Ffrench, Warden of Galway and its District, to Mrs McLoughlin, Presentation Convent Kilkenny, 17 October 1815. Quoted in Hutch, *Nano Nagle*, pp. 180–2 and Scully, 'Galway Schooling', pp. 4–5.

115 *The Connaught Journal*, 27 March 1823. Quoted in Scully, 'Galway Schooling', pp. 11–12.

116 Ibid., p.12. The notice stated that the Rev Thomas Maguire would give the sermon and that the 'acknowledged talents of the eloquent Preacher, as well as the truly Christian and humane occasion on which they will be exerted, will, we doubt not, call forth the charitable sympathies of the public in a liberal subscription'.

117 Presentation Convent (Sexton Street) Limerick Annals, p. 7, p. 14, p. 17, p. 26. Rev Theobold Matthew, strongly associated with the Temperance Movement, was the preacher in 1839.

118 Presentation Convent Clondalkin Annals, Vol. II, p. 22. The Annals note that the charity sermon was held on the Sunday within the octave of the Feast of the Assumption which falls on the 15 August.

119   George's Hill Convent Annals, p. 493.

120   Ibid., pp. 494–5. Presentation Convent Listowel Annals, p. 19.

121   South Presentation Convent Annals, p. 266.

122   George's Hill Convent, Expenditure Account Sheets, Cash Received from January 54 to December 31/54, GHAD, IE PBVM [GHD] 3/AD/1 (2); George's Hill Community Annual Accounts 1874–1936, Cash Received from January 1ˢᵗ to December 1874, GHAD, IE PBVM [GHD] 3 / AD / 2. The 1854 Accounts also note £11.8s.6d that was collected at *Quarant Ore*, part of the ceremony of adoration to the Sacred Heart.

123   Dublin Diocesan Archives (hereafter DDA) Hamilton Papers, MS File 37 / 4 1853– 60 Ordinary 1855 AH No. 48. The schools were completed in 1862. George's Hill Convent Annals, p. 476.

124   Presentation Convent Wexford Annals (1820). The collections were organised by Mother Baptist Frayne who also drew up the plan for the new chapel.

125   Presentation Convent Wexford Annals (1866).

126   Commissioners of Irish Education Inquiry, *Appendix to Second Report of the Commissioners of Irish Education Inquiry (Abstract of Returns in 1824, from the Protestant and Roman Catholic Clergy in Ireland, of the state of education in their respective parishes)*, pp. 92–3.

127   *Copy of letter in possession of Count Douglas O'Donnel of Austria*, 2 August 1850, IE PBVM GAL, uncatalogued.

128   Presentation Convent Listowel Annals (1855), p. 20.

129   Presentation Convent Wexford Annals (1861; 1862).

130   Presentation Convent Wexford Annals (1868).

131   Presentation Convent (Sexton Street) Limerick Annals, p. 104.

132   Presentation Convent Wexford Annals, pp. 57–179, *passim*.

133   Ibid., pp. 142–3.

134   Presentation Convent Clondalkin Annals, Vol. 1, pp. 7–8, p. 144 and p. 179. The Annals note that in 1862 the pension of a Mrs Shields, a wealthy widow who wished to enter the novitiate, proved 'a means of helping the community, as yet poor and struggling'. A similar situation arose in 1875 when another widow, Mrs Keenan, boarded with them for nine months, for which time she paid a total of £45.

## CHAPTER 4

1   The Presentations quickly became a major force in Newfoundland education and had established at least fifteen schools by the time D.W. Prowse published his *History of Newfoundland from the English Colonial and Foreign Records* (London: Eyre and Spottiswoode, 1896). His work became the island's most widely read historical study, and influenced generations of scholars, yet it ignored the role that the Sisters played. In the five communities of women religious that settled in the US between 1790 and 1815, there were Irish emigrant women

and Irish-American women. These were the Ursulines (New Orleans, 1727), the Carmelites (Port Tobacco, 1790s), the Visitation Sisters (Georgetown, 1799), the Sisters of Charity (Maryland, 1809), the Sisters of Loreto (Kentucky, 1812) and the Sisters of Charity of Nazareth (Kentucky, 1812). The Ursuline Sisters, who settled in Massachusetts and New York in 1813, came from Cork. They returned to Cork in 1815. See Daniel Murphy, *A History of Irish Emigrant and Missionary Education* (Dublin: Four Courts Press, 2000), pp. 195–6. Two years after the Presentations went to Newfoundland, the Irish Sisters of Mercy made an overseas foundation in England. The steady growth of Irish congregations in overseas missions dates from the 1830s, and grew significantly from the 1840s onwards.

2   The concept and practice of chain migration is used by scholars working on diaspora history, with reference to ways in which kinship networks provided the means for successive generations of families to emigrate; Raftery uses this concept to analyse ways in which Orders of Irish women religious brought generations of aspirants, novices and nuns from Ireland to America, Canada and Australia in the nineteenth century. See Raftery, *'"Je suis d'aucune Nation"'*.

3   Several sources have been used to compile the list of Newfoundland and Canada convents and their founding dates; they are here indicated by the place they were located, with additional information where more than one foundation was made in one place. The convents were founded in St John's (1833); Harbor Grace (1851); Carbonear (1852); Fermeuse (1853); Harbor Main (1853); St John's West/ St Patrick's (1856); Ferryland (1858); St Mary's Bay (1859); Witless Bay (1860); Placentia (1864); Torbay (1865); Harbor Breton (1872); Renews (1876); Trepassey (1882); St Jacques (1894); Stephenville (1925); Corner Brook/Sacred Heart (1927); Grand Falls/Immaculate Conception (1933); Windsor (1943); Bishop's Falls (1945); Corner Brook/St FX (1947); Humbermouth (1949); Port-au-Port West (1950); Badger (1953); Buchans (1953); Deer Lake (1953); Freshwater (1954); Avondale (1957); Gander (1957); St John's/Assumption (1957); Port-au-Port East (1959); St Vincent's (1962); Benoit's Cove (1962); Cape St George (1962); Mt Pearl (1964); St John's/Carpasian Road (1964); Grand Falls/St Catherine's (1967); St Alban's Bay (1967); St Mary's Bay/Mt Carmel (1967); Piccadilly (1967); Brent's Cove (1968); St Bride's (1969); Harbor Breton/Stella Maris (1970); St John's/Bon Ave (1970); Toronto (1977); Presentation Generalate (1981); Davis Inlet (1984). Other 'houses' were established after this period, as convents closed and Sisters moved into smaller accommodation.

4   See John Mannion, 'Irish migration and settlement in Newfoundland: the formative phase, 1697–1732', *Newfoundland and Labrador Studies*, 17, 2 (2001), pp. 257–93.

5   Ibid., p. 288.

6   Captain James Story, 'Answers to enquiries', 1 September 1681, CO 1/47, 115. Cited in Mannion, 'Irish migration and settlement in Newfoundland', p. 262.

7   Ibid., p. 286.

8   Ibid., p. 274.

9 Governor Samuel Gledhill to Lords of Trade, 2 October 1725, CO 194/8, 52. Cited in Mannion, 'Irish migration and settlement in Newfoundland', p. 275.

10 Ibid, p. 287.

11 Mannion records the earliest ethnic intermarriage in Newfoundland, between an Irish stonemason and a French woman, as taking place in 1689. See Mannion, 'Irish migration and settlement in Newfoundland', p. 264.

12 Thomas F. Necmec, 'The Irish emigration to Newfoundland', in Joseph R. Smallwood (ed.), *The Book of Newfoundland*, Vol. VI (St John's, NL: Newfoundland Book Publishers, 1967), p. 186.

13 Ibid., pp. 186–7.

14 Ibid., p. 187; Mannion, 'Irish migration and settlement in Newfoundland', p. 272.

15 See Necmec, 'The Irish emigration to Newfoundland', p. 189.

16 See Anthony MacDermott, 'Some Irish Families and their influences in Newfoundland', in Smallwood, *The Book of Newfoundland*, Vol. VI, p. 191.

17 See James Fleming, *History of the Catholic Church in Newfoundland and Labrador* (Newfoundland: Transcontinental, 2006); Thomas Flynn, 'The Roman Catholic Church in Newfoundland' in Smallwood, *The Book of Newfoundland*, Vol. II (St John's, NL: Newfoundland Book Publishers, 1937).

18 Flynn, 'The Roman Catholic Church in Newfoundland', p. 376. See also Fleming, *History of the Catholic Church in Newfoundland*, pp. 7–9. Fleming (p. 10) notes that after the Treaty of Utrecht in 1713, Roman Catholic Newfoundland was under the Vicar Apostolic of the London District of England, who had jurisdiction over the British possessions of America. In 1784, John Carroll of Baltimore was nominated Prefect Apostolic for the thirteen colonies in the US.

19 Governor Dorrell to the Magistrates, Harbor Grace (1775), cited in Paul O'Neill, *A Seaport Legacy: The Story of St John's, Newfoundland*, Vol. 2 (Ontario: Porcepic Press, 1976), p. 724.

20 O'Neill notes that parish records in port towns in southern Ireland contain marriage and baptismal entries referring to 'Terra Nova'; Irish Catholics in Newfoundland sometimes married by common consent and had their marriage solemnised later in Ireland, at which time these couples also had their children baptised. See Parish Records, Old St Patrick's, Waterford, cited in O'Neill, *A Seaport Legacy*, p. 725. Travellers' accounts suggest that in harbours remote from St John's, the practice of common consent continued into the nineteenth century. See Constant Carpon, *Voyage à Terre-Neuve* (1852), cited in Ronald Romkey, 'The representation of Newfoundland in nineteenth-century French travel literature', *Newfoundland and Labrador Studies*, 25, 2 (2010), p. 187.

21 Order of Vice Admiral John Campbell, Governor of Newfoundland (1784), cited in Fleming, *History of the Catholic Church in Newfoundland*, p. 12. See also Prowse, *History of Newfoundland*, p. 363.

22 There are three steps towards the development of a bishopric: firstly a priest is appointed Prefect Apostolic, and assumes responsibility for the area (the Prefecture Apostolic), under the supervision of Rome. Then he, or his successor, is ordained

bishop, and the area becomes known as a Vicariate Apostolic. Finally, the area is made a bishopric, and the bishop has authority over it.

23  See O'Neill, *A Seaport Legacy*, p. 731.

24  Ibid. Scallan paid at least one social visit to the Anglican bishop, John Inglis, at his residence on Star Hill; he also accompanied Inglis into the Protestant church, to the horror of Irish Catholics. The incident was reported to Rome and Scallan was sent a reprimand.

25  Fleming went over the head of the Governor and wrote repeatedly to the Secretary of State for the Colonies; he set sail for England in 1836, went to Rome in 1837, and it is suggested he even managed to meet Queen Victoria and press his case for land to build a cathedral in St John's. See O'Neill, *A Seaport Legacy*, pp. 735–7.

26  Sr Mary Xaverius Lynch to Mother M. John Power, 6 January 1834. Presentation Archives, Newfoundland (hereafter PANFL), uncatalogued.

27  O'Neill, *A Seaport Legacy*, p. 775.

28  Irish migrants to Newfoundland in the eighteenth century may themselves have been educated in hedge schools, and would have known how to hide a Catholic schoolmaster. For a study of the hedge schools see McManus, *The Irish Hedge School*.

29  O'Neill, *A Seaport Legacy*, p. 776.

30  The Benevolent Irish Society was founded in Newfoundland in 1806, as a non-denominational philanthropic society for men. All denominations of Christians were admissible to its ranks, as long as they were Irishmen or descendants of Irishmen. In time, the society became exclusively Catholic. See M.F. Howley, *Ecclesiastical History of Newfoundland* (Boston: Doyle and Whittle, 1888), p. 228.

31  Ibid., p. 231.

32  Ibid., p. 235.

33  Sr Mary Xaverius Lynch to Mother M. John Power, 6 January 1834, PANFL.

34  Bishop Fleming recounted his founding of the convent in his *Relatio* (1836), translated into English and published as *Report of the Catholic Mission in Newfoundland in North America, Submitted by the Vicar Apostolic of that Mission, Monsignor Michael Fleming, to His Eminence the Cardinal Prefect of Propaganda, Rome* (Rome: Printing Press of the Sacred Congregation, 1837). He also rehearsed the same story in *The State of the Catholic Religion in Newfoundland, Reviewed in Two Letters* (Rome: 1836), which was inserted into the *Freeman's Journal* for circulation in Ireland, and recounted it again in *Letters on the State of Religion in Newfoundland addressed to the Very Rev. Dr A. O'Connell* (Dublin: James Duffy, 1844).

35  Fleming, *The State of the Catholic Religion in Newfoundland*.

36  Fleming, *Report of the Catholic Mission in Newfoundland*.

37  Howley's *Ecclesiastical History of Newfoundland*, p. 263, indicates that in 1830, while there were seven priests in Newfoundland, three suffered from physical and/ or mental illnesses, and one was in his eighty-second year. Fleming had, therefore, only three active priests.

38   Fleming, *The State of the Catholic Religion in Newfoundland*, p. 4.
39   Ibid.
40   Ibid., p. 18.
41   Fleming, *Letters on the State of Religion in Newfoundland*, p. 18.
42   Ibid.
43   Mary Aikenhead's Sisters of Charity were established in 1815, but their mission to work with hospitals and orphanages, as well as with schools, may have precluded them from Fleming's consideration.
44   The two main types of labour for women in Newfoundland were fish and berry processing, and they continued to work in all-female groups in these industries well into the twentieth century. See Linda Cullum, "'It was a woman's job, I 'spose, pickin' dirt outa berries": negotiating gender, work and wages at Job Brothers, 1940–1950', *Newfoundland and Labrador Studies*, 23, 2 (2008), pp. 185–213.
45   See Patricia A. Thornton, 'Newfoundland's frontier demographic experience: the world we have not lost', *Newfoundland and Labrador Studies*, 1, 2 (1985), pp. 141–62.
46   See Cullum, 'It was a woman's job', and Thornton, 'Newfoundland's frontier demographic experience'.
47   Developing a full understanding of how Presentation education impacted on the experience of women in Newfoundland would benefit from historical research using the methodology of family reconstitution.
48   Presentation Convent Galway Annals, p. 5. Mother Angela Martin returned to the Presentation Convent Kilkenny, in September 1819.
49   The first Superior of Presentation Convent Galway, Mother Angela Martin, had come from Presentation Convent Kilkenny to make the Galway foundation in 1815. Dr French requested that when she returned to Kilkenny in 1819, a replacement should be sent from Kilkenny: this was Sr M. John Power, who was appointed Superioress of the Galway convent.
50   The Galway convent flourished under Mother Power's leadership, and made a foundation in Limerick on 2 May 1833. Those who went to found the Limerick convent were Sr M. Joseph Nolan (Superioress), Sr M. Evangelist Hally, Sr M. Paul French, and Sr M. Stanislaus Lynch. The same month, a new convent was founded in Blackrock, Galway; the Sisters who were sent to found that convent were M. de Sales Coppinger (Superioress), M. Catherine Martin, M. Elizabeth Browne, M. de Pazzi O'Donnell, and M. Agnes Nolan.
51   There were about thirty-three nuns in the Galway convent in 1833, and it continued to attract vocations; parting with a small group to Newfoundland was, therefore, a manageable proposition.
52   Mother M. John Power to Dr Michael Fleming, 22 July 1833, PANFL.
53   Dr Michael Fleming to Mother M. John Power, 17 July 1833, IE PBVM GAL, uncatalogued.
54   Ibid.
55   Ibid.

56   Ibid., Mother M. John Power's independent wealth is discussed in Howley, *Ecclesiastical History of Newfoundland*, p. 279.

57   Dr Michael Fleming to Mother M. John Power, 17 July 1833.

58   Ibid.

59   Mother M. Xavier Moloney to Mother M. John Power, 22 September 1833, PANFL.

60   Mother Magdalen O'Shaughnessy, cited in Howley, *Ecclesiastical History of Newfoundland*, p. 289.

61   The *Lady of the Lake* sank east of Newfoundland having struck an iceberg early in the morning of 11 May, 1833. It had sailed from Belfast, on 8 April.

62   In January 1833, the *Emily* was wrecked while sailing to St John's, Newfoundland, from Nova Scotia; the same month the British-owned *Hume* had to be abandoned off the coast of St John's, and the *Guysbro*, which sailed from Newfoundland on 26 January, bound for Devon, was lost at sea. For lists of shipwrecks see *Lloyd's Register of Shipping*; see also 'Research References' (Irish Shipwrecks, n.d.). Available at: http://www.irishshipwrecks.com/site_pages.php?section=References   (accessed on 31 May 2018) and 'List of shipwrecks in 1833' (Wikipedia, n.d.). Available at: https://en.wikipedia.org/wiki/List_of_shipwrecks_in_1833 (accessed on 31 May 2018).

63   Mother M. Xavier Moloney to Mother M. John Power, 22 September 1833.

64   Ibid.

65   Mother M. Magdalen O'Shaughnessy, cited in Howley, *Ecclesiastical History of Newfoundland*, p. 289.

66   Mother M. Xaverius Lynch to Mother M. John Power, 22 September 1833, PANFL.

67   M. James Dinn, *Foundation of the Presentation Congregation in Newfoundland* (Presentation Convent, Newfoundland, privately published pamphlet, 1975), pp. 16–17.

68   Mother M. Magdalen O'Shaughnessy to Mother M. John Power, 24 November 1833, PANFL.

69   Mother M. Xaverius Lynch to Mother M. John Power, 22 September 1833.

70   The first temporary convent was attached to a slaughterhouse at the foot of Pilot Hill. Dr Fleming, upon seeing a cow being driven through the convent to reach the slaughter yards, decided to move the nuns to more suitable premises.

71   This house, on King's Road, was owned by Archdeacon Wix, who leased it to Dr Fleming for £80 per annum. The Sisters lived there from December 1833 until August 1843.

72   Mother M. Xaverius Lynch to Mother M. John Power, 6 January 1834, PANFL.

73   Ibid.

74   Mother M. Magdalen O'Shaughnessy to Mother M. John Power, 24 November 1833, PANFL.

75   Giacomo Filippo Franzoni, Cardinal Prefect, Office of the Sacred Congregation for the Propagation of the Faith, Rome, to the Rt Rev Michael Fleming, 3 December 1834. Fleming Papers, Diocesan Archives, Newfoundland.

76   Mother M. Xaverius Lynch to Mother M. John Power, 6 January 1834.

77   Ibid.

78   Mother M. Magdalen O'Shaughnessy to Mother M. John Power, 24 November 1833.

79   Entry for 1840 in *Leaves from the Annals of the Sisters of Mercy in Three Volumes*, Vol. 1 (New York: The Catholic Publication Society Co., 1881). This edition: General Books, Tennessee, 2010, p. 221.

80   Ibid. Catherine McAuley had friends who were Presentations, including Sister M. Louis, in Galway. When McAuley went to Galway in 1840, to make a Mercy foundation, she stayed with the Presentation Sisters. See Presentation Convent Galway Annals, p. 13.

81   Mary C. Sullivan, *In the Path of Mercy: The Life of Catherine McAuley* (Dublin: Four Courts Press, 2012), p. 302. Sullivan suggests that Dr Fleming may have visited Mary Francis Creedon at the Mercy Convent, Baggot Street, Dublin, in July 1840; he consulted with Mother Catherine McAuley about a Newfoundland foundation around that time. McAuley refers to Bishop Fleming as 'my Bishop' in a letter to Sister M. Teresa White, 27 July 1840. See M. Angela Bolster, *The Correspondence of Catherine McAuley, 1827–1841* (Privately published by the Congregation of the Sisters of Mercy, Diocese of Cork and Ross, 1989), p. 139.

82   Dr Fleming's niece, Mary Justina Fleming, was a 'sickly' young woman during some of her time at the novitiate. See Mary C. Sullivan, *Catherine McAuley and the Tradition of Mercy* (Dublin: Four Courts Press, 1995), p. 22.

83   Mother Catherine McAuley died on 11 November 1841; Sr M. Justina Fleming died on 10 December 1841.

84   Bishop Fleming had built a new convent for the Presentation Sisters in 1844, and the little community moved into it in December. After the convent was destroyed by fire in 1846, the Sisters lived in part of the Mercy convent for five years. During that time a new school building was erected for them. See Annals of the Presentation Convent, St John's, Newfoundland, PANFL.

85   Catherine Phelan from Wexford, and Amelia Shanley from Dublin, entered the Presentation Convent, St John's, in 1842, and were professed in 1846. They had been invited to Newfoundland by Bishop Fleming, who 'visited Ireland for the purpose of procuring recruits for his missions'. Annals of the Presentation Convent, Carbonear, 1852–1962, PANFL.

86   Presentation Convent Galway Annals, p. 14.

87   Presentation Convent Harbour Grace Annals (1851–1972), PANFL.

88   Presentation Convent Fermeuse-Renews Annals (1851–1972), PANFL.

89   Presentation Convent Harbour Grace Annals (1851–1972).

90   Presentation Convent Riverhead (St Patrick's), (1856–1990), PANFL.

91   Presentation Convent Fermeuse-Renews Annals (1851–1972).

92   Presentation Convent Witless Bay Annals (1860–1989), PANFL.

93   Presentation Convent Fermeuse-Renews Annals (1851–1972).

94   Presentation Convent Harbour Main Annals (1853–1965), PANFL.

95   Presentation Convent Fermeuse-Renews Annals (1851–1972).

96   Presentation Convent Harbour Grace Annals (1851–1972).

97   Presentation Convent Riverhead (St Patrick's).

98   Ibid.

99   Cloister was rigidly observed; when Mother M. Gonzaga Murphy left the Harbour Main convent to attend a meeting in St John's in 1916, 'it was the first time she had been outside the enclosure in almost fifty years'. Presentation Convent Harbour Main Annals (1853–1965).

100  Ibid.

101  Ibid.

102  Presentation Convent St Mary's Annals (1859–1986), PANFL.

103  Presentation Convent Harbour Main Annals (1853–1965).

104  Ibid.

105  Ibid.

106  MS copybook entitled 'Architecture', and MS copybook entitled 'Questions on Various Subjects'. Uncatalogued early documents, PANFL.

107  *Journal of the House of Assembly of Newfoundland* (1867), p. 639. Provincial Archives, Newfoundland (hereafter PROANFL).

108  'Report on the Inspection of Catholic Schools, 1864' in *Journal of the House of Assembly of Newfoundland* (1865), p. 537. PROANFL.

109  Ibid.

110  Joseph Lancaster, a Quaker educator, opened his first school in London in 1797; it attracted the same large numbers that Nano Nagle's Cork schools attracted. He developed a system whereby pupils who knew a little, taught pupils who knew less. The more advanced pupils were known as monitors. The system, working efficiently, could enable one schoolmaster to manage the teaching of a thousand pupils. In 1803, he published a book on the system, *Improvements on Education*.

111  See Susan M. Parkes, *Kildare Place: The History of the Church of Ireland Training College, 1811–1969* (Dublin: Church of Ireland College of Education, 1984).

112  Appendix to the *Sixteenth Report of the Commissioners of National Education in Ireland*, 1849, p. 158.

113  Women who had trained as teachers at the Presentation Convent, St John's, were able to set up small schools around the island. Misses Power, Lawlor, Dutton, Jackman, Gearin, Fowler and O'Leary all trained at St John's before operating schools on the south side of Renews, and in Board Cove, Chance Cove, Clam Cove, and Kingman's Cove. See Frank Galgay, Michael McCarthy, Sister Teresina Bruce, and Sister Magdalen O'Brien, *A Pilgrimage of Faith: A History of the Southern Shore* (St John's: Harry Cuff Publications, 1983), p. 94.

114  Presentation Convent Harbour Main Annals (1853–1965), PANFL.

115  *Journal of the House of Assembly of Newfoundland* (1836), pp. 100–1; PROANFL.

116  See Frederick W. Rowe, *The Development of Education in Newfoundland* (Toronto: The Ryerson Press, 1964), p. 119.

117  *Journal of the Legislative Council of Newfoundland*, 1881, p. 200, cited in MS 'Vision and Courage' in uncatalogued file entitled Presentation Roots in Newfoundland, PANFL.

118  Dinn, *Presentation Congregation in Newfoundland*, p. 26.

119  *The Newfoundlander*, 5 August 1961, n.p.

120  Ibid.

121  Howley, *Ecclesiastical History of Newfoundland*, p. 235.

122  For example, among the early community at the Presentation Convent, Fermeuse, were nuns who had been educated by other congregations in Ireland; Sr M. Joseph O'Donnell had been educated by the Ursulines in Thurles, and Mother Teresa Maher had attended the St Louis Convent, Monaghan. See Presentation Convent Fermeuse-Renews Annals (1851–1972).

123  Though the nuns initially taught in very modest conditions, convent Annals hint at their aspirations to introduce 'genteel' subjects to the girls, and they were delighted in 1881 when fundraising at the Presentation Convent, St Mary's, allowed them to buy a grand piano. See Presentation Convent St Mary's Annals (1859–1986).

124  Sr M. Rose Mullally, from Bonavista, is recorded as the first Newfoundland woman to enter the Presentations as a Choir Sister. See Presentation Convent Fermeuse-Renews Annals (1851–1972). Sr Veronica Collins is recorded as the first Newfoundland woman to enter the order as a Lay Sister, at the Presentation Convent, Carbonear. See Presentation Convent Carbonear Annals (1852–1962). They probably entered the novitiate in the late 1840s.

## CHAPTER 5

1  Nano Nagle to Miss Fitzsimons, 17 July 1769; MS 'Rules Observed in the Schools for Poor Girls which began in May 1766 in St Mary's Lane', GHAD, IE PBVM [GHD] 3 /FD / 49 / (1).

2  *Rules and Constitutions*, Ch. 2, quoted in Consedine, *Listening Journey*, pp. 407–8.

3  Ibid., pp. 219–22. Consedine highlights the impracticality of dividing pupils into 'classes of ten or twelve according to number', especially in the early years of a convent's existence.

4  *Directory of the Religious of the Presentation Order*. The task of writing the *Directory* had been commenced by Mother Joseph McLoughlin (Presentation Convent, Kilkenny). She began the process of compiling a history and customs of the order, but she died in 1838.

5  See 'The Stanley Letter' in Hyland and Milne, *Irish Educational Documents, Vol. I*, pp. 98–103.

6  See Akenson, *The Irish Education Experiment*; Norman Atkinson, *Irish Education: A History of Educational Institutions* (Dublin: Allen Figgis, 1969); Hyland and Milne, *Irish Educational Documents, Vol. I*.

7  James Kavanagh, *Mixed Education, The Catholic Case Stated; or, Principles, Working, and Results of the System of National Education; with suggestions for the settlement*

*of the education question. Most respectfully dedicated to the Catholic Archbishops and Bishops of Ireland* (Dublin: John Mullany, 1859), p. 233.

8  *Appendix to Twentieth Report of the Commissioners of National Education in Ireland for the year 1853* (1854), H.C. 1854, XXX, pt. i, p. 319; *Appendix to Twenty-fourth Report … for the year 1857* (2456–1), H.C. 1859, VII, pp. 252–5; *Appendix to Thirty-first Report … for the year 1864* (3496), H.C. 1865, XIX, pp. 262–5; *Appendix to Thirty-seventh Report … for the year 1870* (C.360), H.C. 1871, XXIII, pp. 656–9.

9  Presentation Convent Doneraile School Register, Vol. I, 1818–1962, PSCA, IE PBVM DON/67/(1), pp. 1–11; Presentation Convent School Mitchelstown School Register, 4 July–5 August 1853, PSCA, IE PBVM MTN, uncatalogued.

10  *Rules and Constitutions*, Ch. 2, quoted in Consedine, *Listening Journey*, pp. 407–8; *Presentation Directory*, pp. 13–14. The *Constitutions* state that there was vacation from the schools every Saturday; from the Feast of our Blessed Lady of Mount Carmel, 16 July, until the Monday after the Octave of the Feast of Her Assumption on 15 August; from the 20 December until the Monday immediately after New Year's Day and from the Wednesday of Holy Week until the Monday after Low Sunday. They were also closed on every holy day of obligation and on the eve and Feast of the Presentation of our Blessed Lady, 20 and 21 November. The feasts of the Conception, Nativity and Purification fall on the 8 December, 8 September and around the 2 February each year. The feast of the Purification of Our Blessed Lady is also known as Candlemas and the Feast of the Presentation of Jesus in the Temple.

11  *Presentation Directory*, p. 14. The recommendation was that, if possible, the clock should strike once every half hour.

12  NAI, ED 1, MS Files on Application.

13  *Appendix to Twenty-second Report … for the year 1855* (2142–11), H.C. 1856, XXVII, pt. ii, pp. 39–49. The General Lesson was a statement of the benign neighbourliness that should exist between Christians, compiled from the Scriptures by Dr Richard Whately, the Anglican Archbishop of Dublin and a member of the Board of Commissioners until his resignation in 1853. The Commissioners required that the principles of the Lesson, or a Lesson of similar import approved by them, be strictly inculcated during the hours of combined instruction and a copy of the Lesson be hung up in each school.

14  *Appendix to Twenty-second Report … for the year 1855*, pp. 39–49.

15  NAI, ED 1, MS Files on Application. Changes to the Rules of National System in 1855 meant that convents were entitled to receive assistance in relation to only one of the schools they were operating. Yet, in the case of the Limerick community the Sexton Street Infant School, Roll Number 5711, that had been in receipt of grant aid from the Board from 1849 was struck off on 1 January 1852 and the grants transferred to their Female National School, Roll Number 5547, 'it being a convent School'. Six years earlier the Commissioners refused to grant assistance to the Sisters in Thurles towards a separate Infant School, on the grounds that the

average attendance was insufficient (NAI, ED 1 / 82, MS No. 85, Applications; NAI, ED 2 / 27, MS Folio 169, Registers).

16 Presentation Convent Galway, Rahoon Female National School Registers 1872–1886, IE PBVM GAL, uncatalogued; Presentation Convent Wexford, Wexford Female No. 1 National School Registers 1863–1909, IE PBVM WEX, uncatalogued; NAI, MFA 31/32 (pt. 4); Presentation Convent Clondalkin School Registers, IE PBVM CDN.

17 *Presentation Directory*, p. 20. This echoed the address given by Eliza Caldbeck in May 1810 on the type of education that was provided in her school in Clondalkin: 'The domestic economy of a family is entirely a poor woman's province, if ever you come to have the charge of a family, it ought to engage much of your time and attention. The intention of your being taught needlework, knitting, spinning and such like, is to teach you industry and enable you to fill up some of the many solitary hours you must necessarily pass at home'. (Mrs Eliza Caldbeck, *Address to Females of Clondalkin*, quoted in Presentation Convent Clondalkin Annals, Vol. I, pp. 13–24).

18 *Presentation Directory*, pp. 24–5.

19 Ibid, pp. 41–53.

20 *Appendix to Twenty-second Report ... for the year 1855*, pp. 122–6.

21 *Appendix to the Twenty-fifth Report ... for the year 1858* (2594), H.C. 1860, XXVI, p. 168.

22 *Appendix to the Twenty-sixth Report ... for the year 1859* (2706), H.C., XXVI, Vol. II, pp. 136–7.

23 The introduction of a system of payment-by-results was one of the recommendations of the Powis Commission 1870, which was established to review the operation of primary education in Ireland. *Royal Commission of Inquiry into Primary Education (Ireland), Vol. I, Pt. I: The Report of the Commissioners, with an appendix*, [C.6], H.C. 1870, XXVIII, pt. i.

24 *Appendices to the Forty-seventh Report ... for the year 1880* (C.2925), H.C. 1881, XXXIV, pp. 400–1.

25 *Forty-second Report ... for the year 1875* (C.1503), H.C. 1878, XXIV, p. 23; *Appendices to the Thirty-ninth Report ... for the year 1872* (C.805), H.C. 1874, XIX, p. 109; *Forty-second Report ... for the year 1875*, p. 23. In 1872 the four compulsory subjects in First and Second Classes were Reading, Writing, Spelling, and Arithmetic. Geography and Needlework for girls became compulsory, whilst Fourth, Fifth and Sixth had all seven subjects. Needlework became compulsory for girls in Second Class from 1875 onwards.

26 NAI, ED 2 / 166, MS Folio 64, 1/4/1864; ED 2 / 150, MS Folio 64, 28/3/1862 and 1/4/1864; ED 2 / 186, MS Folio 15, 23/12/1867; ED 2 / 121, MS Folio 130–133, 15/8/1863, Registers. Dugan's difficulties focused on the low numbers receiving instruction in the Theory and Practice in Vocal Music and a concern that whilst singing was taught regularly it was taught without Theory and Practice.

27 NAI, ED 2 / 212, MS Folio 50, 1/3/1856–26/2/1858; ED 2 / 212, MS Folio 40, 14/3/1862, Registers. Whilst Mr Shiel and his two assistants were paid by the

lesson, Ellen McKenna received a salary of £50 per annum, which included travelling expenses and was 'to be occupied in bona fide teaching for 2½ hours on each of the first five week days'.

28  NAI, ED 2 / 27, MS Folio 162, 29/9/1852–11/11/1853, Registers.

29  NAI, ED 2 / 18, MS Folio 75, 12/8/1850 and 26/9/1850, Registers. The original arrangement was to have two teachers in Galway and two more in Sligo. Wallace changed this to having all four in the Galway school. A similar arrangement was recorded in the Register for the school in Cashel for August 1851; see NAI, ED 2 / 43 MS Folio 194, 30/8/1851, Registers.

30  Presentation Convent Galway, Rahoon Female National School Registers 1872–1886; Presentation Convent Wexford Female No. 1 National School, School Registers 1863–1909; NAI, MFA 31/32 (pt. 4), Clondalkin Convent School Registers; Presentation Convent Kilkenny, Reports from Results Examinations, 1885–1900 PBVM 6/7/2. The Crosshaven Annals recorded that their pupils were examined in seven extra subjects in the Results Examination for 1885, see Presentation Convent Crosshaven Annals (1885).

31  Presentation Convent Kilkenny, District Inspector's Observation Book 1856–1898, pp. 47–8, GHAD, IE PBVM [KKY] 6/7/1.

32  South Presentation Convent School, District Inspector's Observation Book 1856–1936, pp. 35 and 41, PSCA, IE PBVM [SPC] 1, uncatalogued.

33  Presentation Convent Kilkenny, Reports from Results Examinations 1885–1900, GHAD, IE PBVM [KKY] 6/7/2.

34  Presentation Convent Wexford Female No. 1 National School Registers 1863–1909, pp. 33–114; NAI, MFA 31/32 (pt. 4), Clondalkin Convent School Registers, pp. 17–119. In addition to the increase in children who met the attendance requirements, the numbers who were recorded as being absent on exam days reduced from 40 to 21 in the case of Wexford and 22 to 0 in Clondalkin.

35  *Rules and Constitutions*, Ch. 1, quoted in Consedine, *Listening Journey*, p. 406; *Presentation Directory*, pp. 17–20.

36  Consedine, *Listening Journey*, pp. 226–7. Consedine explains that in the letter accompanying the *Decretum Laudis* of 1791, Bellarmine's work was recommended as the basis for teaching Christian Doctrine. The letter also suggested the Roman Catechism if wider instruction was needed. See 'Letter of the Sacred Congregation, Rome, to Bishop Moylan, 6 August 1791', in O'Farrell, *Breaking of Morn*, pp. 158–63.

37  *Rules and Constitutions*, Ch. 1, quoted in Consedine, *Listening Journey*, p. 406; *Presentation Directory*, p. 30.

38  *Presentation Directory*, pp. 18–32. The nuns were advised that to prepare themselves for giving general instructions in or explaining the Catechism, they should occasionally read over *The Poor Man's Catechism*, *The Catechism of the Council of Trent*, *The Sincere Christian*, *The Duties of a Christian*, *Familiar Instructions* or any other approved book of instruction.

39  *Presentation Directory*, pp. 33–7.

40  Ibid., pp. 51–4.

41  Presentation Convent Thurles Annals (1824), pp. 10–12. Dr Robert Laffan was Archbishop of Cashel from 1823 to 1833.

42  Presentation Convent Thurles Annals (1859–1862), pp. 28–33.

43  Presentation Convent Cahirciveen Annals (1861), IE PBVM CAH, uncatalogued.

44  Presentation Convent Cahirciveen Annals (1885).

45  Presentation Convent Fermoy Annals (1863), IE PBVM FER, uncatalogued.

46  Presentation Convent Crosshaven Annals (1878 and 1881).

47  Presentation Convent Limerick Annals, pp. 93–4. Monsignor Gualdi was secretary to the Envoy. Persico paid similar visits to the convent in Thurles on 29 August 1887 and Wexford on 3 October 1887. See Presentation Convent Thurles Annals, pp. 74–5; Presentation Convent Wexford Annals, 1887.

48  *Presentation Directory*, pp. 10–12.

49  Ibid. The author continued, 'Her zeal ought to be firm – nothing should daunt her courage – nothing should be to her a subject of discouragement in her important and arduous pursuit. The tediousness and irksomeness of her school duties, may often seem to strew her path with thorns, but her heart must still remain turned towards, and steadfastly fixed upon, that one great object of all her solicitude – her God. She must uphold her courage, and preserve her love for Him, and hope for no reward, but from Him alone.'

50  *Appendix to Twenty-eighth Report … for the year 1861*, p. 4.

51  *Presentation Directory*, pp. 30–3.

52  Presentation Convent Clondalkin Annals, Vol. II, pp. 137–8.

53  *Presentation Directory*, pp. 41–2.

54  Ibid., pp. 45–6. The numbers in the groups depended on the size of the school.

55  Ibid., p. 48. The author noted that, whilst the new skills may be more difficult, they were not more necessary.

56  Ibid., p. 48–9. The Sister was also expected to foster an environment of silence and recollection, and never to engage in useless discourse with them. She was also advised never to give way to murmuring or complaints when the children disappointed and perplexed her; rather she was to be an example of humility, patience, meekness and forbearance to them.

57  *Presentation Directory*, pp. 24, 42, 45, 46.

58  Mother Baptist Frayne was the Superioress of the Wexford Convent.

59  J. Campbell to Sr Baptist Frayne, 16 January 1832, The Campbell Letters Collection, Presentation Convent Wexford, IE PBVM WEX.

60  J. Campbell to Sr Baptist Frayne, 27 November 1832, The Campbell Letters Collection.

61  Ibid. Campbell had moved from the Kildare Place Society to work for the National Board in 1833.

62  Powis Commission, *Vol. III, Minutes of Evidence*, 24 and 25, Right Hon Alexander MacDonnell. According to MacDonnell's evidence, Organising Teachers were paid £150 per annum by that time. He also stated that they were paid travelling expenses.

63   NAI, ED 2 / 18 MS Folio 75, 3/6/1853–1/9/1853, Registers. The entry for September reads: 'B.O. on Let. 6323 Under the circumstances the Comms. Will allow Miss Doyle to remain for two months after the termination of the Quarter {i.e. from the time of her appt.} but they cannot sanction any further extension. M. Doyle is listed under the names of teachers as organising. Teacher.' As the relevant Quarters ended 30 June and 30 September, this probably meant that her extra two months were to run into October and November.

64   NAI, ED 2 / 159 MS Folio 40, 27/2/1857 and 6/2/1876, Registers; NAI, ED 2 / 194 MS Folio 4, 3/12/1858, Registers. Cashel was organised again in 1869. The schools in Kilkenny, Drogheda, Enniscorthy and Stradbally were all noted to have benefited from working with this scheme of organising in the 1864 *Special Report on Convent Schools*. See *Special Report made to the Commissioners of National Education on Convent Schools in Connection with the Board*, H.C. 1864 (405) XLVI.

65   Presentation Convent Tralee Annals (1869).

66   *Special Report on Convent Schools*, p. 121; Presentation Convent Tralee Annals (1869); Presentation Convent Bandon Annals (1869), p. 19.

67   Presentation Convent Wexford Annals (1872).

68   NAI, ED 2 / 27 MS Folio 162, 1884 and 15/7/1885, Registers.

69   *Appendices to the Forty-fourth Report ... for the year 1877*, pp. 174–5.

70   South Presentation Cork, District Inspector's Observation Book. Presentation Convent Kilkenny District Inspector's Observation Book, GHAD, IE PBVM [KKY] 6/7/1.

71   District Inspector John E. Sheridan, 10 April 1856. South Presentation Cork District Inspector's Observation Book, p. 1, PSCA, IE PBVM [SPC] 1, uncatalogued.

72   District Inspector Edward Sheehy, 24 and 25 October 1860. South Presentation Convent District Inspector's Observation Book, p. 13. Sheehy finished his assessment by saying: 'I am sure from the zeal of the lady in charge of the schools and her anxiety to introduce every improvement into them, that my next report on the Schools will be very Satisfactory.'

73   District Inspector L B/Sillie (?), 28 May & 2 June 1868. South Presentation Convent District Inspector's Observation Book, p. 27. His previous inspection had taken place on 17 and 18 July 1867.

74   District Inspector B. MacSheehy, 9 February 1883, South Presentation Convent District Inspector's Observation Book, p. 45.

75   'Queries which are answered in the following Special Reports', in *Special Report on Convent Schools*, p. 2.

76   *Special Report on Convent Schools*, pp. 3–230, *passim*.

77   Ibid.

78   Ibid. In assessing the adequacy of accommodation the inspectors were given a formula of six square feet for each pupil in average attendance. Sheehy's concerns were echoed by Assistant Commissioner W. Scott Coward, Esq in his Report for the Powis Commission six years later. He stated: 'The South Presentation Nuns in Cork have a school with 1,228 on the books, and an average attendance of 645,

for a greater number than which, however, they have no accommodation, which occasions much overcrowding when the weekly average attendance rises, as it does in every school during certain weeks of the year, above the annual average' ('Report of W. Scott Coward, Esq', in Powis, *Vol. II, The Reports of the Assistant Commissioners*, p. 103).

79  *Special Report on Convent Schools*, pp. 3–230, *passim*.

80  Ibid.

81  Ibid.

82  Report of P. Le Page Renouf, Esq, in Powis, *Vol. II, The Reports of the Assistant Commissioners*, p. 315.

83  Report of James Stuart Laurie, Esq, in Powis, *Vol. II*, p. 302.

84  *Presentation Directory*, pp. 7–8. It continued further, 'The instruction of poor children, is a wearisome but pleasing toil; they are, if the expression may be used, but half formed beings, who are organised only with time, and those who instruct them, make them reasonable creatures: – they are little pagans, whom they make Christians.'

85  *Presentation Directory*, pp. 14–17.

86  Ibid., pp. 21–9.

87  Presentation Convent Doneraile Annals 1845.

88  NAI, ED 1 / 73 No. 2, Applications.

89  NAI, ED 2 / 186 MS Folio 15, 10/7/1865, Registers.

90  NAI, ED 2 / 212 MS Folio 63, 27/2/1879 and 9/5/1883, Registers.

91  NAI, ED 2 / 121 MS Folio 130–133, 5/2/1858; ED 2 / 121 MS Folio 130–3, 27/7/1863, Registers.

92  *Rules and Constitutions*, Chp. 2, 'Of the Election of the Mother Superior', in Consedine, *Listening Journey*, pp. 418–20.

93  NAI ED 1 / 33, MS No. 10; ED 1 / 92, MS No. 116, Applications.

94  NAI ED 2 / 38 MS Folio 141; ED 2 / 159 MS Folio 40, Registers.

95  NAI ED 1 / 88 No. 94 Applications; ED 2 / 184 MS Folio 29, Registers.

96  NAI ED 2 / 212 MS Folio 63, Registers; South Presentation Convent, The Keenan Letters, 4 January 1889–17 May 1890, PSCA IE PBVM [SPC] 1, uncatalogued. This is a collection of four autograph letters, three from Keenan and the fourth from a Mr Nash in Keenan's office. Three relate to the appointment of a Manager in succession to Dean Neville, a fourth relates to a request for sanctioning the appointment of monitors before July 1890.

97  Sir Patrick Keenan to Rev Mother de Sales White, 4 January 1889, The Keenan Letters.

98  Presentation Convent Galway Annals, p. 6; Scully, 'Galway Schooling', p. 14. The Annalist wrote: 'Mother Angela Martin … through excessive anxiety, seeing all that was done, and all that was still to be done, got extremely nervous and delicate – her recovery being totally despaired of – it was thought better by herself and her friends that she should return to her own Convent. She departed from this in September 1818.'

99 Presentation Convent Thurles Cemetery. Joseph Bradshaw died in 1863, John Aherne in 1893, Magdalen Hely in 1843 and Magdalen Fitzharris in December 1831. Sr John Fitzharris also died in June 1831.

## CHAPTER 6

1 Burke Savage, *A Valiant Dublin Woman*, p. 58.

2 See Presentation Convent Tralee Annals (1809–12).

3 Presentation Convent Galway Annals, pp. 3–7.

4 Presentation Convent Thurles Annals, p. 205.

5 See Presentation Convent Wexford Annals (1818).

6 Nano Nagle to Miss Mulally, 29 July 1780, GHAD, IE PBVM [GH] 3/1/1/8.

7 Rosario Allen, *A Story of Love and Faith* (Cork: South Presentation Convent, 1979). This also meant that the Sisters were able to move between their convent and schools without having to go out on the street as all of the buildings were inside the street wall.

8 The Annals record that the foundation stone of the new convent was laid by Dr Moylan on 10 February 1808: 'The convent, now so happily commenced, lies a little further back in the garden than our present house which was built by Mother Nagle. We have no funds to defray the expense of the building, but a loan of £300 given by our kind friend Mrs Kelleher. We have only to trust to Providence for future resources.' South Presentation Convent Annals, p. 114.

9 *Appendix to Second Report of the Commissioners of Irish Education Inquiry*, pp. 90–1.

10 South Presentation Convent Annals, pp. 170–5; pp. 183–5. Dr Collins raised the initial £300 for the purchase and the Presentation community agreed to pay the additional £200. They leased the convent they vacated to the Presentation Brothers, whose school became known as the South Monastery of Cork. The Ursuline community put the Blackrock campus up for sale in 2002.

11 South Presentation Convent Annals, p. 266. Mary Anne Mahon was recommended to them by the Christian Brothers in Dublin.

12 NAI, ED 1/16, MS No. 183, Applications; South Presentation Convent District Inspector's Observation Book. The first visit by Inspector John Sheridan was on 10 April 1856. The dimensions of the various rooms are recorded here and vary slightly from those available in the Applications. The Infant School (an irregular shape) measured 30 feet 6 inches long, by 18 feet 6 inches wide, by 20 feet high. It contained six long seats. Number 1 Book Room measured 28 feet 6 inches long, by 22 feet 3 inches wide, by 10 feet high. It contained six desks and nine seats. Number 2 Book Room measured 39 feet 6 inches long, by 25 feet 6 inches wide, by 10 feet high. It had ten desks and twelve seats. Number 3 Book Room measured 31 feet long, by 25 feet 6 inches wide, by 9 feet high. It had seven desks and nine seats. Number 4 Book Room measured 39 feet 6 inches long, by 25 feet 6 inches wide, by 9 feet high. It had ten desks and twelve seats. The Sequel Room was 22 feet 5 inches

long, by 23 feet wide, by 10 feet high. It had four desks and five seats. Finally, the Work Room measured 22 feet 3 inches long by 20 feet 7 inches wide by 9 feet high. It had four desks, two seats and two worktables.

13   NAI, ED 1/16, MS No. 183, Applications. The name of the school changed in January 1861 to St Finbarr's Female National School, NAI, ED 2/212, MS Folio 63, Registers.

14   South Presentation Convent Annals, pp. 312–14. South Presentation Convent Photographic Collection, IE PBVM PSCA [SPC], uncatalogued; Allen, *Walk with Nano in Cove Lane*. The building cost £3,000, a portion of this was collected and the rest given from the house, with the stained-glass windows presented by friends of the community.

15   Copy of Edmund Ffrench to Cardinal Fontana, 12 October 1820, *Archives of the Congregation of the Propaganda Fide, Scritture Riferite Irlanda*, Vol. XIII ff. 286–9, IE PBVM GAL, uncatalogued.

16   *Appendix to Second Report of the Commissioners of Irish Education Inquiry*, pp. 92–3. The Protestant Returns gave the number of pupils in attendance as 272, while the Roman Catholic returns listed 395.

17   NAI, ED 1/33 MS No. 10; NAI ED 1/33 No. 203, Applications; NAI, ED 2/17, MS Folio No. 14, Registers.

18   NAI, ED 1/33 MS No. 10; NAI ED 1/33 No. 203, Applications; 'Register of School Expenses' quoted in Scully, 'Galway Schooling', p. 25. NAI, ED 2/136, MS Folio No. 7.

19   Presentation Convent Wexford Annals, p. 1. The running of the Orphanage was later taken over by the Sisters of Mercy.

20   *Appendix to Second Report of the Commissioners of Irish Education Inquiry*, pp. 94–5.

21   NAI, ED 2/48, Folio No. 16, Registers.

22   NAI, ED 1/92, MS No. 116, Applications. The second room was listed as being 'the under floor of the house (lately orphanage?) to the large schoolroom'. Mother Baptist Frayne's signature was the only one on either the Protestant or Catholic side of the Application form. Her signature was given as Jayne M. Frayne, Superioress, Presentation Convent, Wexford.

23   Ibid. The school was called Wexford Female National School with the assigned Roll Number 969.

24   Presentation Convent Wexford Annals (1859–63). Chief among the benefactors was Richard Devereux, who supplied the balance owing on the work. Evangelist Butler, who died in 1859, was a niece of Baptist Frayne's. The last fundraiser was a two-day Bazaar held in the Town Hall in July 1862, which raised £450.

25   Presentation Convent Wexford Annals (1867 and 1869).

26   Presentation Convent Wexford Annals (1867 and 1882). Michael Warren was Bishop of Ferns, 1876–84. Mrs Connell from Bettyville donated the money for the workroom; Richard Devereux provided the finance for the boys' school. Mrs Connell also provided the money for another new school for infant boys in 1882.

27  Presentation Convent Clondalkin Annals, Vol. 1, pp. 26–8.

28  Presentation Convent Clondalkin Annals, Vol. 2, p. 152.

29  Ibid., pp. 53–4 and p. 57.

30  Thurles joined on 1 July 1844, and as Thurles Female National School was assigned the Roll Number 4068; Limerick joined in November 1844 and was known as Sexton Street Female National School, with Roll Number 5547. South Presentation joined on 1 August 1850; George's Hill on 1 January 1850. NAI, ED 2/10, MS Folio 2; ED 2/16, MS Folio 77; ED 2/44 MS Folio, 10; ED 2/27, Folio 162, Registers.

31  Walsh, *Nano Nagle*, p. 217. Although the foundation of the Convent in Millstreet did not take place until 28 May 1840, Patrick Fitzpatrick PP made two applications to the Commissioners for aid – the first dated 20 December 1839. In this he requested assistance in fitting up the school, for which he received £37.10s; the second requested a Teacher's Salary, which was granted from 1 July 1840. With the assigned Roll Number 2278, the school was known to the Board as Millstreet Female National School. NAI, ED 1/13, MS No. 168; ED 1/14 MS No. 183.

32  Frayne's correspondence with Julia Campbell over the years is represented by The Campbell Letters Collection (1832–1842), a collection of eight letters from Julia Campbell and a ninth letter from a Sister Mary Xavier Hennessy of the Sisters of Charity in Gardiner Street, Dublin. The Murray Papers in the Dublin Diocesan Archives contain two letters from March and April 1848 written by Sr M. O'Donel of the Presentation Convent in Galway. While the primary purpose of these letters is to thank Murray for donations towards their work during the Famine, she finishes one letter with 'We all feel anxious to forward the great cause of National Education' and offers prayers for Dr Kelly, the late Archbishop of Tuam and uncle to the Secretary of the National Board in the other, and signs herself on both as 'M. O'Donel, N. Teacher'. Presentation Convent, Wexford, The Campbell Letters. DDA MS File 32/4, Murray 1848, AH No. 12; MS File 32/4, Irish Famine 1848.

33  John Murphy succeeded Francis Moylan as Bishop of Cork and Ross in 1815, and was one of the Irish bishops who supported the National System through the dispute between Dr McHale and Dr Murray in the late 1830s. Akenson, *The Irish Education Experiment*, pp. 206–12.

34  Burke Savage, *A Valiant Dublin Woman*, p. 237.

35  The George's Hill Annals describe Dr Murray as 'most amiable and affable in his manners, yet his noble and dignified demeanour commanded the respect of all. It is said he was most penetrating in point of knowledge of the human character; he was seldom or ever found wrong in his estimation of those upon whom he had occasion to offer an opinion. He did everything coolly, orderly and without hurry or embarrassment; his punctuality with regard to time was edifying; his deportment private and professional, was truly majestic, he was most exact in his celebration of the Holy Sacrifice every morning. … Of his wisdom we need say very little; indeed the Spirit of Wisdom, Understanding, Counsel, fortitude, piety and the fear of the Lord seems to have descended on this great Bishop. The private charities of Dr. M.

were far more extensive, than supposed. He dreaded the appearance of ostentation or display in the distribution of his charities. He founded numerous Churches, Convents, Monasteries, Religious Societies and charitable institutions. He was particularly partial to the Sisters of Charity and the Loreto Convents which were established in Dublin by him as also the Sisters of Mercy. In his intercourse with this Convent he was cool but kind, for many years received our interest, and until the latter years of his life officiated at all the ceremonies and at some elections'. Presentation Convent George's Hill Annals, p. 8.

36  NAI, ED 1/28, MS No. 3, Applications; NAI, ED 2/15, MS Folio 45, Registers.

37  NAI, ED 1/29, MS No. 46, Applications. Called George's Hill Female National School, it was assigned the Roll Number 5933.

38  Presentation Convent Doneraile School Register, Vol. 1 (1818–1962), PSCA, IE PBVM DON 67/(1); Presentation Convent Mitchelstown School Register, PSCA, IE PBVM MTN, uncatalogued; Mitchelstown Presentation Convent School opened 4 July 1853. Presentation Convent Waterford Daily Attendance Register, St Agnes Section, GHAD, IE PBVM WAT 7/2/3/2.

39  *Appendix to the Second Report of the Commissioners of Irish Education Inquiry, 1826*, pp. 90–5; *Appendix to the Minutes of Evidence taken before the select committee of the house of lords appointed to inquire into the practical working of national education in Ireland, 1854*, pp. 1452 and 1453; *Special Report made to the Commissioners of National Education on Convent Schools*, pp. 1–230; *Powis Report, Vol. VI, Educational Census: Returns showing number of children actually present in each primary school, 25 June 1868, with introductory observations and analytical index, 1870*, pp. 2–191.

40  The figures for 1826 represent an average of three months in the autumn of 1824 and are those supplied by the Roman Catholic clergy (*Second Report*, pp. 3–6). The figures for the 1854 Report are Average Daily Attendance figures for the quarter ending 30 June 1853. Five of the convents (Waterford, North Presentation, Dungarvan, Carrick-on-Suir and Clonmel) included in the 1826 Report were not included in the 1854 returns.

41  *Special Report on Convent Schools*, pp. 3–234. The phrase used by the Commissioners is 'Total number of Distinct Pupils on Rolls during the Year 1863'. The school in Wexford is included in the Report twice, pp. 224–6 and pp. 229–30 as the Sisters had opened their new school on 12 January 1863. Presentation Convent Wexford Annals (1863).

42  While the 23.4 per cent average attendance for South Presentation is the lowest, this figure is placed within the context of 2,575 'distinct' pupils who registered, by far the highest total across all the convent schools.

43  Compiled from the *Twenty-eighth Report of the commissioners of National Education in Ireland, for the year 1861*, (3026), H.C. 1862, XX, p. 5; *Thirty-seventh Report of the commissioners of National Education in Ireland, for the year 1870*, (C.360), H.C. 1871, XXIII, p. 7; *Forty-seventh report of the commissioners of National Education in Ireland, for the year 1880*, (C.2925), H.C. 1881, XXXIV, p. 3.

44  *Royal Commission on Primary Education (Ireland), Vol. VI: Educational Census*, H.C. 1870 (C.6-V) XXVIII, pt. v, xxxviii–xlvi. Of the nine schools not connected with the System, the attendance recorded for 25 June 1863 in Waterford, North Presentation, Dungarvan, Clonmel and Mitchelstown was above the 243.5 average at 318, 546, 294, 441 and 435 respectively. Of the other four, only Castlecomer was above the average of 141.7 achieved in non-national convent schools. Carrick-on-Suir, Tuam and Lismore recorded 134, 138 and 118 pupils in attendance on the day. The raw figure for average attendance in ordinary national schools given by Powis is 60.3, four times less than that given for the convent schools.

45  James Kelly, 'The 1798 Rebellion', in Sean Duffy (ed.), *Atlas of Irish History* (Dublin: Gill and Macmillan, 2000), p. 92; E.R.R. Green, 'The Great Famine 1845–50', in T.W. Moody and F.X. Martin (eds) *The Course of Irish History* (Cork: Mercier Press, 2001), pp. 218–27.

46  North Presentation Convent Annals (1845–86), p. 6.

47  Presentation Convent Tralee Annals (1847).

48  DDA, MS File 32/4 Murray, 1848 AH No. 12.

49  Presentation Convent Thurles Annals, p. 17.

50  Presentation Convent Wexford Annals.

51  Presentation Convent Portlaoise Annals (1838–1856) p. 55.

52  Presentation Convent Dingle Annals (1847).

53  Presentation Convent Listowel Annals, pp. 7–12.

54  Presentation Convent (Sexton Street) Limerick Annals, p. 43.

55  Presentation Convent Doneraile Annals (1845).

56  NAI ED 1/33 No. 10; NAI ED 1/33, No. 203, Applications.

57  NAI ED 1/81, No. 26, Applications.

58  NAI ED 1/51, No. 115; ED 1 / 14, No. 183, Applications.

59  NAI, ED 1/82, No. 32, Applications.

60  NAI ED 1/51, No. 115, Applications.

61  *Appendix to Twenty-fifth Report … for the year 1858*, Vol. II, pp. 130–1.

62  *Appendix to Twenty-fifth Report … for the year 1859*, Vol. II, pp. 136–7; *Appendix to Twenty-eighth Report … for the year 1861*, Vol. II, pp. 144–5; *Appendix to Thirty-fourth Report … for the year 1867*, p. 498; *Appendix to Thirty-sixth Report … for the year 1869*, (C.119, C.120), H.C. 1870, XXIII, p. 557; *Appendix to Forty-seventh Report … for the year 1880*, pp. 286–7.

63  *Appendix to Twenty-seventh Report … for the year 1860*, Vol. II, pp. 140–1; *Appendix to Twenty-ninth Report … for the year 1862*, Vol. II (3235), H.C. 1863, XVII Pt. I, pp. 148–9; *Appendix to Thirtieth Report … for the year 1863*, Vol. II, pp. 232–3; *Appendix to Thirty-first Report … for the year 1864*, Vol. II, pp. 156–7; *Appendix to Thirty-second Report … for the year 1865*, Vol. II, pp. 184–5; *Appendix to Thirty-eighth Report … for the year 1868*, p. 343; *Appendix to Thirty-seventh Report … for the year 1870*, p. 343; *Appendix to Thirty-eighth Report … for the year 1871*, (C.599), H.C. 1872, XXIII, p. 510; *Appendix to Thirty-ninth Report … for the year*

*1872*, p. 563; *Appendix to Fortieth Report … for the year 1873*, p. 535; *Appendix to Forty-first Report … for the year 1874*, p. 185.

64　*Appendix to Forty-fourth Report … for the year 1877*, p. 339; *Appendix to Forty-seventh Report … for the year 1880*, pp. 286–7; *Appendix to Fiftieth Report … for the year 1883*, pp. 520–1.

65　Presentation Convent Tralee Annals (1830 and 1850).

66　South Presentation Convent Annals (1846) p. 266.

67　Presentation Convent Listowel Annals, pp. 17–18.

68　Presentation Convent Thurles Annals, pp. 32–3; p. 54. Sr Peter made the contribution to be used in whatever way was deemed beneficial for the poor children. Until 1861, the yearly interest was given in clothing. In 1871, a workroom was added to the schools.

69　Presentation Convent (Sexton Street) Limerick Annals (1839; 1840; 1843).

70　Presentation Convent Clondalkin Annals, Vol. II, pp. 21–179.

71　*Appendix to the Twenty-second Report … for the year 1855*, p. 48.

72　Ibid., p. 55. Amounts ranged from £10 for an Average Daily Attendance of fifty children to £111 for an average of 600. Averages above 600 received an increase of £15 per annum.

73　Presentation Convent Tralee Annals (1874); Presentation Convent Killarney Annals, p. 12. Presentation Convent Dingle Annals, p. 43.

74　*Appendices to Fifty-second Report … for the year 1885*, pp. 46 and 50.

75　Ibid.

76　Although the Annual Reports of the Commissioners were given for the calendar year from January to December, the school year generally ran from September/October to the following August/September. For the purposes of this study, all figures regarding finance are for the twelve months from January to December.

77　NAI, ED 4 Salary Books; *Annual Reports of the Commissioners of National Education 1858–1885*.

78　Presentation Convent Killarney Annals, p. 9; Presentation Convent Tralee Annals (1833).

79　Powis Report, *Vol. VII, The Returns*, pp. 395–415.

80　NAI, ED 4 Salary Books – National Schools (1834–1918), Vols 153–161, 923–7, 944 and 946–9. These volumes record salary payments to all national school teachers and are arranged according to roll number. Teachers' names were listed under their schools and the details of their earnings and status in the school were recorded. In the case of convent schools, however, only the names of lay assistants and monitors were recorded. The Sisters who taught in the convent schools were recorded under the heading 'Nuns'.

81　Ibid. The monetary amounts are expressed according to contemporary usage and not in their decimal equivalent. There were twelve pennies in one shilling and twenty shillings in one pound. Thus, £22.3s.4d is twenty-two pounds, three shillings and four pence.

82　NAI, ED 2 / 150, MS Folio 64, Registers, 27/7/1860, 6/2/1863 & 1/4/1864.

83  NAI, ED 2 / 150, MS Folio 64, Registers, 1860–1871; NAI, ED 4 / MS Vols 155–61, 923 & 924, Salary Books.

84  *Appendix to Twenty-fifth Report ... for the year 1858*, Vol. I, p. 355.

85  *Forty-second Report ... for the year 1875*, (C.1503), H.C. 1876, XXIV, pp. 23–6.

86  *Forty-fourth Report ... for the year 1877*, (C.2031), H.C. 1878, XXIX, p. 22.

87  *Forty-second Report ... for the year 1875*, p. 23. A revised scale of fees was introduced in 1882/3, which among other changes allowed 4s payment for children in organised infant schools and introduced Book-keeping and a Girls' Reading Book, as extra subjects for girls in Fifth and Sixth Classes, earning 2s 6d and 3s respectively.

88  Presentation Convent Tralee Annals (1875); Presentation Convent Crosshaven Annals (1877–1886).

89  Presentation Convent Dingle Annals, Vol. 2, p. 40.

90  Presentation Convent Galway, Senior Girls Register 1872–89, IE PBVM GAL, uncatalogued; Presentation Convent Wexford, Senior Girls Register 1863–82, pp. 33–114, IE PBVM WEX, uncatalogued; NAI, MFA 31/32 (part 4), Senior Girls Register 1872–94.

91  South Presentation Convent, Daily Report Book for St Finbarr's Female National School, June 1880–April 1884 and January 1888–December 1891, PSCA, IE PBVM [SPC], uncatalogued. Presentation Convent Waterford, Daily Report Books, January 1881 and July 1888, GHAD, IE PBVM WAT 7/1/8/1. These books were issued by the Commissioners of National Education and contained general details regarding the school, a record of the number of children in attendance every day, any visitors to the school and their comments in relation to what they saw, and a section for recording the amounts of money paid by the Board in grants to the school.

92  Ibid. These totals include all payments made in the calendar year 1883 and 1888 irrespective of whether or not they related to the previous year.

## CHAPTER 7

1  The Presentations were followed just three years later by Catherine McAuley's Sisters of Mercy and in 1851 by the Irish Institute of the Blessed Virgin Mary (Loreto). See Walsh, *Roman Catholic Nuns*, pp. 65–6.

2  While the arrival of the Presentation Sisters in Manchester was undoubtedly significant in the immediate post-Catholic emancipation era, it has not been recognised as such in many seminal works regarding Roman Catholicism and female religious in England. See Walsh, *Roman Catholic Nuns*, and Carmen Mangion, *Contested Identities: Catholic Women Religious in Nineteenth Century England and Wales* (Manchester: Manchester University Press, 2008). Indeed, the work of the Presentation Sisters in England, particularly in the field of education, has been largely neglected in academic scholarship. For the purpose of this chapter, research has been drawn mainly from Presentation archives in England and Ireland.

3   For example, in 1842 the Presentations in Manchester opened a night school for poor women and young girls, and in 1845 they took in twenty Catholic orphan children. A Sunday School was established by the Presentation Sisters in Buxton shortly after their arrival in 1898. An orphanage was founded by the Sisters in Pickering in 1919, and in 1927 the community in Matlock commenced a Sunday School in the local parish church.

4   In 1842, a group of Presentation Sisters from Rahan and Maynooth commenced a foundation in Madras, India. By the early twentieth century, the Order had spread to Vepery, Royapuram, Church Park, Perambur and Egmore. The success of the Presentation Sisters in India depended on a continuous supply of Sisters from England and Ireland. In 1919, the Superioress of the Presentation Convent, Madras, decided to establish a novitiate in England for the sole purpose of recruiting and training postulants for the Indian missions. The first novitiate was established in Liverpool in 1919 and was transferred to Matlock in 1927. See Anon., *Mother Xavier Murphy, First Superior General of the Presentation Sisters, South India* (n.d., n.p.), PSCA.

5   See Akenson, *The Irish Education Experiment*.

6   In 1851 and 1894, the community in Livesey Street had been invited to establish foundations in Salford and Rishton, respectively. These foundations failed due to lack of financial support and difficulties regarding the Rule of the Order.

7   A total of twenty convents were established in England (excluding Castleconnell, Ireland) but three had closed by 1958: Salford (1851–52), Rishton (1894–96) and Liverpool (1919–27).

8   Unlike the native foundations in Ireland, where Sisters were invited to establish a convent in a particular area and subsequently organise a school, in England, for the most part, the schools had already been established but for one reason or another had failed to prosper. The Presentation Sisters were regularly invited to assume responsibility for such institutions.

9   Nano Nagle to Miss Mulally, 30 October 1779, GHAD, IE PBVM [GHD] 3/1/1/1/7.

10  David Fitzpatrick, 'Irish emigration in the later nineteenth century', *Irish Historical Studies*, 22, 86 (September 1980), p. 136.

11  John M. Werly, 'The Irish in Manchester, 1832–49', *Irish Historical Studies*, 18, 71 (March 1973), p. 346.

12  Ryan Dye, 'Catholic protectionism or Irish nationalism? Religion and politics in Liverpool, 1829–1845', *Journal of British Studies*, 40, 3 (July 2001), p. 360.

13  Werly, 'The Irish in Manchester', pp. 351–2.

14  Friedrich Engels, *The Condition of the Working Class in England* (Leipzig: 1845), p. 71. Cited in Werly, 'The Irish in Manchester', p. 347.

15  Werly, 'The Irish in Manchester', p. 356.

16  *Manchester Guardian*, 3 July 1847. Cited in Werly, 'The Irish in Manchester', p. 357.

17  Dye, 'Catholic protectionism or Irish nationalism?', p. 359.

18  Fitzpatrick, 'Irish emigration in the later nineteenth century', p. 135.

19  New Town, also known as Irish Town, was situated between the River Irk and St George's Road. Little Island was located in the south of Manchester within a bend in the River Medlock. New Town was the largest of the two districts and during the 1830s boasted a population of approximately 20,000. See Werly, 'The Irish in Manchester', p. 346.

20  Alexis de Tocqueville, *Journeys to England and Ireland* (Paris: 1865). Cited in Werly, 'The Irish in Manchester', p. 350.

21  M. Leon Faucher, *Manchester in 1844, its present condition and future prospects* (Manchester: 1844), p. 31. Cited in Werly, 'The Irish in Manchester', p. 350.

22  Until 1832, the religious and spiritual needs of the Catholic population in Manchester were provided for in three parishes: St Augustine's in Granby Row, St Mary's in Mulberry Street and St Chad's located in Rook Street.

23  *Silver Jubilee Souvenir, St Patrick's Livesey Street, Manchester* (1961), Presentation Archive and Heritage Centre, Matlock (hereafter PAHCM).

24  The chapel was constructed in the shape of a cross, 'after the style so often seen in Ireland' and three galleries provided additional accommodation for the ever-growing Catholic population. See, *Silver Jubilee Souvenir*.

25  Fr Hearne was a native of Waterford and had been educated in Maynooth. Until his appointment as parish priest of St Patrick's in 1832, he had worked as an assistant priest in St Mary's parish, Mulberry Street. Fr Hearne served as parish priest of St Patrick's from 1832–46 and was a key figure in the establishment of the first Presentation foundation in England. See, *Silver Jubilee Souvenir*.

26  On 12 July 1819, 2,000 Catholics attacked an Orange procession, which subsequently enticed many English and Scottish labourers to join the cause. Throughout the nineteenth century, sectarian division was a prominent feature of society in Liverpool. See Dye, 'Catholic protectionism or Irish nationalism?', pp. 362–3.

27  Ibid., p. 363.

28  E.P. Thompson, *The Making of the English Working Class* (New York: Victor Gollancz, 1963), p. 435. Cited in Werly, 'The Irish in Manchester', p. 355.

29  In 1832, during the cholera epidemic, a young boy was treated for the disease in a local hospital in Manchester. However, the young boy died and on the day of his funeral it was discovered that his head had been cut off by a medical attendant and sold for dissection. Rumours about the boy's death spread throughout Manchester and soon after a crowd gathered at the hospital, sacked it and lit a bonfire in the yard. Fr Hearne was called to defuse the situation. His words of reason subdued the angry mourners and the crowd dispersed. During the 1830s, Fr Hearne sued a British minister for libel when he accused the parish priest of imposing tyrannical practices on his congregation. The jury found in favour of Fr Hearne, marking a notable victory for the Catholic Church in the early days of emancipation. In 1843, Fr Hearne introduced the Temperance Hall to Manchester and during his time as parish priest of St Patrick's convinced many Irish Catholic immigrants to take the pledge. See *Silver Jubilee Souvenir*.

30  *Report on the State of the Irish Poor in Great Britain*, H.C. 1836 (40) xxxiv, p. 549. Cited in Werly, 'The Irish in Manchester', p. 355.

31  Edmund Hogan, *The Irish Missionary Movement: A Historical Survey, 1830–1980* (Dublin: Gill and Macmillan Ltd., 1990), p. 2.

32  In 1842, a seminary, All Hallows, was founded in Dublin for the sole purpose of training priests for missionary activity oversees. While it was intended that the seminary would provide recruits for non-Catholic missions, the political, religious and social conditions in Ireland during the nineteenth century made such endeavours extremely difficult, particularly during the Great Irish Famine when thousands emigrated. See Hogan, *The Irish Missionary Movement*, pp. 16–24.

33  Some of the most notable literature within this genre include S.M. Lewis, *The Monk* (1794), Charles Maturin, *Melmoth the Wanderer* (1820), Maria Monk, *Awful Disclosures* (1836), and Ann Radcliffe, *The Italian* (1797).

34  Ingram Cobbin, 'Essay on Popery' in *Foxe's Book of Martyrs* (London: 1875), iv. Cited in E.R. Norman, *Anti-Catholicism in Victorian England* (London: Wilmer Brothers Ltd., 1968), p. 15. See also Philip Ingram, 'Protestant patriarchy and the Catholic priesthood in nineteenth century England', *Journal of Social History*, 24, 4 (Summer 1991), pp. 783–97.

35  Dye, 'Protectionism or Irish Nationalism?', pp. 361–3; Norman, *Anti-Catholicism*, pp. 13–18; Werly, 'The Irish in Manchester', pp. 351–4.

36  Norman, *Anti-Catholicism*, p. 17.

37  Norman has suggested that the number of Roman Catholics in England at this time was 610,000 while Walsh has argued that the figure was probably closer to 700,000. It is difficult to ascertain the exact number of Catholics living in England in the mid-nineteenth century as the religious census was based on church attendance alone and did not factor in the non-practising Catholic. See Norman, *Anti-Catholicism*, p. 17 and Walsh, *Roman Catholic Nuns*, pp. 24–5.

38  Mangion, *Contested Identities*, p. 49.

39  Ibid., p. 34.

40  Rene Kollar, 'Foreign and Catholic: a plea to Protestant parents on the dangers of convent education in Victorian England', *History of Education*, 31, 4 (2002), p. 336.

41  Susan O'Brien, 'Terra Incognita: the nun in nineteenth-century England' in *Past and Present*, 121, 1 (November 1988), pp. 111–12.

42  Mangion, *Contested Identities*, p. 50.

43  Walsh, *Roman Catholic Nuns*, pp. 15–16.

44  Mangion, *Contested Identities*, p. 50.

45  Gerald Grace, 'The State and Catholic schooling in England and Wales: politics, ideology and mission integrity', *Oxford Review of Education*, 27, 4 (2001), p. 492.

46  Walsh, *Roman Catholic Nuns*, p. 14.

47  From 1839, voluntary bodies in receipt of the grant aid were also required to submit to government inspection. However, such examinations were irregular and infrequent. Moreover, the inspectors were not permitted to interfere with the organisation or governance of the school nor were they allowed to comment on

the discipline or religious practices. See S.J. Curtis and M.E.A. Boultwood, *An Introduction to the History of English Education Since 1800* (London: University Tutorial Press, 1964), pp. 56–61.

48  Walsh, *Roman Catholic Nuns*, p. 26.

49  Ibid.

50  Cited in Grace, 'The State and Catholic Schooling', p. 490.

51  Ibid., p. 491; Walsh, *Roman Catholic Nuns*, p. 26.

52  While the first Presentation Sisters arrived in Manchester from Clonmel in Co. Tipperary, Walsh has incorrectly stated that they travelled from Cork. Similarly, Mangion has indicated that only one Presentation foundation was established in England during the nineteenth century. A second branch of the Order was actually founded in Buxton in 1898. See Walsh, *Roman Catholic Nuns*, p. 13; Mangion, *Contested Identities*, p. 189.

53  *Silver Jubilee Souvenir*. The *Silver Jubilee Souvenir* was published to celebrate the twenty-fifth anniversary of the new St Patrick's church which had been built in 1936. The original church was established in 1832, just four years before the Presentation Sisters arrived in Manchester.

54  The Annals of the Presentation Convent, Livesey Street, indicated that Mr Lavery was originally from Navan in Co. Down. However, this has been accepted as a misprint and corrected in the main body of this text. See Presentation Convent Livesey Street Annals (1836–1936), p. 1, PAHCM.

55  It is not clear why Lavery was so keen that his bequest should be used for the establishment of a Presentation foundation. The Order had no existing houses in his hometown of Navan and there is no evidence to suggest that he had any prior relationship with any members of the congregation. It could simply be that Lavery favoured a congregation of his own faith and heritage, who would understand more easily the needs of his Irish, Catholic employees in the Lancashire district. Moreover, as the Presentation Sisters were bound by their constitutions to serve the needs of the poor above all others, their apostolic work would be of greater benefit to the working-class in Manchester than a congregation from the continent.

56  According to the Annals of the Presentation Convent, Livesey Street, 'Under the existing laws it was not safe for any money to be given to a Director for Charitable purposes'. See Presentation Convent Livesey Street Annals, p. 1.

57  Ibid.

58  Ibid.

59  Ibid.

60  Ibid.

61  According to the *Constitutions* of the Presentation Sisters: 'As the Poor are the main object and particular end of this pious institute, it is hereby enacted as a statute inviolably to be observed, that the Sisters of the Religious Institute shall admit none into their schools but poor children; nor can they receive money, or any other temporal emolument for instruction.' See *Presentation Constitutions*, p. 12.

62  It is estimated that by 1832, the interest on Mr Lavery's bequest had generated more than £800.

63  The exact figure raised for the Presentation foundation in Manchester is unclear and the Annals recorded that 'the sums obtained were not known at any time to the Nuns'. See Presentation Convent Livesey Street Annals, p. 2.

64  Ibid.

65  The laying of the foundation stone of the Presentation Convent was a momentous occasion attended by Rev D. Hearne and several other priests with a procession of about 600 children, the girls wearing white frocks and caps trimmed with white, having a white ribbon with a cross on their breasts as was the custom with Catholic processions. See Presentation Convent Livesey Street Annals, p. 2.

66  The Clonmel community had originally intended to send Sr M. Aquin Rivers, M. Angela Dillon and M. Magdalen Sargent. However, due to issues surrounding the dowries of the two former mentioned Sisters it was decided to send Sisters M. Francis and M. Baptist in their place. See Presentation Convent Livesey Street Annals, p. 2.

67  Ibid.

68  Ibid.

69  Ibid.

70  Ibid., p. 3.

71  Ibid.

72  Ibid.

73  *Constitutions* (1809), p. 12.

74  While the *Constitutions* directed that the Sisters were not allowed to charge fees for instruction in their poor schools, certain circumstances permitted the Sisters to provide instruction to pupils of affluent means provided that any money received was given 'to the relief of the poor children'. The Rev Mother of the Clonmel community undoubtedly used this clause to permit the Sisters in Manchester to charge a fee to their pupils. See *Constitutions* (1809), p. 13.

75  Presentation Convent Livesey Street Annals, p. 3.

76  Ibid.

77  Ibid., pp. 3–4.

78  It is possible that Fr Hearne had the Sisters transported via a horse-drawn carriage as it was considerably less expensive than travelling by train to the capital.

79  It was recorded in the Annals that 'They were very much encouraged and edified by the pious conversation of Brother Ignatius Rice .... To him Mother Magdalen J. Sargent was indebted for the support and consolation he gave her during the long term of nine years which she had spent in the novitiate of the several houses of Waterford and Cork and Clonmel on account of the delay her father had made in granting her dowry in the hope that she would tire and give up the idea of being a Presentation nun. She bore towards Mr Rice a most loving respect. He gave her [a] small plain watch which she wore when she came to Manchester and it was given to the Christian Brothers after the death of Mr Rice. They treasured

it as a relic of that holy man.' See Presentation Convent Livesey Street Annals, p. 4.

80 It is not clear how, but while in George's Hill, Sr M. Baptist Murphy sprained her ankle, 'the effects of which she suffered very much'. See Presentation Convent Livesey Street Annals, p. 4.

81 Ibid.

82 Ibid.

83 Dr Penswick served as Vicar Apostolic of the northern district from 1831–1836. He died shortly after the Presentation Sisters arrived in England, on 29 January 1836.

84 Presentation Convent Livesey Street Annals, p. 4.

85 Ibid.

86 Ibid.

87 Ibid., p. 6.

88 Ibid., p. 4.

89 Ibid., pp. 4–5.

90 Ibid.

91 Ibid., p. 4.

92 Ibid., p. 5.

93 Ibid.

94 Ibid.

95 Ibid. In 1845, the Christian Brothers took responsibility for a boys' school which had been built opposite the church in Livesey Street. Br Phelan, or 'Daddy Phelan' as he was known by his pupils, was appointed headmaster. See *Silver Jubilee Souvenir*.

96 *Silver Jubilee Souvenir*.

97 Presentation Convent Livesey Street Annals, p. 5.

98 Ibid.

99 Ibid.

100 *Constitutions* (1809), p. 42.

101 Presentation Convent Livesey Street Annals, p. 8.

102 Ibid.

103 Ibid.

104 Ibid.

105 Ibid.

106 Ibid.

107 Ibid.

108 *Silver Jubilee Souvenir*.

109 Ibid.

110 Presentation Convent Livesey Street Annals, pp. 7–11.

111 *Catholic Directory* (1838), p. 85, cited in Mangion, *Contested Identities*, p. 127.

112 Presentation Convent Livesey Street Annals, pp. 15–18.

113 *Silver Jubilee Souvenir*.

114 Walsh has indicated that in 1857 there were 100 convents in England and Wales. By 1897 this number had increased to 469 and by 1917 there were 800 female religious houses in operation. See Walsh, *Roman Catholic Nuns*, p. 177.

115 Mangion, *Contested Identities*, p. 230.

116 Between 1839 and 1900, the Mercy Sisters opened 119 convents in England and Wales, eighteen of which had closed before the turn of the century. See Mangion, *Contested Identities*, p. 230.

117 In 1851, the hierarchy of bishops in England was renewed with the appointment of twelve bishops and one archbishop. Lancashire was divided into two separate ecclesiastical districts, Liverpool and Salford. The Rt Rev Dr Turner was thereafter appointed bishop-elect of Salford. See Presentation Convent Livesey Street Annals p. 23.

118 Presentation Convent Livesey Street Annals, pp. 23–4.

119 Ibid.

120 Ibid.

121 Ibid.

122 Ibid.

123 Ibid.

124 Ibid.

125 Ibid.

126 Susan O'Brien, 'French nuns in nineteenth-century England', *Past and Present*, 154 (February 1997), p. 149.

127 Walsh, *Roman Catholic Nuns*, pp. 15–16.

128 Mangion, *Contested Identities*, p. 50.

129 Presentation Convent Livesey Street Annals, pp. 23–4.

130 Ibid.

131 Ibid., p. 56.

132 Ibid.

133 Ibid.

134 Ibid., p. 57.

135 Ibid.

136 Ibid., p. 59.

137 Ibid., pp. 58–9.

138 Ibid., p. 59.

139 Ibid.

140 Ibid.

141 Ibid.

142 See Peckham Magray, *The Transforming Power of the Nuns*, pp. 15–31.

143 Mangion, *Contested Identities*, p. 229.

144 Presentation Convent Livesey Street Annals, pp. 43–4.

145 The Sisters were accompanied on their trip by a student from Freshfield College, J. Crowley.

146 Presentation Convent Livesey Street Annals, pp. 43–4.

147 According to the constitutions, 'The schools for the poor children shall be within the enclosure, and shall be proportioned to the number of Religious capable of attending.' Moreover, it was directed that 'after having made their Religious Profession, it shall be no longer in their power to pass the limits of Enclosure, which shall be marked out'. See *Constitutions* (1809), p. 13; pp. 20–1.

148 Presentation Convent Livesey Street Annals, p. 47.

149 Ibid.

## CHAPTER 8

1 Department of Education, *Annual Report, 1924/25* (Dublin, 1926), p. 44 (hereafter DE, *Annual Report*).

2 Coolahan, *Irish Education*, p. 57.

3 Ibid., p. 58.

4 Desmond Bowen, *Paul Cardinal Cullen and the Shaping of Modern Irish Catholicism* (Dublin: Gill and Macmillan Ltd., 1983), p. 129.

5 Bowen, *Paul Cardinal Cullen*, p. 292.

6 Dr Cullen to Mrs William Grey, 16 November 1871. Cited by Ann V. O'Connor, 'The revolution in girls' secondary education in Ireland, 1860–1910,' in Mary Cullen (ed.), *Girls don't do honours: Irish women in education in the nineteenth and twentieth centuries* (Dublin: Arlen House, 1987), p. 36.

7 Judith Harford and Deirdre Raftery, 'The education of young girls within the national system,' in Raftery and Parkes, *Female Education in Ireland*, p. 52.

8 Ibid.

9 Ibid.

10 O'Connor, 'The revolution in girls' secondary education,' pp. 38–9.

11 The Brigidine Sisters managed four schools located in Tullow, Mountrath, Abbeyleix and Goresbridge; the Mercy Sisters operated a school in Ennis and the Holy Faith Sisters conducted a boarding school in Glasnevin. See O'Connor, 'The revolution in girls' secondary education,' p. 38.

12 O'Connor, 'The revolution in girls' secondary education,' p. 42.

13 Ibid.

14 When asked his opinion regarding extending intermediate education to the labouring class, Cullen stated that 'Too high an education will make the poor oftentimes disconnected, and will unsuit them for following the plough, or for using the spade, or hammering iron or building walls. The poor ought to be educated with a view to the place they hold in society.' See *Royal Commission of inquiry into primary education (Ireland), Vol. I* (Dublin, 1870), p. 506.

15 Katherine Tynan, *Twenty-five Years: Reminiscences* (London, 1913) cited in Maria Luddy, *Women in Ireland: A documentary history, 1800–1918* (Cork: Cork University Press, 1995), p. 115.

16 O'Connor, 'The revolution in girls' secondary education,' pp. 42–3.

17 Ibid., 43.

18  Kieran Waldron, *Out of the Shadows: Emerging Secondary Schools in the Archdiocese of Tuam, 1940–69* (Tuam: Nordlaw Books, 2002), p. 157. See also *Nationalist and Leinster Times*, 1 December 1883.

19  Presentation Convent Listowel Annals (1844–1882).

20  Presentation Convent Clondalkin Annals, Vol. I (1857–1925), p. 26.

21  Presentation Convent Clondalkin Annals, Vol. I. According to the constitutions of the Presentation Order, the Sisters were permitted to open a benefit school in areas 'where there are no proper schools for the education of girls' provided that 'the emoluments received on those occasions are not to be applied to the use of the Sisters, but to the relief of the poor children'. See *Constitutions of the Institute of the Religious Sisterhood of the Presentation of the Ever Blessed Virgin Mary* (Cork: 1935), pp. 21–2.

22  Presentation Convent Clondalkin Annals, Vol. II, pp. 101–3.

23  Hutch, *Nano Nagle*, pp. 409 and 447.

24  Presentation Convent Tralee Annals (1812–1897).

25  Presentation Convent Ballingarry Annals and Accounts (1878–1955), IE PBVM BAL, uncatalogued.

26  Coolahan, *Irish Education*, p. 61.

27  Irish MPs such as The O'Conor Don and William Monsell, the barrister and teacher, Edward Howley, Fr Leman, President of the French College in Blackrock, and Sir Patrick Keenan, Resident Commissioner for National Education, were all instrumental in highlighting the need for a more formal system of intermediate education. See Coolahan, *Irish Education*, pp. 61–2.

28  Áine Hyland, 'Intermediate education' in Hyland and Milne, *Irish Educational Documents, Vol. I*, p. 201.

29  See Coolahan, *Irish Education*, p. 63.

30  Hyland, 'Intermediate Education', p. 201.

31  Presentation Convent Tralee Annals, Vol. 2 (1857–1910).

32  Ibid. While the Presentation Sisters in Tralee were providing intermediate education to their pupils, the school was not selected as a centre for the examinations. As a result, their pupils were required to sit their examinations in the Loreto Convent School in Killarney.

33  Presentation Convent Killarney Annals (1793–1953).

34  *Forty-eighth Report of the Commissioners of National Education in Ireland, 1881*. Cited in O'Connor, 'The revolution in girls' secondary education', p. 51.

35  Presentation Convent Bandon Annals (1829–1919).

36  Hyland, 'Intermediate Education', p. 201.

37  Ibid.

38  Reporting on the Intermediate Examination results in 1887, the *Freeman's Journal* noted that convent schools were superior in the teaching of modern languages, but Protestant schools had outpaced them at mathematics. See O'Connor, 'The revolution in girls' secondary education', p. 46.

39  Coolahan, *Irish Education*, p. 72.

40   Ibid., pp. 72–3.

41   Ibid., p. 74.

42   DE, *Annual Report, 1924/25*, p. 5.

43   Ibid., p. 7.

44   In 1924, Seosamh O Neill and Proinnsias O Dubhthaight, Intermediate Education Commissioners, produced the first programme for secondary schools. The purpose of the programme was to provide school managers with direct guidelines relating to the Intermediate Education (Ireland) Acts, 1878 and 1924. See Department of Education, *Rules and Programmes for Secondary Schools, 1925* (Dublin, 1925) (hereafter, DE, *Rules and Programmes*), p. 3.

45   DE, *Annual Report, 1924/25*, p. 54.

46   O'Connor, 'The revolution in girls' secondary education', p. 44.

47   Ibid.

48   DE, *Annual Report, 1924/25*, p. 106.

49   DE, *Rules and Programmes, 1938/39*, p. 66. The conditions for recognition of secondary tops remained largely unchanged since their initial implementation and were still being used by the Department of Education during the school year 2004/05. See DE, *Rules and Programmes, 2004/05*, pp. 22–3.

50   In 1892, national school education became free and as a result many pupils stayed on in primary schools well into their teenage years. See Coolahan, *Irish Education*, p. 56.

51   DE, *Annual Report, 1940/41*, p. 102.

52   'The Beginning of the Presentation Sisters in Milltown' (n.d., n.p.)

53   Sr Oliver Byrne, *A Record of Eighty-four Years: Presentation Sisters Durrow* (Laois: Presentation Sisters, 1998), p. 13.

54   James S. Donnelly Jr, 'Bishop Michael Browne of Galway (1937–76) and the regulation of public morality', *New Hibernia Review*, 17 (Spring 2013), p. 16.

55   Presentation Convent Galway Annals, Vol. II (1815–1999), p. 47.

56   Ibid.

57   The final date for acceptance of applications differed from year to year but tended to range between 15 August and 1 September. See individual *Rules and Programmes, 1924–58*. See *Rules and Programmes, 1938/39*, p. 6.

58   DE, *Rules and Programmes, 1940/41*, pp. 6–7.

59   DE, *Annual Report, 1940/41*, p. 94.

60   Presentation Convent Waterford Annals.

61   Presentation Convent Cahirciveen Annals (1840–1994).

62   Gerald Ahern (ed.), *The Story of the Presentation Sisters, Scoil Chroí Naofa and Presentation College, Athenry, 1908–2008* (Galway: Presentation Sisters, 2009), pp. 258–60.

63   As the Presentation Sisters were still an enclosed Order at this time, the Sisters teaching in the secondary school had to be accompanied to and from Canton Hall. The subjects taught by the Sisters included Irish, English, Maths, French, history, geography, music, art, drawing, cookery, needlework and Christian Doctrine. The

pupils also had to attend school on Saturdays up to 12:30 pm. See Ahern, *The Story of the Presentation Sisters*, p. 258.

64    Presentation Convent Galway Annals, Vol. II (1815–1999), p. 55.

65    *Constitutions* (1935), pp. 59–60.

66    Presentation Sisters, 10 December 1947, Dublin Diocesan Archives, McQuaid Papers, 1/AB/8B. Hereafter DDA, McQ.

67    Presentation Sisters, 15 January 1948, DDA, McQ, 1/AB/8B.

68    Ibid.

69    Presentation Sisters, 29 January 1948, DDA, McQ, 1/AB/8B.

70    *The Irish Catholic Directory*, 1951 (Dublin, 1951), p. 286.

71    Ibid., pp. 225–320.

72    Eileen Randles, *Post-primary Education in Ireland, 1957–1970* (Dublin: Veritas Publications, 1975), p. 18.

73    Tom O'Donoghue, *The Catholic Church and the Secondary School Curriculum in Ireland, 1922–62* (New York: Peter Lang, 1999), p. 22.

74    A junior pupil could not be less than twelve years of age. If the pupil was less than twelve years old on the first day of the school year the Department of Education could offer a capitation grant of £8 provided the pupil had a minimum of 130 attendances during that school year. See DE, *Rules for the Payment of Grants to Secondary Schools, 1957/58* (Dublin, 1957), pp. 4–5 (hereafter *Rules for the Payment of Grants*).

75    DE, *Rules for the Payment of Grants, 1957/58*, p. 16.

76    Ibid., p. 4.

77    DE, *Rules for the Payment of Grants, 1937/38*, pp. 7–8.

78    See DE, *Annual Reports, 1940–52*.

79    DE, *Annual Reports, 1958/59*, p. 17.

80    *Irish Catholic Directory* (1930), p. 247.

81    Post-primary day fees, 1961–68, George's Hill Archive Directory, GHAD, IE PBVM [GHD] 3/A/34/6.

82    Presentation Convent George's Hill Annals (1775–1983).

83    Presentation Convent Ballingarry Accounts.

84    Ibid.

85    Presentation Sisters, 15 February 1949, Galway Diocesan Archives, Browne Archive, B/3/109. Hereafter GDA, BA.

86    St Joseph's School Accounts, Oranmore, Co. Galway (1947–75). GDA, Oranmore Papers, C51/67.

87    St Joseph's Accounts (1953) and St Philomena's Accounts (1935–65), GDA, A/30.

88    St Joseph's School Accounts (1947–75).

89    Presentation Convent Ballingarry Annals.

90    Ibid.

91    Presentation Sisters, 6 June 1946, GDA, BA, B/3/108.

92    Ibid. According to the *Constitutions* of the Presentation Sisters 'if they [the sisters] receive any present from their relatives, or others, it must be applied to the

community, and not to the particular use of the receiver'. See *Constitutions*, (1935), p. 26.

93   Presentation Sisters, 24 January 1947, GDA, BA, B/3/110.

94   Presentation Sisters, 7 September 1950, GDA, BA, B/3/111.

95   Presentation Convent Ballingarry Annals.

96   Ibid.

97   Presentation Convent Ballingarry Accounts.

98   Ibid.

99   St Joseph's School Accounts (1947–75).

100   Presentation Sisters, 26 September 1949, GDA, BA, B/3/111.

101   Ibid.

102   Ibid.

103   *Presentation Constitutions* (1935), p. 28.

104   Patrick Duffy, *The Lay Teacher* (Dublin: Fallons, 1967), pp. 49–50.

105   O'Donoghue, *The Catholic Church*, pp. 111–12.

106   Department of Education, *Report of the Council of Education as presented to the Minister for Education, the Curriculum of the Secondary School* (Dublin, 1962), p. 256 (hereafter, DE, *The Curriculum of the Secondary School*).

107   Ibid.

108   Department of Education, *Report of the Survey Team Appointed by the Minister for Education, Investment in Education, Ireland* (Dublin, 1965), (hereafter, DE, *Investment in Education*), p. 10.

109   Government of Ireland, *Bunreacht na hEireann* (Dublin, 1975).

110   O'Donoghue, *The Catholic Church*, p. 49. The Conference of Convent Secondary Schools was first established in 1929. The aim of the organisation was 'to watch over Catholic interests in all matters concerning our schools and to take such steps as may be considered advisable to ensure the due consideration of such interests'. Furthermore, it facilitated the 'interchange of ideas and information in all school matters including teaching, examinations, internal management and organisation in general'. See Séamas O'Buachalla, *Education policy in twentieth-century Ireland* (Dublin: Wolfhound Press, 1988), pp. 138–49.

111   Fr Edward Leen CSSp, *What is Education?* (London: Burns, Oates and Washbourne, 1943), cited in O'Donoghue, *The Catholic Church*, pp. 48–9.

112   *Cork Examiner*, 10 August 1940.

113   *Irish Press*, 17 August 1940.

114   *Kerryman*, 28 June 1952.

115   Presentation Convent Waterford Annals.

116   Coolahan, *Irish Education*, p. 76.

117   Presentation Convent Rahan, Notebook A6, 'The Irish courses', 1922–26, IE PBVM RAH, uncatalogued.

118   Presentation Convent Portlaoise Annals.

119   Presentation Convent Clondalkin Annals, Vol. I (1857–1925), p. 37.

120   South Presentation Convent Annals.

121 Presentation Convent Portlaoise Annals.

122 Presentation Convent Rahan, Notebook A6.

123 Presentation Convent Killarney Annals.

124 South Presentation Convent Annals.

125 Ibid.

126 Ibid.

127 Ibid.

128 Presentation Convent Cahirciveen Annals.

129 Ibid.

130 O'Donoghue, *The Catholic Church*, p. 93.

131 DE, *Investment in Education*, p. 11.

132 Presentation Convent Rahan, Notebook A6.

133 DE, *Rules and programmes, 1941/42*, p. 6.

134 Many congregations established their own university residences in cities where their members were attending universities and colleges, and they sometimes offered hospitality to members of other Orders; the daily routines in these houses had to reflect the fact that the Sisters were out attending lectures during the day.

135 Susan O'Brien, *Leaving God for God: The Daughters of Charity of St Vincent de Paul in Britain, 1847–2017* (London: Darton, Longman and Todd Ltd., 2017), p. 17.

136 Presentation Convent Ballingarry Annals, October 1958.

## CHAPTER 9

1 Sr M. Aquinas suffered from rheumatism and had been advised by the community's First Superior, the Rt Rev J. Billsborrow, Bishop of Salford and the Rt Rev Dr Carroll, Bishop of Shrewsbury, to travel to Buxton and avail of the 'pure air and mineral waters' there. See Presentation Convent Buxton Annals (1898–1912).

2 Ibid.

3 Ibid.

4 Ibid.

5 Ibid.

6 Ibid.

7 Ibid.

8 Ibid.

9 Ibid.

10 Ibid.

11 Ibid.

12 Ibid.

13 Ibid.

14 Ibid.

15 Ibid.

16 Ibid.

17 Ibid.

18 Form of agreement, circa February 1898. Presentation Convent Buxton Annals (1898–1976).

19 Ibid.

20 Although the Sisters had agreed to commence their work on 1 May, the teacher at the Buxton school could not remain until that time. As a result, Canon Hoeben was required to contact the Manchester community and inquire if the Sisters could come at an earlier date. But the Sisters were unable to leave Manchester until 22 April 1898 and consequently the elementary school in Buxton had to close for a period of three weeks. See Presentation Convent Buxton Annals (1898–1976).

21 Presentation Convent Buxton Annals (1898–1912).

22 Canon Hoeben had engaged a number of workmen to carry out alterations and improvements on the convent and had hoped that the work would have been finished prior to the Sisters' arrival. However, due to an attack of bronchitis Canon Hoeben's project was delayed.

23 Presentation Convent Glossop Annals (1904–20).

24 Ibid.

25 Ibid.

26 Ibid.

27 Ibid.

28 Ibid.

29 Presentation Convent Buxton Annals (1898–1976).

30 Ibid.

31 The Annals record that salary increases were awarded to the teaching Sisters in July and November 1917, while an increase of £14 was provided in October 1918. See Presentation Convent Glossop Annals (1904–20).

32 Presentation Convent Buxton Annals (1898–1976).

33 Ibid.

34 Ibid.

35 Ibid.

36 Ibid.

37 It should be noted that the Presentation constitutions directed that 'Pensioners, or lodgers, whether young or old, shall not, on any account, be received into their convents.' Nonetheless, it seems that in light of wartime measures the Presentation Sisters frequently admitted lodgers into their convents. See *Rules and constitutions of the institute of the religious sisterhood of the Presentation of the Ever Blessed Virgin Mary* (Cork, 1809), p. 13 (hereafter, *Presentation Constitutions*).

38 Presentation Convent Glossop Annals (1904–20).

39 Ibid.

40 Presentation Convent Pickering Annals (1919–75).

41 Ibid.

42 Ibid.

43 Plans of the proposed convent were sent from Galway to Pickering. It was expected that the property would consist of 'a stone mansion standing in its own

grounds with orchards no. 1 and 2'. See Presentation Convent Pickering Annals (1919–75).

44  Ibid.

45  Ibid.

46  Ibid.

47  Ibid.

48  Fr Bryan had intended to establish an orphanage 'chiefly for the benefit of little girls whose fathers had been killed in the war'. See Presentation Convent Galway Annals, Vol. 2 (1815–1999), p. 3.

49  Presentation Convent Pickering Annals (1919–75).

50  Ibid.

51  Ibid.

52  Ibid.

53  Anon., *Presentation Convent Galway, 1815–1965, Sesquicentenary Souvenir* (Galway, 1965), p. 28.

54  Presentation Convent Pickering Annals (1919–75).

55  Ibid.

56  Ibid.

57  Ibid.

58  Ibid.

59  Ibid.

60  Ibid.

61  Ibid.

62  Ibid.

63  Anon., *Presentation Convent Galway, 1815–1965*, p. 28.

64  Presentation Convent, Pickering Annals, (1919–75).

65  Ibid.

66  *Nano Nagle* (Matlock, 1961), pp. 18–19.

67  Presentation Convent Castleconnell Annals (1945–77), PAHCM, uncatalogued.

68  Account of Etonfield (1941), Typescript, n.n., PAHCM.

69  Ibid.

70  At the time, there were already schools in operation under the direction of other female religious. See 'The Convent on the Hill, Matlock' (Typescript, n.n., n.d.), PSCA, IE PBVM 90/1/9/5/1.

71  In 1919, the houses in India had not yet amalgamated and the foundation in Liverpool had to depend on voluntary subscriptions and donations from independent Presentation communities. See Account of Etonfield (1941).

72  Account of Etonfield (1941).

73  'The Convent on the Hill, Matlock'.

74  Presentation Convent Liverpool and Matlock Annals (1918–76).

75  Anon., *Mother Xavier Murphy*, p. 17.

76  Account of 'The Convent on the Hill, Matlock'.

77  Anon., *Mother Xavier Murphy*, p. 17.

78   Ibid., p. 18.

79   'The Convent on the Hill, Matlock'.

80   Anon., *Mother Xavier Murphy*, p. 18.

81   'The Convent on the Hill, Matlock'.

82   Ibid.

83   Presentation Convent Liverpool and Matlock Annals (1918–76).

84   Presentation Convent Matlock Annals (1927–61), Vol. II. During the Second
     World War, the site of the former novitiate in Liverpool was bombed. See Anon.,
     *Mother Xavier Murphy*, p. 18.

85   Prior permission had been granted by the Sacred Congregation of Religious to
     transfer the novitiate from Etonfield to Chesterfield. See Presentation Convent
     Liverpool and Matlock Annals (1918–76).

86   Among the first Sisters in Matlock were Mother Dominic Murphy and Sr Clare
     Conway, Lelia MacNamara, Ursula McGarrett, Oliver McEvoy, Victoire Carroll,
     Mildred Flynn and Barbara Fleming. See 'The Convent on the Hill, Matlock'.

87   Ibid.

88   The Sisters first undertook to provide religious instruction to the poor children of
     Matlock in the convent. Fr Cossins later decided that it would be best to run the
     Sunday School in the parish church, as it was more easily accessible to the children.
     The convent was situated on top of a large hill which many children may have
     found too difficult to climb. See 'The Convent on the Hill, Matlock'.

89   Ibid.

90   The exact number of pupils who attended Mount St Joseph's on the first day is
     unclear, but there were about twenty-seven pupils in total.

91   These Sisters included Sr Agnes Loughran, Christine Loughran, Josepha McEvoy,
     Liguori McEvoy, Paula O'Connell and St John Ryder. See 'The Convent on the Hill,
     Matlock'.

92   'The Convent on the Hill, Matlock'.

93   *Nano Nagle* (Matlock, 1961), p. 29.

94   Presentation Convent Liverpool and Matlock Annals (1918–76).

95   Anon., *Mother Xavier Murphy*, p. 26.

96   'The Convent on the Hill, Matlock', p. 6.

97   Presentation Convent Liverpool and Matlock Annals (1918–76).

98   Ibid.

99   'The Convent on the Hill, Matlock', p. 6.

100  Presentation Convent Matlock Annals Vol. 2 (1927–61).

101  Ibid.

102  Ibid.

103  Presentation Convent Buxton Annals (1898–1976).

104  Presentation Convent Pickering Annals (1919–75).

105  Presentation Convent Buxton Annals (1898–1976).

106  'Benfleet Community Archive'. Available at: www.benfleethistory.org.uk (accessed
     29 January 2018).

107  Ibid.

108  Presentation Convent Matlock Annals, Vol. 2 (1927–61).

109  Presentation Convent Buxton Annals (1898–1976).

110  Ibid.

111  Ibid.

112  Ibid.

113  Presentation Convent Pickering Annals (1919–75).

114  Ibid.

115  Ibid.

116  Ibid.

117  Ibid.

118  Presentation Convent Buxton Annals (1898–1976).

119  Presentation Convent Castleconnell Annals (1945–77).

120  Ibid.

121  Ibid.

122  Ibid.

123  Ibid.

124  Ibid.

125  Ibid.

126  Most Rev Dr Fogarty, Bishop of Killaloe, to Rev Mother Liguori McEvoy, Superior of the Presentation Convent, Matlock, 2 March 1945. Recounted in the Presentation Convent Castleconnell Annals (1945–77).

127  Presentation Convent Castleconnell Annals (1945–77).

128  Ibid.

129  Ibid.

130  Ibid.

131  Ibid.

132  Ibid.

133  'The Convent on the Hill, Matlock'.

134  *To Protestant Parents* (Loughborough: Daniel Cartwright, 1830), p. 3. Cited in Kollar, 'Foreign and Catholic', p. 341.

135  Presentation Convent Livesey Street Annals (1836–1936), p. 5.

136  Ibid. Although the Annals do not expand on what 'the world said it (the convent) was', this observation would indicate that the Presentation Sisters were aware of the 'No popery' literature and the frequent comparison of female religious houses to 'dens of sin and vice', 'torture and orgy', and 'brothels of the worst description'. See Ingram, 'Protestant patriarchy', pp. 783–97; Kollar, 'Foreign and Catholic', pp. 335–50; Norman, *Anti-Catholicism*.

137  Presentation Convent Buxton Annals (1898–1976).

138  Presentation Convent Buxton Annals (1898–1912).

139  Presentation Convent Pickering Annals (1919–75).

140  Ibid.

141  A.H. Guinness was a member of the Protestant Alliance, a political society which had been established in 1851 and regularly produced anti-Catholic publications. See A.H. Guinness, *Education by nuns: its failures and injurious tendencies* (London: Protestant Alliance, 1890), p. 5. Cited in Kollar, 'Foreign and Catholic', pp. 337–38.

142  Presentation Convent Livesey Street Annals (1836–1936), p. 15.

143  Ibid., p. 38.

144  Presentation Convent Buxton Annals (1898–1976).

145  One set of rosary beads was subsequently returned. See Presentation Convent Buxton Annals (1898–1976).

146  Presentation Convent Buxton Annals (1898–1912).

147  *The Month* (1894), p. 520. Cited in Mangion, *Contested Identities*, p. 80.

148  The night school was first opened in 1842 for the benefit of poor women and young girls who were employed during the day in factories. See Presentation Convent Livesey Street Annals (1836–1936), p. 15; pp. 27 and 49.

149  The Catholic hierarchy supported convent schooling because they believed it helped to create devout and good Catholics. The middle-class believed that religious-run educational institutions helped reinforce the social status quo by ensuring that a broad education was denied to the labouring class, making it less likely for them to become dissatisfied with their traditional roles of employment. Finally, as the home was considered the rightful and natural place of the woman in Victorian society, there was little point in providing instruction in anything outside the sphere of domesticity. See W.B. Stephens, *Education in Britain, 1750–1914* (London: Macmillan Press Ltd., 1998), pp. 12–13.

150  At the turn of the nineteenth century, the education system which existed in England consisted of a broad and varied network of largely inefficient institutions. The composition of these schools was complex and included parish, charity, voluntary, private, private middle-class and endowed grammar foundations all of which operated independently of one another. Catholic religious congregations, for the most part, were involved in the operation of voluntary schools for poor children and, to a lesser degree, the provision of private education to middle-class girls. The level of instruction provided in each of these autonomous institutions also varied greatly and generally depended on local circumstances, social class and denominational interests in the curricular content of the subjects taught in the schools. Lack of a regular, sustained income also affected the level of instruction and the efficiency and operation of these schools. In any case, despite the apparent multitude of educational institutions which operated in England at this time, participation rates in all types and levels of schooling were extremely low.

151  From 1847, pupil teachers were employed to replace the traditional monitorial system and during the 1850s, ragged or industrial schools which provided trade or craft training were awarded government aid. In the 1860s, payment-by-results was also introduced for the first time. See Stephens, *Education in Britain*, pp. 7–10.

152   Presentation Convent Livesey Street Annals (1836–1936), pp. 22–3.
153   Ibid.
154   Ibid.
155   Stephens, *Education in Britain*, p. 17.
156   Presentation Convent Buxton Annals (1898–1912).
157   Ibid.
158   Board of Education, Local Education Authority, report by HMI Miss E. Luce, 23 January 1925, PAHCM.
159   Presentation Convent Livesey Street Annals (1836–1936), p. 23. The position of the Catholic Church in Manchester was further reinforced following the Education Act 1902, which saw the transfer of management, from a financial point of view, from voluntary bodies to Local Education Committees. 'Catholic managers, the priests of the mission, retained the right of appointing and dismissing teachers subject to the approval' of the Manchester Education Committee. See Presentation Convent Livesey Street Annals (1836–1936), p. 69.
160   Ibid., p. 26.
161   Ibid.
162   Presentation Convent Buxton Annals (1898–1912).
163   Diocese of Salford, Religious Inspection of Schools, 14 December 1915, PAHCM, uncatalogued.
164   Diocese of Salford, Religious Inspection of Schools, 6 July 1920, PAHCM, uncatalogued.
165   *Silver Jubilee Souvenir*.
166   'Centenary of the Presentation Convent, Buxton' compiled by Mrs Joyce Stack, retired teacher of St Anne's school and Sr Christine Loughran (n.d., n.p.).
167   Presentation Convent Glossop Annals (1904–20).
168   In August 1934, an old conservatory was converted into a library for the pupils and in December three new music rooms were built. In 1937, a second storey consisting of nine cubicles and a bathroom was built over the convent dining room. See Matlock Annals, Vol. 2 (1927–61).
169   Presentation Convent Ryde Annals (1948–70).
170   Presentation Convent Livesey Street Annals (1836–1936), p. 23.
171   According to the Annals, 'The first parlour, a fine, large, well lighted and airy room was furnished and converted into a schoolroom and … formed … the Sacred Heart School.' See Presentation Convent Buxton Annals (1898–1912).
172   Presentation Convent Livesey Street Annals (1836–1936), pp. 29–30.
173   Presentation Convent Glossop Annals (1904–20).
174   Presentation Convent Buxton Annals (1898–1912).
175   As the Presentation Sisters were an enclosed Order, special arrangements were made for Sr Dominic during her time in the training college. For example, she was to have her meals and take her recreation in a large sitting room in the college and was only permitted to mix with the secular students during her lectures and study hours. See Presentation Convent Buxton Annals (1898–1912).

176  Ibid.
177  Presentation Convent Matlock Annals, Vol. 2 (1927–61).
178  Ibid.


## CHAPTER 10

1  For a discussion of mission territories see Angelyn Dries, *The Missionary Movement in American Catholic History* (New York: Orbis Books, 1998). For excellent accounts of nuns in American life see Margaret McGuinness, *Called to Serve: A History of Nuns in America* (New York and London: New York University Press, 2013), and Anne M. Butler, *Across God's Frontiers: Catholic Sisters in the American West, 1850–1920* (Chapel Hill, NC: University of North Carolina Press, 2012).

2  Indian Province Annals, Madras (MS copy), PSCA, IE PBVM 90/1/9/5/1.

3  Ibid.

4  See Gerard Moran, *Sending out Ireland's Poor: Assisted Emigration to North America in the Nineteenth Century* (Dublin: Four Courts Press, 2004), pp. 14–15.

5  Ibid.

6  Ibid., p. 21.

7  See Raftery, '"Je suis d'aucune Nation"', p. 524; see also Hasia R. Diner, *Erin's Daughters in America: Irish Immigrant Women in the Nineteenth Century* (Baltimore and London: Johns Hopkins University Press, 1983), p. 35.

8  David Fitzpatrick, '"A share of the honeycomb": education, emigration and Irishwomen', in Mary Daly and David Dickson (eds), *Language, Change and Educational Development, 1700–1920* (Dublin: Trinity College Dublin and University College Dublin, 1990), p. 173.

9  Assisted by the Poor Law unions, thousands of girls aged 16 to 20 years were sent to the Cape of Good Hope and Van Dieman's Land (now Tasmania); they were also sent to Australia and Canada.

10  For a discussion of women religious and emigration in the nineteenth century, see Raftery, '"Je suis d'aucune Nation"'.

11  Diner, *Erin's Daughters in America*, p. 5. See also Kerby A. Miller, *Emigrants and Exiles: Ireland and the Irish Exodus to North America* (New York: Oxford University Press, 1985).

12  Diner, *Erin's Daughters in America*, pp. 30–1.

13  Ibid., p. 33.

14  Gerald Shaughnessy, *Has the Immigrant Kept the Faith? A Study of Immigration and Catholic Growth in the United States, 1790–1920* (New York: Macmillan Co., 1925), p. 110.

15  Diner, *Erin's Daughters in America*, p. 41.

16  Robert A. Burchell, *The San Francisco Irish, 1848–1880* (Manchester: Manchester University Press, 1979), p. 85.

17  Patrick O'Farrell, *The Irish in Australia: 1788 to the Present* (Notre Dame, IN: University of Notre Dame Press, 1992), p. 63.

18  Mary Rosa MacGinley, *A Dynamic of Hope: Institutes of Women Religious in Australia* (Darlinghurst, NSW: Australian Catholic University/Crossing Press, 2002), p. 139. Bishop William Willson (1794–1866) was the first Roman Catholic Bishop of Hobart.

19  Some of the pioneering groups who died in India included: Sr M. Regis Kelly (d. 1844); Sr Martha Kelly (d. 1846); Mother de Sales Nugent (d. 1852), and Sr Aloysius Neville (d. 1853). The Irish Loreto Sisters, who arrived in India a year before the Presentations, were equally affected by the heat and by diseases including cholera; forty-two Loreto Sisters died in Calcutta within the first twenty years of the mission.

20  Barry Crosbie, *Irish Imperial Networks: Migration, Social Communication and Exchange in Nineteenth-Century India* (Cambridge and New York: Cambridge University Press, 2011), p. 2.

21  Crosbie, *Irish Imperial Networks*, pp. 3–6, *passim*.

22  Ibid. See also Hayden J.A. Bellenoit, *Missionary Education and Empire in Late Colonial India, 1860–1920* (London: Pickering & Chatto, 2007), and Sanjay Seth, *Subject lessons: The Western education of colonial India* (Durham, NC: Duke University Press, 2007).

23  An exception is the work of Tim Allender, who has included research on women religious in *Learning Femininity in Colonial India, 1820–1932* (Manchester: Manchester University Press, 2016). Though Crosbie's ground-breaking work in *Irish Imperial Networks* provides a study of Catholicism in India, it is almost silent on the work of women religious.

24  For further work in this area see Deirdre Raftery and Marie Clarke (eds), *Transnationalism, Gender and the History of Education* (London and New York: Routledge, 2016).

25  Crosbie, *Irish Imperial Networks*, p. 151.

26  Ibid., p. 152.

27  Dr Patrick Joseph Carew (1800–1855). Carew was appointed Apostolic Vicar of Western Bengal in 1840.

28  A Loreto Sister, *Joyful Mother of Children: Mother Frances Mary Teresa Ball* (Dublin: M.H. Gill and Son Ltd., 1961), p. 190.

29  Indian Province Annals, Madras. While Walsh, *Nano Nagle*, p. 302, suggests that Carew brought the Presentations to India, the Annals record the arrival of the pioneering group, accompanied by Bishop Fennelly. Dr Stephen Fennelly (1806–1868) was appointed Vicar Apostolic of Madras in 1841. Dr Carew was Bishop of Calcutta by the time the Presentations arrived in India.

30  Dr John Fennelly to Fr David Moriarty, 1 June 1841. Cited in T.G. Duffy, 'An Irish Missionary Effort: the Brothers Fennelly', *Irish Ecclesiastical Review*, XVII (May 1921), pp. 464–84.

31  Crosbie, *Irish Imperial Networks*, pp. 156–7.

32  Notebook A2, 'Registry of the Foregoing Acts', p. 33, IE PBVM RAH, uncatalogued.

33  Indian Province Annals, Madras.

34 Ibid.

35 Allender, *Learning Femininity in Colonial India*, p. 43.

36 Ibid.

37 Ibid., p. 73.

38 Ibid., p. 74.

39 Indian Province Annals, Madras.

40 Sr Ignatius Murphy returned to Ireland, when her health broke down.

41 Fox, *An Acorn Grows*, p. 40.

42 Several of the early groups of Presentations who came from Ireland had been educated by the Ursulines, the Society of the Sacred Heart, Roscrea, and the Faithful Companions of Jesus, Laurel Hill. See MacGinley, *A Dynamic of Hope*, p. 139; see also Mary Rosa MacGinley, *Roads to Sion: Presentation Sisters in Australia, 1866–1980* (Queensland: Sisters of the Presentation of the Blessed Virgin Mary, 1983), p. 103.

43 MacGinley, *Roads to Sion*, p. 113.

44 Ibid., p. 132.

45 Ibid., p. 135.

46 Ibid., p. 168.

47 Sandra Myres, *Westering Women and the Frontier Experience, 1800–1915* (Albuquerque, NM: University of New Mexico Press, 1982), p. 183.

48 Ibid.

49 See Ruth B. Moynihan, Susan Armitage and Christiane Fischer Dichamp, *So Much to Be Done: Women Settlers on the Mining and Ranching Frontier* (Lincoln, NE and London: University of Nebraska Press, 1990), p. 237. The recent scholarship of Anne M. Butler has been important in assessing the role of Catholic Sisters and the 'frontier experience'. See Butler, *Across God's Frontiers*.

50 Butler, *Across God's Frontiers*, pp. 44–5.

51 Ibid., pp. 45–6.

52 Ibid.

53 Ibid., p. 187.

54 Ibid.

55 There are many instances in Presentation history where clergy quested for nuns while visiting Europe. For example, Fr Patrick Bermingham visited many convents while home from Australia in 1874; he tried unsuccessfully to get Sisters at the Presentation Convent in Clonmel, but then secured a founding group for Wagga Wagga through his visit to the Presentation Convent, Kildare. Similarly, when Bishop Doyle travelled from Australia to Rome in 1891, he continued on to Ireland where he visited schools and convents; he secured a former pupil of Presentation Convent, Castleisland, and a professed Sister from the Presentation Convent, Mountmellick, who returned with him for the foundation in Lismore, New South Wales.

56 Comerford acknowledged that she was the 'unworthy Foundress of our Convents in California'. Mother M. Teresa Comerford to Cardinal [Simeoni], 25 January 1878, Administration Records, 1855–1889, PASF.

57   Bishop of Salford [Herbert Vaughn] to Mother M. Teresa Comerford, 27 January
     1879, Administration Records, 1855–1889, PASF.
58   Annals of the Presentation Convent, San Francisco (1854–1906), p. 10. See also
     *Memoir of Rev. Mother Mary Teresa Comerford: Foundress of the Convents of
     the Presentation Order on the Pacific Coast* (San Francisco: P.J. Thomas, 1882),
     p. 28.
59   For a discussion of the 'first wave' and 'second wave' of Irish women religious who
     went to the United States, see Suellen Hoy, 'The Journey Out: The Recruitment and
     Emigration of Irish Religious Women to the United States, 1812–1914', *Journal of
     Women's History*, 6:4/7:1 (1995), pp. 65–98.
60   Annals of the Presentation Convent, San Francisco (1854–1906), p. 7;
     Administration Records, 1855–1889, PASF.
61   The Presentations in nineteenth-century San Francisco included ninety-four Irish-
     born; some came over as professed religious, some were Irish emigrants who
     entered in the US and fifteen were from the novitiate which Comerford founded in
     Kilcock, Ireland. See Membership database, 'Sisters born in Ireland', PASF.
62   'Irish Missioners in California' (*Kilkenny Journal*, 2 March 1867) and 'Irish Nuns in
     California' (*idem.*, 30 March 1867). Cited in Hoy, 'The Journey Out', p. 74.
63   Mother M. Teresa Comerford to Cardinal Simeoni, 25 January 1878. Mother Mary
     Teresa Comerford's Kilcock Correspondence, Administration Records, 1855–1889,
     PASF.
64   Ibid.
65   Ibid.
66   Hoy, 'The Journey Out', p. 76.
67   Bishop Herbert Vaughn to Cardinal Simeoni, 3 November 1878, Comerford
     Correspondence Transcriptions, Administration Collection, 1855–1889, PASF.
68   St Brigid's Missionary School, Mercy Convent, Callan, was established in 1884, and
     closed in 1958; during its lifespan it prepared over 1,900 women for religious life in
     the US, Australia and New Zealand.
69   For the history of the Presentations in California see Forest, *With Hearts of Oak*.
70   The four women who came from Ireland in 1885 were Sr Mary Clare Brown, Mary
     Aloysius Chriswell, Nora Tanner and Mary Ellen Butler.
71   Anon., *Presentation Women: Sisters of the Presentation, San Francisco, California,
     1854–2004* (San Francisco: Sisters of the Presentation, Masonic Avenue, 2004),
     p. 20.
72   Martin Marty OSB (1836–1896) was appointed Vicar Apostolic of Dakota in 1879.
73   The Catholic Church was granted Standing Rock and Fort Totten, in the Dakota
     Territory, along with six other Indian agencies, while the various Protestant
     denominations were awarded thirty between 1870 and 1880. See Susan Carol
     Peterson and Courtney Ann Vaughn-Roberson, *Women With Vision: The
     Presentation Sisters of South Dakota, 1880–1985* (Urbana and Chicago: University
     of Illinois Press, 1988), p. 46.
74   Peterson and Vaughn-Roberson, *Women With Vision*, p. 59.

75  People lived in 'dug-outs', which were mud houses dug into the earth, or built stone-and-sod houses with materials around them. Sod houses collapsed in heavy rains; the houses in towns that were built from thin wooden slats had no form of insulation, and if a fire broke out a town could be destroyed quickly.

76  See Kenneth M. Hammer, 'Come to God's Country: Promotional Efforts in Dakota Territory, 1861–1889', *South Dakota History*, 10, 4 (2000). Cited in Caroline Fraser, *Prairie Fires: The American Dreams of Laura Ingalls Wilder* (New York: Metropolitan Books, 2017), p. 101.

77  Fraser, *Prairie Fires*, p. 100.

78  Mother M. John Hughes to Sister Bridget [January 1881]. Presentation Convent Archives, Fargo. Cited in Mooney, *Doing What Needs to be Done*, p. 22.

79  Galvin, *From Acorn to Oak*, p. 59.

80  Peterson and Vaughn-Roberson, *Women With Vision*, p. 67.

81  Forest, *With Hearts of Oak*, p. 92.

82  Murphy, *Pakistan Presentation Story*, p. 15.

83  Butler, *Across God's Frontiers*, p. 71.

# Select Bibliography

## Primary Sources

The archives used for this book are mainly private archives; they vary in the extent to which they are organised, classified and catalogued. Many of the convent collections from Irish Presentation convents have been deposited at one of the two Presentation Archives (Cork or Dublin), and they are mainly in the process of being organised, classified and catalogued as this book goes to print. The collections at Cork and Dublin are open to researchers, by arrangement.

## A. Presentation Archives

### (i) Presentation Sisters Congregational Archives, Cork, Ireland

*Presentation Convent Cahirciveen Collection*
Community Annals, 1840–1939; 1940–2012.
Profession Register, 1839–1944.

*Presentation Convent Carlow Collection*
Community Annals, 1811–1887; 1888–1952.
Registers of postulants, novices and religious.
Directory for religious of the Presentation Order, 1870.
Reports of Results Examinations, 1886–1899.
New buildings, 1838–1913.
Circulars from office of National Education, 1898–1913.
Other incomes [dowries and annuities, 1786–1900].

*Presentation Convent Crosshaven Collection*
Community Annals, 1876–2005.
Entrance Register, 1876–1992.
Receipts and Expenditure Book.
Photographic Files.

*Presentation Convent Dingle Collection*
Community Annals, Vol. 1 (1829–1868) 1/1; Vol. 2 (1869–1898); Vol. 3 (1898–1969).
Profession Registers, Vol. 1 (1831–1918); Vol. 2 (1928–1966).

*Presentation Convent Doneraile Collection*
Annals of the convent in two volumes: 1818–1912; 1912–1968.
Register of acts of reception and profession, 1818–1975.
Noviceship Register, 1818–1967.
Gould letters, 1825–1826.
Last Will and Testament of Angelina Gould, 1829.
Monthly Account Books, 1818–1960.
Statutes for a central novitiate for the Sisters of the Presentation of the Blessed Virgin Mary in the Diocese of Cloyne at the Presentation Convent, Fermoy, 1932.

*Presentation Convent Listowel Collection*
Community Annals, Vol. 1 (1844–1944); Vol. 2 (1944–1994).

*Presentation Convent Millstreet Collection*
Documentary Account of the Convent (n.d.).
Accompt Book for Monthly Expenditures, 1840–1865.

*Presentation Convent Mitchelstown Collection*
Community Annals (1853–2002).
Entrance and Profession Register (1856–1970).
Yearly Account Books (1853–1910).

*Presentation Convent Monasterevin Generalate Collection (Indian Province)*
Annals of Presentation Convent Georgetown, Madras 1842–1922.

*North Presentation Convent Collection*
Community Annals, Vol. 1 (1799–1845); Vol. 2 (1845–1886); Vol. 3 (1886–1924).
Entrance Register, Vol. 1 (1799–1903); Vol. 2 (1906–1980).

*South Presentation Convent Collection*
Community Annals, 1771–1892; 1916–1944.
Funds of the Convent Income, 1824–1974.

Profession Registers.
MS Letter, Mother Clare Callaghan to Bishop Coppinger (n.d) [1800–1804].
Nano Nagle Collection.
Alfred O'Rahilly Papers.
T.J. Walsh Papers.

## (ii) George's Hill Archives, Dublin

*George's Hill Collection*
George's Hill Community Annals, 1874–1936.
MS Letter, Nano Nagle to Teresa Mulally, 24 August 1778.
MS Letter, Abbess Lynch to Teresa Mulally, 24 February 1784.
MS Letter, Abbess Lynch to Teresa Mulally, 13 August 1784.
MS Letter, Sr Angela Fitzsimons to Teresa Mulally, 21 May 1784.
Post-primary day fees, 1961–68, George's Hill Archive Directory.

*Presentation Convent Kildare Collection*
Community Annals.
TS History of Presentation Convent, Kildare.
Correspondence of M. Stanislaus Dunne, Wagga Wagga, NSW.

*Presentation Convent Kilkenny Collection*
Annual income and expenditure of the Presentation Convent, Kilkenny,
    1883–1972.

*Presentation Convent Portlaoise Collection*
Community Annals.

*Presentation Convent Waterford Collection*
Annals of the Presentation Convent, Holy Cross, Waterford, 1795–1970.
Saint Philomena's School, Annual Accounts, 1935–65.
Saint Joseph's School, Accounts, Receipts and Expenditure.

## (iii) Presentation Convent Archives, Ireland (not deposited)

*Presentation Convent Ballingarry Collection*
Community Annals, 1926–1978.
Annals and Accounts, 1878–1955.
Pioneer Total Abstinence Association of the Sacred Heart, Registers and
    Minute Book, 1940–1970.

*Presentation Convent Bandon Collection*
Convent Annals, Vol. 1 (1829–1937); Vol. 2 (1939–2000).
Entrance and Profession Registers, Vol. 1 (1829–1877); Vol. 2 (1885–1937);
    Vol. 3 (1935–1984).
Novitiate Register, 1889–1979.
Yearly Accounts.

*Presentation Convent Clondalkin Collection*
Community Annals, Vol. 1 (1857–1925); Vol. 2 (1862–1885).

*Presentation Convent Fermoy Collection*
Receipts and Expenditures, 1838–1888.

*Presentation Convent Galway Collection*
Community Annals, 1815–1999.
MS Letter, Bishop Michael Fleming to Mother M. John Power, 17 July 1833.

*Presentation Convent Hospital Collection*
Community Annals, 1891–1976.

*Presentation Convent Killarney Collection*
Community Annals, 1793–1953.
Entrance and Profession Register, 1793–1977.
MS PBVM Rule, Dr Moylan.
Photographic Files.

*Presentation Convent Kilcock Collection*
MS 'Founding Stories'.
Miscellaneous Papers.

*Presentation Convent (Sexton Street) Limerick Collection*
Community Annals, 1837–1932.
Presentation Convent Limerick Register, 1837–1973.

*Presentation Convent Midleton Collection*
TS 'Nagles of Saint Germain-en-Laye'.

*Presentation Convent Rahan Collection*
Notebook A2, Registry of the Foregoing Acts.

Notebook A3, Register of the Members Enrolled in the Confraternity of the Sacred Heart of Jesus in the Presentation Convent, Killina, Rahan.
Notebook A5, Visitations, 1826–1882.
Album A4, Rahan's Contribution to the Indian Mission.

*Presentation Convent Thurles Collection*
Community Annals, 1817 – to the present.

*Presentation Convent Tralee Collection*
Community Annals, Vol. 1 (1809–12); Vol. 2 (1812–1897).

*Presentation Convent Wexford Collection*
Community Annals, 1818; 1820; 1835; 1856; 1861–68; 1883.

*Presentation Convent Youghal Collection*
Convent Annals, Vol. 1 (1834–1933).
Entrance Register, 1834–1966.
Photographic Files.

**(iv) Presentation Convent Dubuque, Iowa**
TS Annals of the Sisters of the Presentation, Dubuque, Iowa.

**(v) Presentation Archives, St John's, Newfoundland**
Annals of the Presentation Convent, Carbonear, 1852–1987.
Annals of the Presentation Convent, Harbour Breton, 1872–1943.
Annals of the Presentation Convent, Harbour Grace, 1851–1972.
Annals of the Presentation Convent, Harbour Main, 1853–1965.
Annals of the Presentation Convent, Ferryland, 1858–1962.
Annals of the Presentation Convent, Fermeuse-Renews, 1851–1972.
Annals of the Presentation Convent, Riverhead (St Patrick's), 1856–1990.
Annals of the Presentation Convent, Placentia, 1864–1989.
Annals of the Presentation Convent, St John's, 1833–1855.
Annals of the Presentation Convent, St Mary's, 1859–1986.
Annals of the Presentation Convent, Torbay, 1865–1931.
Annals of the Presentation Convent, Trepassey, 1882–1955.
Annals of the Presentation Convent, Witless Bay, 1860–1989.
TS Collection, 'Foundresses' letters to Ireland, 1833'.
MS Letter, Mother M. John Power to Bishop Michael Fleming, 22 July 1883.

MS Letter, Mother M. Xavier Moloney to Mother M. John Power, 22 September 1833.

MS Letter, Mother M. Xaverius Lynch to Mother M. John Power, 22 September 1833.

MS Letter, Mother M. Magdalen O'Shaughnessy to Mother M. John Power, 24 November 1833.

MS Letter, Mother M. Xaverius Lynch to Mother M. John Power, 6 January 1834.

MS copybook, 'Architecture'.

MS copybook, 'Questions on Various Subjects'.

MS document, 'Vision and Courage'.

### *(vi) Presentation Archive and Heritage Centre, Matlock*
*Presentation Convent Bicester Collection*
60th Anniversary of the Presentation Sisters in Bicester, 1953–2013 (n.d., n.p.).

*Presentation Convent Buxton Collection*
Community Annals, Vol. 1 (1898–1912); Vol. 2 (1898–1976).
TS account 'Centenary of the Presentation Convent, Buxton' compiled by Mrs Joyce Stack, retired teacher of St Anne's school and Sister Christine Loughran, PBVM (n.d., n.p.).

*Presentation Convent Castleconnell Collection*
Community Annals, 1945–1977.
Novitiate Log Book.
Rosary Hill Log Book, 1955–1977.

*Presentation Convent Glossop Collection*
Community Annals, 1904–1920.

*Presentation Convent Livesey Street Collection*
Community Annals, 1836–1936.
Religious Inspection Reports, 1911–1948.
Reports by Education Committee, 1912–1935.
*Silver Jubilee Souvenir, St Patrick's Livesey Street, Manchester* (1961).

*Presentation Convent Market Harborough Collection*
Newsletter of the English Province, PBVM, *Focus on ... Market Harborough* (December 1983).

*60th Anniversary of the Presentation Sisters in Market Harborough 1954–2014* (n.d., n.p.).

*Presentation Convent Matlock Collection*
Convent Annals, Vol. 1 (1918–1976); Vol. 2 (1927–1961); Vol. 3 (1954–1960); Vol. 4 (1963–1975).

*Presentation Convent New Moston Collection*
The Rt Rev George Andrew Beck, Bishop of Salford, *The souvenir of the opening of St Margaret Mary's Church* (n.p., 16 March 1957).

*Presentation Convent Pickering Collection*
Community Annals, 1918–1975.

*Presentation Convent Ryde Collection*
Community Annals, 1948–1970.
Account Book, 1948–1954.
School Inspections and Reports, 1949–1964.

*Presentation Convent Scunthorpe Collection*
Ashby Log Book.
Newsletter of the English Province PBVM, *Focus on … Scunthorpe with Crowle* (April 1979).

**(vii) Presentation Convent New Windsor, New York**
TS Annals of the Presentation Sisters' Foundation in New York at St Michael's Convent, 1784–1966.

**(viii) Presentation Archives, San Francisco**
MS Letter, Nano Nagle to Miss Fitzsimons, 17 December 1770.
Mother M. Teresa Comerford's Kilcock Correspondence, Administration Records, 1855–1889.
MS Directions and Spiritual Examen, written by a Sister.

## B. Manuscripts

*Dublin Diocesan Archives*
McQuaid Papers.

*Galway Diocesan Archives*
Browne Archive.

*St John's Diocesan Archives, Newfoundland*
Fleming Papers.

*National Archives of Ireland*
ED Files.


## C. Printed Primary Sources

Coppinger, W., *Life of Miss Nano Nagle* (Cork: James Haly, 1794).

Fleming, Rt Rev M., *The State of the Catholic Religion in Newfoundland.* Extracted from the Annals of Religious Science of Rome, Vol. 11, FASC. V, March and April 1836 (Rome: 1836).

————, *Report of the Catholic Mission in Newfoundland in North America, Submitted by the Vicar Apostolic of that Mission, Monsignor Michael Fleming, to His Eminence the Cardinal Prefect of Propaganda, Rome* (Rome: Printing Press of the Sacred Congregation, 1837).

————, *Letters on the State of Religion in Newfoundland addressed to the Very Rev. Dr A. O'Connell* (Dublin: James Duffy, 1844).

'Annual report of the asylum for aged and destitute women, Douglas Street, Cork for the year ending the 31st of December, 1863' (*Cork Examiner*, 20 February 1864).

'Report on the Inspection of Catholic Schools, 1864', *Journal of the House of Assembly of Newfoundland* (1865).

*Leaves from the Annals of the Sisters of Mercy in Three Volumes*, Vol. 1 (New York: The Catholic Publication Society Co., 1881. This edition: General Books, Tennessee, 2010).

*Memoir of Rev. Mother Mary Teresa Comerford, Foundress of the Convents of the Presentation Order on the Pacific Coast* (San Francisco: PJ Thomas, 1882).

*Rules of the Youghal Co-operative Lace Society Limited* (Dublin: Sealy, Bryers and Walker, 1897).

*The Youghal Lace Industry* (n.n., Dublin: Browne and Nolan, 1898).


## D. Parliamentary Papers and Reports

*Act of Uniformity*, 1665, 17 and 18 Car. II. c. 6.

*Act to Restrain Foreign Education*, 1695, 7 Wm. III. c. 4; 1703. 2 Anne, c. 6; 1709. 8 Anne, c. 3.

*Royal Commission of Inquiry into Primary Education (Ireland)*, Vol. 1, Pt. I: *The Report of the Commissioners, with an appendix*, (C.6.), H.C. 1870, XXVIII, pt. i.

*Royal Commission of Inquiry into Primary Education (Ireland), Vol. VI, educational Census: Returns showing the number of children actually present in each primary school 25th June 1868; with introductory observations and Analytical Index*, (C. 6V), H.C. 1870, XXVIII, pt. v. 1.

*First Report of the Commissioners of Irish Education Inquiry; 1825* (400) XII. 1.

*Second Report of the Commissioners of Irish Education Inquiry (Abstract of Returns in 1824, from the Protestant and Roman Catholic Clergy in Ireland, of the state of Education in their respective Parishes)*, 1826–27 (12) XII. 1, 6–18.

*Special Report made to the Commissioners of National Education on Convent Schools in Connection with the Board*; H.C. 1864 [405] XLVI.

*Twenty-fifth Report of the Commissioners of National Education in Ireland, for the year 1858; with an appendix*, (2593), H.C. 1860, XXV.

*Twenty-seventh Report ... for the year 1860.*

*Twenty-eighth Report ... for the year 1861.*

*Twenty-ninth Report ... for the year 1862.*

*Thirtieth Report ... for the year 1863.*

*Thirty-first Report ... for the year 1864.*

*Thirty-second Report ... for the year 1865.*

*Thirty-fourth Report ... for the year 1867.*

*Thirty-sixth Report ... for the year 1869.*

*Thirty-seventh Report ... for the year 1870.*

*Thirty-eighth Report ... for the year 1871.*

*Thirty-ninth Report ... for the year 1872.*

*Fortieth Report ... for the year 1873.*

*Forty-first Report ... for the year 1874.*

*Forty-second Report ... for the year 1875.*

*Forty-fourth Report ... for the year 1877.*

## E. Newspapers and Journals

*Freeman's Journal*, 18 February 1771.

*The Connaught Journal*, 27 March 1823.

*Manchester Guardian*, 3 July 1847.

*Cork Examiner*, 20 February 1864.

*Journal of the House of Assembly of Newfoundland*, 1865; 1867.

*Journal of the Legislative Council of Newfoundland*, 1881.

*Nationalist and Leinster Times*, 1 December 1883.

*The Month*, 1894.

*Irish Ecclesiastical Review*, XVII, May 1921.

*Irish Press*, 17 August 1940.

*Cork Examiner*, 10 August 1940.

*Kerryman*, 28 June 1952.

## Secondary Sources

## A. Books

Ahern, G. (ed.), *The Story of the Presentation Sisters, Scoil Chroí Naofa and Presentation College, Athenry, 1908–2008* (Galway: Presentation Sisters, 2009).

Akenson, D.H., *The Irish Education Experiment: The National System of Education in the Nineteenth Century* (London: Routledge & Kegan Paul, 1970).

———, *A Mirror to Kathleen's Face: Education in Independent Ireland, 1922–1960* (Montreal and London: McGill-Queen's University Press, 1973).

Allen, R., *A Story of Love and Faith* (Cork: South Presentation Convent, 1979).

Allender, T., *Learning Femininity in Colonial India, 1820–1932* (Manchester: Manchester University Press, 2016).

A Loreto Sister, *Joyful Mother of Children: Mother Frances Mary Teresa Ball* (Dublin: M.H. Gill and Son Ltd., 1961).

Anon., *Mother Xavier Murphy, First Superior General of the Presentation Sisters, South India* (n.d, n.p.).

Anon., *Presentation Convent Galway, 1815–1965, Sesquicentenary Souvenir* (Galway, 1965).

Anon., *Presentation Women: Sisters of the Presentation, San Francisco, California, 1854–2004* (San Francisco: Sisters of the Presentation, Masonic Avenue, 2004).

Anon., *The Charitable Mistresses of the Holy Infant Jesus, Known as the Dames de St Maur, 1662* (Dornach: Braun and Co., 1925).

Anon., *The Sisters of St Joseph of Carondolet* (St Louis, MO: B. Herder Books, 1966).

Atkinson, N., *Irish Education: A History of Educational Institutions* (Dublin: Allen Figgis, 1969).

Bellenoit, H.J.A., *Missionary Education and Empire in Late Colonial India, 1860–1920* (London: Pickering & Chatto, 2007).

Bolster, M.A., *The Correspondence of Catherine McAuley, 1827–1841* (Privately published by the Congregation of the Sisters of Mercy, Diocese of Cork and Ross, 1989).

Bourke, R., *Empire and Revolution: The Political Life of Edmund Burke* (Princeton, NJ and Woodstock, Oxon.: Princeton University Press, 2015).

Bowen, D., *Paul Cardinal Cullen and the Shaping of Modern Irish Catholicism* (Dublin: Gill and Macmillan Ltd., 1983).

Brown, M., *The Irish Enlightenment* (Cambridge, MA: Harvard University Press, 2016).

Burchell, R.A., *The San Francisco Irish, 1848–1880* (Manchester: Manchester University Press, 1979).

Burke, C. and Grosvenor, I., *School* (London: Reaktion Books, 2008).

Burke Savage, R., *A Valiant Dublin Woman: The Story of George's Hill (1766–1940)* (Dublin: M.H. Gill and Son Ltd., 1940).

Butler, A.M., *Across God's Frontiers: Catholic Sisters in the American West, 1850–1920* (Chapel Hill, NC: University of North Carolina Press, 2012).

Byrne, Sr O., *A Record of Eighty-four Years: Presentation Sisters Durrow* (Laois: Presentation Sisters, 1998).

Callan, L., *The Society of the Sacred Heart in North America* (New York: Longmans, Green & Co., 1937).

———, *Philippine Duchesne: Frontier Missionary of the Sacred Heart, 1769–1852* (Westminster, MD: Newman Press, 1957).

Choudhury, M., *Convents and Nuns in Eighteenth-Century French Politics and Culture* (Ithaca, NY and London: Cornell University Press, 2004).

Clarke, U., *The Ursulines in Cork Since 1771* (Cork: Privately published by the Ursuline Convent, Blackrock, 1996).

Clear, C., *Nuns in Nineteenth-Century Ireland* (Dublin: Gill & Macmillan, 1987).

Coldrey, B.M., *Faith and Fatherland: The Christian Brothers and the Development of Irish Nationalism, 1838–1921* (Dublin: Gill and Macmillan, 1988).

Connolly, S.J., *Priests and People in Pre-Famine Ireland, 1780–1845* (Dublin: Four Courts Press, 2001).

Consedine, R., *Listening Journey: A Study of the Spirit and Ideals of Nano Nagle and the Presentation Sisters* (Victoria: PBVM, 1983).

———, *Nano Nagle Seminars July–August 1984* (Cork: Nano Nagle House, Douglas Street, 1984).

Coolahan, J., *Irish Education: its History and Structure* (Dublin: Institute of Public Administration, 1981).

————, *Towards the Era of Lifelong Learning: A History of Irish Education 1800–2016* (Dublin: Institute of Public Administration, 2017).

Crosbie, B., *Irish Imperial Networks: Migration, Social Communication and Exchange in Nineteenth-Century India* (Cambridge and New York: Cambridge University Press, 2011).

Crowley, J. Devoy, R., Linehan, D. and O'Flanagan, P., Murphy, M. (eds), *Atlas of Cork City* (Cork: Cork University Press, 2005).

Cullen, M. (ed.), *Girls Don't Do Honours: Irish Women in Education in the Nineteenth and Twentieth Centuries* (Dublin: WEB Press, 1987).

Cunningham, B. and Kennedy, M. (eds), *The Experience of Reading: Irish Historical Perspectives* (Dublin: Economic and Social History Society of Ireland, 1999).

Cunningham, H. and Innes, J. (eds), *Charity, Philanthropy and Reform from the 1690s to 1850* (London: Macmillan Press, 1998).

Cunningham, P. and Gardner, P., *Becoming Teachers: Texts and Testimonies, 1907–1950* (London: Woburn Press, 2004).

Curtis, S.A., *Civilizing Habits: Women Missionaries and the Revival of French Empire* (Oxford & New York: Oxford University Press, 2010).

Curtis, S.J. and Boultwood, M.E.A., *An Introduction to the History of English Education Since 1800* (London: University Tutorial Press, 1964).

Daly, M. and Dickson, D. (eds), *The Origins of Popular Literacy in Ireland: Language, Change and Educational Development, 1700–1920* (Dublin: Trinity College Dublin and University College Dublin, 1990).

Dickson, D., *Old World Colony: Cork and Munster 1630–1830* (Cork: Cork University Press, 2005).

Diner, H.R., *Erin's Daughters in America: Irish Immigrant Women in the Nineteenth Century* (Baltimore and London: Johns Hopkins University Press, 1983).

Dinn, Sr M.J., *Foundation of the Presentation Congregation in Newfoundland* (Presentation Convent, Newfoundland, privately published pamphlet, 1975).

Dowd, B. and Tearle, S. (eds), *Centenary History of the Presentation of the Blessed Virgin Mary, Wagga Wagga, New South Wales, 1874–1974* (Published by the Sisters of the PBVM, Wagga Wagga, NSW, 1973).

Dries, A., *The Missionary Movement in American Catholic History* (New York: Orbis Books, 1998).

Duffy, P., *The Lay Teacher* (Dublin: Fallons, 1967).

Duffy, S. (ed.), *Atlas of Irish History*, second edition (Dublin: Gill and Macmillan, 2000).

Flanagan, B., O'Brien, M.T., O'Leary, A. (eds), *Nano Nagle and an Evolving Charism: A Guide for Educators, Leaders and Care Providers* (Dublin: Veritas, 2017).

Fleming, J., *History of the Catholic Church in Newfoundland and Labrador* (Newfoundland: Transcontinental, 2006).

Forest, M.R., *With Hearts of Oak: The Story of the Sisters of the Presentation of the Blessed Virgin Mary in California, 1854–1907* (Privately published by the Sisters of the PBVM, San Francisco, 2004).

Fox, N.M., *An Acorn Grows among the Gums: The Presentation Sisters in Tasmania, 1866–2006* (Tasmania: Presentation Sisters Property Association, 2006).

Fraser, C., *Prairie Fires: The American Dreams of Laura Ingalls Wilder* (New York: Metropolitan Books, 2017).

Galgay, F., McCarthy, M., Bruce, T. and O'Brien, M., *A Pilgrimage of Faith: A History of the Southern Shore* (St John's: Harry Cuff Publications, 1983).

Galvin, C., *From Acorn to Oak: A Study of Presentation Foundations, 1775–1968* (Published by the Sisters of the PBVM, Fargo, North Dakota, 1968).

Geser, F., *Canon Law Governing Communities of Sisters* (London: B. Herder, 1938; 1950).

Grosvenor, I., Lawn, M. and Rousmaniere, K. (eds), *Silences and Images: The Social History of the Classroom* (New York: Peter Lang, 1999).

Guinness, A.H., *Education by Nuns: its Failures and Injurious Tendencies* (London: Protestant Alliance, 1890).

Harrison, V.V., *Changing Habits: A Memoir of the Society of the Sacred Heart* (New York and London: Doubleday, 1988).

Hellinckx, B., Simon, F. and Depaepe, M., *The Forgotten Contribution of the Teaching Sisters* (Leuven: Leuven University Press, 2009).

Hogan, E., *The Irish Missionary Movement: A Historical Survey, 1830–1980* (Dublin: Gill and Macmillan Ltd., 1990).

Howley, M.F., *Ecclesiastical History of Newfoundland* (Boston: Doyle and Whittle, 1888).

Hutch, W., *Nano Nagle: Her Life, Her Labours and Their Fruits* (Dublin: McGlashan and Gill, 1875).

Hyland, Á. and Milne, K. (eds), *Irish Educational Documents, Vol. I* (Dublin: CICE, 1987).

Kavanagh, J., *Mixed Education, The Catholic Case Stated; or, Principles, Working, and Results of the System of National Education; with suggestions for the settlement of the education question. Most respectfully dedicated to the Catholic Archbishops and Bishops of Ireland* (Dublin: John Mullany, 1859).

Kealy, M., *Dominican Education in Ireland, 1830–1930* (Dublin: Irish Academic Press, 2007).

Keogh, D., *Edmund Rice and the First Christian Brothers* (Dublin: Four Courts Press, 2008).

Kilroy, P., *Madeleine Sophie Barat: A Life* (Cork: Cork University Press, 2000).

———, *The Society of the Sacred Heart in Nineteenth-Century France, 1800–1865* (Cork: Cork University Press, 2012).

Leen, E., *What is Education?* (London: Burns, Oates and Washbourne, 1943).

Lillis, Sr M., *Two Hundred Years A-growing: The Story of the Ursulines in Thurles 1787–1987* (Privately published: A Bicentenary Commemorative Publication, 1987).

Luddy, M., *Women and Philanthropy in Nineteenth-Century Ireland* (Cambridge: Cambridge University Press, 1995).

———, *Women in Ireland, 1800–1918: A Documentary History* (Cork: Cork University Press, 1995).

MacCurtain, M. and O'Dowd, M. (eds), *Women in Early Modern Ireland* (Dublin: Wolfhound Press, 1991).

MacGinley, M.R., *Roads to Sion: Presentation Sisters in Australia, 1866–1980* (Queensland: Sisters of the PBVM, 1983).

———, *A Dynamic of Hope: Institutes of Women Religious in Australia* (Darlinghurst, NSW: Australian Catholic University/Crossing Press, 2002).

MacLellan, A. and Mauger, A. (eds), *Growing Pains: Childhood Illness in Ireland, 1750–1950* (Dublin: Irish Academic Press, 2016).

Malcolm, E. and Jones, G. (eds), *Medicine, Disease and the State in Ireland, 1650–1940* (Cork: Cork University Press, 1999).

Mangion, C., *Contested Identities: Catholic Women Religious in Nineteenth Century England and Wales* (Manchester: Manchester University Press, 2008).

Marchant James, R., *Cork to Capricorn: A History of the Presentation Sisters in Western Australia, 1891–1991* (Published by the Congregation of the Presentation Sisters of Western Australia, 1996).

McBride, I., *Eighteenth Century Ireland* (Dublin: Gill Books, 2009).

[McCarthy, M.] *Edmund Ignatius Rice and the Christian Brothers* (Dublin: Gill and Son, 1926).

McCulloch, G. and Richardson, W., *Historical Research in Education Settings* (Maidenhead: Open University Press, 2000).

McGuinness, M., *Called to Serve: A History of Nuns in America* (New York and London: New York University Press, 2013).

McManus, A., *The Irish Hedge School and its Books, 1695–1831* (Dublin: Four Courts Press, 2002).

McNamara, J.A.K., *Sisters in Arms: Catholic Nuns Through Two Millennia* (Cambridge, MA: Harvard University Press, 1996).

Milne, K., *The Irish Charter Schools, 1730–1830* (Dublin: Four Courts Press, 1997).

Moody, T.W. and Martin, F.X. (eds), *The Course of Irish History*, revised edition (Cork: Mercier Press, 2001).

Mooney, M.M., *Doing What Needs to Be Done: Sisters of the Presentation of the Blessed Virgin Mary, Fargo, 1882–1997* (Published by the Sisters of the PBVM, Fargo, 1997).

Moran, G., *Sending out Ireland's Poor: Assisted Emigration to North America in the Nineteenth Century* (Dublin: Four Courts Press, 2004).

Moynihan, R.B., Armitage, S. and Fischer Dichamp, C., *So Much to Be Done: Women Settlers on the Mining and Ranching Frontier* (Lincoln, NE and London: University of Nebraska Press, 1990).

Murphy, D., *A History of Irish Emigrant and Missionary Education* (Dublin: Four Courts Press, 2000).

Murphy, M., *Pakistan Presentation Story* (Rawalpindi: Privately published by the Army Press, 1986).

Myres, S., *Westering Women and the Frontier Experience, 1800–1915* (Albuquerque, NM: University of New Mexico Press, 1982).

Norman, E.R., *Anti-Catholicism in Victorian England* (London: Wilmer Brothers Ltd., 1968).

Normoyle, M.C., *A Tree is Planted: The Life and Times of Edmund Rice* (Dublin: privately published, 1976).

O'Brien, S., *Leaving God for God: The Daughters of Charity of St Vincent de Paul in Britain, 1847–2017* (London: Darton, Longman and Todd Ltd., 2017).

O'Buachalla, S., *Education policy in twentieth-century Ireland* (Dublin: Wolfhound Press, 1988).

O'Conchúir, B., *Scríobhaithe Chorcaí 1700–1850* (Dublin: An Clóchomhar, 1974).

O'Connor, T. and Lyons, M.A. (eds), *Irish Communities in Early Modern Europe* (Dublin: Four Courts Press, 2006).

O'Donoghue, T., *The Catholic Church and the Secondary School Curriculum in Ireland, 1922–62* (New York: Peter Lang, 1999).

O'Dowd, M. and Wichert, S. (eds), *Chattel, Servant or Citizen: Women's Status in Church, State and Society* (Belfast: Institute of Irish Studies, QUB, 1995).

O'Farrell, P., *The Irish in Australia: 1788 to the Present* (Notre Dame, IN: University of Notre Dame Press, 1992).

O'Farrell, M.P., *Nano Nagle: Woman of the Gospel* (Cork: Cork Publishing, 1996).

———, *Breaking of Morn: Nano Nagle (1718–1784) and Francis Moylan (1735–1815)* (Cork: Cork Publishing, 2001).

Ohlmeyer, J., *Making Ireland English: The Irish Aristocracy in the Seventeenth Century* (New Haven, CT and London: Yale University Press, 2012).

O'Neill, L., *The Sacred Heart Pioneer Association* (Brisbane: 1963).

O'Neill, P., *A Seaport Legacy: The Story of St John's, Newfoundland*, Vol. 2 (Ontario: Porcepic Press, 1976).

O'Reilly, L., *The Impact of Vatican II on Women Religious: Case Study of the Union of Irish Presentation Sisters* (Newcastle upon Tyne: Cambridge Scholars Publishing, 2013).

O'Sullivan, E., *Ascendancy Women and Elementary Education in Ireland: Educational Provision for Poor Children, 1788–1848* (Basingstoke: Palgrave Macmillan, 2017).

Paavola, R.C., *Upon the Rock: A Centennial History of the Presentation Sisters of the Blessed Virgin Mary, Aberdeen, South Dakota, 1886–1986* (privately published, 1986).

Parkes, S.M., *Kildare Place: The History of the Church of Ireland Training College, 1811–1969* (Dublin: Church of Ireland College of Education, 1984).

Peckham Magray, M., *The Transforming Power of the Nuns: Women, Religion and Cultural Change in Ireland, 1750–1900* (Oxford: Oxford University Press, 1998).

Peterson, S.C. and Vaughn-Roberson, C.A., *Women With Vision: The Presentation Sisters of South Dakota, 1880–1985* (Urbana and Chicago: University of Illinois Press, 1988).

Prowse, D.W., *History of Newfoundland from the English, Colonial and Foreign Records* (London: Eyre and Spottiswoode, 1896).

Raber, K. (ed.), *Ashgate Critical Essays on Women Writers in England, 1550–1700*, Vol. 6 (Abingdon, Oxon.: Routledge, 2009).

Raftery, D., *Women and Learning in English Writing, 1600–1900* (Dublin: Four Courts Press, 1997).

Raftery, D. and Clarke, M. (eds), *Transnationalism, Gender and the History of Education* (London and New York: Routledge, 2016).

Raftery, D. and Fischer, K. (eds), *Educating Ireland: Schooling and Social Change, 1700–2000* (Dublin: Irish Academic Press, 2014).

Raftery, D. and Parkes, S.M., *Female Education in Ireland, 1700–1900: Minerva or Madonna* (Dublin: Irish Academic Press, 2007).

Randles, E., *Post-primary Education in Ireland, 1957–1970* (Dublin: Veritas Publications, 1975).

Rapley, E., *The Dévotes: Women and Church in Seventeenth-Century France* (Montreal and London: McGill-Queen's University Press, 1990).

Raughter, R. (ed.), *Religious Women and their History* (Dublin: Irish Academic Press, 2005).

Robins, J., *The Lost Children: A Study of Charity Children in Ireland, 1700–1900* (Dublin: Institute of Public Administration, 1980).

Rowe, F.W., *The Development of Education in Newfoundland* (Toronto: The Ryerson Press, 1964).

Rushe, D., *Edmund Rice: The Man and His Times* (Dublin: Macmillan, 1982).

Seth, S., *Subject Lessons: The Western Education of Colonial India* (Durham, NC: Duke University Press, 2007).

Shaughnessy, G., *Has the Immigrant Kept the Faith? A Study of Immigration and Catholic Growth in the United States, 1790–1920* (New York: Macmillan Co., 1925).

Smallwood, J.R. (ed.), *The Book of Newfoundland*, Vol. II (1937) and Vol. VI (1967) (St John's, NL: Newfoundland Book Publishers).

Smyth, E.M. (ed.), *Changing Habits: Women's Religious Orders in Canada* (Ottawa: Novalis, 2007).

Stephens, W.B., *Education in Britain, 1750–1914* (London: Macmillan Press Ltd., 1998).

Sullivan, M.C., *Catherine McAuley and the Tradition of Mercy* (Dublin: Four Courts Press, 1995).

———, *In the Path of Mercy: The Life of Catherine McAuley* (Dublin: Four Courts Press, 2012).

Thomas, E., *Footprints on the Frontier: A History of the Sisters of St Joseph, Concordia, Kansas* (Westminster, MD: Newman Press, 1948).

Trimingham Jack, C., *Growing Good Catholic Girls: Education and Convent Life in Australia* (Melbourne: Melbourne University Press, 2003).

Vacher, M., *Nuns Without Cloister: Sisters of St Joseph in the Seventeenth and Eighteenth Centuries* (Lanham, MD: University Press of America, 2010).

Van Dijck, M., de Maeyer, J., Tyssens, J. and Koppen, J. (eds), *The Economics of Providence: Management, Finances and Patrimony of Religious Orders and Congregations in Europe, 1773–1930* (Leuven: Leuven University Press, 2012).

Waldron, K., *Out of the Shadows: Emerging Secondary Schools in the Archdiocese of Tuam, 1940–69* (Tuam: Nordlaw Books, 2002).

Walsh, Barbara, *Roman Catholic Nuns in England and Wales, 1800–1937: A Social History* (Dublin: Irish Academic Press, 2002).

Walsh, Brendan, *The Pedagogy of Protest, the Educational Thought and Work of Patrick H. Pearse* (Bern: Peter Lang, 2007).

Walsh, T.J., *Nano Nagle and the Presentation Sisters* (Dublin: M.H. Gill & Son, 1959).


## B. Chapter within an Edited Volume

Ashford, G., 'Children's Smallpox and Inoculation Procedures in Eighteenth-Century Ireland', in A. MacLellan and A. Mauger (eds), *Growing Pains: Childhood Illness in Ireland, 1750–1950* (Dublin: Irish Academic Press, 2016).

Barnard, T., 'Reading in eighteenth-century Ireland: public and private pleasures', in B. Cunningham and M. Kennedy (eds), *The Experience of Reading: Irish Historical Perspectives* (Dublin: Economic and Social History Society of Ireland, 1999).

Cobbin, I., 'Essay on Popery' in *Foxe's Book of Martyrs* (London, 1875).

Connolly, S.J., 'Family, Love and Marriage: Some Evidence from the Early Eighteenth Century', in M. MacCurtain and M. O'Dowd (eds), *Women in Early Modern Ireland* (Dublin: Wolfhound Press, 1991).

Coppinger, W., 'The Life of Miss Nano Nagle' (1794), Reprinted in T.J. Walsh, *Nano Nagle and the Presentation Sisters* (Dublin: M.H. Gill & Son, 1959).

Cullen, L.M., 'Patrons, Teachers and Literacy in Irish: 1700–1850', in M. Daly and D. Dickson (eds), *The Origins of Popular Literacy in Ireland: Language Change and Educational Development, 1700–1920* (Dublin: Trinity College Dublin and University College Dublin, 1990).

Dolan, F.E., 'Reading, Work and Catholic Women's Biographies' in K. Raber (ed.), *Ashgate Critical Essays on Women Writers in England, 1550–1700*, Vol. 6 (Abingdon, Oxon.: Routledge, 2009).

Fahy, T., 'Nuns in the Catholic Church' in M. Cullen (ed.), *Girls Don't Do Honours: Irish Women in Education in the Nineteenth and Twentieth Centuries* (Dublin: WEB Press, 1987).

Fitzpatrick, D., '"A share of the honeycomb": education, emigration and Irishwomen' in M. Daly and D. Dickson (eds), *The Origins of Popular Literacy in Ireland: Language, Change and Educational Development,*

*1700–1920* (Dublin: Trinity College Dublin and University College Dublin, 1990).

Flynn, T., 'The Roman Catholic Church in Newfoundland' in J.R. Smallwood (ed.), *The Book of Newfoundland*, Vol. II (St John's, NL: Newfoundland Book Publishers, 1937).

Green, E.R.R., 'The Great Famine 1845–50', in T.W. Moody and F.X. Martin (eds), *The Course of Irish History* (Cork: Mercier Press, 2001).

Harford, J. and Raftery, D., 'The education of young girls within the national system,' in D. Raftery and S.M. Parkes, *Female Education in Ireland 1700–1900: Minerva or Madonna* (Dublin: Irish Academic Press, 2007).

Hickey, K. and Devoy, R., 'Weather and Natural Disasters', in J. Crowley et al. (eds), *Atlas of Cork City* (Cork: Cork University Press, 2005).

Kelly, J., 'The Emergence of Scientific and Institutional Medical Practice in Ireland, 1650–1800', in E. Malcolm and G. Jones (eds), *Medicine, Disease and the State in Ireland, 1650–1940* (Cork: Cork University Press, 1999).

———, 'The 1798 Rebellion' in S. Duffy (ed.), *Atlas of Irish History* (Dublin: Gill and Macmillan, 2000).

Luddy, M., 'Religion, philanthropy and the state in late eighteenth and early nineteenth-century Ireland' in H. Cunningham and J. Innes (eds), *Charity, Philanthropy and Reform from the 1690s to 1850* (London: Macmillan Press, 1998).

———, '"Possessed of Fine Properties": Power, Authority, and the Funding of Convents in Ireland, 1780–1900', in M. Van Dijck et al., *The Economics of Providence* (Leuven: Leuven University Press, 2012).

MacCurtain, M., 'Late in the field: Catholic Sisters in twentieth-century Ireland and the New Religious History', in M. O'Dowd and S. Wichert (eds), *Chattel, Servant or Citizen: Women's Status in Church, State and Society* (Belfast: Institute of Irish Studies, QUB, 1995).

MacDermott, A., 'Some Irish Families and their influences in Newfoundland', in J.R. Smallwood (ed.), *The Book of Newfoundland*, Vol. VI (St John's, NL: Newfoundland Book Publishers, 1967).

Moloney, M., 'Limerick in Emancipation Days' in *Presentation Convent, Limerick Centenary 1837–1937* (Limerick: City Printing Company, 1937).

Necmec, T.F., 'The Irish emigration to Newfoundland', in J.R. Smallwood (ed.), *The Book of Newfoundland*, Vol. VI (St John's, NL: Newfoundland Book Publishers, 1967).

Nowlan-Roebuck, C., 'The Presentation Order and National Education in Nineteenth-Century Ireland' in D. Raftery and K. Fischer (eds),

*Educating Ireland: Schooling and Social Change, 1700–2000* (Dublin: Irish Academic Press, 2014).

O'Connor, A.V., 'The revolution in girls' secondary education in Ireland, 1860–1910; in M. Cullen (ed.), *Girls Don't Do Honours: Irish Women in Education in the Nineteenth and Twentieth Centuries* (Dublin: Arlen House, 1987).

O'Sullivan, E., 'Irish women and elementary education for the poor in early nineteenth-century Ireland' in D. Raftery and K. Fischer (eds), *Educating Ireland: Schooling and Social Change, 1700–2000* (Dublin: Irish Academic Press, 2014).


## C. Journal Articles

Burley, S., 'Engagement with Empires: Irish Catholic Female Religious Teachers in Colonial South Australia, 1868–1901', *Irish Educational Studies*, 3, 2 (2012).

Castle, J. and O'Brien, G., '"I am building a house": Nano Nagle's Georgian convents', *Irish Architectural and Decorative Studies*, 19 (2016).

Chisick, H., 'French Charity Schools in the Seventeenth and Eighteenth Centuries – with Special Reference to the Case of Amiens', *Social History*, 16, 32 (1983).

Connolly, S.J., 'A woman's life in mid-eighteenth-century Ireland: the case of Letitia Bushe', *The Historical Journal*, 43, 2 (2000).

Coonerty, P., 'The Presentation Sisters and the Education of "Poor Female Children" in Limerick, 1837–1870', in *The Old Limerick Journal*, 33 (Winter 1996).

Cullum, L., '"It was a woman's job, I 'spose, pickin' dirt outa berries": negotiating gender, work and wages at Job Brothers, 1940–1950', *Newfoundland and Labrador Studies*, 23, 2 (2008).

Daniel, T.M., 'The history of tuberculosis', *Respiratory Medicine*, 100, 11 (2006).

Donnelly Jr, J.S., 'Bishop Michael Browne of Galway (1937–76) and the regulation of public morality', *New Hibernia Review*, 17 (Spring 2013).

Duffy, T.G., 'An Irish Missionary Effort: the Brothers Fennelly', *Irish Ecclesiastical Review*, XVII (May 1921).

Dye, R., 'Catholic protectionism or Irish nationalism? Religion and politics in Liverpool, 1829–1845', *Journal of British Studies*, 40, 3 (July 2001).

Fitzpatrick, D., 'Irish emigration in the later nineteenth century', *Irish Historical Studies* 22, 86 (September 1980).

Fogel, N., 'Tuberculosis: A disease without boundaries', *Tuberculosis*, 95 (2015).

Grace, G., 'The State and Catholic schooling in England and Wales: politics, ideology and mission integrity', *Oxford Review of Education*, 27, 4 (2001).

Hoy, S., 'The Journey Out: The Recruitment and Emigration of Irish Religious Women to the United States, 1812–1914', *Journal of Women's History*, 6:4/7:1 (1995).

Ingram, P., 'Protestant patriarchy and the Catholic priesthood in nineteenth-century England', *Journal of Social History*, 24, 4 (Summer 1991).

Kelly, J., 'The abduction of women of fortune in eighteenth-century Ireland', *Eighteenth Century Ireland*, 9 (1994).

Kennedy, M., 'Reading the Enlightenment in Eighteenth-Century Ireland', *Eighteenth-Century Studies*, 45, 3 (2012).

Kollar, R., 'Foreign and Catholic: a plea to Protestant parents on the dangers of convent education in Victorian England', *History of Education*, 31, 4 (2002).

Lei, C., 'The Material Culture of the Loretto School for Girls in Hamilton, Ontario 1865–1971', *Canadian Catholic Historical Association Historical Studies*, 66 (2000).

Luddy, M., 'Presentation Convents in County Tipperary 1806–1900' in *Tipperary Historical Journal* (1992).

Mannion, J., 'Irish migration and settlement in Newfoundland: the formative phase, 1697–1732', *Newfoundland Studies*, 17, 2 (2001).

McBride, I., 'The Edge of Enlightenment: Ireland and Scotland in the Eighteenth Century', *Modern Intellectual History*, 10, 1 (2013).

O'Brien, S., 'Terra Incognita: the nun in nineteenth-century England' in *Past and Present*, 121 (November 1988).

———, 'French nuns in nineteenth-century England', *Past and Present*, 154 (February 1997).

O Comdealbáin, S., 'The Charter Schools of Cork County', *Journal of Cork Historical and Archaeological Society*, 39 (1944).

Raftery, D., 'The "Mission" of Nuns in Female Education', *Paedagogica Historica*, 48, 2 (2012).

———, '"Je suis d'aucune Nation": the recruitment and identity of Irish women religious in the international mission field, c. 1840–1940', *Paedagogica Historica*, 49, 4 (2013).

———, 'The "third wave" is digital: researching histories of women religious in the twenty-first century', *American Catholic Studies*, 128, 2 (2017).

Romero-Maroto, M. and Sáez-Gómez, J.M., 'Mouth ulcers: a deadly disease for children from the sixteenth to eighteenth centuries', *Irish Journal of Medical Science*, 182, 2 (2013).

Romkey, R., 'The representation of Newfoundland in nineteenth-century French travel literature', *Newfoundland and Labrador Studies*, 25, 2 (2010).

Thornton, P.A., 'Newfoundland's frontier demographic experience: the world we have not lost', *Newfoundland and Labrador Studies*, 1, 2 (1985).

Trimingham Jack, C., 'Sacred Symbols, School Ideology and the Construction of Subjectivity', *Paedagogica Historica*, 34, 3 (1998).

———, 'The Lay Sister in Educational History and Memory', *History of Education*, 29, 3 (2000).

Werly, J.M., 'The Irish in Manchester, 1832–49', *Irish Historical Studies*, 18, 71 (March 1973).

## D. Unpublished Thesis

Scully, M., 'Galway Schooling and the Presentation Sisters: An Account of the Work of a Religious Body in the Practice of Education (1815–1873)' (unpublished MEd thesis, University College Cork, 1973).

## E. Online Sources

'Benfleet Community Archive'. Available at: http://www.benfleethistory.org.uk (accessed 29 January 2018).

'Research References' (Irish Shipwrecks, n.d.). Available at: http://www.irishshipwrecks.com/site_pages.php?section=References (accessed on 31 May 2018).

# Index